BUSINESS CYCLES: THEORIES, EVIDENCE AND
ANALYSIS

# Business Cycles: Theories, Evidence and Analysis

Proceedings of a conference held by the International
Economic Association, Copenhagen, Denmark

Edited by
Niels Thygesen
Kumaraswamy Velupillai
and
Stefano Zambelli

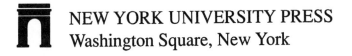

NEW YORK UNIVERSITY PRESS
Washington Square, New York

First published in the U.S.A. in 1991 by
NEW YORK UNIVERSITY PRESS
Washington Square
New York, N.Y. 10003

Printed in Great Britain

Library of Congress Cataloging-in-Publication Data
Business cycles: theories, evidence, and analysis: proceedings of a
conference held by the International Economic Association at
Copenhagen, Denmark/edited by Niels Thygesen,
Kumaraswamy Velupillai, and Stefano Zambelli.
p.cm.
Conference held in June 1989.
Includes indexes.
ISBN 0–8147–8194–2
1. Business cycles—Congresses.   I. Thygesen, Niels.
II. Velupillai, Kumaraswamy, 1947–   .   III. Zambelli, Stefano.
IV. International Economic Association.
HB3711.B94   1991
338.5'42—dc20                                          91–21976
                                                          CIP

In Memoriam
Sir John Hicks and Karl Brunner

# Contents

*Contents*

# Preface

Soon after Professor Jean-Paul Fitoussi took over as the Secretary-General of the International Economic Association he suggested, to Kumaraswamy Velupillai, the possibility of a conference on 'Business Cycles: Theory and Evidence'. The original suggestion was mooted as far back as 1984 when Fitoussi and Velupillai were colleagues at the European University Institute in Fiesole. Indeed, the original proposal to the IEA was to hold the conference in Florence in 1985. These plans had to be shelved in view of the departure, first of Fitoussi to Paris and then of Velupillai to Copenhagen and Aalborg. The ideas were taken up again after Velupillai had settled down in Denmark and were finally brought to fruition in June 1989. The result is this volume.

As anyone who has organised conferences knows only too well there are trials and tribulations in any such endeavour. It would be dishonest to deny that we had our share of these. In proportion, however, to the excitement, interest, willingness and goodwill shown by all concerned the traumas were quite insignificant.

Our greatest indebtedness, as all participants would testify, goes to Rigmor Lundgaard and Else-Marie Pedersen, the conference secretaries. Every detail was meticulously planned and pleasantly executed by them. In this they – and we – also had the invaluable help of Bjarne Skarin. Whatever administrative success the conference had is due entirely to their valiant efforts.

At an early stage and then all the way through to the completion of the preparation the co-chairmen, Niels Thygesen and Vela Velupillai, had the expert help and excellent advice of an advisory board. The advisory board of Professors Charles Feinstein, Jean-Paul Fitoussi, Lars Jonung and Axel Leijonhufvud were instrumental in helping with the organisation of various sessions. In particular Professor Charles Feinstein was responsible for Part V; Professor Lars Jonung for the session on 'Political Business Cycle Theories'; Professor Leijonhufvud for Part III and Professor Velupillai for Part IV. To all of them we are deeply grateful.

We had the privilege of honouring a past Vice-President of the International Economic Association, Professor P. Nørregaard Rasmussen of the University of Copenhagen, on the occasion of his retirement. The farewell dinner on the last day was held in his honour.

The one sadness to report was the death of Professor Karl Brunner a few weeks before the conference. He had, quite enthusiastically, agreed to contribute and had also been in correspondence with us literally till the day of his untimely and sad death. We hope that, in some sense, this volume is a tribute to his lifelong dedication to a critical approach to economic analysis. We are sure that all participants would agree with our decision to dedicate these proceedings to the memory of Karl Brunner.

We were generously funded by the Danish Social Science Research Council, the Carlsberg Foundation and, through the good offices of Professor Lars Jonung, also the Swedish Central Bank (Sveriges Riksbank). We thank all these organisations.

# The International Economic Association

A non-profit organisation with purely scientific aims, the International Economic Association (IEA) was founded in 1950. It is in fact a federation of national economic associations and presently includes fifty-eight such professional organisations from all parts of the world. Its basic purpose is the development of economics as an intellectual discipline. Its approach recognises a diversity of problems, systems and values in the world and also takes note of methodological diversities.

The IEA has, since its creation, tried to fulfil that purpose by promoting mutual understanding of economists from the West and the East as well as from the North and the South through the organisation of scientific meetings and common research programmes, and by means of publications on problems of current importance. During its forty years of existence, it has organised eighty-six round-table conferences for specialists on topics ranging from fundamental theories to methods and tools of analysis and major problems of the present-day world. Nine triennial World Congresses have also been held, which have regularly attracted the participation of a great many economists from all over the world.

The Association is governed by a Council, composed of representatives of all member associations, and by a fifteen-member Executive Committee which is elected by the Council. The present Executive Committee (1989–92) is composed as follows:

|  |  |
|---|---|
| President: | Professor Anthony B. Atkinson, UK |
| Vice-President: | Professor Luo Yuanzheng, China |
| Treasurer: | Professor Alexandre Lamfalussy, Belgium |
| Past President: | Professor Amartya Sen, India |
| | |
| Other members: | Professor Abel Aganbegyan, USSR |
| | Professor Kenneth J. Arrow, USA |
| | Professor Edmar Lisboa Bacha, Brazil |
| | Professor B. R. Brahmananda, India |
| | Professor Wolfgang Heinrichs, GDR |
| | Professor Edmond Malinvaud, France |

xiii

# List of Participants and Contributors

* denotes contributors to this volume

* **Professor Ralph Abraham**, Department of Mathematics, University of California, USA

  **Professor Michael Bordo**, Department of Economics, University of South Carolina, USA

  **Dr Helge Brink**, Department of Economics, Politics and Public Administration, University of Aalborg, Denmark

  **Professor Meyer Burstein**, Department of Economics, York University, Ontario, Canada

* **Professor Forrest Capie**, The City University Business School, London, UK

* **Professor Barry Eichengreen**, University of California at Berkeley, California, USA

* **Professor Revold M. Entov**, Institute of World Economy and International Relations, Moscow, USSR

  **Professor Charles Feinstein**, Nuffield College, Oxford, UK

* **Professor Chaim Fershtman**, Foerder Institute for Economic Research, Tel Aviv University, Israel

* **Professor Arthur Fishman**, Foerder Institute for Economic Research, Tel Aviv University, Israel

  **Professor Jean-Paul Fitoussi**, Observatoire Français des Conjonctures Economiques, Paris, France

\* **Professor Joshua S. Goldstein**, School of International Relations, University of Southern California, USA

\* **Professor Richard M. Goodwin**, Università degli Studi di Siena, Facoltà di Scienze Economiche e Bancarie, Siena, Italy

**Dr Christian Groth**, Institute of Economics, University of Copenhagen, Denmark

**Professor Daniel Heymann**, Comision Economica Para America Latina Y El Caribe, Buenos Aires, Argentina

**Dr Carsten Heyn-Johnsen**, Department of Economics, Politics and Public Administration, University of Aalborg, Denmark

**Professor Douglas Hibbs**, Trade Union Institute for Economic Research, Stockholm, Sweden

**Dr Jesper Jespersen**, Institute of Financing, Copenhagen School of Business, Frederiksberg, Denmark

**Professor Lars Jonung**, Stockholm School of Business, Sweden

\* **Professor Charles P. Kindleberger**, Department of Economics, Massachusetts Institute of Technology, Cambridge, Massachusetts, USA

**Professor Alan Kirman**, Department of Economics, European University Institute, Firenze, Italy

\* **Professor Finn E. Kydland**, Graduate School of Industrial Administration, Carnegie-Mellon University, Pittsburg, USA

\* **Professor J. P. Laffargue**, University of Paris and Centre d'Etudes Prospectives d'Economie Mathematique Appliqueés à la Planification, Paris, France

**Professor Axel Leijonhufvud**, Department of Economics, University of California at Los Angeles, California, USA

* **Professor Marco Lippi**, Università degli Studi di Modena, Facoltà Economica e Commercio, Modena, Italy

* **Professor Hans-Walter Lorenz**, Georg-August Universität, Göttingen, West Germany

* **Professor Pierre Malgrange**, Centre d'Etudes Prospectives d'Economie Mathematique Appliqueés, à la Planification, Paris, France

* **Professor John McCall**, Department of Economics, University of California at Los Angeles, California, USA

  **Professor Anders Ølgaard**, Institute of Economics, University of Copenhagen, Denmark

* **Professor Martin Paldam**, Institute of Economics, University of Aarhus, Denmark

  **Professor Edmund Phelps**, Department of Economics, Columbia University in the City of New York, USA

* **Dr Andrey V. Poletayev**, Institute of World Economy and International Relations, Moscow, USSR

* **Professor Edward C. Prescott**, Department of Economics, University of Minnesota, Minneapolis, Minnesota, USA

  **Professor Poul Nørregaard Rasmussen**, Institute of Economics, University of Copenhagen, Denmark

* **Dr Lucrezia Reichlin**, Observatoire Français des Conjonctures Economiques, Paris, France

  **Dr Berc Rustem**, Department of Electrical Engineering, Imperial College of Science and Technology, London, UK

  **Professor Björn Thalberg**, Department of Economics, University of Lund, Sweden

* **Professor Niels Thygesen**, Institute of Economics, University of Copenhagen, Denmark

* **Professor K. Velupillai**, Institute of Economics, University of Copenhagen, Denmark

* **Dr Stefano Zambelli**, Department of Economics, Politics and Public Administration, University of Aalborg, Denmark

# Abbreviations and Acronyms

| | |
|---|---|
| AE | adaptive expectations |
| AI | artificial intelligence |
| ANU | Australian National University |
| CEPAL | Comision Economica Para America Latina Y El Caribe |
| CEPREMAP | Centre d'Etudes Prospectives d'Economie Mathematique Appliquées à la Planification |
| CPI | Consumer Price Index |
| ECT | elementary catastrophe theory |
| EMS | European Monetary System |
| FDIC | Federal Deposit Insurance Corporation |
| FSLIC | Federal Savings and Loan Insurance Corporation |
| GNP | gross national product |
| IRI | Instituto per la Riconstruzione Italiana |
| LTP | long-term potential |
| NE | no expectations |
| NBER | National Bureau of Economic Research |
| OECD | Organisation for Economic Cooperation and Development |
| OFCE | Observatoire Français des Conjunctures Economiques |
| OLS | ordinary least squares |
| RE | rational expectations |
| RFC | Reconstruction Finance Corporation |
| UCLA | University of California at Los Angeles |

# Introduction

Niels Thygesen, Kumaraswamy Velupillai and
Stefano Zambelli

From the outset our intention was to try to represent the widest possible alternatives in the theoretical and empirical analysis of fluctuations in industrial societies. This implied, somewhat regrettably, that the real and deep issues of fluctuations in the developing countries was not something for consideration at this conference. Perhaps a more specialised theme, concentrating on issues of relevance to the developing countries, from the point of view of business-cycle theory should be the natural sequel to this conference. Some of us have been thinking along these lines.

Even apart from this we did not fully succeed in encompassing all the theories at the frontiers of research. In particular the new Keynesian approaches and the financial instability models had no proponents in the formal sessions. It is also regrettable that Marxian theories of the crisis and other stagnation theories were not presented or discussed. Again, we hope the record of the proceedings will lead to a wider and deeper analysis both at the theoretical and empirical levels.

Given the above shortcomings – and others – it was felt that a wide spectrum of theories and issues were presented, discussed, attacked and defended. The most characteristic features of the presentations, discussions and lectures were their eclectic nature and good-humoured openness. Almost no dogmatism was displayed by any proponent of any view or school. A willingness to accept criticism, modify assumptions and be sceptical seemed also to be a feature of the whole of the proceedings. This is reflected in the fact that several contributions were modified significantly as a result of the discussions.

In this introduction an effort is made to provide a summary view of the distinguished lectures and the main papers. Some of the more debatable points are published as comments by the discussants and where applicable the relevant responses are also recorded. Finally a summary of the issues taken up during the 'panel discussion' is also presented.

Before plunging into the topics and lectures and their substance it may well be useful to recall the late Professor Erik Lundberg's opening paragraph to introduce an earlier business cycle conference also held under the auspices of the International Economic Association:

> It is difficult to say how far the papers presented at the Oxford Conference in September 1952 give a representative picture of the present position of business cycle research. To describe a number of economists, their papers and contributions to discussions as representative has no very precise meaning. There are a great number of economists all over the world working on business-cycle problems with widely diverging methods of approach. There is the further implication that this particular subject of research varies from country to country, and changes with the economist at the same time as the economist (*qua* economist) changes with it. In such a flux of mind and matter the statement that our proceedings were representative certainly cannot be proved by some kind of significance test. It is, however, a statement that I should like to make, and that can be made.
>
> (Lundberg, 1955, p. ix)

It is quite remarkable how apposite these words are for a conference on the same issues held after a period of thirty-seven years. The warnings, the caveats and the claims all apply almost word for word. With the qualifications above we also feel that this conference was representative of the broad spectrum of topics going under the name of 'Business Cycles: Theories, Evidence and Analysis'. Our defence for this claim – with the caveats above – is based on the 'survey' lecture by Velupillai (cf. Chapter 1, below). To the extent that the 'survey' is comprehensive it will be evident that the conference was a fair representation of current research activity at the frontiers of analysis of economic fluctuations. We can now turn to summarising, albeit inadequately, the different contributions.

We begin with the three distinguished lectures by Kindleberger, Abraham and McCall in that order. They present, on a broad canvas, the historical, phenomenological and structural perspectives on the facts of economic fluctuations, the analytics of it and their foundations in tastes and technology respectively. Kindleberger builds upon his celebrated earlier studies, in particular his justly famous monograph on 'A History of Financial Crises' (Kindleberger, 1978) and, for example, chapters 8 and 9 of Kindleberger (1985). The basic point, however, is an analysis of *the international character* of the famous ten-year-cycles – the fountain-head of business-cycle *theory* ever since Juglar, Marx and Sombart. A key assertion and a point in the agenda for future research – theoretically and empirically – must be his well-reasoned point about the failure of collective memory in conjunction with financial crises. It is an assertion which rational-expectations economists must take seriously. On the other hand the peculiar case of the Krueger-crash in Sweden in the early 1930s and the fact that the Stockholm stock market remained dormant for almost fifty years is a counterexample that cuts both ways: the rational-expectations way and the Kindleberger way. An interesting observation by Kindleberger leads smoothly to the basic topics in the lectures by Abraham and, then, McCall:

> Any analogy between predictable cyclical paths of stars and galaxies and the economy is flawed in my judgement. Economics less resembles celestial mechanics than evolutionary biology in which mutations can be confidently predicted to occur, and later explained, but forecasting their nature and timing is hazardous.
>
> (Kindleberger, 1985 p. 4)

Abraham's masterly survey of the mathematics of dynamical systems emphasised the importance of non-linearities in behavioural phenomena – be they systems in the natural sciences or social sciences. Ralph Abraham, almost more than any other single person since the halcyon days of Poincaré, Birkhoff (the elder) and the Russian disciples of Andronov and Mandelstam, has made a passionate plea for the *geometry* of non-linear dynamics to be taken seriously in the analysis of fluctuations of all phenomena. His masterpiece (in four-volumes so far) *Dynamics: The Geometry of Behaviour* (Abraham and Shaw, 1984 a, b, c; 1988) has made this vast and interesting field available to a large audience. In this lecture the emphasis was on the intricate dynamics generated in non-linear forced oscillatory systems with the Rayleigh–van der Pol equations being canonical. The use of bifurcation diagrams to tame these complex dynamics in forced oscillators was presented with deceptive simplicity. The opening remarks on the personalities and events that have shaped the development of the theory of non-linear dynamical systems gave this highly technical lecture a historical perspective indicating that exciting breakthroughs were in the offing at the frontiers of research. In particular, the vexing disjunction between the experimental and numerical *facts* of chaos and the lack of *a theory* of chaos may soon have a solution – perhaps in terms of bifurcation diagrams. At least that seemed to be the implicit message. Alas it is no longer the case that there are 'predictable cyclical paths of stars and galaxies' (Kindleberger, this volume); even Hamiltonian systems have succumbed to the magic of non-linearities.

Almost exactly a century ago three disparate events had their origins: Poincaré's systematisation of non-linear dynamics; Hilbert's proof of Gordon's theorem; Raman y Cajal's anatomical geometry of the brain. The confluence of the by-products of the latter two is manifested in the classic work by McCulloch and Pitts (1943). The updating of that in the theories of neural nets at the frontiers of research in neurology, neurophysiology, computability and complexity is the further confluence of flowering of Poincaré's research agenda. McCall, accepting the neoclassical closure in terms of preferences, endowments and technology made a strong and reasoned case for going to the basics of preferences – i.e. tastes – and technology in terms of, and within the formalism of, neural networks. This is an audacious as well as an exciting research programme which will ultimately make economics a truly experimental science. The origins of fluctuations should be sought within the framework of neural nets and the constraints imposed by meaningful (physiological, neurological, psychological) thresholds. The first basic casualty of this approach will surely be the non-satiation assumption at the micro level and hence elementary reliance on Walras's law as a conservation principle in proofs of existence. The ramifications, however, are many-faceted. It was also a genuine plea for a truly interdisciplinary research programme harnessing the results, methods and concepts of physiologists, neurologists, computer scientists, physicists, mathematicians, economists and psychologists. The canvas is vast; the details intricate; the scope almost daunting; the prospects exciting.

So much for the distinguished lectures. We felt that their purpose was well served – broad surveys which took many of us, gently, to some of the frontiers with a glimpse of pastures beyond the walls.

The summary of the more concrete contributions can, now, be relatively brief in view of the survey in Chapter 1 and some of the discussion material.

In reading Chapter 5 at least two points must be kept in mind:

(a) The basic framework of real business-cycle (RBC) variants of
    new-classical economics;
(b) The irrelevance of traditional supply–demand analysis;

RBC theorists accept a fundamentalist position with respect to the
neoclassical closure in terms of preferences, endowments and technology. Such a closure has neither scope nor need for money and its
institutional ramifications. Once these fundamentals are specified
equilibrium *is* rational behaviour *and* consistent dynamic solutions.
No nonsense about supply-and-demand functions. The mistake is
often made that RBC theorists rely exclusively on technology shocks;
this is not necessarily the case although it is the usual assumption.
Against this background Kydland and Prescott relax some of the
more traditional assumptions: specifically, capacity utilisation and its
manning are allowed to be choice variables. The calibration, unlike
earlier models or share variables, is to national income and product
account but also to household survey data. The repeated use of the
phrase 'computable general equilibrium model' is, strictly speaking,
an infelicity. This does *not* refer to *computability* in the strict foundational sense.

In Chapter 6 Fershtman and Fishman set a search model in its
paces by investigating the feasibility of cyclical activity resulting from
'equilibrium *interaction* between economic agents at the micro level'
(Introduction to Chapter 6, italics added). There is, in our opinion, a
conceptual infelicity in assuming *a continuum* of agents and firms in
search models – as Fershtman and Fishman do, explicitly in the
illuminating section 4 of their contribution. The essence of the
Stigler–McCall approach to search as an individual activity was to
restore some semblance of meaning to the behaviour of real agents.
By definition an agent or a firm is insignificant in a continuum model.
The analytical infelicity can be removed by working with non-
standard models and using, for example, a consistent theory of
probability for such models as provided by Nelson (1987). If we let
this infelicity pass the analysis by Fershtman and Fishman is an
elegant alternative to the somewhat *ad hoc* sun-spot or bootstrap
approach to endogenous cycles outside the non-linear tradition. Alan
Kirman's insightful remarks as a discussant provides a wealth of
constructive suggestions for further explorations.

The two papers by Malgrange and Lorenz in Part IV belong to
what may usefully still be called the 'Keynesian tradition'. There is a
plethora of econometric models of varying degrees of 'Coarseness'

proliferating international organisations, national agencies and even universities. In spite of the fundamental criticism by Lucas practitioners continue to forecast with princely unconcern. Many of these models are Ptolemaic in nature: epicycles upon epicycles to explain away mounting discrepancies; i.e. *ad hoc* assumptions, one upon the other over many layers, obscure the fact that underlying all the massiveness is a simple (linear) multiplier–accelerator model doing all the work. This point is made and its implications are forcefully brought out by Laffargue and Malgrange. There is no money in their model – yet another feature of the traditional multiplier–accelerator model. It is also a closed economy. They are not to be blamed for claiming microfoundations in a representative agent model. Such is the practice in the profession. They are quite French in assuming exogenously given wage and interest rates. We have, therefore, a traditional fix-price, closed-economy, real model. The virtue is the blatant honesty with which the authors state every assumption. Essentially theirs is an exercise in adjustment dynamics under different hypotheses about expectations, parameters and shocks. Fluctuations as adjustment dynamics is an old story. It is, however, told with modern, expectational, themes in the foreground. The points raised by the discussants, Thalberg and Jespersen, provide additional food for thought.

In Chapter 8 Hans-Walter Lorenz presents, essentially, a tutorial in some of the more elementary aspects of the theory of non-linear dynamical systems. It is also a minor survey of the traditional application of results from the theory of non-linear dynamical systems to various standard economic models to generate periodic and aperiodic dynamics. However, the central point in his contribution is the use of a modified Metzler model to apply and discuss Shil'nikov's celebrated theorem. In discussing this paper Christian Groth correctly pointed out that the '*minor* modification to Metzler's (1941) cycle model with inventories' (Lorenz; italics added) was, after all, not quite 'minor'. However, basically, Lorenz's paper is not about specific models but – apart from the tutorial aspect – is about the methodology of modelling fluctuations. His is a case, based on non-linear dynamics, for a revival of interest in the classics by Kaldor, Hicks and Goodwin. There is, however, a strange omission: why no discussion of *solitons*? All the models and the underlying mathematics – even when non-linear – are about systems whose limit sets are, ultimately, confined to some bounded region of the phase-space. The spirit of Lorenz's discussion calls for a thoroughly disequilibrium methodology and that means dynamical systems persisting not simply in oscillation but also in *far-from-equilibrium regions* of the phase-space. A wider notion of persistence is surely on the agenda in the further applications of results at the frontiers of non-linear dynamics. If fluctuations in economic activity embody true unpredictability in some significant sense, then they have to be generated by dynamical systems capable of universal computation. None of the cases in Lorenz's illuminating paper satisfy that requirement.

Capie in Chapter 9 investigates the relationship between money and fluctuations in economic activity for Britain for the period 1870–1913. It is a study judiciously combining standard hypotheses on the influence of money on economic activity with statiscal methods for time-series analysis on data on which the author has himself worked in collecting, updating and refining. A theme which is basic to the paper is the classic methodology of Friedman and Schwartz. Essentially the author wishes to repeat the exercise for the United Kingdom. His negative conclusion that 'There is no clear relationship between money and the business cycle in Britain over this period at least' and the more guarded statement that: 'this exercise in measurement has shown that the relationship between money and the business cycle in Britain is far from unambiguous', is subject to a searching criticism by Burstein in his lengthy discussion. A few remarks on Capie's thorough analysis may not be irrelevant at this point:

(i) It is curious that the 'historiography' – however brief – fails to mention Hayek's classic of 1933.
(ii) All the statistical techniques employed – including his use of the Kalman filter – are within a linear framework. A non-linear monetary transmission mechanism, even in the presence of a stable banking system, may couple the real economy in such a way as to generate fluctuations in economic activity. The linear Kalman filter used by Capie and Mills is not necessarily an improvement. The decomposition by an optimal non-linear filter may unravel different, more fluctuating, stories – even if not series. These remarks are related to the literature discussed in the contribution to these proceedings by Lippi and Reichlin. The impressive efforts that have resulted in Capie's access to important data should, perhaps, be analysed by non-linear, non-stationary models.

In Chapter 10 Barry Eichengreen examines exactly what the title of the paper indicates: 'The Comparative Performance of Fixed and Flexible Exchange Rate Regimes: Inter-war Evidence'. However, in the context of this conference it is perhaps best read as a study of the effects of alternative policy regimes on international aspects of business cycles. In this sense it provides empirical flesh in an analytical way to some aspects of issues taken up by Charles Kindleberger at a much broader level. When Gottfried Haberler wrote his classic survey (Haberler, 1937) he was able to say (and substantiate the statement with numerous references) that 'the literature on international trade has become more "cycle conscious" in recent times and contains frequent references to cycle problems' (Haberler, 1937, p. 303, fn). The literature on business cycle *theory* does not seem to have become, even in the intervening five decades, more 'international-trade conscious'. Eichengreen's impressive *statistical analysis* of three policy regimes in the inter-war period and their impact on real and nominal measures of (international) economic activity cries out for formalisation within *the theoretical* framework of a business-cycle model. The generalised queries posed by Eichengreen are:

(a) To what extent and how are flexible policy regimes and fluctuations related?;
(b) The (welfare) costs of the (resulting) fluctuations;
(c) The relationship between flexibility and the predictability of fluctuations;

and finally:

(d) The relationship between the flexibility of the policy regime and factor mobility (in this case, capital);

All these issues are highly topical and Eichengreen has done a signal service in relating the statistics and the discussion of the inter-war period with current events and debates. There is one interesting conclusion which should, surely, whet the appetite of those interested in formalising the dynamics underlying the descriptive statistics, 'whether a reduction in exchange rate variability confers economic benefits depends on *how* that reduction is achieved' (Eichengreen, italics added).

'*Corsi e ricorsi*', the enigmatic utterance of the great Vico haunts
the destiny of myth-makers, story-tellers *and business cycle theorists*.
Someday someone will write on the theories and theorists of cycles
from Charlemagne to Lucas via Pacioli and Marx. Till that blissful
day arrives we must rest content with the imagination and audacity of
long-cycle theorists. Goldstein ranged far and wide in his search for
hypotheses to 'explain' long cycles in his recent book (cf. Goldstein,
1988). There is an admirable, albeit short – as it must be – survey of
the literature and the phenomena in the compact contribution by
Entov and Poletayev (Chapter 17). It is the one approach to fluctuations in the zoo of business-cycle theories which seems to be indisput-
ably empirical. The sources that theorists of long-cycles can mine are
inexhaustible. The warning, by the authors, on this count, is worth a
moment's reflection:

> Another non-negligible factor is the quality of the available long-
> term series. The constructing of such series still remains a chal-
> lenging task, and because of that the reliability of the obtained
> results are often questionable. Unfortunately, the methods of
> constructing the long-term series, which are sometimes cited by the
> proponents of long cycles to support their arguments, perhaps
> won't stand a mild criterion of reliability.

A point neglected in their compact survey deserves some mention.
In section 2.2 of their paper Entov and Poletayev discuss the reinvestment cycle (the 'echo effect') as a basis for long-cycle theories. Oddly
enough they fail to mention the early mathematical (Tinbergen) and
empirical (Einarsen) work on the shipbuilding cycle. Had they integrated these approaches the separation between the section on 'the
innovations process' and 'the investment mechanism' may have been
shown to be somewhat artificial. Few will disagree that the subject of
'Political Economy' owes as much to Petty, Malthus and Wicksell for
its development as to anyone else. They emphasised demographic
factors – sometimes even to the exclusion of most other influences. It
is, therefore, a poignant fact that Entov and Poletayev are able to
note that 'Up to now there have been practically no serious empirical
studies of the long-term demographic fluctuations.'
    At the frontiers of theoretical and time-series research on business
cycles it is, once again, fashionable to discuss growth cycles. The
many and esoteric models of growth dynamics proliferating the

mathematical macrodynamic literature has almost never been integrated with the empirical facts of long cycles. The authors of Chapter
11 ruefully make a note of this anomaly. The hope is that the
techniques of the recent advances in growth cycle analysis may also
encompass the problem of long cycles.

Whilst Entov and Poletayev seem to assert that the dating of long
cycles remains unsolved, Goldstein (Chapter 12) almost predicates
his analysis of the exact opposite assertion 'Past empirical studies of
long waves have *agreed on the dating of long waves historically* but
not on the scope of those waves in terms of variables encompassed,
relevant time periods, or causal mechanisms.' Thus the tone is set for
the scope of *his* investigation. Just as much as Eichengreen's is a
statistical study, Goldstein's is a descriptive time-series analysis.
Goldstein's hypotheses are bold; his scope is vast; but his predictions
hopeful – the possibility of getting 'off the merry-go-round of great
power war once and for all'. Goldstein's themes are similar to those
in Paul Kennedy's much-discussed recent best-seller written from a
historian's perspective (Kennedy, 1989); Goldstein's is the perspective of the political scientist. What are the messages for the political
economist? There are, of course, the familiar elements too: innovational waves and speculations on the future of some of these. Curious
that the effect of foundational and theoretical issues in the pure
sciences on the development of new waves of innovations is com-
prehensively neglected in this otherwise interesting study of long
swings.

The two quite heterogeneous papers of Part VII (appropriate for a
section including a contribution by Lippi who has devoted more time
than most theorists to analyse 'heterogeneity'!) are on two widely
differing problems at the frontiers of business-cycle theory and its
empirical handmaidens: mathematical underpinnings of some aspect
of time-series analysis and empirical studies of a view of political
business cycles.

Lippi and Reichlin, in Chapter 13, take us to the frontiers of some
of the recent methodological issues stemming from the time-series
analysis of real business-cycle theories. Three issues must be kept in
mind when reflecting upon the results and critique in the Lippi–
Reichlin contributions:

(a) the emphasis on the growth-cycle aspects of fluctuations in real
business cycle theories;
(b) advances in the study of non-stationary time-series data;

(c) the fundamental Frischian methodological prism of impulse-propagation *hilfenkonstruktion*.

Since the related issues of segmented trends is a part of this framework of analysis of fluctuations one would have expected appeals to, or utilisation of, Girsanov-type theorems (cf. Wong, 1971, ch. 6); moreover the order of the systems studied in these classes of models remains low, which would have led one to believe that advances in non-linear and non-stationary time-series analysis could also have been harnessed (cf. for example, Priestly, 1988, for an excellent exposition). Curiously, neither of these classes of results has been exploited – thus far.

The analysis of election statistics to reveal political and economic aspects of fluctuations was a virgin territory when Tingsten published his studies in the heyday of business-cycle theories: 1937 (Tingsten, 1937). After the early speculative theoretical works by Kalecki and Åkerman in the 1940s the field remained fallow, so to speak, till the age of stagflation in the late 1960s and early 1970s. The work till the early years of this decade has been expertly surveyed, summarised and extended in the monograph by Borooah and van der Ploeg (1983). The only advances in the orthodox approaches since then seems to be the incorporation of elements of new classical macroeconomics, especially versions of the rational-expectations hypothesis. Paldam's contribution addresses the issue of economic policies as effected by political parties in governments of *democracies* within the framework of the so-called Alesina RE Partisan cycle theory. It is, essentially, an empirical study.

Since much of this literature pertains to the election statistics of democracies it is curious that the political science literature is totally neglected. In particular the fundamental paper by Gerald Kramer (1977) could provide much of the microeconomic buttressing these theories lack in spite of the lip service – and no more – paid to new classical foundations. The necessity of the buttressing is evident from the fact that the analysis is of *competitive voting processes*. That is an indication of the links also with social choice theory. Whither impossibility theorems, then? Heyn-Johnsen's contributions as a discussant is, partly, also a background survey and critique of this class of models.

And so we come to Part VIII. The report of the panel discussion under the chairmanship of Michael Bordo speaks for itself. The last chapter is a piece of history – a link with a great past and many

futures. Richard Goodwin was our link with an earlier IEA conference on the same topic: the Oxford one of 1952. No one has worked
systematically at the mathematical formalism of non-linear theories
of economic fluctuations for so long with so much success as Goodwin
has. His lecture needs no summary nor introduction. A minor piece
of background information may be useful for the unwary reader
unacquainted with the details of cubic non-linearities in second-order
non-linear differential equations.

The celebrated Lorenz equations are:

$$\dot{x}_1 = \alpha(x_2 - x_1) \tag{1}$$

$$\dot{x}_2 = -x_1x_3 + \beta x_1 - x_2 \tag{2}$$

$$\dot{x}_3 = x_1x_2 - \gamma x_3 \tag{3}$$

Equations (2) and (3) contain the non-linear terms $(-x_1x_3)$ and $(x_1x_2)$
respectively. Otto Rössler sought a 'simpler' system and produced:

$$\dot{x}_1 = -x_2 - x_3 \tag{4}$$

$$\dot{x}_2 = x_1 + \delta x_2 \tag{5}$$

$$\dot{x}_3 = \varepsilon + x_1x_3 - \eta x_3 \tag{6}$$

At the cost of an inhomogeneity in his third equation he was able to
⁻oduce a system with the one non-linearity, viz. $(x_1x_3)$ in equation
₁o). For parameter values, for example, of $\delta = 0.55$, $\varepsilon = 2$, and $\eta = 4$
the system exhibits 'strange attractors'.

In Chapter 1 there is a sketch of the story behind the so-called
'Goodwin oscillator' (cf. Velupillai, 1990, for the romance of the
story); no wonder, then, that the Rössler system appeals so much to
the ever-fertile mind of a supreme theorist of cycles looking eternally
for the simplest hypotheses to describe events at the phenomenological level. However, events have even overtaken this artist: we now
know that not only are there limit points, limit cycles and strange
attractors but that there is a fourth class – a class capable of universal
computation; a class lying delicately balanced between the limit
cycles of Poincaré and the 'chaotic' attractors of Birkhoff. Not even
the great Poincaré foresaw such a possibility. As our analytical tools
develop, our perception of phenomena sharpen and we discuss

details of finer and more significant structure. That, almost, is the path of civilisation and Goodwin's non-linear path is the story of growth-cycle theory.

It is appropriate to end this introduction with remembrances of yet another anniversary; it is exactly fifty years ago that Schumpeter's monumental two-volume study of 'Business Cycles' was first published. In the 'Preface' to that influential work he wrote that he 'had [his] own tale to tell' (Schumpeter, 1939, p. vi) about Business Cycles; and then went on to note that 'there is in fact little in the work done by economists during the last two or three decades that does not bear upon problems of economic cycles in one way or another', (Schumpeter, 1939, p. vi). It is a sobering thought that these words are equally apposite today – fifty years later. It puts in perspective for many futures, the theme of the 'Panel Discussion'.

**References**

Abraham, R. and Shaw, C. D. (1984, a) *Dynamics: The Geometry of Behaviour. Part One: Periodic Behaviour* (Santa Cruz: Aerial Press).
Abraham, R. and Shaw, C. D. (1984, b) *Dynamics: The Geometry of Behaviour. Part Two: Chaotic Behaviour* (Santa Cruz: Aerial Press).
Abraham, R. and Shaw, C. D. (1984, c) *Dynamics: The Geometry of Behaviour. Part Three: Global Behaviour* (Santa Cruz: Aerial Press).
Abraham, R. and Shaw, C. D. (1988) *Dynamics: The Geometry of Behaviour. Part Four: Bifurcation Behaviour* (Santa Cruz: Aerial Press).
Borooah, V. K. and van der Ploeg, F. (1983) *Political Aspects of the Economy* (Cambridge: Cambridge University Press).
Goldstein, J. S. (1988) *Long Cycles: Prosperity and War in the Modern Age* (New Haven: Yale University Press).
Haberler, G. von (1937) *Prosperity and Depression: A Theoretical Analysis of Cyclical Movements* (Geneva: The League of Nations).
Kennedy, P. (1989) *The Rise and Fall of Great Powers: Economic Change and Military Conflict from 1500 to 2000* (London: Fontana).
Kindleberger, C. (1978) *Manias, Panics and Crashes: A History of Financial Crises* (London: Macmillan).
Kindleberger, C. (1985) *Keynesianism vs. Monetarism and Other Essays in Financial History* (London: Allen & Unwin).
Kramer, G. (1977) 'A Dynamical Model of Political Equilibrium', *Journal of Economic Theory*, vol. 16, no 2, December, pp. 310–34.
Lundberg, E. (1955) Introduction to Erik Lundberg and A. D. Knox (eds) *The Business Cycle in the Post-War World: Proceedings of a Conference Held by the International Economic Association* (London: Macmillan).
McCulloch, W. S. and Pitts, W. H. (1943) 'A Logical Calculus of the Ideas Immanent in Nervous Activity', *The Bulletin of Mathematical Biophysics*, vol. 5, pp. 115–33.

Metzler, L. A. (1941) 'The Nature and Stability of Inventory Cycles', *Review of Economics and Statistics*, vol. 23, pp. 113–29.

Nelson, E. (1987) *Radically Elementary Probability Theory*, Annals of Mathematics Studies: # 117 (Princeton: Princeton University Press).

Priestly, M. B. (1988) *Non-linear and Non-stationary Time Series Analysis* London: Academic Press.

Schumpeter, J. A. (1939) *Business Cycles: A Theoretical, Historical, and Statistical Analysis of the Capitalist Process* (New York: McGraw Hill).

Tingsten, H. (1937) *Political Behaviour: Studies in Election Statistics* (London: P. S. King & Son).

Velupillai, K. (1990) 'The (Non-linear) Life and (Economic) Times of Richard M. Goodwin', in K. Velupillai (ed.) *Non-linear and Multisectoral Macrodynamics: Essays in Honour of Richard Goodwin* (London: Macmillan).

Wong, E. (1971) *Stochastic Processes in Information and Dynamical Systems* (New York: McGraw Hill).

# Part I

# Introductory

# 1 Theories of the Trade Cycle: Analytical and Conceptual Perspectives and Perplexities

Kumaraswamy Velupillai
UNIVERSITY OF COPENHAGEN

## 1 INTRODUCTION

[V]an der Pol believes that even periodic business cycles show a
certain analogy to the relaxation oscillation of a physical system.
The essential condition for such oscillations is negative damping
for small deviations and a rather rapidly increasing positive damping for large deviations from the equilibrium position. The psychological response of certain groups of people to changing business
conditions shows doubtless some analogy to the behaviour of
mechanical systems capable of relaxation oscillations (von Kármán,
1940, p. 624).

Denote by:

| | |
|---|---|
| $y$ | level of output |
| $c$ | level of consumption |
| $k$ | capital stock |
| $\dot{k}$ | net investment $(\dot{k} = \dfrac{dk}{dt})$ |
| $l(t)$ | autonomous investment |
| $\phi(\dot{y})$ | induced investment |
| $\alpha, \beta, \varepsilon$ | positive constants |

Then, on the basis of standard flow identities and simple assumptions
about behaviour and adjustment dynamics, we have:

3

$$y = c + \dot{k} \tag{1.1}$$

$$c = \alpha y + \beta \tag{1.2}$$

$$\dot{k} = \phi(\dot{y}) + \ell(t) \tag{1.3}$$

$$\dot{y} = \frac{(1-\alpha)}{\varepsilon} \left\{ \frac{\beta + \dot{k}}{1-\alpha} - y \right\} \tag{1.4}$$

put:

$$\Phi(\dot{y}) \equiv \phi(\dot{y}) - \varepsilon\dot{y} \tag{1.5}$$

Therefore:

$$y = \frac{1}{1-\alpha} \left\{ \beta + l(t) + \phi(\dot{y}) - \varepsilon\dot{y} \right\} \tag{1.6}$$

Relation (1.3), as will be seen, depicts a non-linear accelerator, relation (1.4) is the incorporation of the dynamic multiplier where $y$ adjusts ($\dot{y} \gtreqless 0$) to the deficiency

$$\left\{ \frac{\beta + \dot{k}}{1 - \alpha} \right\}$$

with a speed of adjustment given by

$$\left\{ \frac{(1 - \alpha)}{\varepsilon} \right\}.$$

Note also that we retained, notationally, the explicit time dependence of autonomous investment $[\ell(t)]$. We shall suppress this time dependence in what follows.

To get from Figure 1.1 to the phase-plane dynamics of Figure 1.2, we proceed as follows:[1]

Put:

$$x = \frac{dy}{dt} \tag{1.7}$$

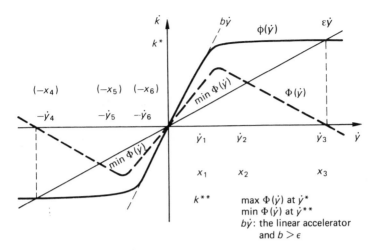

*Figure 1.1*

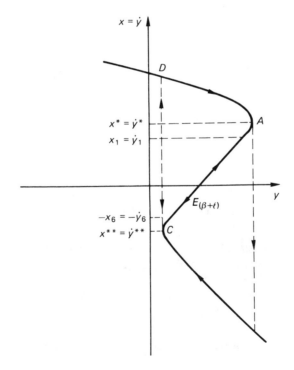

*Figure 1.2*

Then (1.6) is:

$$y = \frac{1}{(1 - \alpha)} \{ \beta + 1 + \phi(x) - \varepsilon x \} \tag{1.8}$$

Assuming the validity of an appropriate form of the implicit function theorem we can write (1.8) as:

$$x = \Omega(y) \tag{1.9}$$

and

$$(1 - \alpha)dy = \phi'(x)dx - \varepsilon dx \tag{1.10}$$

and hence

$$\frac{dx}{dy} = \frac{(1 - \alpha)}{\{\phi'(x) - \varepsilon\}} \tag{1.11}$$

Thus:

1. In the range where the normal accelerator assumptions are satisfied $(k = b\dot{y})$, $\frac{dx}{dy}$ is constant. This is in the range $-x_6 \leqslant x \leqslant x_1$.
2. $\frac{dx}{dy} > 0$ for $-x^{**} < x < x^*$.
3. $\frac{dx}{dy} < 0$ for $x > x^*$
   and for $x < -x^{**}$
4. At $x = x^*$ and $x = x^{**}$, $\frac{dx}{dy}$ is *undefined*.
   This is translated into behavioural dynamics of infinitely fast jumps from $A$ and $C$ to $B$ and $D$ (Figure 1.2).
5. Since $b > \varepsilon$, the equilibrium at $E$ is (locally) unstable.
6. It is clear from Figure 1.1 that there is the standard assumption on the existence of a 'ceiling', $k^*$, and a 'floor' $k^{**}$.

The connoisseur of business cycle theory will recognise the above as Goodwin's celebrated model of 'The Nonlinear Accelerator and the Persistence of Business Cycle' (Goodwin, 1951). The version I have presented is the model without an investment lag – the introduction of which removes the discontinuous jump in $\dot{y}$. The final form, in Goodwin (1951), of the model with an investment lag is given as a Rayleigh-type equation:

$$\ddot{x} + X(\dot{x}) + x = 0 \qquad (1.12)$$

(cf. Goodwin, 1951, p. 13, equation 7b).

This can be reduced to a van der Pol-type equation by redefining:

$$q = \dot{x} \qquad (1.13)$$

and differentiating (1.12) w.r.t. time we get:

$$\ddot{q} + X'(q)\dot{q} + q = 0 \qquad (1.14)$$

If we choose:

$$X(q) = \tau(q^3/3 - q) \qquad (1.15)$$

We get the classical form of the van der Pol-type equation:

$$\ddot{q} + \tau(q^2 - 1)\dot{q} + q = 0 \qquad (1.16)$$

with the phase-plane dynamics depicted in Figure 1.2 – i.e., relaxation oscillations.

Why should we model business cycles as relaxation oscillations (or strange attractors, or . . .)? What are the behavioural and institutional bases for output to oscillate in accordance with the dynamics represented by van der Pol's fascinating equation? Goodwin was not alone in exploiting the rich geometry of this (and related) equations: Le Corbeiller (1933), Hamburger (1934), Samuelson (1947), Georgescu–Roegen (1951), Yasui (1953), Ichimura (1955), and no doubt many others, all made a case for formalising the dynamics of business cycles in terms of van der Pol-type equations. Eugene Wigner (1960), in a celebrated Courant lecture with the fascinating title 'The Unreasonable Effectiveness of Mathematics in the Natural Sciences' gave a possible answer to our query above (provided we substitute 'economist' for 'physicist'!):

A possible explanation of the physicist's use of mathematics to formulate his laws of nature is that he is a somewhat irresponsible person. As a result, when he finds a connection between two quantities which resembles a connection well-known from mathematics, he will jump at the conclusion that the connection *is* that discussed in mathematics *simply because he does not know of any other similar connection*. (Wigner, 1960, p. 8, italics in final two lines added).

On the other hand, the *concept* of maintained oscillations – i.e., the persistence of economic fluctuations – was an independent economic phenomenon. In order to encapsulate this particular aspect of economic fluctuations Kaldor developed an ingenious model of the business cycle which was only subsequently recognised – for special functional forms of the Kaldorian behavioural relations – as being mathematically equivalent to van der Pol-type relaxation oscillations. (Much later, more general functional forms and an appeal to Poincaré–Bendixson results led to formal proofs of the existence of limit cycles in Kaldor-type models; even later, this pretty model became chaotic. No doubt in the years to come it will be transmogrified into Fokker–Planck equations and solitons.) Reading 'economics' for 'physics' it can be seen that Wigner was not as ungenerous to the 'physicist' (≡ 'economist') as the above quote may suggest:

It is true, of course, that physics chooses certain mathematical concepts for the formulation of the laws of nature, and surely only a fraction of all mathematical concepts is used in physics. It is true also that the concepts which were chosen were not selected arbitrarily from a listing of mathematical terms but were *developed*, in many if not most cases, *independently by the physicist and recognized then as having been conceived before by the mathematician* (Wigner, 1960, p. 7; italics added).

There is, surely, a case for the 'pro' – as there is for the 'con'. I have begun this paper in this unusual fashion so as to facilitate the setting of the main theme, or subject matter: to view conceptual developments in business cycle theory from the point of view of the interactions with developments in 'theoretical technology' (Lucas, 1981, p. 9).

To be more specific about the theme, I would like to pose a few more questions (without pretending to know any of the answers – or even presupposing that interesting answers are possible). Would we have thought up the 'non-linear accelerator' with the shape given in Figure 1.1 had we been innocent of the theoretical technology[2] of second-order non-linear differential equations? Indeed, had we thought up the 'non-linear accelerator' in that shape (for strictly economic reasons) would we – as analytical economists – have developed the theory of second-order non-linear differential equations? These are questions about the mutual interaction between theoretical technology and conceptual development. There is one view – the dominant one in economics at least from the point of view of practice, most forcefully expressed by Lucas (1981) – which gives priority to the developments in theoretical technology.

In reviewing 'recent developments in business cycle theory', Lucas claims that 'developments' arise from 'two quite different kinds of forces outside the subdisciplines of monetary economics or business cycle theory' (1981, p. 272):

> Of these forces the most important, I believe, in this area and in economics generally, consists of purely technical developments that enlarge our abilities to construct analogue economies. Here I would include both improvements in mathematical methods and improvements in computational capacity. The neglect in traditional history of doctrine of this force for change in our thinking is a serious omission and contributes to the common but mistaken sense that everything has been said before or 'its all in Marshall'. (Lucas, 1981, pp. 272–3).

and also:

> There is no reason to view our ability to think as being any less limited by available technology then is our ability to act (if, indeed, this distinction can be defended). (Lucas, 1981, p. 286).

Lucas is not alone in approaching the problem of theoretical formalisation and conceptual developments along such 'uni'-directional paths; Richard Gregory seems to be on his side – at least *pro tempore* – albeit in a slightly different but not dissimilar context:

> I wish to explore the notion that the most abstract notions of philosophy and theories of Mind stem directly from technology.

*Technological innovations typically come before conceptual bases by which they are understood*; as understanding grows, principles can be described with increasing generalization to allow deeper analysis (Gregory, 1981, p. 43, italics added).

Most practitioners of mathematical trade cycle theory – if not mathematical economics in general – seem to be followers of this particular Lucasian methodological philosophy. Indeed the example I have chosen, by a leading Keynesian, is squarely in that tradition – of causality running from developments in theoretical technology to conceptual innovations (the 'cubic' characteristic in the van der Pol equation – $\tau(q^3/3 - q)$ – to the 'non-linear accelerator'). I do not believe that the causal theory – as I will call any articulation of the Lucasian methodological philosophy as stated above – is tenable; it is more likely that there is a shifting balance of interactions. The story of Einstein's discovery of Riemannian geometry is, perhaps, one of the most colourful counter-examples to the causal theory (cf. Pais, 1982, pp. 210–25) – although the Dirac-delta function and its 'formal' acceptance is almost equally colourful, and equally useful in countering excessive claims made by the causal theorists.

Whether the causal theory is tenable or not it is a fact that business cycle theory is a highly mathematical subject as it is practised today. Within the main theme of exploring the interconnections between developments in analytical concepts and theoretical technology, it is surely legitimate to ask the more specific question whether the mathematical formalisms that have been used to encapsulate the phenomenon of business cycles is adequate – even accepting the causal view; if not, why not? If adequate why do competing formalisms exist? Underlying these queries is the more basic one of enquiring into the nature of the assumptions that go into the formalism of economic man himself. Can (s)he live, as Rational Economic (Wo)man, with all these formalisms?

## 2   VARIETIES OF BUSINESS CYCLE THEORIES

[T]he diversity of our opinions, . . ., does not arise from some being endowed with a larger share of reason than others, but solely from this, what we conduct our thoughts along different ways, and do not fix our attention on the same objects (Descartes, *A Discourse on Method*, Everyman edn, 1965, p. 3).

A possible catalogue of theories of economic fluctuations that have been given a mathematical formalism could be as follows:[3]

| | |
|---|---|
| 1. Marx | – Mark I (vol. 1 of *Das Kapital*): a distribution cycle – in its modern version elegantly formalised by Goodwin in the Dobb *Festschrift* as 'A Growth Cycle' (cf. Goodwin, 1967). |
| 2. Marx | – Mark II (vol. 2 of *Das Kapital*): reinvestment Cycles (cf. for example, Einarsen, 1938). |
| 3. Marx | – Mark III (vol. 3 of *Das Kapital*): underconsumption Theories of the Cycle (cf, for example, Sweezy, 1968, Ch. X, §2). Hobson (cf. Hamburg, 1954, Pt II, pp. 66–8) |
| 4. Long Waves | – in Money and Prices; in Real Variables; in general (cf. for example, van Duijin, 1983, Goldstein, 1988). |
| 5. Political Business Cycles | – Kalecki, Åkerman, Kramer, Frey. |
| 6. The Modern Classics I | – linear Keynesians (Hansen–Samuelson, Metzler). |
| 7. The Modern Classics II | – non-linear Keynesians (Kaldor, Hicks, Goodwin). |
| 8. The Modern Classics III | – non-linear Neoclassicals I (Rose, Schinasi). |
| 9. The Modern Classics IV | – non-linear Neoclassicals II (Day, Grandmont). |
| 10. The Modern Classics V | – 'French' Keynesians (Benassy, Malinvaud, Blad–Zeeman, Honkhapohja). |
| 11. The Modern Classics VI | – New Classicals I (Lucas, Barro, Sargent). |
| 12. The Modern Classics VII | – New Classicals II (Kydland–Prescott, King–Plosser). |
| 13. The Modern Classics VIII | – New Keynesians (Phelps, Hall, Summers, Akerlöf, Yellen, Mankiew, Rotenberg). |
| 14. Debt-Deflation and Financial Instabilities | – Hybrid Classicals (Irving Fisher, Minsky, Foley). |
| 15. Psychological- | – Extrinsic Uncertainty in *RE*-equilibrium |

| 'Sunspot' Theories | fluctuations (Pigou, Cass–Shell). |
|---|---|
| 16. Delay-Differential | – Phenomenological Macrodynamics (Af- |
| Dynamics | talion, Frisch, Kalecki, Tinbergen) |
| 17. Schumpeterian | |
| innovational | |
| business cycles. | |

It would be idle pretension on my part even to imagine the above to be an acceptable classification – let alone an exhaustive one (even under the qualification 'mathematised' theories of the business cycle). The rough guideline has been to take Frisch's Cassel *Festschrift* article to be the starting point for 'Mathematical Theories of the Business Cycle'; but even a cursory glance reveals names like Marx, Aftalion, Fisher and Pigou. Why leave out Spiethoff, Robertson, Hawtrey, Lavington, Wicksell, Lundberg, Harrod, Hammarskjöld, Cassel, Palomba and many others? I would have had to claim space in the form of several volumes for a fairly accurate and reasonably complete classification to include all these pioneers; in addition, for my purposes, a classification that included many or all these pioneers would have been less than useful. Even making these lame excuses Harrod, Lundberg and Steindl – at least – should have been included. Their natural places are in 6 (for Lundberg and one version of Harrod) and 13 (for another perspective on Harrod and Steindl). My classification includes all those theories whose theoretical technologies are relevant for the theme of this paper. Implicitly or explicitly, they will all be considered in the sequel (mostly implicitly – an extensive treatment is published in Velupillai, 1990).

Two remarks are in order:

(a) The dynamics in the mathematical formalisms of *all* of the above theories are in terms of one of the following forms:

1. ordinary differential equations;
2. (linear) difference equations and one-dimensional maps;
3. stochastic differential or difference equations;
4. delay-differential equations;

These, in turn, can all be studied from the unified point of view of (the theoretical technology of) dynamical systems theory.

(b) It is significant that partial differential equations do not appear in the *direct* formalisation of any of the classified theories. This, by itself, has meant the exclusion of a great deal of the theoretical technology of dynamics – and, hence, according to the causal theory, stunting possible advances in theorising about business cycles.

Let me return to the elementary example of section #1 before concluding this section. I will give few preambles even before that. Keynesian economics[4] can be characterised, with some justification, as a system of postulates based on a judicious combination of assumptions linking *behavioural, technological* and *institutional* factors; they were given quantitative embodiment in the form of the *marginal propensity to consume, the marginal efficiency of capital* and *liquidity preference theory*.[5] (The corresponding elements, in neoclassical economics are, of course, *preferences, technology* and *endowments*.) Keynes himself made the strong assertion that a claim to have provided a theory of the level of employment and output 'must be capable' – within that theory – also 'of explaining the phenomena of the Trade Cycle' (Keynes, 1936, p. 313). Indeed he went on to note in the famous 'Notes on the Trade Cycle' (1936, Ch. 22):

> we shall find that fluctuations in the propensity to consume, in the state of liquidity-preference, and in the marginal efficiency of capital have all played a part (in any actual instance of the Trade Cycle). But I suggest that the essential character of the Trade Cycle . . . is mainly due to the way in which the marginal efficiency of capital fluctuates (Keynes, 1936, p. 313).

Since the monetary factor has been left out of the examples in section 1 the Keynesian features of the cycle can be encapsulated only by assumption about the other two elements: consumption and investment. Keynes, as noted above, seems to have admonished us to look for the essential conditions of the cycle in fluctuations in investment.

Returning explicitly to the example in section 1 we see that van der Pol states 'the essential conditions for [relaxation] oscillations' in physical terms – as befits the insights of one of the great applied mathematicians of this century: 'negative damping', 'rapidly increasing positive damping', 'deviations from equilibrium', etc. This is not unnatural since the famous equation which now bears his name (and, essentially, also Reyleigh's name) came about as a result of a study of a basic electronic circuit: the multivibrator (cf. Minorsky, 1962). The mathematical formalisation of the conditions for planar (relaxation) oscillations had been available, in the works of Henri Poincaré and

Ivar Bendixson, for about a quarter of a century *before* even van der Pol's earliest works in 1920. This is, in many senses, a classic methodological example for the sentiments expressed in the first of the Wigner quotes above. But van der Pol's work, method and gifts were such that Dame Cartwright was able to observe, in her remarkable Presidential Address to the London Mathematical Society that:

> Mathematical ideas may be wrapped up in physical statements, and I think that van der Pol was quite exceptional in making so many of these ideas available to us [the mathematicians?] (Cartwright, 1964, p. 194; italics added).

Indeed van der Pol's classic paper of 1927 (van der Pol, 1927) – which had, in fact, appeared in Dutch in 1924 – has no references whatsoever to the works (or even the mathematical language) of Poincaré, Bendixson, Birkhoff or Denjoy. Contrast this with papers on the non-linear theory of the business cycle between, say, 1933 and 1983 (not that the situation is very different after 1983). The point I wish to make can be started in terms of the following points.[6]

1. Van der Pol grappled with the problem of a triode oscillator, the *purpose* of which was to deliver power to a load at a definite frequency – i.e., a frequency transformer to *maintain oscillations*.
2. The mathematical formalisation of electrical circuits in terms of linear (differential or difference) equations cannot account for the functioning of such a triode oscillator – except by fluke.
3. Rayleigh found, by the addition of non-linear expressions to the linear equations of a circuit containing a triode, that maintained oscillation was feasible.
4. The physical realisation of the non-linear element(s) leads to a new mathematical formalisation.
5. The analysis of this mathematical formalism (of a physically realised circuit) uncover deep mathematical ideas cloaked in physical terms.

Thus the path leads from Rayleigh and van der Pol via Cartwright, Littlewood, Levinson and Smale back to Poincaré, Birkhoff, Denjoy, and then forward again via Kolmogorov, Arnold, Moser, Smale, Lorenz and others (not least the Russian predecessors of Kolmogorov) to Strange Attractors and chaotic Dynamics. The ramifications are immense. The beginnings are humble: the study of second-order non-linear differential equations. The causal theory must have a hard time disentangling the knotted (*sic*!) sequence of events.

Can we reconstruct a related sequence for the example in section 1? Recall the 'Keynesian notes' above. The economic paradigm, being Keynesian minus 'the state of liquidity preference', is set in motion by the interaction between the marginal propensity to consume (MPC) and the marginal efficiency of capital (MEC) – given a theory of the level of output and employment (i.e., given the underemployment equilibrium of Keynesian theory); hence the interaction between the multiplier and the accelerator – embodiments of MPC and MEC – and the early model of Samuelson. To this we add Harrod's concept of an unstable growth equilibrium and fluctuations determined by the interaction between the multiplier and accelerator in an economy ostensibly neither exploding nor collapsing must be constrained by some sort of upper and lower bounds; hence the non-linear accelerator of Goodwin, the 'ceilings' and 'floors' of Hicks and the S-shaped investment and savings curves of Kaldor – the non-linear Keynesians as I have called them in the list above.

A plausible reconstruction of the sequence of events leading to the contributions by the non-linear Keynesians can be depicted as follows:

Keynesian theory of the determination of the level of output.
↓
Harrod's dynamic closure of the Keynesian static model?

Hansen–Samuelson Multiplier–Accelerator     Harrod's unstable growth equilibrium

$\left\{\begin{array}{c}\text{Search for 'essential non-linearities' in the Multiplier–Accelerator}\\\text{interaction for a theory of 'maintained oscillations' in a model}\\\text{with an unstable growth equilibrium}\end{array}\right\}$
↓

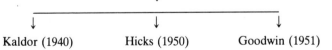

Kaldor (1940)          Hicks (1950)          Goodwin (1951)

The crucial 'mathematical ideas wrapped up in [economic] statements' are, of course, the idea of an *unstable (growth) equilibrium* and *persistence* (or *maintained oscillations*). The presupposition is of a vision of the (capitalist) economic system as being inherently unstable and the resolution of this instability in periodic crises. These three 'visionaries' grasped, intuitively and technically, the necessity of 'non-linearities' and the inadequacy of the theoretical technology of linear deterministic theory.[8] Hence:

> economists will be led, *as natural scientists* have been led, to seek in non-linearities an explanation of the *maintenance of oscillations* (Goodwin, 1951, p. 2, italics added).

And, significantly, Goodwin began his paper by pointing out that:

> for directing attention to the basic elements of oscillations – . . . *we must turn to non-linear (structural relations). With them we are enabled to analyze a much wider range of phenomena,* and in a manner at once more advanced and more elementary (Goodwin, 1951, p. 1, italics added).

Such a strong statement is, of course, not a general truth independent of the economic theoretical underpinnings of the phenomena under analysis. The new classical economists make an equally plausible case for turning to linear stochastic structural relations simply because they accept a vision of a stable growth equilibrium–Solow closure of the Harrod–Domar model.[9]

Summing up this digression, we can state the position as follows: given the constraints imposed by the theoretical technology of planar dynamical systems on the one hand and an economic model in unstable growth equilibrium having to generate persistent fluctuations by means of an interaction between the embodiments of MPC and MEC on the other, the class of *feasible* non-linear structural relations is almost obvious. Although there are some similarities with the five-part sequence summarised above for van der Pol's work and its sequel, nothing like the last two steps seem ever to have resulted from the work in non-linear business cycle theory.[10]

A passing question to conclude this section. Let us grant the non-linear Keynesians (and their neoclassical brethren) the second-order non-linear differential equation as the representation of fluctuations in output, say, in the following form: (cf. equation (1.14):

$$\ddot{q} + f(q)\dot{q} + q = 0 \qquad\qquad (2.1)$$

Why, then, should attempts not be made to dampen the amplitude of fluctuations in the great tradition of Keynesian stabilisation policy? Such an attempt leads, for example to:

$$\ddot{q} + f(q)\dot{q} + q = u(t) \tag{2.2}$$

where:

$u(t)$: a control variable (government expenditure?).

This is, now, treacherous territory so far as theoretical technology is concerned. Going from (1.15) to (1.16) has taken us from a two-dimensional system to a three-dimensional system with a fascinating menu of attractors going beyond conventional fixed points and limit cycles.[11]

In defence of the non-linear Keynesians one could say that there was not much point in trying to stabilise a system around an unstable growth equilibrium. But then is one to accept eternal fluctuations? Is it not in the Keynesian tradition to try to use policy to achieve configurations that imply a desirable equilibrium growth path which is stable – i.e., sustainable? If so, we are talking about a system with multiple equilibria and the next legitimate question would be whether 'endogenous' fluctuations, in the sense of maintained oscillations, are compatible with a stable growth equilibrium. That the answer is in the affirmative seems to have been neglected in the business cycle literature only because of some ignorance of the available theoretical technology. It is a point in favour of the causal theory.

Finally, it is more than surprising that the long reign of the theoretical technology of non-linear dynamics on the plane to model business cycles did not bring with it a more sustained effort to develop an associated theoretical technology of estimation – rather than simulation (but cf. Klein and Preston, 1969). Advances on this front have wholly bypassed business cycle theory and, in turn, have been bypassed by business cycle theorists (cf. for example Tong and Lim, 1980). Perhaps Wigner must be invoked: the economist is somewhat irresponsible, at least when he theorises about business cycles.

## 3 THE CONFLUENCE OF EVENTS AND THEORIES OF MACROECONOMIC FLUCTUATIONS

Reviewing the current explanations for the business cycle that are offered to us by monetarists, rational expectationists and supply siders, we may even convince ourselves that there is a genuine fifty year cycle – not a business cycle but *a cycle of business cycle theories* (Simon, 1984, p. 36, italics added).

There are many ways to tell a plausible story. The classification of theories of the business cycle as given in section 2 above is for the specific purpose of telling a plausible story about the interaction between developments in theoretical technologies and theories of macroeconomic fluctuations.[12] It would be almost 'Machiavellian' to claim that concepts in business cycle theories were fashioned to fit theoretical technologies – although one implication of the causal theory seems to be exactly that. In any case, a short summary of the chronological development of theoretical technologies, used in the formalisms of business cycle theories, may be useful as a preamble to this section.[13] In section 2 a list of four items was given as the forms in which the dynamics of economic fluctuations were formalised. In the 'panoramic' view of the technological development of theoretical technologies to be listed below, the above list and its broad sweep must be kept in mind. On the basis of the deterministic–stochastic divide (rather than equilibrium – disequilibrium, endogenous – exogenous or stable – unstable divides) a plausible sequence of relevant (i.e., utilised) development would be as follows:

(A) Deterministic *non-linear* systems

1. Earliest uses of relaxation oscillation techniques (Le Corbeiller, Hamburger, Goodwin, Yasui, Ichimura) mid-1930s to mid-1950s. van der Pol–Rayleigh equation, Liénard's methods and implicit appeals to the Poincaré–Bendixson theorem.
2. Explicit uses of the formal methods and techniques of planar dynamical systems (with vestiges or utilization of special equations) (Goodwin, Rose, Schinasi, Torre, Benassy, Chang–Smyth) mid-1960s to mid-1980s. Lotka–Volterra equations and Kolmogorov's generalisations, structural stability theorems, Poincaré–Bendixson theorem and its explicit use, Levinson–Smith-type theorems, elementary bifurcation theory, Olech's theorem.
3. Ordinary differential equation with discontinous right hand sides. (Henry, Itoh) a 'flash' in the late 1970s; generalised solution of the Filippov type.
4. Singularity theory, bifurcation and elementary catastrophe theory (Zeeman, Blad, Varian) mid-1970s to early 1980s; Thom's classification theorem and its ramifications.

5. Strange Attractors, chaotic dynamics and dynamical systems theory (Day, Benhabib, Pohjola, Grandmont – and countless others) late 70s to 1990; one-dimensional maps and the associated concepts and theorems (Schwarzian derivatives, Sarkovskii's theorem, period doubling sequences, kneading theory, Lyapunov exponents, etc.), forced oscillators and associated concepts and theorems (homoclinicity, Poincaré maps, the Smale–Levinson horseshoe fractal dimensions, etc.).

(B) Stationary stochastic processes[14]

1. Earliest developments of moving average and autoregressive processes and representation theorems (Slutsky, Yule, Frish, Wold) mid-1920s to mid-1940s.
2. Martingale theory (von Mises, Levy, Ville, Church, Doob, McCall) mid-1930s to early 1940s; mid-1950s; mid-1960s to 1970s.
3. Stochastic differential equations (Ito, Stratanovich, Kushner) 1950s and 1960s.
4. Theories of optimal filters, prediction and smoothing (Lucas, Prescott, Sargent and their new classical followers) mid-to-late 1960s up to the present time; Wiener–Hopf theory (rarely), Kalman–Bucy theory, separation theorems (certainty equivalence), implicit use of the theory of sufficient statistics, representation theory, etc.

(C) Non-stationary stochastic processes
(Nelson, King and other new classicals with particular emphasis on real business cycle theories) early 1980s to the present time; essentially ad-hoc application of elementary results; ideally towards Girsanov-type theorems and Cameron–Martin transformations.

Much of this, at least in the case of (B), is enhanced also by the theoretical technology of Optimal Control Theory and Dynamic Programming – both extended to the stochastic domain. In almost all of the above cases the frontiers are being pushed towards a formulation of business cycle theories in terms of recursive and computable models.[15]

The confluence of economic events and macroeconomic fluctuations of the past half-century or so can also be told as a plausible story in many different ways. To suit my aims in this paper, I shall adopt the following sequence:

(a) Keynesian beginnings, Harrod's dynamic closure and movement towards the non-linear Keynesians (cf. section 1 for a reasonably detailed description): mid-1930s to early 1950s.

(b) Phillips curve results, its incorporation as the 'missing equation' in the neo-classical synthesis and the age of fine-tuning: mid-1950s to mid-1960s.

(c) From fine tuning to optimal growth, welfare and distribution: the interlude in the late 1950s to the late 1960s (heavily dominated by the theoretical technology of optimal control theory, dynamic programming and large-scale econometric stabilisation policy exercises).

(d) The *end* of a Keynesian era: the onset of stagflationary scenarios and theoretical disquiet. The search for the theoretical foundations of stagflation, and the perplexities of reconciling neo-classical Keynesianism with Walrasian economics. The first search leads to the Phelps–Friedman expectational revolution. The second perplexity leads to the pioneering work by Clower and Leijonhufvud: mid-1960s to late 1960s.

(e) The blossoms of microeconomics as the foundation of macro-economic and macrodynamic dust. The first of the above searches, via the famous 'Phelps conference', leads towards the beginnings of equilibrium macroeconomics. A new view of the agent – the agent as a 'signal processor' – and a new framework for macrodynamics – Samuelson's 'overlapping generation model' – is set in motion by Lucas and his followers. With a remarkable amalgam of the paradigm of the agent as a 'signal processor' in a Phelpsian island economy generating noisy signals within a framework of a monetary economy as encapsulated by the overlapping generation model Lucas, almost single-handedly, transforms the whole fabric of macrodynamics and its theoretical technology.

The second of the above perplexities leads, via the French Keynesians, to so-called fix-price dynamics: the reversal of tra-ditional Walrasian dynamics in favour of Marshallian-quantity dynamics. Neither cross-field dynamics nor simultaneous price-quantity dynamics was given extensive consideration (but not totally ignored: cf. Beckman–Ryder, 1969 and Mas–Colell, 1986 for elementary examples and some references).[16]

(f) If the 1960s and early 1970s were dominated by the search for the theoretical foundations for the phenomenon of stagflation and for the microfoundations of macroeconomics, then the mid-1970s and early 1980s were dominated by the search for the foundations of the traditional 'theory of economic policy'. In the hiatus created by the apparent failure of neoclassical Keynesianism as a prop for the theory and practice of policy, it was easy for a well-oiled monetarism to step in. Rules rather than discretion received a theoretical boost as the Lucasian programme matured and gave a rationale for the ineffectiveness of policy. (The brief interlude by supply-siders does not seem to warrant a specific discussion in a panoramic setting!).

(g) The next steps in these confluences are quite fascinating. The resurgence of growth, after two supply shocks, as an empirical fact (to some extent phantom) on the one hand and the rejection of Lucasian monetary shock theories of the business cycle on empirical grounds (cf. for example Boschen and Grossman, 1983) on the other leads to the development of so-called 'real business cycle' theories. Returning to Solow's stable closure of Harrod's dynamics, and fully exploiting the theoretical technologies of the intervening years – optimal stochastic growth, dynamic programming, differential games and linear stochastic control theory – the agent as a 'signal processor', instead of inhabiting Phelpsian islands and recursively filtering noise from information due to monetary shocks, separates control from estimation in a model where the shocks are to technology. The basic vision of a stably growing economy is retained; business cycles as fluctuations around a trend are emphasised and, hence, the field becomes 'business cycles as growth cycles'.

(h) Almost as a natural sequel to this growth cycle interpretation, the first steps away from the theory of stationary stochastic processes begin to be taken. The immediate future is surely going to see the extensive application of the theoretical technology of non-stationary stochastic processes and, if the causal theory is to be believed, hence the encapsulation of hitherto neglected (or even ignored) phenomena to enrich business cycle analysis; perhaps, eventually, even leading to the demise of real business cycle theories.

(i) But after (f) a rearguard action was generated by a motley group all purporting to show that conclusions regarding ineffectiveness of policy were too hasty. The spillover of this rearguard action into the field of business cycle theories is one clear example in favour of the causal theory. It seems to be somewhat of a misplaced emphasis to battle the ideological shift to the right in most Western economies in the early 1980s (a shift which began in the late 1970s) on the theoretical plane. But that is what, seemingly, happened. New classical economics ostensibly supported, via neutrality theorems, Ricardian equivalence theorems and policy ineffectiveness propositions, the rightward ideological shift in policy. All Keynesian hands were harnessed to wage a theoretical crusade against these theoretical underpinnings of the new right. Harnessing the early work by Day (which, in turn, comes down from Scarf, Samuelson and David Gale), Grandmont, as deftly as Lucas a decade earlier, combined the theoretical technology of non-linear dynamics and the economic dynamics of overlapping generation models to refute ineffectiveness propositions, and tried to resurrect the desirability of (and the necessity for) stabilisation policies. In passing, he was able to resurrect also an endogenous vision of business cycles. It was, however, a return also to a vision of fluctuations generated by instability.

(j) The vision of Keynesian economics as the economics of nominal rigidities never left the centre stage of macroeconomics. An attempt to provide rational foundations for rigidities – nomimal and otherwise – has led to a *new Keynesian* approach to business cycles. Combining imperfections in market structure, incomplete rationality, sluggish adjustment processes and quite standard theoretical technologies, this genre has attempted to refute, empirically, all and every new classical proposition within the framework of the analysis of business cycles. At the frontiers of theoretical *ideology*, the battle for the minds of the young seems to be between the *new Keynesians* and *variants of real business cycle theories*. Whether the frontiers of *theoretical ideology* contributes to an understanding of the macroeconomic phenomenon of business cycles seems, however, to be quite another question.

This ten part chronological summary (a) – (j) of the confluence of events and the development of macroeconomic theories of fluctuations is both incomplete and, undoubtedly, biassed.[17] It does, however, hopefully, provide a setting – a backdrop – against which to view the interactions between developments in theoretical technologies and conceptual advances in business cycle theory. To these issues, in a more concretely analytical way, we now turn.

## 4  THE PERPLEXITIES

> I realized you had found what no one had been able to find since
> 1927, an example of a stable oscillator differing essentially from
> that of Lord Rayleigh and van der Pol (Letter from Ph. Le
> Corbeiller to Richard Goodwin, 28 March 1958, reprinted in
> Velupillai, 1990).

All the richness – perhaps only 'almost' all – of non-linear dynamics
can be understood by studying the four canonical equations: van der
Pol (Rayleigh), Duffing, Lorenz and Lotka–Volterra; but of course
this means also their coupled, forced and higher-dimensional variations too. If, then, something 'differing essentially' from one of
these exotic equations is found it must be a significant event; if,
moreover, it was developed out of simple economic considerations
the significance becomes remarkable; if, in addition, it is instrumental in resolving, however partially, a part of one of Hilbert's famous
'Mathematical Problems' it should be considered sensational; and,
finally, it poses a serious counter-example to the causal view.

When de Figueiredo mentions, *en passé*, the use of a 'Goodwin
oscillator' to settle an issue raised by Hilbert for the Lienard
equation, readers of *Nonlinear Analysis: Theory, Methods and Applications* (de Figueiredo, 1983) would be referred to Le Corbeiller
(1960). That reference, in turn, would be little help: being referred to
'personal communication'. Only recently, but with no reference to
any of these connections, has it been possible to go beyond 'personal
communication' – but not linking up Hilbert, Liénard, van der Pol,
etc. (cf. Goodwin and Puzo, 1987).

The story is simple:

(a) Hilbert, in his famous address of 1900 (Hilbert, 1902), posed as
the second part of the 16th of his 23 'Mathematical Problems' the
question of the number and positions of limit cycles in planar
dynamical systems. (Economists, somewhat cavalier in their use
of high-dimensional non-linear dynamics, may well be surprised
to know that the problem remains unresolved to this day.)

(b) Soon after the appearance of Hick's classic 'A contribution to the
theory of the Trade Cycle' Goodwin and Duesenberry wrote
masterly reviews (Goodwin, 1950, and Duesenberry, 1950); both
pointed out that it was not necessary to assume a 'floor' and a

'ceiling' to generate self-sustained fluctuations (Goodwin p. 318 and Duesenberry, p. 468, respectively).

(c) Goodwin went further: his own celebrated non-linear multiplier–accelerator model had been analysed in the Lienard plane and reduced to a Rayleigh-type equation (cf. however, section 1 above) where the necessity of the cubic characteristic played a prominent part in the formulation of economic hypotheses as well (cf. equation (1.15) above) – a case to bolster the causal view. If it was sufficient with a 'floor' or a 'ceiling' it meant that a cubic characteristic was not necessary and, hence, a formalism must be possible with one 'bend' (cf. Goodwin and Punzo, 1987, part I; Le Corbeiller, 1960, for the diagrams). This 'possibility' was described graphically by Goodwin to Le Corbeiller (1960) who suggested the characteristic given by $(e^{-\dot{q}}-2)$, instead of the 'usual' one (cf. for example, equation (1.15) above). This, and all such one-bend characteristics he proposed to call 'the Goodwin characteristic'. The notation is in terms of equations (1.14) and (1.15). The economic implications are that the system spends a relatively high proportion of the time, in any one phase, in the stable region and, conversely, a short period of time (relatively) in the unstable region. This realistic economic asymmetry was the propelling reason for Goodwin to question the necessity of the 'floor' and 'ceiling'; from this it is a short step to the graphical description and, via Le Corbeiller, to a possible form for a non-cubic characteristic:

$$X(q) = (e^{-\dot{q}}-2). \tag{4.1}$$

(d) The problem of making all this analytical was then passed on, by Le Corbeiller, to his gifted pupil: Rui Jose Pacheco de Figueiredo, who achieved it in his remarkable Harvard Ph.D. thesis in 1958 (cf. de Figueiredo, 1958).

I will break this sequence at this point to state Hilbert's 16th problem. The second part of Hilbert's 16th problem was posed as follows:

> I wish to bring forward a question which, it seems to me, may be attacked by the same method of continuous variation of coefficients, and whose answer is of corresponding value for the topology of families of curves defined by differential equations. This is the question as to the maximum number and

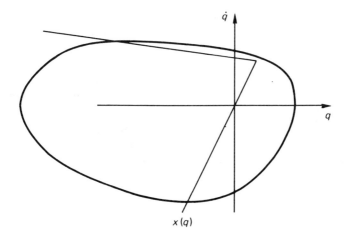

*Figure 1.3*

position of Poincaré's boundary cycles (*cycles limites*) for a differential equation of the first order and degree of the form

$$\frac{dy}{dx} = \frac{Y}{X}$$

where $X$ and $Y$ are rational integral functions of the nth degree in $x$ and $y$. Written homogeneously,

$$X\left( y \frac{dz}{dt} - z \frac{dy}{dt} \right) + Y\left( z \frac{dx}{dt} - x \frac{dz}{dt} \right)$$

$$+ Z\left( x \frac{dy}{dt} - y \frac{dx}{dt} \right) = 0$$

where $X$, $Y$ and $Z$ are rational integral homogeneous functions of the nth degree in $x$, $y$, $z$ and the latter are to be determined as functions of the parameter $t$ (Hilbert, 1902, p. 465).

The older notation may seem a little jarring, but interested and analytically minded readers can be referred to any number of contributions that bridge the gap – Lloyd (1988) for example. The full details of the colourful attempts – successes, failures and obfuscation – to solve Hilbert's 16th problem, as it pertains to the story here, I have described in Velupillai (1989). The problem, as I mentioned earlier, remains unsolved. The most celebrated attempt, by Dulac (1923), has apparently, been resolved recently with a proof that is over a hundred pages! Unlike the 4-colour problem, it is not even combinatorial. Who will check it! Or, are we destined to go through the Dulac story all over again. Back to our sequence.

(e) De Figueiredo's contribution to the resolution of a part of Hilbert's 16th problem was as follows. For the second-order equation called the Liénard equation:

$$q + f(q)\dot{q} + g(q) = 0 \qquad (4.2)$$

and, putting:

$$f(q) = F'(q) \qquad (4.3)$$

for an analysis in the Liénard plane (rather than the normal state space):

$$\dot{q} = p - F(q) \qquad (4.4)$$

$$\dot{p} = -g(q) \qquad (4.5)$$

de Figueiredo assumed Goodwin characteristics for $f(q)$ (or $F'(q)$) to show the topological structure and the existence of a prescribed number $n$ of periodic solutions (cf. de Figueiredo, 1983). The origins of the Goodwin characteristic are the 'facts' of asymmetric economic fluctuations.

As mentioned earlier, the interested analytically minded doctrine-theorist can refer to the literature I have been signposting all along; the simple point I wish to make is the following: had we relied solely on mastering the theoretical technology of second-order non-linear differential equations and then applying it to formalise observed events in the economic sphere would we not have emasculated its conceptual richness? The almost blind series of assumptions: unstable singular point in a closed and bounded region so as to apply Poincaré–Bendixson is the sorry story of one series of business cycle 'theories' – a clear application, not a vindication, of the causal story.

Non-linearities, non-stationarities and infinities are the tricky and treacherous territory upon which economic dynamics must operate. I have used the subtleties of non-linearities, in the above simple example, to question the causal theory. I may add, in passing, that the fascination the Rössler system poses for Goodwin should now be clear; it is that ubiquitous 'one-bend' in the Rössler system which, surely, reminds Goodwin of the discovery (or was it the 'invention'!) of the characteristic which has now entered the pure and applied mathematical folklore of planar dynamical systems. Because of obvious time and space constraints I will not be able to take up the issue of 'perplexities' due to non-stationarity. I should abscond from tackling perplexities due to infinities for the same reason – but I shall not do so. The reason is a little lame. Given that I have mentioned – at least – van der Pol, etc., I can make the point I wish to make quite simply and with little extra space and time. For the van der Pol equation given by equation (1.16):

$$q + \tau(q^2 - 1)\,\dot{q} + q = 0 \tag{1.16}$$

the usual assumption is that the parameter $\tau \gg 1$. In the Liénard form this would be:

$$\varphi\,\frac{dq}{dt} = p - \left(\frac{1}{3}\,q^3 - q\right) \tag{4.5}$$

and

$$\frac{dp}{dt} = -q \tag{4.6}$$

where now $\varphi$ is positive but 'very' small (i.e., $0 < \varphi \ll 1$, (since $\tau \gg 1$)). The 'very' large $\tau$ and the 'very' small $\varphi$ are obverse sides of the coin which has 'infinitely fast' behavioural dynamics on one of the sides – as desired capital and actual capital mesh and unmesh. Both analytically and behaviourally these are inelegant assumptions – to say the least. If we are to be consistently analytical we must be serious about infinitesimals and that means the addition of predicates to our mathematical language to allow 'non-standard' entities; alternatively, serious series expansions at the turning points must be used. For if not we risk missing – not looking for – phenomena that are 'there' but the mesh in the sieve has been too coarse to capture them.

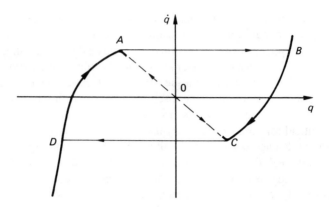

*Figure 1.4*

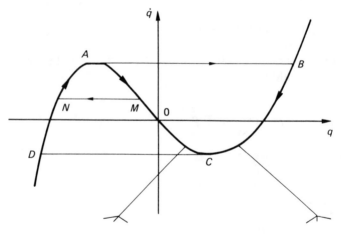

*Figure 1.5*

Again, I refer you to my earlier cited works for some of the analytical details. For the present, and for my purposes here, it will be sufficient to give a few of the geometric details. The standard relaxation oscillations phase portrait for equation (1.16) and their Liénard representations are as in Figure 1.4.

The point seems to be that the equilibrium at 0 is (locally) unstable and hence the phase-portraits at A and C cannot curve 'inwards' – as shown in Figure 1.5.

As pointed out in n. 11 (and equations (1N.1) and (1N.2) in n.11) the complete model of Goodwin (1951) includes a forcing term which is taken to be a constant. Even granting that (in Liénard form):

$$\varphi \, \frac{dq}{dt} = p - \left( \frac{1}{3} q^3 - q \right) \tag{4.7}$$

and

$$\frac{dp}{dt} = - (q + \delta) \tag{4.8}$$

(where $\delta$ is the forcing term)

it can be shown, either using non-standard analysis to make 'rigorous' sense of 'infinitely' fast and 'infinitesimal' or using standard series expansions (cf., for example, Grasman, 1987, Ch. 2) that the fluctuations are richer in structure than has been implied by 'blind' applications of van der Pol's equations. An example, easily detectable in a standard simulation, say using Phaser (cf. Kocak, 1989), is the cycle AMN, where the AM portion seems to be counter-intuitive (given that 0 is locally unstable).

My point in trying to show the existence of 'counter-intuitive' phenomena in theoretical technologies by way of van der Pol's 'ducks' is, again, to caution adherents of the causal view in a field as complex as business cycle theory. If we must be causalists then we must handle infinities and infinitesimals with care – even reverence.[18]

I have used just one equation – the van der Pol – and its variants to discuss a few conceptual and analytical perplexities. I should stop here. However, I wish to make a few observations on the most fashionable of the new theoretical technologies – for the moment – being applied (with causal vengeance) to business cycle theory: it comes in the name of chaos, although discerning people know that there is, as yet, no 'theory' of chaos.

Much has been made of the feasibility of combining the modelling of rational behaviour with the generation of maintained oscillations. Indeed a leading theorist and an exponent of this particular theoretical technology would have us:

> look more closely at the sort of mechanisms that may be responsible for significant nonlinearities in the economic system if they wish

to have a proper foundation upon which to build a sound economic theory (Grandmont, 1985, p. 1039).

This is both too strong and too narrow a view, and is an almost whole-hearted endorsement of the causal view; but it is narrow in another sense – even granting the causalist view: it is not only the non-linearity that is important, it is also the iterative, recursiveness. Put another way it is the algorithmic structure of rational behaviour coupled to non-linearity that causes the unpredictability. Briefly the points I wish to make are the following:

1. The dynamics in most of the chaos-inspired literature can be formulated, in terms of symbolic dynamics, as words from an alphabet to which a group theoretic formalism can be given.
2. The complex dynamics will then be equivalent to word problems for Post systems – or in Automata language, to the halting problem for Turing Machines.
3. If these authors are serious about rational economic agents being behind the decision algorithms – the dynamical systems – then the whole enterprise is very peculiar for the following reason:

   (a) either the agents – rational economic man – compute foreever;
   (b) or they halt the computation suboptimally.

   In case (a) no decisions are ever taken; in case (b) they are knowingly irrational.

I discuss these issues in Rustem and Velupillai (1988, 1990) and in my forthcoming book (Velupillai, 1991). I believe an element of caution and a dose of moderation is now necessary to curb the over-enthusiastic indulgence in applying chaos 'theory' to understanding the complexities of economic fluctuations.


## 5  CONCLUDING NOTES

my subject does not appear to me to be ripe for methods of precision (Wicksell, 1936, p. xxx).

These cautionary words, although over half a century old, must be remembered, from time to time, lest the causal view blinds us to the obvious in phenomena.

It is said that in the distant island of Serendip there is a library of dynamical systems in the garden of the temple of the order of Roubakists – an ancient order whose origins are traced to a mendicant mathematician who is supposed to have left the Pythagoreans after a strange dispute; he is supposed to have disagreed with Pythagoras himself about the supremacy and the divine power of numbers.

In any case in this library of dynamical systems there is only one book and one librarian. He is blind and the book is the library. As many as those who wish to read the book at any one time can do so. In that book all the conceivable laws of dynamics have already been written; all the dynamical systems, all the rules of combinations over dynamical systems and the laws of all the dynamics of dynamical systems and so on are all written down.

It is, however, written by a people in a language which has no concept of numbers – neither cardinal nor ordinal. Moreover, neither their culture nor their speculations have any concept of measurement; they have, thus, no understanding of, no need for, the distinction between the discrete and the continuous. It is said that when they were given copies of some of Poincaré's great works on global analysis the 'court' academicians deciphered them within a few minutes. The result was curious: the works had been interpreted as exquisite poetical renderings of a deeply emotional person.

Very few who have had the privilege of finding the locations of, and entering the world of, the Roubakists ever leave it. (It is sometimes said that the best place to start the pilgrimage is from the city centre of Lucerne in Switzerland.) The few who abandoned the rigorous apprenticeship returned to tell strange stories – or, in one celebrated case, no story at all. Some, like Galileo, were severely punished for telling their stories about dynamical systems; others, like Majorana, remained silent. Still others, the select few, claimed to have understood the book of dynamical systems and chose to popularise it to the world at large. They went around, like the travelling teachers and sanyasis of ancient times, weaving epic tales into which they spun lesssons about dynamical systems. Catastrophes, fractals, chaos, solitons, excitons and strange attractors are some of these epics. Many read such tales, as they have read other epics from other cultures, to discern moral and practical wisdom.

But in all this they forgot that the book of dynamical systems was written in a language and by a people who had no concept of number, nor of measurement. Galileo, when he returned from Serendip – as his great ancestor Marco Polo once did – claimed to have interpreted the book correctly and proclaimed that the laws of nature were written in the language of mathematics; if so, it was a mathematics without number.

From Frisch to Lucas all the mathematical business cycle theorists seem to have returned from Serendip. Their serendipitous output seems to be aesthetically ever more exquisite. Since the book in the library has all the laws, anyone with sufficient patience can write down all the future business cycle theories; whether it will correspond to the events of the phenomenological world is quite another, and more difficult, matter.

On the other hand we are, perhaps, too charitable to our gods. As David Ruelle noted:

> We like to think of the discovery of mathematical structure as walking upon a path laid out by the Gods. But, as Antonio Machado wrote, maybe there is no path:
>
> 'Caminante, son tus huellas
> el camino y nada más;
> caminante, no hay camino,
> se hace camino al andar' (Ruelle, 1988, p. 266).

I do not believe mathematical business cycle theory has 'made the path by walking'. The time, however, will come when 'our footsteps will make the [mathematical] path'.

### Notes

1. The variables are measured as deviations from their 'equilibrium' values (cf. Goodwin, 1951, p. 9).
2. I shall, henceforth, drop the inverted commas and direct the interested reader to Lucas, 1981, p. 9 for the origins of this serendipitous phrase.
3. The explicit references are given only where secondary sources are cited.
4. This is, of course, controversial territory. I refer, substantially, to the *General Theory*.
5. I do not imply that there is a bijection between these double trinities.
6. It must be remembered that Cartwright and Littlewood, *pure* mathematicians *par excellence*, were literally enlisted by the engineers to help in taming, theoretically, forced and unforced van der Pol-type equations (cf. Cartwright, 1964, pp. 193–4).
7. As Goodwin notes:

The similarities [between Hicks and myself] are not purely accidental, partly because we have both started from the unsatisfactory, but profoundly stimulating, dynamical closure of the Keynesian system put forth by Mr Harrod in his book, *The Trade Cycle* (Goodwin, 1951, p. 2, n. 3).

8. One, at least, of the reasons for ignoring the vision of an inherently stable economic system fluctuating around an equilibrium growth path due to erratic – but not necessarily random – shocks becomes quite clear in this reconstruction. This alternative vision lies, now, at the frontiers of research in business cycle theory. We will return to this theme in the research in business cycle theory.

9. An equally strong objection can be made, on the same grounds, to the remark made by Grandmont in his influential and interesting paper (Grandmont, 1985, p. 1039); cf, below, the quote in section 4.

10. With one exception to which we shall return later.

11. Recall that we began our elementary example of section 1 with autonomous investment $\ell(t)$ depending explicitly on time. In fact introducing Aftalion–Frisch-type decision lags in investment and retaining the time-dependent autonomous investment leads to the following equation even in the elementary, phenomenological Goodwin model of section 1:

$$\varepsilon\theta\ddot{y} + [\varepsilon + (1 - \alpha)\theta]\dot{y} - \phi(\dot{y}) + (1 - \alpha)y = 0^*(t) \qquad (1.\text{N1})$$

(This is equation 5e in Goodwin, 1951). In slightly simplified notation it can be written as:

$$\ddot{y} + f(\dot{y}; \alpha, \varepsilon, \theta) + \tau y = \frac{0^*(t)}{\varepsilon\theta} \qquad (1\text{N.2})$$

It is easily seen that this is a forced oscillator with potentially exotic dynamics going beyond fixed points and limit cycles. If, in addition, it is remembered that the elementary model of section 1 is that of a closed economy it becomes even more perplexing that theorists did not try to analyse the dynamics of coupled (interdependent) economies. The dynamics of coupled oscillators is even more fascinating and quite exotic. We shall return, albeit briefly, to this as well.

12. In one of his many classics on *Business Cycles*, Mitchell, in comparing his classification of business cycle theories with the one by Warren Persons, noted:

> Persons' classification is the first stage of a critical examination of 'the theories of business fluctuations'. My classification is the first stage of a constructive study of business cycles. Persons is interested primarily in the causes of business fluctuations stressed by different writers: I am interested primarily in those parts of a theory which offer working hypotheses which I can use. *This difference between our aims leads us at times to classify the same writer under quite different heads* (Mitchell, 1927, p. 49, n. italics added).

13. This is not meant to be anything other than a panoramic view. The reader is warned that much of the fine texture is left out and the rich details that provide the flesh to the story are almost as important as the structure. A detailed exposition is in preparation in Velupillai (1991).
14. The neat, almost simultaneous, interaction between theoretical technology and business cycle theory catalogued in section A becomes diffuse in section B. Here lies, paradoxically, a weak link in the causal theory. Why were developments in the theoretical technology of non-linear deterministic dynamical systems absorbed and utilised almost 'instantaneously', whereas developments in the theory of stochastic processes were utilised, at least for the first forty years, with a considerable lag (in business cycle theory, of course)? Sargent, perceptive as always, did note:

> it just happened that economists in general and macroeconomists in particular learned the tools of optimal control (e.g., calculus of variations) somewhat before they learned the tools of optimal prediction and filtering (Sargent, 1987, p. xxi).

Sargent is, surely, a mild causalist since he notes, a few pages earlier:

> as economic analysts we are directed by, if not prisoners of, the mathematical tools that we possess (Sargent, 1987, p. xix).

Contrast this with the wholly different view of Einstein who, while making a strong case for the use and, indeed, the need for mathematics in the physical sciences is able to say:

> To throw out geometry and keep [physical] laws is equivalent to describing thoughts without words. We must search for words before we can express thoughts. What must we search for at this point? . . . I realized that the foundations of geometry have physical significance . . . So I asked my friend whether my problem could be solved by Riemann's theory (Pais, 1982, pp. 211–12).

15. But in neither case with any systematic understanding of the foundational questions related to such formulations. In other words, the iterative processes underlying recursive methods and the nature of computability from the point of view of the foundations of mathematics is rarely – if at all – acknowledged as being in need of investigation.
16. This literature is closely related to the 'dual stability' genre of input–output dynamics, although the two strands seem not to be aware of each others' existence (*sic!*). All of them have missed two classics straddling both groups: Goodwin (1953) and Leijonhufvud (1971). Neither of these references nor, indeed, the two in the main body of the text to which this note corresponds are about business cycles. In view, however, of the nature of some of the theoretical formalisms of business cycles at the frontiers these days (cf. for example Grandmont, 1985) and also because

of the almost indiscriminate use of Sonnenschein–Debreu-type theorems (cf. Debreu, 1974) to generate 'relevant' curvatures and arbitrary 'Walrasian dynamics', these references do have a place here.

17. I have, quite deliberately, left out theories of long waves in money and prices, innovations and institutions; equally consciously, I have excluded crisis theories based on financial instabilities and theories of the political business cycle. These important and interesting phenomenological approaches have been left out not because they are irrelevant; they do not seem to have been coupled to novel theoretical technologies at any level and, hence, remain peripheral for the main theme in this paper.

18. Mindless statements, like indexing over a continuum, in modelling business cycles should be subject to some sceptical thoughts (for examples of this sort, indexing over a continuum and even a continuum of monopolists also indexed, see the series of papers, each a minor variant of the other, by Professor Torben Andersen; a representative piece is in Andersen, 1988).

**References**

Andersen, T. M. (1988) 'Coordination and Business Cycles', Papers and Proceedings of the Second Annual Congress of the European Economic Association , *European Economic Review*, vol. 32, pp. 221–5.

Beckman, M. J. and Ryder, H. E. (1969) 'Simultaneous Price and Quantity Adjustment in a Single Market', *Econometrica*, vol. 37, no 3 (July) pp. 470–84.

Boschen, J. and Grossman, H. (1983) 'Monetary Information and Macroeconomic Fluctuations', in J.-P. Fitoussi (ed.) *Modern Macroeconomic Theory* (Ch. 8) (Oxford: Basil Blackwell) pp. 173–84.

Cartwright, M. L. (1964) 'From Non-Linear Oscillations to Topological Dynamics', *Journal of the London Mathematical Society*, vol. 39, pp. 193–201.

de Figueiredo, R. J. P. (1958) *Existence and Uniqueness of Periodic Solutions in Autonomous Oscillators*, unpublished Ph.D. thesis, the Division of Engineering and Applied Physics, Harvard University (December).

de Figueiredo, R. J. P. (1983) 'On the Existence of *N* periodic Solutions of Liénard's equation', *Nonlinear Analysis: Theory, Methods and Applications*, vol. 7, no 5, pp. 483–99.

Duesenberry, J. J. (1950) 'Hicks on the Trade Cycle', *Quarterly Journal of Economics*, vol. 64, pp. 464–76.

Dulac, H. (1923) 'Sur les cycles limités', *Bulletin du Société Mathematique France*, vol. 51, pp. 45–188.

Einarsen, J. (1938) *Reinvestment Cycles*, (Oslo: J. Chr. Gundersens Boktryckeri).

Georgescu-Roegen, N. (1951) 'Relaxation Phenomena in Linear Dynamic

36 *Introductory*

Models', in T. C. Koopmans (ed.) *Activity Analysis of Production and Allocation* (Ch. V) Cowles Foundation Monograph, 13 (New Haven: Yale University Press) pp. 116–31.

Goldstein, J. (1988) *Long Cycles* (New Haven: Yale University Press).

Goodwin, R. M. (1950) 'A Non-linear Theory of the Cycle', *The Review of Economics and Statistics*, vol. XXXII, no 4 (November) pp. 316–20.

Goodwin, R. M. (1951) 'The Nonlinear Accelerator and the Persistence of Business Cycles', *Econometrica*, vol. 19, no 1 (January) pp. 1–17.

Goodwin, R. M. (1953) 'Static and Dynamic Linear General Equilibrium Models', in Netherlands Economic Institute (ed.), *Input–Output Relations: Proceedings of a Conference on Inter-Industrial Relations*, Driebergen, Holland (Leyden: H. E. Stenfert Kroese NV).

Goodwin, R. M. (1967) 'A Growth Cycle', in C. H. Feinstein (ed.) *Socialism, Capitalism and Economic Growth* (Cambridge: Cambridge University Press).

Goodwin, R. M. and Punzo, L. F. (1987) *The Dynamics of a Capitalist Economy: A Multisectoral Approach* (Cambridge: Polity Press).

Grandmont, J.-M. (1985) 'On Endogenous Competitive Business Cycles', *Econometrica*, vol. 53, no 5 (September) pp. 995–1045.

Grasman, J. (1987) *Asymptotic Methods for Relaxation Oscillations and Applications*, Applied Mathematical Sciences, vol. 63 (New York: Springer-Verlag).

Gregory, R. (1981) *Mind in Science: A History of Explanations in Psychology and Physics* (London: Weidenfeld & Nicolsen).

Hamburg, D. (1954) 'Steady Growth and Theories of Cyclical Crisis: Pt I and Pt II', *Metroeconomica*, vol. VI (fascida, I, II) (April and August) pp. 11–30 and 55–68.

Hamburger, L. (1934) 'Note on Economic Cycles and Relaxation Oscillations', *Econometrica*, vol. 2, no 1 (January) p. 112.

Hicks, J. R. (1950) *A Contribution to the Theory of the Trade Cycle* (Oxford: Clarendon Press).

Hilbert, D. (1902) 'Mathematical Problems', *Bulletin of the American Mathematical Society*, vol. 8 (July) pp. 437–79.

Ichimura, S. (1955) 'Toward a General Nonlinear Macrodynamic Theory of Economic Fluctuations', in K. K. Kurihara (ed.) *Post-Keynesian Economics* (Ch. 8) pp. 192–226.

Kaldor, N. (1940) 'A Model of the Trade Cycle', *Economic Journal*, vol. L (March) pp. 78–92.

Keynes, J. M. (1936) *The General Theory of Employment, Interest and Money* (London: Macmillan).

Klein, L. R. and Preston, R. S. (1969) 'Stochastic Nonlinear Models', *Econometrica*, vol. 37, no 1 (January) pp. 95–106.

Kocak, H. (1989) *Differential and Difference Equations Through Computer Experiments* (New York: Springer-Verlag) 2nd edn.

Le Corbeiller, Ph. (1933) 'Les Systèmes Autoentretenus et les Oscillations de Relaxation', *Econometrica*, vol. 1, no 3 (July) pp. 328–32.

Le Corbeiller, Ph. (1960) 'Two-stroke Oscillators', *IRE Transactions on Circuit Theory*, vol. 7, pp. 387–98.

Leijonhufvud, A. (1971) 'Notes on the Theory of Markets', *Institute of*

*Government and Public Affairs*, UCLA, publication no 64.

Lloyd, N. G. (1988) 'Limit Cycles of Polynomial Systems – Some Recent Developments', in T. Bedford and J. Swift (eds) *New Directions in Dynamical Systems*, London Mathematical Society, Lecture Note Series, vol. 127.

Lucas, R. E. Jr (1981) *Studies in Business-Cycle Theory* (Oxford: Basil Blackwell).

Mas-Colell, A. (1986) 'Notes on Price and Quantity Tatônnement Approach to Competitive Equilibrium', in H. Sonnenschein (ed.) *Models of Economic Dynamics*, Lecture Notes in Economics and Mathematical Systems, vol. 264 (Heidelberg: Springer-Verlag).

Minorsky, N. (1962) *Nonlinear Oscillations* Princeton, NJ: Van Nostrand.

Mitchell, W. C. (1927) *Business Cycles: The Problem and its Setting* (London: Pitman).

Pais, A. (1982) *'Subtle is the Lord . . .': The Science and the Life of Albert Einstein* (Oxford: Oxford University Press).

Ruelle, D. (1988) 'Is Our Mathematics Natural? The Case of Equilibrium Statistical Mechanics', *Bulletin (New Series) of the American Mathematical Society*, vol. 19, no 1 (July) pp. 259–68.

Rustem, B. and K. Velupillai (1988) 'Computability, Complexity and Decision Processes in Economics', Aalborg (August) (mimeo).

Rustem, B. and K. Velupillai (1990) 'Rationality, Computability and Complexity', *Journal of Economic Dynamics and Control*, vol. 14, pp. 419–32.

Samuelson, P. A. (1947) *Foundations of Economic Analysis* (Cambridge: Massachusetts: Harvard University Press).

Sargent, T. J. (1987) *Macroeconomic Theory* (New York: Academic Press) 2nd edn.

Simon, H. A. (1984) 'On the Behavioural and Rational Foundations of Economic Dynamics', *Journal of Economic Behaviour and Organization*, vol. 5.

Sweezy, P. M. (1968) *The Theory of Capitalist Development* (New York: Monthly Review Press).

Tong, H. and Lim, K. S. (1980) 'Threshold Autoregression, Limit Cycles and Cyclical Data', *Journal of the Royal Statistical Society, Ser. B*, vol. 42, no 3, pp. 245–92.

Van der Pol, B. (1927) 'Forced Oscillations in a Circuit with non-linear Resistance (Reception with reactive Triode)', *The London, Edinburgh and Dublin Philosophical Magazine and Journal of Science*, vol. 3, pp. 65–80.

Van Duijin, J. J. (1983) *The Long Wave in Economic Life* (London: George Allen & Unwin).

Velupillai, K. (1989) 'Hilbert's 16th Problem, Nonlinear Dynamics and Economic Fluctuations: A Curiosum in the History of Dynamical Systems', Svanshall. (mimeo).

Velupillai, K. (ed.) (1990) *Nonlinear and Multisectoral Macrodynamics: Essays in Honour of Richard Goodwin* (London: Macmillan).

Velupillai, K. (1991) *Mathematical Theories of the Trade Cycle: From Frisch to Lucas – and Beyond* (London: Macmillan) (forthcoming).

Von Kármán, T. (1940) 'The Engineer Grapples with Nonlinear Problems',

*Bulletin of the American Mathematical Society*, vol. 46, pp. 615–83.

Wicksell, K. (1936) *Interest and Prices* (London: Macmillan).

Wigner, E. (1960) 'The Unreasonable Effectiveness of Mathematics in the Natural Sciences', *Communications in Pure and Applied Mathematics*, vol. 13, no 1 (February) pp. 1–14.

Yasui, T. (1953) 'Self-Excited Oscillations and Business Cycles', *Cowles Commission Discussion Paper*, no 2065.

# Part II

# The Distinguished Lectures

# 2 Business Cycles, Manias and Panics in Industrial Societies

Charles P. Kindleberger
MASSACHUSETTS INSTITUTE OF TECHNOLOGY

Let me clear the decks by first limiting my discussion to the cycles of about ten years, disregarding the Braudel cycle of 150 years (with peaks in 1350, 1650, 1817 and 1973–4 (Braudel, 1984, p. 78), the Kondratieff (1935) of fifty years, and the Kuznets cycle of twenty years (Kuznets, 1958), not to mention the Brinley Thomas international cycles linked across the Atlantic by migration, again of twenty years (Thomas, 1954). I have in mind much more the nineteenth- and twentieth-century cycles with breaks in 1816, 1825, 1836, 1847, 1857, 1866, 1873, 1890, 1907, 1914, 1921, 1929, 1937, perhaps 1949, and then again perhaps 1974–5 and 1981–2. I will have great difficulty in explaining the cyclical character of the movements, but am unwilling to accept that there is anything in nature, apart from human nature, that makes for the regularity, such as it is.

My interest, moreover, is in the international character of these events. Many observers write about cycles in a given country as if they were purely local, and some insist that the origin of a given international cycle is purely local (Friedman, 1970, p. 78, on 1929; Clapham, 1910, II, p. 267 on 1866; four economic historians on the 1893 Australian financial crisis which they denied was connected with the Baring crisis in London in 1890 (Butlin, 1961, p. 280; Hall, 1963, p. 148; Boehm, 1971, chs 9, 10; Pressnell, 1982, p. 160). There have been many accounts of the 1873 crises in Germany and Australia on the one hand, and in the USA on the other, but few connect the two.

The other salient issue is the extent to which given cycles, or all cycles are primarily financial, primarily real insofar as they involve a structural disequilibrium or misallocation of resources, or some combination of the two.

On the international front, I assert that the connections between the course of economic events in one country and one or more others

41

are many and varied. Friedman and Schwartz (1963) base the judgement that the USA was responsible for the depressions of 1921 and
1929 on the fact that at both turning points the flow of gold was
toward the USA. Money flows, including gold flows, form one
connection, working through monetary changes and changes in
short-term interest rates. Long-term capital movements – especially
when they are suddenly cut off – form another. In 1866 tight money in
France and Britain cut off lending to Italy and pushed that country
into recession and inconvertibility of the lira. In 1873 the German
and Austrian boom interrupted the capital flow to the USA, cutting
down railroad investment there. The Baring crisis of 1890 led to a
halt in British lending not only to Argentina but also to Brazil, Chile,
South Africa, Australia and the USA. The brilliant rise in the New
York stock market from March 1928 interrupted lending through
foreign bonds to Germany and Latin America and pushed those
countries into relapse. Tight money in the USA starting in 1979
halted long-term lending to the Third World, although policy
measures were taken after 1982 to ease it down, rather than cut it
abruptly. In these cases, especially 1928–9, the downturn in the
borrower deprived of capital may well feed back to the lender in the
third sort of connection – i.e. through reduced imports – by way of a
fall in national income and the foreign-trade multiplier.

A fourth connection runs through arbitrage that reduces the prices
of internationally traded commodities and internationally traded
securities in two or more markets, and has an effect on the incomes of
producers and the wealth of asset-holders. Some observers deny that
price changes within an economy can lead to depression, as they deny
the existence of money illusion. In their analysis, consumers gain
from price declines, offsetting the losses of producers. But this is a
static view that overlooks the dynamics of the matter. Producers
know rapidly that they must cut back spending when the prices of
their outputs fall, while consumers are slower to recognise and
respond to a gain in real income. Moreover, the bankruptcy of
producers may cause banks to fail, whereas the gains of consumers
are not only slow to be recognised but are likely to lead to new banks.

The fifth and final connection is purely psychological, though it is
connected with arbitrage in securities traded in common. In 1929
when the New York Stock Market crashed, all stock markets over the
world marked down their prices, even though the number of stocks
traded on more than one exchange was limited. The same phenomenon was observed in 1987 on Black Monday, 19 October.

I see no way to measure the relative weight of each of these five connections – gold, money and interest rates as one; long-term capital flows and their cut-off; income changes that lead to changes in foreign trade; commodity and security arbitrage, and psychological connections that lead to marking prices up or down in two markets not directly joined. No doubt, the weights will differ from case to case, and I am sceptical that an average of the weights over a significant number of cycles would be helpful in enabling economists to forecast what may happen in the next international cycle, just as I doubt that there is a typical business cycle such as Wesley C. Mitchell tried to measure at the National Bureau of Economic Research in the 1920s and 1930s. That effort produced superb by-products such as the studies in income and wealth, but the direct output can be said to have been exiguous. In my judgement any analogy between predictable cyclical paths of stars and galaxies and the economy is flawed. Economics less resembles celestial mechanics than evolutionary biology in which mutations can be confidently predicted to occur and later explained, but forecasting their nature and timing is hazardous.

In my lexicon, there are two general models of business cycle with strong but variable links between them. One is real, sometimes called structural, sometimes resulting from overinvestment because of too low a rate of interest (Hayek), or a market rate below the natural rate (Wicksell). The other derives from the title of this paper and is financial in origin. It is sometimes called the Fisher–Minsky model. I start describing the latter.

The Fisher–Minsky model starts with some autonomous event, shock or 'displacement', which alters investment priorities. It can be real: the start of a war; the end of a war; a good harvest; a bad harvest; the coming to fruition of a major and wide-ranging innovation such as the railroad; a discovery; and also of wide-ranging impact – some salient political event such as the independence of the Spanish colonies in Latin America around 1822. It may also be almost entirely financial: a refunding of maturing high-interest government debt, as in 1822 and 1888; a change in financial legislation, as the adoption of limited liability; banking deregulation; a financial innovation, the unexpected success of a large security issue (the Baring loan of 1817, the Thiers *rentes* of 1871 and 1872, the Dawes loan of 1924, or the many-times oversubscribed Guinness public issue of 1886, the success of which was like 'the crack of a starting pistol' for the issuance of other brewery shares not only in England but in Canada and the USA (Cottrell, 1980, pp. 168–70).

The altered investment opportunities lead to a shift in investor interest and new investment which may – I do not say must – lead to overshooting. Rational expectations holds that new information leads a market economy to establish a new set of prices according to some widely-recognised economic model, presumably a new set of equilibrium prices. This no doubt does happen. It is my contention, however, that it occasionally does not. Rational expectations assumes that the participants in the market all have equal sophistication, information, and purposes, or at least that the market is dominated, so that prices are established by a dominant group that is intelligent, sophisticated and well-financed. History shows, however, that participants in a market often have very different interests, degrees of experience, purposes, information and the like. To take one example, early railroad investment in England that led to the railway mania of the 1840s was undertaken by the gentry along the right of way, hoping to enhance the value of their land, especially when it contained deposits of coal and other minerals; by manufacturers served by a given line gaining access to inputs and transport for outputs; by pure investors seeking income from dividends and interest; by sophisticated speculators who bought the securities with the intention of selling them for capital gain; and by unsophisticated speculators, sometimes referred to as 'servant girls and greengrocers', who observed the early capital gains of the professional speculators and entered the game late (Reed, 1975). In addition to these, when the mania collapsed in 1847, half-built lines made a determined effort to sell securities to their suppliers of construction materials and rolling stock, speculating in a different way by buying so-called vendor's issues. Without more research than has been given to the problem it is not self-evident that any one group was sufficiently dominant for its notion of an equilibrium price to prevail in the market.

Assume that the market for railway shares, brewery shares, Latin American bonds, whatever asset is subject to revised valuations, does develop euphoria and positive feedback, as rising prices entice more numerous and less-sophisticated speculators to enter the market and bid prices up still further. At some point expectations of continuously rising prices will moderate, and more sophisticated investors may judge that the market has gone too high. They begin to sell. Investors along the right of way (of a railroad), manufacturers hoping to gain from the finished line, and pure investors, typically unleveraged, buy securities to hold. The last two groups, however, seek action.

They hope to buy low and sell dear. Their purchases are leveraged by borrowed funds or instalment purchases. So long as new investors continue to enter, the early ones can sell and pull out. But uncertainty may come to prevail. This is a period that I call 'distress', by analogy with a term in corporate finance that obtains when a company can contemplate the possibility that it may be unable to meet its obligations. No certainty is involved, merely recognition of a possibility. Distress may subside and leave a given market in equilibrium with market-clearing prices, balancing new demands and supply from former holders. Or the expectations of higher prices that led to rapid advances may give way to expectations of a large decline, on the ground that the rise has been overdone. In these circumstances a crash and perhaps a panic may ensue. The rush out of money into the asset or assets gives way to a rush out of assets into money. Prices fall.

The bare bones of this model must be fleshed out in a number of directions, especially covering the propaganda of euphoria and overshooting from one market to another, and one country to another; the possibility of curbing an excited market with monetary policy or even by moral suasion, and the possibility that a market crash of some sort may lead to business depression.

A plausible case can be made that overshooting and collapse in a single market are of no general macroeconomic interest. The Florida land boom that crashed in 1925, for example, burned unwary investors, but had only localised effects. For a mania to have serious potential, it must spread. In the 1820s, for example, the independence of Spanish colonies that started a boom in Latin-American bonds and mining shares coincided with the 1822 refunding of British debt from the Napoleonic wars which stimulated a boom in domestic shares, especially in insurance, as investors sought to maintain their incomes in the face of lower interest rates by buying higher-paying and riskier securities. In the 1830s the boom was in cotton, public lands in the USA, and British industries exporting to the USA; in 1847 in railroad shares (the mania), and in grain which soared in price because of the short crop and the potato blight in 1846. In the boom leading to crisis in 1866, there was a rise in cotton and in shipping to countries that might overcome the cotton famine produced by the Civil War in the USA, plus an Italian boom brought on by public works, especially railroads, in the newly unified country. The German boom that spilled over to Austria was partly financial in origin, based on receipt of the Franco–Prussian indemnity with more than

500 million francs paid in gold and silver, partly construction from the so-called *Gründungsfieber* – exultation over the establishment of the German Reich, and partly a railroad boom in the USA, financed in part by German and Austrian investors. These examples could be multiplied.

Of particular interest for contemporary observers is the link between the 1981 oil-price collapse and the financial crises of Mexico, Venezuela, etc. on the one hand, and the south-west banking community on the other. Also in the south-west, but elsewhere in the USA as well, is the connection between financial crises in security markets and those in real estate. The two cycles have different patterns. A stock-market crash as in 1921 or 1987 has effects which are completed – unless the deflation spreads relentlessly as in 1929 – in a few months or at most one or two years. In real estate, the profile of difficulty is different (Hoyt, 1933, ch. vii). At the time that the stock market collapses, real-estate speculators congratulate themselves. They own real assets instead of pieces of paper. Their debts consist in term loans, not demand obligations. But demand for real estate falls sharply. As real-estate prices level off and start downward people stop buying, waiting for the bottom, but taxes and interest keep up. Attrition among the real-estate speculators is slow, but if there has been a boom in office buildings, shopping malls, luxury houses, condominia and the like to parallel that in shares, the shake-out of open positions may go on for four, five even eight years, with strong negative effects on the industry and on banks lending to it.

Something of the propagation from one country to another has been indicated for Britain–Latin America (1826), Britain–USA (1836), Germany–Austria and the USA (1873). The collapse in London in 1847 can be traced throughout the world by a record of the number of bankruptcies (though the volume of assets involved would be better). In 1857 the collapse started in the Ohio Life and Trust Company in New York, spread to London, Scandinavia and Hamburg. One of the more interesting possibilities is for a convulsive deflation to be transmitted from $A$ to $D$ through $B$ and $C$ without $B$ and $C$ being much affected. In 1866 Paris did not suffer greatly but communicated the tightness of money from London and Berlin to Milan and Genoa by cutting off French lending. In 1907, a stock-market panic in New York sent a shock wave through London and Paris to Italy again, without significant consequences for the mediating markets. Some of these connections, both up and down, are monetary or involve capital flows; some psychological. The foreign-trade multiplier seems less involved for financial boom and bust as they work slowly when most of the propagation is close to instantaneous. The table of spreading failures starting in London in August 1847 and arriving in the USA in October to December 1848 (Kindleberger, 1978, p. 127) may well have been caused by declining British imports.

In explaining the euphoric phase of a boom, Minsky places great stress on the growth of debt of dubious quality (Minsky, 1982). His taxonomy of debt is not universally applauded (e.g. Goldsmith, 1982), and it is moreover, difficult to establish a characterisation of debt by quality. Monetarists such as Friedman and Schwartz (1963), however, believe that the expansionary phase of the cycle could be curbed by holding the money supply constant or growing at some predetermined rate. This view presupposes, first, that the velocity of money is constant, and second, that there are no innovations that relate to means of payments. Neither assumption seems warranted historically, Short-term variations in money turnover are frequent. Of greater importance, however, has been the fact that the definition of money is constantly undergoing change, as new means of payment and new forms of credit are devised. Coin, banknotes, deposits, bills of exchange, brokers' loans, other forms of selling in instalments, savings deposits as well as demand deposits, certificates of deposit, NOW accounts, credit cards, options, repos, etc., can extend the amounts available for payments to buy assets, and so, successively, under conditions of agitated speculation. Along with an outrush of money into some form of assets in euphoria, there will be extensions of credit in new forms and new directions, based on a given amount of 'money', however defined. Monetary control of manic investment booms is a theoretical construct that is belied by historical experience.

On the down-side, as debt is paid off, the money supply shrinks rapidly. To prevent a market crash from leading to depression, and the price collapse in the agitated area from spreading to other assets, especially goods and services, there should be a lender of last resort, as rationalised by Bagehot in *Lombard Street* (Bagehot, 1873). Such measures take many forms: suspending the Bank Act of 1844 that limited the amount of banknotes the Bank of England could issue, open-market operations in the USA, relaxation of rigid rules of central-bank discount, guarantees of bank liabilities as in the Baring crisis, the actions of the Federal Deposit Insurance Corporation (FDIC) or the Federal Savings and Loan Insurance Corporation (FSLIC) in guaranteeing deposits up to a limit which has been

increasingly raised, governmental loans of the Reconstruction
Finance Corporation (RFC) or Istituto per la Riconstruzione Italiana
(IRI) type. All have political implications and sometimes require
political action – for example, to expand the resources of the FDIC or
FSLIC after its appropriated funds and borrowing authority have
been exhausted. This may be particularly anxiety-provoking in a
situation when the executive and legislative branches of the US
government are in different hands, when the contending parties have
just emerged from a bitter electoral campaign and when there is a
substantial budget deficit that the executive wants eliminated but for
which it is unwilling to raise taxes.

It is my contention that financial crises lead to depression only
when there is no lender of last resort to halt the spreading collapse of
credit and money. Using the meteorological metaphors that are
frequently encountered in the popular literature, one may say that a
financial crisis halted by a lender of last resort is like a summer storm,
short, sharp, useful in clearing the air of the oppressive atmosphere
of the period of distress, but without serious consequence. Where
there is no lender of last resort to check the spread of deflation from
one asset to another, and from assets to banks that have made loans
to asset-holders, financial crisis may lead to prolonged depression.
This, in my view, is what happened in 1873 and 1929. In 1890 the
London financial market was righted by the guarantee of liabilities of
Baring Brothers; the deflation continued in the world overseas –
Latin America, Australia, South Africa and the USA, until the
expanding gold production of the Rand served, after a fashion – and
belatedly – as a lender of last resort, or more accurately as an
ultimate provider of more liquidity. Especially have I maintained that
international markets might have been able to recover if the spreading collapse in 1931 from Austria in May, to Germany in July, Britain
in September, Japan in December, the USA in 1933 and the gold
bloc in September 1936 had been arrested in timely fashion by a
significant lender-of-last-resort action by the USA and France to prop
up Austria as the first casualty of the causal chain (Kindleberger,
1986, 2nd edn, ch. xiv). Failure to take such action internationally
can be ascribed to the lack of international government on the one
hand, to the politicisation of the process by France, over foreign
policy, and to the isolationism of the USA. It should be noted,
however, that this view is contested by Moggridge, who holds that
the 1929 Crash was far more structural than purely financial, and
needed some more, thoroughgoing therapy, perhaps some such

measure as the Marshall Plan after the Second World War (Mog-gridge, 1982). At the same time, a number of respectable economists felt then, and feel now, that the Marshall Plan was not needed and the recovery of Europe from the Second World War could have been accomplished by such elementary measures as halting the inflation and depreciating the exchange rate (in still more elementary terms, balancing the budget and setting the exchange rate at the purchasing-power parity (for this brand of opinion, see Kindleberger, 1982, ch. 14). It is evident that the distinction between financial business cycles and structural ones, and the links running between the two, are a matter of some debate and confusion.

Within the financial causes of business cycles, there is a distinction between those who think in monetary terms, believing that the quantity of money determines the course of national income, and that mistakes in monetary policy are responsible for excessive expansions and contractions which would be non-existent or perhaps only greatly moderated, if monetary policy were perfect, and those who follow a Keynesian mode of thought, ascribing the cycle to changes in investment, consumer, or government spending, autonomously determined. In his recent Robbins lectures, Peter Temin, for example, ascribes the 1929 depression to deflationary policies of the British, French, German and US governments, and the recovery to a change in 'regimes', with their altered expectations, that led to enlarged investment (Temin, forthcoming; see also Temin, 1976). Opposed to this class of views is a more structural view that emphasizes the misallocation of investment. The classic example is the Empire State Building, finished in 1930, and not fully occupied until 1940 during the first year of the European war, a 'stranded investment' in the terminology of Hayek, that may have had monetary origins in too low an interest rate that caused investment to be too roundabout and capital-intensive, but produced a structure of investment unsuited to final demand.

In one of his semantic essays, Fritz Machlup excoriated the use of the term 'structural', calling it a weaselword, from which all the meaning had been sucked out, as a weasel sucks the meat out of an egg (Machlup, 1958, reprinted 1964). I took exception to this characterisation, especially as he quoted something I had written about 'structural disequilibrium', in which I had defined precisely what I had meant. In the second reprint of the paper, he added a footnote saying he had not meant to impugn my use of the term. By structural disequilibrium I meant a failure of markets to adjust to changes in

underlying conditions of demand and supply, including those produced by nature, war or discoveries. In a different context relating to
calculations of purchasing-power parity, I specifically included such
changes as a loss of foreign assets (sold off during war), or the
necessity – because of a peace treaty – to pay reparations, or because
of aid during a war, to pay war debts. The need to service old debts
could be subsumed under the term. In all this, it is assumed that other
things are equal, or that they change, if they happened to consist of
macroeconomic variables such as national income, the money supply,
and the budget, in some appropriate amount. Typically structural
disequilibria result from failure of resources to adjust as required by
some change in demand, supply, institutional condition or arrange-
ment, and are to be distinguished from a purely macroeconomic
expansion or contraction. The distinction is of course overdrawn,
since not all income elasticities are identical and any expansion or
contraction requires some rearrangement of resource allocation. But
at a heuristic level one can distinguish such cycles or disequilibria that
can be handled with merely monetary and/or fiscal policy (excluding
from the former, exchange-rate adjustment that directly alters relative prices of foreign-trade and non-traded goods) and with the
appropriate microeconomic adjustment left to the market to achieve
the appropriate allocation of resources, from those cycles or disequilibria occasioned by changes in demand, supply or institutional
arrangements that require more deep-seated therapy.

As already indicated, judgement will differ from case to case.
Viner, Machlup, Graham and Lutz believed that the disequilibrium
after the destruction caused by the Second World War could be
handled by macroeconomic policy. Moggridge and I did not. I
thought that the disequilibrium after the First World War, including
some destruction but more fundamentally the institutional trauma
involved in war debts and reparations, plus the recovery of European
production in lines that had expanded greatly outside Europe during
the war, could have been corrected by the market, provided that the
spreading collapse that started in Austria could be rapidly halted.
Moggridge (1982) did not.

A business cycle that starts as a simple expansion and then goes too
far, or as a simple contraction and spreads too widely and deeply
because of the absence of a lender of last resort, can convert a
Fisher–Minsky model of debt expansion and deflation into a structural cycle. On the up-side, investment in a set of industries or assets
may go so far as to strand Hayek-type investments that have to be

worked off slowly over time if they are not taken over by government to rescue their owners from bankruptcy, and the banks that financed their owners rescued from failure in their turn. On the down-side, especially in the international cycle that proceeds from a boom in lending that goes too far and is then cut off, the accumulation of interest and principal repayments to the overseas creditors may mount so high as to be beyond the capacity of macroeconomic policy, in this case even including exchange depreciation, to service the debt and at the same time discharge normal obligations to domestic resources. This is the issue today in Third World debt, where bankers and until recently the World Bank and the US Treasury have been insisting that sensible macroeconomic policies in the Third World would enable them to pay up, while the countries themselves seek wider measures, such as limits on debt service or partial forgiveness and write-offs, suggesting that the boom in Third World lending after 1970 went so far as to constitute a structural disequilibrium.

Simple cyclical and structural disequilibrium do not exhaust the possibilities. In the second and third editions of *International Economics* (1958 and 1963) I suggested there might be secular disequilibria as well, in which balance-of-payments disequilibrium could be ascribed to long-run income forces related to growth and decline rather than to cycles. There are pervasive structural changes not necessarily connected with either cycles or secular change. These include the discovery of the route to the Far East around the Cape of Good Hope, of the New World by Columbus, the sharp decline in ocean freights from the introduction of the iron-clad vessel, steam, diesel, refrigerated ships, etc., in the second half of the nineteenth century. Secular disequilibria are connected with economic growth and decline. Some economists dismiss such analysis as Spenglerian nonsense, but the the facts that Britain was overtaken by Germany and the USA at the end of the last century, and that the USA is being overtaken by Germany and Japan currently, raises the question. If one believes unreservedly in the equilibrating capacity of the market, all that is needed to correct the US balance of payments currently is to fiddle with tax and other incentives in the USA and Japan, to raise savings in the USA, lower them in Japan, and increase research and development in the USA to bring it up to or beyond the Japanese level along with adjusting the exchange rate further. If the trouble lies deeper in the growth process, however, American profligate spending, Japanese hoarding and the steady decline of productivity increases in the USA are unlikely to be readily reversed in the short run. The monetary and fiscal policy measures needed for the cycle, and the price measures such as depreciation of the exchange rate to assist the reallocation of resources from non-traded to traded goods will not go all the way to restore balance.

This paper is addressed to international business cycles on the one hand and manias, panics and crashes on the other. It is not therefore incumbent upon me to discuss anti-cyclical policy with its problems of recognition, decision and action lags, the choices in fiscal policy whether to act in the spending or tax field, and the possibility of gridlock in action from vested interests, called by Mancur Olson (1982) 'distributional coalitions', with opposing programmes. (In this last connection, the difficulty in raising taxes in the USA today offers a powerful illustration). Instead, I pose two questions: first, why have these financial crises occurred on an average of one every ten years up to 1949? and why did the early rhythm that had prevailed for close to 400 years then break? The first question is the harder, so that I take the second one first.

It seems evident that even without purposeful design, government finances serve as a built-in stabiliser of the economy. To the extent that government taxation varies with the cycle, rising in boom and falling in recession or depression, and to the extent that expenditure for such matters as unemployment assistance or relief of the poor behaves counter-cyclically, there is an inherent tendency, without policy decision, for governments to run surpluses, or at least relative surpluses, in boom and deficits in depression. Before the Second World War, government budgets formed a relatively small portion of gross national product, except in war-time, so that the dampening of national-income changes initiated in the private economy under capitalism was small. With the growth of expenditure and taxation after the Second World War, however, from the order of 10 per cent of gross national product (GNP) or less around 1900 to more than 20 per cent after the Second World War, the different behaviour of government from private expenditure patterns, altered the macro-economic scene.

The first question – why booms followed by busts repeated themselves at intervals of about a decade – is harder to answer. One would have thought that economic actors would learn. Sometimes they do – as in US government policy after the First and Second World Wars – insistence on collecting war debts and the sanctity of commercial loans after the First World War and relief, rehabilitation, grants and reconstruction loans on generous terms and the Marshall Plan after the Second World War. On the other hand, the French general staff failed to learn after the First World War and built a Maginot line that was circumvented through the undefended French border along the Low Countries.

Two possible theories can be adduced on an *ad hoc* basis, without, so far as I can see, any adequate means to test which of the two is superior. First, there is the hypothesis that as the nature of the displacement and the objects of speculation change from time to time the participants in the manic phase are persuaded on each occasion that this is different – i.e. that the freedom of the Spanish colonies in the 1820s, the demand for cotton in the 1830s that drove expansion west from Georgia and led to booms both in public land and in purchases of British goods in the USA, the railway boom of the 1840s, and so on were so unlike that the old pattern was by no means certain to be reproduced. The second possible hypothesis is that the astute speculators may learn, and repeat their successful manoeuvres of the past decade, but the amateur, inexperienced and late-coming crowd that gets caught up in the excitement of a rising market is a new group each time. Some individuals may learn and move from the large class of outsiders that gets fleeced in the crash into the charmed circle of insiders that consciously or unconsciously does the fleecing, perhaps, but their places are taken by newcomers as uninitiated as they were the first time. A third possible theory is that the players recognise the nature of the game and its dangers, but enjoy the action thoroughly and sustain their hopes of winning even though in a contemplative mood they would realise that the chances of emerging successful are not high. Lotteries are played continuously on this basis, both by the unintelligent who focus upon the winnable amounts rather than the chances of losing – in cognitive dissonance – and by intelligent players who hope to get in and out fast – like the originators of chain-letters, but are sufficiently sophisticated to realise that they may not. I see no way to determine which of these theories explains the repetition of the pattern for 400 years. Especially is this the case when there is no agreement in the economics profession, first, on why the 1929 depression was so extended and, second, why the Stock Market crash of 1929 was followed by prolonged and deep depression, when those of 1921 (in the USA at least) and 1987 were not.

Let me conclude with a series of short blunt declarative sentences:

1. The persistent pattern of financial crises at ten year intervals is impossible to explain in terms of the theory of rational expectations.

2. Financial crisis may turn into depressions if there is no lender of last resort.
3. Business cycles may have primarily financial, primarily structural (resulting from changes in demand, supply or institutional relationships) or mixed origins.
4. It is hard to explain why economic actors in capitalist societies have not learned from experience so as to avoid financial crises.
5. The larger role of government in national income expenditure since the Second World War has both dampened financial crises and extended their periodicity.
6. Financial crises are generally international in character, with the connections between a crisis in one country and others running through money and capital flows, including changes in interest rates, asset and commodity arbitrage, the foreign-trade multiplier, and purely psychological infection.
7. One particular pattern frequently encountered is that of a flow of foreign lending burgeoning in manic or quasi-manic form and then being suddenly cut off, leaving the borrowing country with a recession or depression that may feed back to the original lender.

**References**

Bagehot, Walter (1873) *Lombard Street: A Description of the Money Market*, (London: John Murray, 1917) reprint edition.
Boehm, E. A. (1971) *Prosperity and Depression in Australia, 1887–1897* (Oxford: Clarendon Press).
Butlin, S. J. (1961) *Australia and New Zealand Bank, the Bank of Australasia and the Union Bank of Australia, Limited* (Croyden, Australia: Longmans, Green).
Braudel, Fernand (1984) *Civilization and Capitalism, 15th–18th Century*, vol. 3, *The Perspective of the World* (New York, Harper & Row).
Clapham, Sir John (1910) 'The Last Years of the Navigation Acts', *English Historical Review* (two parts, July and October), reprinted in E. M. Carus-Wilson (ed.) *Essays in Economic History*, vol. 3 (London: Arnold, 1962).
Cottrell, P. L. (1980) *Industrial Finance, 1830–1914: The Finance and Organization of English Manufacturing Industry* (London: Methuen).
Fisher, Irving (1913) *The Purchasing Power of Money: Its Determination and Relation to Credit, Interest and Crises* (New York: Macmillan).
Friedman, Milton (1970) 'Column' in *Newsweek*, 25 May 1970.
Friedman, Milton and Schwartz, Anna J. (1963) *A Monetary History of the United States, 1867–1960* (Princeton: Princeton University Press).

Goldsmith, Raymond W. (1982) 'Comment' on Hyman P. Minsky, 'The Financial-Instability Hypothesis: Capitalist Processes and the Behavior of the Economy', in C. P. Kindleberger and J.-L. Laffargue (eds) *Financial Crises: Theory, History and Policy* (Cambridge: Cambridge University Press, and Paris: Editions de la Maison des Sciences de l'Homme) pp. 41–3.

Hall, A. R. (1963) *The London Capital Market and Australia, 1870–1914* (Canberra: Australian National University, Science Monograph) no 21.

Hayek, Friederich (1931) *Prices and Production* (London: Routledge & Kegan Paul).

Hoyt, Homer (1933) *One Hundred Years of Land Values in Chicago: The Relationship of the Growth of Chicago to the Rise in Its Land Values, 1830–1933* (Chicago: University of Chicago Press).

Kindleberger, Charles P. (1973, 1986) *The World in Depression, 1929–1939* (Berkeley: University of California Press).

Kindleberger, Charles P. (1978) *Manias, Panics and Crashes: A History of Financial Crises* (New York: Basic Books).

Kindleberger, Charles P. (1987) *Marshall Plan Days* (Boston: Allen & Unwin).

Kindleberger, C. P. and J.-P. Laffargue (eds) (1982) *Financial Crises: Theory, History and Policy* (Cambridge: Cambridge University Press, and Paris: Editions de la Maison des Sciences de l'Homme).

Kondratieff, N. D. (1935) 'The Long Waves in Economic Life', in *Review of Economic Statistics*, vol. 17, no 6 (November).

Kuznets, Simon (1958) 'Long Swings in the Growth of Population and in Related Economic Variables', *Proceedings of the American Philosophical Society*, vol. 102, no 1.

Machlup, Fritz (1958, 1964) 'Structure and Structural Change: Weaselwords and Jargon', *Zeitschrift für Nationalokonomie*, no 3, pp. 280–98, reprinted in his *International Payments, Debts and Gold* (New York: Charles Scribner's Sons).

Minsky, Hyman P. (1982) 'The Financial-Instability Hypothesis: Capitalist Processes and the Behavior of the Economy', in Kindleberger and Laffargue (eds) *Financial Crises*, pp. 13–39.

Moggridge, D. E. (1982) 'Policy in the Crises of 1920 and 1929', in Kindleberger and Laffargue, *Financial Crises*, pp. 171–87.

Olson, Mancur (1982) *The Rise and Decline of Nations: Economic Growth, Stagflation and Social Rigidities* (New Haven: Yale University Press).

Pressnell, L. S. (1982) 'The Sterling System and Financial Crises before 1914', in Kindleberger and Laffargue (eds) *Financial Crises*, pp. 148–64.

Reed, M. C. (1975) *Investment in Railways in Britain: A Study in the Development of the Capital Market* (Oxford: Oxford University Press).

Temin, Peter (1976) *Did Monetary Forces Cause the Great Depression?* (New York: Norton).

Temin, Peter (forthcoming) *The Robbins Lectures*, delivered January 1989.

Thomas, Brinley (1954) *Migration and Economic Growth* (Cambridge: Cambridge University Press).

Wicksell, Knut (1935) *Lectures on Political Economy*, vol. 2, *Money* (New York: Macmillan).

# 3 Cuspoidal Nets[1]

## Ralph Abraham[2]
UNIVERSITY OF CALIFORNIA

The ubiquitous cusp catastrophe has been pressed into service by Zeeman as a rough qualitative model for many dynamical systems in the sciences, including a democratic nation. The extension to two nations has been made by Kadyrov, who discovered an interesting oscillation in this context. Here we speculate on the properties of connectionist networks of cusps, which might be used to model social and economic systems.

## INTRODUCTION

Complex and cellular dynamical systems provide useful models for morphodynamic systems, such as neural membranes, heart muscle, reaction-diffusion devices, microeconomic communities.[3] The connectionist neural net is an important example, which uses the simplest standard cell, but achieves complex behaviour through a rich net of connections. In this paper, we suggest properties of a network of cusps. The properties are built up through a sequence of examples, beginning with published works of Zeeman and Kadyrov. A later paper will be devoted to the results of simulations.[4]

## ONE CUSP

The cusp catastrophe of elementary catastrophe theory (ECT) is the canonical bifurcation of codimension two. It occurs with static attractors, periodic attractors,[5] and chaotic attractors.[6] We will adopt the (non-standard) notations of the Isnard and Zeeman model for hawks and doves (see their Sec. 11).[7] Let

$$\phi(x, a, b) = -\frac{1}{4} x^4 + \frac{1}{2} bx^2 + ax$$

Then the dynamical scheme of the cusp is

56

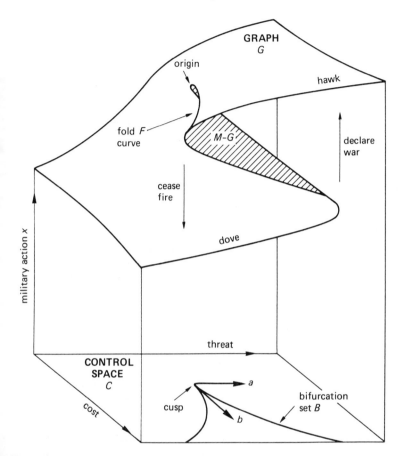

*Figure 3.1* Response diagram of the standard cusp

$$x' = \phi_x (x, a, b) = -x^3 + bx + a$$

where $\phi_x$ denotes the partial derivative of $\phi$ with respect to $x$. This scheme has the familiar response diagram shown in Figure 3.1 (taken from Isnard and Zeeman, Fig. 11). The control parameter $b$ is called the *splitting factor*, while $a$ is the *normal factor*.

TWO CUSPS

In the spirit of complex dynamical systems theory, we may couple
two cusps in a minimal network. Each of the control parameters of
one of the cusps may be expressed as a function of the state of the
other. We consider here only one special case, introduced by Kadyrov's model: let the normal factor of each be proportional to the state
of the other.[8] Thus,

$$x' = - x^3 + ax + by$$

$$y' = - y^3 + cy + dx$$

This is a dynamical scheme with two-dimensional state space, $(x, y)$
$\varepsilon R^2$, and four-dimensional control space, $(a, b, c, d)$ $\varepsilon R^4$. Due to the
source of this dynamical scheme within ECT, we might expect this to
be a gradient system. In general, it is not. For the partial derivative of
the $x'$ function with respect to $y$ is $b$, while that of the $y'$ function with
respect to $x$ is $d$. Thus, in the *symmetric case*, in which we set $b = d$,
the coupled system is a gradient scheme with three-dimensional
control, equivalent to one of the umbilics of ECT (see p. 185 of
Poston and Stewart).[9] Its potential function is

$$\phi(x, y) = - \frac{1}{4} (x^4 + y^4) + \frac{1}{2} ax^2 + bxy + \frac{1}{2} cy^2$$

Its bifurcation set (an algebraic surface in $R^3$) may be visualised in a
plane cross-section by setting any of the three control parameters
equal to a constant. For example, with $b = d = 1$ the bifurcation set
section consists of two crossed umbilics.

But in the general, *asymmetric* case, we have a non-elementary
response diagram. Kadyrov has obtained, for example, the section of
the bifurcation set shown in Figure 3.2 (taken from Kadyrov, Figure
6). In this $(b, d)$ plane section, $a = 1$, and $c = 1$, (or any positive
values in the wedge defined by $2c > a$ and $2a > c$). The cusps
represent degenerate fold catastrophes or blue loops, while the
parabolic curves represent basin folds. We may explain these in more
detail by considering the phase portraits in the seven distinct regimes
of the section $(A-G)$ in Figure 3.2. The jargon from bifurcation
theory may be found in Part Four of Abraham and Shaw (1982–88).[12]

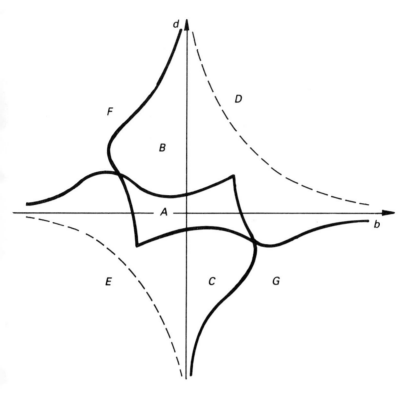

*Figure 3.2*  Section of the bifurcation set

(A) With $(b, d)$ in the central region enclosed by the two cusps, the phase portrait in the $(x, y)$ state space has four static, nodal attractors (one in each quadrant), four saddles (their insets comprising the separators of the four basins), and one central, nodal repellor.
(B) Here there are two point attractors (in quadrants 1 and 3), two saddles, and one central repellor. Across the bifurcation curve between $A$ and $B$ there are two fold catastrophes, in each of which a point attractor and a saddle mutually annihilate. (If non-degenerate, these would occur one at a time across disjoint curves.)
(C) Two attractors as in $B$ (but in quadrants 2 and 4).
(D) Two attractors as in $B$, but across the bifurcation curve between $B$ and $D$ there is a fold in which one saddle and the central repellor or annihilate. Occurring entirely within the separator of two basins, this is an insignificant bifurcation.
(E) Two attractors as in $D$ (but in quadrants 2 and 4).

(F) In this regime there is a single attractor (periodic) and a central, spiral repellor. Across the bifurcation curve separating $B$ (or $C$) from $F$, there is a degenerate blue loop explosion, in which both point attractors (in $B$ or $C$) explode simultaneously. (In a non-degenerate analogue, each blue loop event would occur across its own, distinct, curve. Alternatively, there might be a fold catastrophe, followed by a single, non-degenerate blue loop.)

(G) One periodic attractor, like $F$. In these two regimes, $F$ and $G$, we call the attractor a *Kadyrov oscillator*. The existence of this oscillation in a system of coupled ECT schemes is crucial for the applications we envision, and discuss below. It is reminiscent of the oscillator found by Smale in the context of two coupled cells.[10]

We ignore the degeneracy of this scheme for the present, but will return to this in a future paper, in which a complete unfolding will be suggested.[4]

CUSPOIDAL NETS

We may easily extend our definitions to an ensemble of $N$ cusps. Let $A$ be a real matrix size $N$ by $N$, and consider the vectorfield on $R^N$ defined by

$$\dot{x}_i = -x_i^3 + A_{ij}x_j, \, i = 1, \ldots, N$$

where the Einstein sum convention is implied by the repeated subscripts. This is a dynamical scheme with $N$-dimensional state space, $x \, \varepsilon \, R^N$, and $N^2$-dimensional control space, $A \, \varepsilon \, R^{N \times N}$. From the connectionist point-of-view, this is a neural net, slightly generalised from the usual linear one by the addition of the cubic terms. In the symmetric case, $A_{ij} = A_{ji}$, the system is of gradient type, with potential function,

$$\phi(x_1, \ldots, x_N) = -\frac{1}{4}(x_1^4 + \ldots + x_N^4) + \frac{1}{2}A_{ij}x_ix_j$$

The interpretation of the attractors of the scheme as the local minima of this function, common to ECT and to neural net theory alike, is valid and useful here.[11] Further, between the symmetric and the general cases, intermediate cases may be of interest, such as the case in which $A$ is symplectic. We might suggest that the neural net community experiment with these systems, which have long-term memory properties in their bistable regimes.

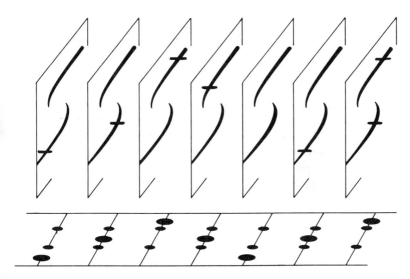

*Figure 3.3* One-dimensional array of double folds

An example of a cuspoidal net is illustrated in Figure 3.3 in which each cusp is reduced to a double fold by fixing its splitting factor, $b = +1$. This net exhibits *memory*, in that the temporary displacement of the local (normal factor) controls $a_i$ from neutral values may effect a catastrophic shift of state, which is remembered after the return to neutral.

Note that if two neighbouring cells are coupled by the Kadyrov scheme of the preceding section, Kadyrov oscillations may result from their interaction. There may even be two or more Kadyrov oscillators within the network. And the coupling of two Kadyrov oscillators may easily result in chaotic behaviour. Thus, a cuspoidal net with four cells and Kadyrov (that is, linear) coupling is capable of multistable behaviour, with static, periodic, and chaotic regimes.

We may conclude that models for social and economic behavior, such as business cycles, may be constructed of cuspoidal nets. These may be *the simplest models* exhibiting such behaviour.


CONCLUSION

Complex dynamical systems, made from a finite set of identical dynamical schemes by a complete graph of coupling functions of adjustable strength, may be regarded as a potentially useful generalisation of neural nets and excitable media. Taking the standard cell from ECT defines an *ECT net*, and provides us with a headstart in the understanding of the global behaviour of the network, and the geometry of its response diagram. In this paper, we have described only one example of an ECT net, *the cuspoidal net*, based on the cusp catastrophe of ECT. The oscillatory cusp of the Duffing system also suggests itself for this treatment.[13] Exploration of these nets will require extensive computation, and will provide serious challenge to our computer-graphic visualisation skills. Massively parallel machines would be particularly well-suited for this research.

### Notes

1. Dedicated to Christopher Zeeman on his sixtieth birthday.
2. It is a pleasure to acknowledge the generosity of Chris Zeeman, Tim Poston, and Gottfried Mayer-Kress in sharing their ideas; Peter Brecke for a translation of Kadyrov's paper; and the University of California's INCOR program for financial support of this work, in connection with a modelling project on international stability, jointly with Gottfried Mayer-Kress. Thanks also to John Corliss and John Dorband at the NASA Goddard Space Flight Center for introducing me to the Massively Parallel Processor.
3. Ralph H. Abraham, 'Cellular Dynamical Systems', pp. 7–8 in *Mathematics and Computers in Biomedical Applications, Proc. IMACS World Congress, Olso, 1985*, ed. J. Eisenfeld and C. DeLisi, North-Holland, Amsterdam (1986).
4. Ralph H. Abraham, Gottfried Mayer-Kress, Alex Keith, and Matthew Koebbe, 'The Double Cusp', (forthcoming).
5. E. Christopher Zeeman, 'Duffing's Equation in Brain Modelling', pp. 293–300 in E. Christopher Zeeman (ed.) *Catastrophe Theory* (Reading, MA: Addison-Wesley, 1977).
6. Ralph H. Abraham and Christopher D. Shaw, *Dynamics, the Geometry of Behavior, Four vols.*, Santa Cruz, CA: Aerial Press, 1982–8).
7. C. A. Isnard and E. C. Zeeman, 'Some Models from Catastrophe Theory in the Social Sciences', (E. C. Zeeman, *Catastrophe Theory*, New York: Addison-Wesley, 1977) pp. 303–59.
8. M. N. Kadyrov, 'A Mathematical Model of the Relations between Two States', *Global Development Processes 3* Institute for Systems Studies, (1984).
9. Tim Poston and Ian Stewart, *Catastrophe Theory and its Applications* (London: Pitman, 1978).
10. Steve Smale, 'A Mathematical Model of Two Cells via Turing's Equa-

tion', in M. MacCracken (ed.) *The Hopf Bifurcation and its Applications* (New York: Springer, 1976).
11. J. J. Hopfield, 'Neural Networks and Physical Systems with Emergent Collective Computational Abilities', *Proceedings of the National Academy of Science, USA* (1982) 79, pp. 2554–8.
12. See note 6 above.
13. See note 5 above.

# 4 A Constructive Approach to Economic Fluctuations[1]

John J. McCall[2]

UNIVERSITY OF CALIFORNIA, LOS ANGELES

## 1 INTRODUCTION

A major goal of this paper is to introduce a constructive approach to the study of economic phenomena. The highlights of this approach are its connections with the recent advances in neuroscience and the earlier research of Turing, McCulloch, Gödel and Church.[3] We claim that the spectacular innovations in computer-neuroscience and bio-logical-neuroscience clarify the limitations of modern economics flowing from both its static foundations and its previous neglect of the interdisciplinary foundations of utility and production theory. It is precisely these two areas of neuroscience which contain the building blocks required for constructing dynamic economic processes of tastes and production. The recent neuroscientific innovations are responsible for this potential construction. Furthermore, an inter-disciplinary network among economics and the disciplines comprising *artificial intelligence* (AI) could enhance the AI disciplines as much as it vitalises economics. We maintain that these gains from trade can be realised only if the *static* and fragile von Neumann–Morgenstern edifice is replaced by flexible foundations less vulnerable to paradox and more tolerant to the faults and errors intrinsic in human decision-making.

A critical component of this interdisciplinary enterprise is prob-ability theory contained in the 'general theory of processes'.[4] It not only is the mortar merging economics, computer science, psychology, neuroscience and physics, but provides a new perspective for appreci-ating the brilliance of the contributions of Adam Smith, Vico and de Finetti and the evolution of economic institutions.

The proposed methodology emphasises the importance of contacts with empirical phenomena, and *contains* the process for accomplishing this induction.

**Outline of the Paper**

In his Hicksian portrait of the diversity and profundity of business cycle theory, K. Velupillai provides an elegant introduction to this paper. We begin by elaborating on Samuelson's insightful piece (1952) and show its relation to the earlier work of Fisher, and the research programme presented here. Section 3 is an attempt to unify the seemingly diverse business-cycle theories presented at this conference, ranging from Goodwin to Prescott, as well as other post-Lucasian contributions. Clearly their economic content varies substantially. Yet they are all variations of Markov processes. Next, the elements of our theory of economic fluctuations are summarised (Section 4) with emphasis on the role of semimartingales. The neuroscience connections are presented in Section 5. The influence of biological-neuroscience on the formation of tastes and the corresponding effect of computer-neuroscience on production processes are outlined, thereby illustrating the constructive approach to economics and exemplifying several of its implications.

## 2 FROM FISHER TO FRIEDMAN AND SAMUELSON TO CHANCE[5]

It is instructive to summarise earlier economic contributions which are related closely to the theory of economic fluctuations proposed here.[6] These contributions include the seminal research of Arrow, Marschak, Alchian, Coase, Fisher, Becker, Stigler, Lucas, Sargent, Samuelson, Winter, Nelson, Friedman and many others. Obviously, it would be impossible to summarise the pertinent contributions of these economists. Hence, we focus on Fisher, Samuelson and Friedman.

**Irving Fisher**

Irving Fisher (1867–1947), one of America's most prominent economists, was the last student of J. Willard Gibbs (1839–1903), America's first great scientist. Gibbs's study of thermodynamics led to the development of statistical mechanics and provided the foundations for quantum mechanics. Gibbs had a profound influence on Fisher's intellectual development which is manifested clearly in his dissertation. Implicit in this extraordinary thesis is a coherent business-cycle theory. It is contained in Fisher's hydrodynamic analogy of consumer behaviour.

Until now the major contributions of Fisher were perceived as his design of a consistent utility theory and his monumental research on investment and the theory of interest. In his famous essay Stigler (1965) observes that:

> The first careful examination of the measurability of the utility function and its relevance to demand theory was made by Fisher. He solved the measurability problem quite satisfactorily for the case in which the marginal utilities of the various quantities are independent of one another . . . Fisher concludes his brilliant dissertation with the argument that the total utility function cannot in general be deduced from the indifference curves and that, for purposes of explaining consumers' reactions to prices and income changes, there is not occasion to introduce total utility:
>
>> Thus if we seek only the causation of the *objective facts of prices and commodity distribution* four attributes of utility as a quantity are entirely unessential, (1) that one man's utility can be compared to another's, (2) that for the same individual the marginal utilities at one consumption-combination can be compared with those at another, or at one time with another, (3) even if they could, total utility and gain might not be integrable, (4) even if they were, there would be no need to determining the constants of integration.

Stigler does not comment on Fisher's hydrodynamic (arbitrage) arguments. This silence may reflect the profession's view that Fisher's interest in the theory and practice of hydrodynamics was merely another sign of a highly eccentric personality. Actually, it was another dimension of his genius – a genius that invented a card-sorting machine and co-founded Remington Rand! We maintain that if the hydrodynamic approach had been applied to stochastic economic fluctuations – clearly a Gibbsian implication – it would have generated a stochastic dynamic macroeconomic theory superior in both elegance and usefulness to most modern macroeconomic models.[7]

It has been shown by Spitzer (1971) that the Gibbs ensemble, the random configuration of points (discrete gas particles) on a lattice, underlying statistical mechanics is equivalent to a Markov random field. The latter is a method for extending one-dimensional (integer values of time) Markov processes to a higher dimensional lattice-valued time-parameter. Thus, since Markov processes are martingales, so too are Gibbs ensembles. The natural model for describing an arbitrage-free (martingale) system is precisely Fisher's hydrodynamic mechanism.

The arbitrage interpretation is more natural for economists. A system is arbitrage-free when movement ceases – the set of prices has achieved an equilibrium configuration, that is, each component of Fisher's hydrodynamic model has attained a stable level. The familiar equilibrium conditions for the utility-maximising consumer is

$$\frac{MU_i}{P_i} = \frac{MU_i}{P_j} , \quad i, j = 1, 2, \ldots, n$$

for each pair of the $n$ commodities.

It was this utility-maximising feature of Fisher's dissertation that captured the profession's attention. But by the middle of the twentieth century Fisher had almost lapsed into obscurity. His brilliant and highly original research on capital theory received a single citation in Lutz's (1951) 'definitive' work on capital theory.[8]

## Paul Samuelson

Samuelson (1952) saw the intimate connections among his own research on linear programming, Fisher's hydrodynamic model, and the electrical network model as exposited by Enke (1951).[9] Samuelson first recognised the similarity between electrical networks and the linear programming formalism. Kirchhoff revealed the conservation principles equilibrating electrical flows and Samuelson saw that these were similar to the dual variables, 'prices or potentials', which conferred equilibrium on linear programming[10] and its close relatives, the Ford–Fulkerson analysis and graph theory. For our purposes, the key connection is the equivalence between random walks (Brownian motion) and electrical networks (potential theory).[11]

Samuelson attributes these economic insights to Koopmans (1949) and Tucker (1950). However, Samuelson frequently employs language from statistical mechanics, for example, 'keep a system in the optimal configuration', which suggests his intuitive urge to convert the entire deterministic system into its stochastic counterpart.

Samuelson was told by Koopmans that his solution to the transportation problem was guided by using the electrical network analogy. Earlier, Maxwell reveals that his discoveries were always achieved by reference to a hydrodynamic analogue. The equivalence between electrical networks and hydrodynamics is contained in the monotonicity law (Doyle and Snell, 1985). The source of these equivalences and much more is revealed with enthusiasm and lucidity in the splendid book by Strang (1986).

Thus we can trace Samuelson's insights back to Fisher's hydrodynamic model via Enke and Morehouse *et al.*[12] Fisher undoubtedly 'saw' the equivalence between hydrodynamics and electrical networks.

For our purposes the practical import of this historical digression is: the no-arbitrage principle is a martingale, potential theory is equivalent to Brownian motion, and the diffusion operator is the Brownian motion transform discovered by Einstein. The *connection* of graphical methods via potential theory to the 'general theory of processes' has not been exploited. It appears to have many applications in economic theory and econometrics. It could also be the path from neuroscience to rigorous estimation via stopping times, the equivalent of the potential – theoretical concept – Choquet capacity.[13]

Samuelson's seminal work has not gone unnoticed. For example, see Takayama and Judge (1971), the recent survey and extension by Tobin (1988), and Hammond and Magnanti (1987). Samuelson mentions (in a private communication) that his paper stimulated a vast agricultural economic literature. However, as far as I know no one has pursued its nexus with the stochastic literature.

## Friedman[14]

Friedman was the first economist to recognise randomness *as an essential ingredient of economic processes*. The transient component of the time-series was not measurement error, but *transient income*. His permanent-income hypothesis was designed *at the level of individual decision-making*, equilibrated by prices, and modified as new information unfolded. This brilliant research was also stimulated by *Irving Fisher's* path-breaking work on the theory of interest. Friedman's permanent income process was 'fair' or 'natural' as long as the individual could distinguish the transient from the permanent component of the income process. In this fundamental sense, inflation violates the 'rules of the game' in that 'noise detection' becomes costly. The individual can no longer rely on prices to conduct this separation and convey information about changing opportunities. It is this contamination of information which corrupts society's 'fair game'. Inflation is a capricious *tax*; it is unpredictable, but, more importantly, it 'taxes' the allegiance of the citizen to his country. When viewed from this perspective, the monetary research of Friedman becomes an integral part of his overall research programme – comparing actual individual decision-making with their behaviour in stable societies.

## 3 A UNIFIED FRAMEWORK FOR COMPARING THE SEEMINGLY DIVERSE MACROECONOMIC LITERATURE

Several papers contained in this volume appear to be unrelated. Indeed, this appearance is characteristic of much of the post-Lucasian macroeconomic literature. This diversity can be mollified by observing a common *thread* connecting many of these models – the Markov process or more specifically, the optional stopping time.

Consider the resurgence of dynamical models. The papers and comments by Goodwin, Abraham, Lorentz, and Velupillai confirm the influence of this approach to the recent analyses of macroeconomic phenomena. The pioneering research of Goodwin (1951) in dynamic economics, the path-breaking mathematical research by Abraham on chaos and dynamical systems,[15] are finally being studied seriously by the economics profession. The paper by Lorentz[16] is representative of this renaissance.[17]

A critical point has been overlooked by some proponents of dynamical systems. Recall, for example, that the dynamical behaviour of Grandmont's (1984) deterministic model depends critically on the initial conditions. In the early days, econometricians typically estimated naive deterministic models by adding measurement error. Sinai, Freidlin, Glass, Lasota and Mackey have shown that stochastic perturbations transform non-stochastic *discrete* dynamical systems into ergodic stochastic processes. That is, the perturbations produce a stochastic sequence which converges weakly to a unique distribution *independent* of the initial distribution.

When Phelps's famous island metaphor is interpreted in a network setting a reversible Markov process emerges with an invariant distribution. This complex system is reducible to a birth-and-death process possessing all the nice properties of these strong Markov processes.[18]

An important paper, Hopenhayn and Prescott (1987), demonstrates that the seminal articles in the rational expectations literature are strong Markov processes.[19] The distribution of the important functional, the first passage time, is invariant under the weak convergence of the process to its equilibrium distribution. This implies that disorder or structural change can be detected by this functional.

## 4 THE SOURCE OF ECONOMIC OSCILLATIONS

We contend that comprehension of economic fluctuations flows from an understanding of individual oscillations. These oscillations are intrinsic to individual behaviour and are driven by the neurological responses to the continuous vibrations of the environment. A significant source of environmental stimuli is technological change, which in turn is powered by entrepreneurial assessment of changing consumer tastes. The economic consequences of this interaction between tastes and technology[20] is explicable by the recent discoveries in biological and computer neuroscience. Environmental variability extrinsic to the interplay between tastes and technology may ameliorate or exacerbate these 'natural' oscillations. The key point is that economic fluctuations are spatial–temporal phenomena present in every economic activity. The understanding of fluctuations at each level of economic activity requires a separate study, with data corresponding to the nature of the questions being asked of the modules at that hierarchical level and with the appropriate spatio-temporal scaling.

The sources of observed economic fluctuations are the formation and dissolution of contracts and other economic relations by individuals and firms. The entry and exit of individuals and firms from partitions and coalitions are included in the motion induced by 'other economic relations'. The familiar birth-and-death process is used to model contractual relations and these basic movements by economic agents. Because of our reliance on this versatile process, a brief review of its relevant properties is appropriate.

### 4.1 Birth-and-Death Process

Let the state space of a Markov chain be $N^+$, the non-negative integers. The semi-group $P_t$ is the matrix $[P_{ij}(t), i, j \in N^+]$, with

$$P_{ij}(t) = P[X_{t+s} = j \mid X_s = i] \tag{1}$$

Let

$$\lim_{t \downarrow 0} \frac{1 - P_{ii}(t)}{t} = q_i < \infty \tag{2}$$

and

$$\lim_{t \downarrow 0} \frac{P_{ij}(t)}{t} = q_{ij} < \infty \tag{3}$$

These are the *infinitesimal characteristics* of the homogeneous Markov chain, $X_t$. The process $X_t$ is said to be *stable* if

$$q_i < \infty$$

for each $i \in N^+$ and *conservative* if

$$q_i = \sum_{i \neq j} q_{ij} \tag{4}$$

The matrix $Q = \{q_{ij}, i, j \in N^+\}$ is called the $Q$-matrix of the semigroup $P_t$.

The *forward Kolmogorov equations* are:

$$P'_{ik}(t) = -P_{ik}(t)q_k + \sum_{j \neq i} P_{ij}(t)q_{jk}, \quad i, k > 0$$

whereas the backward Kolmogorov equations are:

$$P'_{ik}(t) = -q_i P_{ik}(t) + \sum_{i \neq j} q_{ij} P_{ik}(t), \quad i, k > 0.$$

Under the stipulated conditions, the $P_{ij}$s satisfy the forward equations, but for a countable state space the backward equations need not be satisfied.

Suppose $P_0(k) \equiv \pi_k$ satisfies

$$\pi_k q_k = \sum_{j \neq k} \pi_j q_{jk}, \quad k > 0$$

Then $P_k(t) = \pi_k$ for all $t > 0$ and all $k$; $\pi_k$ is called the equilibrium distribution or the steady-state distribution of $X_t$. It need not be unique.

Specialising to the birth–death process:

$$q_{n,n+1} = \lambda_n, \; n > 0$$

and

$$q_{n+1,n} = \mu_{n+1}, \; n > 0$$

The equilibrium distribution $\pi_n$ is unique provided $\lambda_n \mu_{n+1} > 0$, $n > 0$, and is given by

$$\pi_n = Cr_n, \tag{5}$$

where,

$$r_0 = 1, \quad r_n = \frac{\lambda_0 \ldots \lambda_n}{\mu_1 \ldots \mu_{n+1}}, \; n > 1$$

and

$$C = \frac{1}{\displaystyle\sum_{j=0}^{\infty} r_j} \tag{6}$$

A necessary and sufficient condition for the existence of a unique $\pi_n$ is:

$$\sum_{j=1}^{\infty} r_j < \infty \tag{7}$$

*Example*: At $t = 0$ an industry is formed and thereafter the number of firms $N_t$ evolves as a linear birth–death process with $\lambda(t)$, $\mu(t)$, the birth and death rates, respectively. The average age of the firms that comprise the industry at time $t$ is $a(t)$, where:

$$b_i(t) = 1$$

if firm $i$ has entered the industry by time $t$;

$$d_i(t) = 1$$

if firm $i$ has gone bankrupt (exited the industry) by time $t$.

Then the sequence $[b_i, d_i) = i = 1, 2, \ldots]$ is a Markov process and

$$M_t = N_t \exp \left(-\int_0^t (\lambda_s - \mu_s) \, ds\right)$$

is a martingale. From this observation, we can calculate (using stochastic calculus) the probability that the industry is bankrupt by $t$ and the average age of the surviving firms at $t$.

## 4.2 A Mechanical Analogy

Following Fisher we present a mechanical analogy of economic fluctuations equivalent to his hydrodynamic model. We envisage the economy as composed of two giant box-spring mattresses, one on top of the other. The lower mattress represents the consumer, whereas each coil in the industrial sector corresponds to a firm. The consumer coil is composed of a network of smaller springs. Each of these is a stochastic contract or relationship that the individual has with other members of the economy. The size of the consumer coil fluctuates as new relationships are formed and old ones terminated. Thus each consumer can be viewed as a vibrating network of relationships. There are other birth-and-death processes determining the number of consumers in the economy and their distribution among various subsectors that are deemed important by the analyst. Each consumer continuously modifies his portfolio of contracts in response to the changing environment in which he dwells. His actions are guided by the no-arbitrage condition – he continues to add and delete contracts until no further net benefits are obtainable. In this general setting his tastes and preferences are also random variables and interact with the other environmental oscillations so that the no-arbitrage condition is rarely satisfied exactly.

Each firm is also a vibrating network of contracts. Many of these contractual arrangements are implicit.[21] For example, the firm's contract with an employee is multidimensional. The worker's performance is monitored by the manager and/or by the other member of his production team. His performance may fluctuate according to a semimartingale Markov process composed of both Brownian motion and Poisson jumps.[22] If he can control the drift parameter of the Brownian motion, but has little influence on the jump process, the firm will adjust for this when deciding whether to continue or terminate the contract. The employee reacts in similar fashion to the vicissitudes of the firm, remaining at the firm when an unexpected decline in demand occurs. These implicit arrangements will resolve the moral hazard/adverse-selection problem as best they can in this uncertain environment.[23] Of course, mistakes will be made with probability one, just as the eventual bankruptcy of the firm is an almost sure event. Similar arrangements will characterise the contracts with buyers and other suppliers of inputs. The firm is also continuously adjusting its portfolio of contracts in response to the myriad uncertainties that it must face. These include fluctuating demand and technical change – some of which occurs because of the firm's research and development activities.[24] Once again, it is the no-arbitrage condition that drives these responses.

The industry is composed of similar firms (oscillators). The industrial sector is a box-spring mattress, each spring is an industry. Some springs tend to vibrate in unison, with the box spring being a set of industrial groups. Left on its own, the industrial sector would exhibit the groups that were growing rapidly, groups of relatively constant growth, and declining sectors. External shocks may not only alter the interactions among the fluctuating industries, but also influence their overall course.

The joint response of the consumer sector and industrial sector to endogenous and exogenous shocks generates the semimartingale process composed of economic fluctuations.

The price and wage distributions depend on the precise form of the contractual relations between firms and factors of production and between firms and buyers. For example, there may also be implicit agreements between firms and groups of buyers such that prices remain within a certain band unless an exceptional event occurs.[25] The price distributions are obviously influenced by the rate of technological change, the rate of preference change, and a host of other exogenous shocks many of which are induced by government policy.

### 4.3 Preliminaries[26]

Recall that one of the most significant results emerging from elementary real analysis is the covergence of monotone sequences. The *martingale convergence theorem* is the probabilistic counterpart of this basic result and *supermartingales* are analogous to decreasing functions on the real line. Furthermore, the semimartingales that will preoccupy us here correspond to functions of bounded variation. This is clear in that a semimartingale is simply the difference between two non-negative supermartingales. A more technical interpretation of a semimartingale is to recognise it as a *signed measure*, or to observe that if $X$ is a Markov process on $E$, $f(x)$ is a semimartingale if and only if it is locally the difference between two excessive functions.

Frequently, economic processes $X_t$ possess two different components. The first component $V_t$ is slowly varying and is usually called a 'trend', whereas the second $M_t$ varies rapidly and is sometimes referred to as 'noise'. This is precisely the composition of a semimartingale $\{X_t, t \geqslant 0\}$.

In general, let $\{X_t, t \geqslant 0\}$ be a family of random variables on the probability space $(\Omega, F, P)$ possessing a family of sub-$\sigma$-algebras $\{F_t, t \geqslant 0\}$. Each $F_t$ is right-continuous, i.e. $F_t = F_{t+} = s > t\, F_s$ and $F_0$ is complete, that is, contains the $P$-null sets. Each $X_t$ is $F_{t-}$ measurable and is said to be *adapted*.

## Definitions

The process $\{M_t, t \geqslant 0\}$ is a *super (sub) martingale* if:

$$E[|M_t|] < \infty, \, t \geqslant 0$$

$$E(M_t|F_s) \leqslant (\geqslant)\, M_s, \quad s \leqslant t$$

where $F_s$ is the filtration sigma algebra. Roughly speaking, $F_s$ contains all the information up till time $s$ that is pertinent for any decision made at $s$.

A *martingale* is both a supermartingale and a submartingale.

The martingale was born in a casino and it is fitting that one of the most profound discussions of martingale theory occurs in a monograph entitled *How To Gamble If You Must*, by Dubins and Savage (1965). They maintain that the martingale constitutes a conservation principle, the *conservation of fairness*.

A *local martingale* $M_t$ is an adapted process possessing a sequence of stopping times $(\tau_n)_{n \geqslant 1}$ increasing to $\infty$ such that the stopped processes $M^n = M_{t \wedge \tau_n}$, $n \geqslant 1$, are martingales.

A positive number $\tau$ is called a *stopping time* relative to a sigma-algebra if for each $n$ $\{\tau = n\} \in F_n$.

A process $\{V_t, t \geqslant 0\}$ is *locally bounded variation* if for arbitrary $t \geqslant 0$ and $w \, \varepsilon \, \Omega$

$$\int_0^t |dV_s(w)| < \infty$$

A stochastic process $X_t$ is a *semimartingale* if

$$X_t = V_t + M_t, \quad t \geq 0$$

where $M_t$ is a local martingale and $V_t$ is a process of locally bounded variation.

The class of semimartingales is large, but nevertheless extremely useful.

An arbitrary process $X$ with stationary independent increments is a *semimartingale*.

An arbitrary *Ito process*

$$X_t = X_0 + \int_0^t a_s(w)ds + \int_0^t b_x(w)dW_s$$

where

$$\int_0^t |a_s(w)|ds < \infty$$

and

$$\int_0^t b_s^2(w)ds < \infty, \, t \geq 0 \, a.s.P$$

is a *semimartingale*.

Every stochastic sequence is a *semimartingale*.

The stochastic process $|B_t|^{1/3}$ is not a semimartingale, where $B_t$ is *Brownian motion*.

In counting processes the *dual predictable projection* or *compensator* is an extremely useful concept.[27] The compensator of the counting $\{N(t)\}$ process is simply $\int_0^t \lambda(s)ds$, where $\{\lambda(t)\}$ is a process such that:

$$\lambda(t) = \lim_{h_n \downarrow 0} E[N(t+h_n) - N(t)|F_t]h_n$$

Roughly speaking, the compensator contains all the information present in the appropriate conditional probabilities. That is, it has the information necessary for

$$N(t) - \int_0^t \lambda(s)ds$$

to be a martingale, given the other usual assumptions.

A continuous time parameter stochastic process which possesses the strong Markov property and for which the sample paths $X(t)$ are almost always continuous functions of $t$ is called a *diffusion process*. Brownian motion is the most celebrated diffusion process.

The calculation of functionals connected with diffusion processes is necessary for the analysis of economic fluctuations.

## *Equivalences*

In their lucid monograph Doyle and Snell (1985) (see footnote 9) explain the equivalence between Brownian motion and potential theory[28] via an ingenious study of Polya's famous theorem: a random walk is recurrent iff $d \leqslant 2$; otherwise it is transient, where $d$ is the dimensionality of the lattice. In their analysis they observe the analogy between 'electrical networks' and 'hydrodynamics'. Feynman (1964) elaborates on this analogy:

> In learning electrostatics you have learned at the same time how to handle many subjects in the physics . . . *Why are the equations from many different phenomena so similar?* We might say: 'It is the underlying unity of nature.' But what does that mean? . . . Is it possible that *this* is the clue? That the thing which is common to all the phenomena is *space* . . . as long as things are reasonably smooth in space, then the important things . . . will be the rates of change of quantities with position in space.

The same puzzle was stated exquisitely by Wigner (1960):

> . . . Let us not forget that the Hilbert space of quantum mechanics is the complex Hilbert space, with a Hermitean scalar product. Surely to the unpreoccupied mind, complex numbers are far from natural or simple and they cannot be suggested by physical observations. Furthermore, the use of complex numbers is in this case not a calculational trick of applied mathematics but comes close to being a necessity in the formulation of the laws of quantum mechanics . . . It is difficult to avoid the impression that a miracle confronts us here, quite comparable in its striking nature to the miracle that the human mind can string a thousand arguments together without getting itself into contradictions or to the two miracles of the existence of laws of nature and of the human mind's capacity to divine them . . . A much more difficult and confusing situation would arise if we

could, some day, establish a theory of the phenomena of consciousness, or of biology, which would be as coherent and
convincing as our present theories of the inanimate world.
Mendel's laws of inheritance and the subsequent work on genes
may well form the beginning of such a theory as far as biology is
concerned.

Our contention is that martingale is the source of the equivalence
among the many physical, biological, and social theories. The key
martingale residing in each of these theories is the *no-arbitrage
condition*, the economic statement of the *conservation of fairness
principle*.

Returning to the Doyle–Snell monograph, the set of equivalences
that flow from the basic equivalence between random walks and
electric networks include queueing theory, Markov chain analysis,
network theory, statistical mechanics, quantum mechanics, dynamic
programming, 'dry' hydrodynamics (see Feynman (1964)) and stochastic approximation.

The relevant point is that Fisher's hydrodynamic mechanism has
the martingale property and via potential theory could have been
linked to random walks, the fundamental component of the economic oscillations.

## 4.4   A Stochastic Theory of the Firm

This section presents a theory of the firm based on semimartingale
stochastic processes. As we will see the theory encompasses most of
the firm's major activities: purchasing resources, rearranging the
resources into saleable products, personnel management, inventory
control, and the distribution of the final product. The theory can also
be used either as a microscope or a telescope. As a microscope it can
analyse the relations among the employers and the employees. The
detailed study of these relations is postponed. For now, we merely
note that the relationship was established by mutual search. The
workers' reservation wage was exceeded and the employers' reservation productivity was also exceeded. This gives rise to a stochastic
contract – an optimal stopping rule – with implicit conditions regarding the length and stability of the attachment. We will show that these
implicit arrangements, while perhaps not completely resolving the
adverse selection and moral hazard problems, certainly cast doubt on
the profession's enormous investment in models of asymmetric infor-

mation. Microscopic analysis can also be applied to the contractual relations between the firm and other suppliers of inputs, between the firm and its buyers, and between the firm and its stockholders and management. Semimartingale theory plays a decisive role in all of this microanalysis.

Telescopic analysis will be employed to study industry-wide behaviour including mergers, bankruptcies, and industry-wide fluctuations. Finally, this analysis can be applied to economy-wide fluctuations. Once again the foundation for this work is semimartingale theory. Furthermore, once the economic activities have been formulated as semimartingales the transition to empirical research can be conducted using estimators that are themselves martingales.[29]

The semimartingale model is unique in that the portfolio of stochastic contracts called *the firm* is engaged in arbitrage activity across time and space. Goods and services are purchased at one set of locations and at various times and then reassembled, and sold at another set of locations after a random amount of time has elapsed. The firm continues to grow – adding stochastic contracts to its portfolio – as long as arbitrage opportunities persist. The firm is in stochastic equilibrium (zero expected profit condition) when it has exhausted all arbitrage activities and 'break even' on average.

### The Fluctuation of Sales

Rather than concentrate on the match-making of the previous section, we move on to the firm's output. It is of course the driving force behind the size, number, and composition of the various teams comprising the firm, but we ignore these effects for now and concentrate on the methods available for transforming a fairly general demand process into a diffusion.

The demand per period for the firm's output is assumed to be governed by a pure jump process. This encompass a broad class of stochastic processes including Markov chains, Poisson processes, and queueing models as special cases.[30] In general, the jump process need not possess either the Markov property or the martingale property. Primarily for expository purposes, but also because of its intrinsic value, we focus on jump processes that are semimartingales.

### Jump Processes[31]

The process begins in state $x_0$ and stays there until $\tau_1 > 0$ when it transits to a new state $x_1 \neq x_0$. The process may be inert in which case

$\tau_1 = \infty$. These transitions or jumps occur at the positive random times $\tau_2, \tau_3, \ldots$ so that the state $x(t)$ of the system at $t$ is given by

$$
(?) \quad X(t) = \begin{cases}
x_0, & 0 \leqslant t \leqslant \tau_1 \\
x_1, & \tau_1 \leqslant t < \tau_2 \\
\quad \cdot \\
\quad \cdot \\
\quad \cdot \\
x_j, & \tau_j \leqslant t < \tau_{j+1} \\
\quad \cdot \\
\quad \cdot
\end{cases}
$$

The process $X(t)$ is called a *jump process*. If $X(t)$ behaves so that $\lim_{n \to \infty} \tau_n = \infty$ a.s., $X(t)$ is said to be *non-explosive*. However, if $\lim_{n \to \infty} \tau_n < \infty$ a.s., $X(t)$ is said to *explode*. Assume that $X(t)$ is non-explosive.

The states comprising a jump process are either absorbing or non-absorbing. For each non-absorbing state $X(t_i)$ there is a c.d.f. $F_i$ which controls $\tau_i$ and a transition matrix $Q_{xy}$ such that $Q_{xx} = 0$ and $\Sigma_y \, Q_{xy} = 1$. $F$ and $Q$ are independent so that the probability of starting at $x$, jumping to $y$ by $\tau_1$ and then jumping to $z$ by $\tau_2$ is given by

$$P_x \{\tau_1 \leqslant s, X(\tau \geqslant) = y, \tau_2 - \tau_1 \leqslant, x(\tau_2) = z\}$$
$$= F_x(s)Q_{xy}F_y(t)Q_{yz}$$

The jump process satisfies the Markov property, if and only if (iff) for all non-absorbing states $x$

$$P_x(\tau_1 > t + s \mid \tau_1 > s) = P_x(\tau_1 > t), \, s, t, \geqslant 0$$

This condition obtains iff $F$ is exponential.

Note that:

$$P_x(\tau_1 \geqslant t) = \int_t^\infty q_x e^{-q_x s} ds, \, t \geqslant 0$$

where $q_x = 1/[E_x(\tau_1)]$. In addition, a straightforward calculation shows that the Chapman–Kolmogorov equation is given by:

$$P_{xy}(t + s) = \sum_z P_{xz}(s), \, s \geqslant 0, \geqslant 0. \tag{8}$$

Let the *infinitesimal* parameters of the process be $q_{xy}$. They satisfy the backward equation:

$$P'_{xy}(t) = \sum_z q_{xz} P_{zy}(t), \, t \geq 0$$

The forward equation is obtained by differentiating (8) giving:

$$P'_{xy}(t) = \Sigma P_{xz}(t) \, q_{zy}, \, t \geq 0$$

Important members of the class of Markov jump processes include the birth-and-death process, branching processes, the Poisson process, and a variety of queueing models.

## A Semimartingale Approach to Jump Processes – an Overview

Using methods devised by Dynkin and Metivier, a more general jump process also converges to a *diffusion*.[32]

## A General Jump Process

Suppose that the stochastic process $X$ is a pure Markov jump process with parameter $\mu$, where both $\mu$ and $X$ are $d$-dimensional vectors. Then the *infinitesimal generator*[33] of $X$ is given by

$$Af(x) = \lambda \int_{R^d} [f(x + y) - f(x)] \mu(dy)$$

Letting $X_t^n = (\epsilon_n X_t)/\alpha_n$,[34] this can be rewritten as

$$A^n f(x) = \lambda/\alpha_n \int_{R^d} [f(x + \epsilon y_n) - f(x)] \mu(dy)$$

*The major question is: does $X_n$ converge to a diffusion as $n \uparrow \infty$?* Let $X^n$ be a sequence of Markov processes with generator $A^n$. Assume that $F^i(x) = x^i$ and both $f^i$ and $f^i f^j \, \epsilon \, D(A^n)$, the set of Dynkin semimartingales with $A^n$ generators.

A process $X^n$ is a *Dynkin semimartingale* if its values are in $R^d$ and to every bounded function $f \, \epsilon \, C^2$ on $R^d$ there corresponds a process $[A(f, t, .)]_{t \geq 0}$ such that

$$M_t^f \colon f(X_t) - f(X_0) = \int_0^t A(f, s, .) ds$$

is a *square integrable martingale*. Metivier (1983) demonstrates that these processes converge to diffusions.

We now show that the jump process is one of these processes and derive its diffusion.

Let the infinitesimal drift and variance of the jump process be

$$b^{n,i}(x) = A^n f^i,[35]$$

and

$$a^{n,ij}(x) = A^n f^i f^j - f^i A^n f^j - f^j A^n f^i$$

Application of the Dynkin formula[36] gives:

For all $f \in D(A^n)$ with (a) $E(f(X^n_t)) < \infty$ for all $t$
$$f(x^n_t) = f(x^n_0) + \int_0^t A^n f(x^n)ds + M^n_t(f)$$

where $M^n(f)$ is a martingale.

In the jump process (a) may not hold. However, if the jumps of $X^n_t$ are bounded.

$$X^n_t = X^n_0 + \int_0^t b^n(X^n_s)ds + M^n_t$$

where $M^n_{t\wedge} - n_k$ is a martingale for all $k$. That is, $M^n$ is a local martingale.

Consequently, the jump process $X$ can be characterised as a semimartingale, and the process $X$ can be decomposed into

$$X = V + M$$

where $V$ has finite variation and $M$ is a local martingale.[37]

Using tightness arguments, Metivier demonstrates that this $d$-dimensional stochastic process converges to a diffusion with generator

$$\sum_{i,j=1}^{d} \alpha^{ij} \left( \frac{\partial^2}{\partial^i \partial^j} \right)$$

The final step in this direction proves that for a specific probability law with $f$ twice differentiable,

$$\left[ f(\xi_t) - f(\xi_0) - \int_0^t \sum_{i,j=1}^{d} \alpha^{ij} \left( \frac{\partial^2 f}{\partial x^i \partial x^j} \right) (\xi_s)ds \right] t \geq 0$$

is a martingale, the Stroock–Varandhan martingale characterisation of a diffusion.

This very general stochastic process, which includes birth-and-death processes, Poisson processes, Markov chains, and queueing models, is a semimartingale, and can be characterised as a diffusion process. These are useful results, crucial to the view of the firm presented herein.

Martingales are preserved over addition. Thus an industry-wide diffusion can be obtained by simple aggregation. Similarly, a *pure* process can be calculated for the entire economy. It is pure in that government behaviour is completely ignored and only a portion of consumer behaviour is included.

Returning to the firm's diffusion process, consider two important functionals. Let $\alpha$ be a sales goal established by the firm. For example, assume this is a new product requiring time for consumer acceptance and adaptive pricing. Suppose that it is the considered judgement of the firm's management that if 'all goes wrong' $\beta$ is the corresponding level of sales. The firm wishes to calculate the probability that, after an 'appropriate' marketing investment, the sales diffusion hits $\alpha$ before $\beta$. That is, given the marketing effort, initial sales are $x_0$. The firm calculates

$$P(x_0) = Pr \{T(\beta) < T(\alpha) \mid X(0) = x_0\}$$

where $\beta > \alpha$. If the scale function is natural:[38]

$$P(x_0) = \frac{\beta - x_0}{\beta - \alpha}$$

The firm is also interested in the time it takes to leave any given sales interval. If we let $m(x)$ be the speed at which the process runs when at sales point $x$, then $m(x_0)\varepsilon^2$ is approximately the length of time the process remains in $(x_0 - \varepsilon, x_0 + \varepsilon)$ given $X(0) = x_0$.

To summarise, the firm is a collection of stochastic contracts. Each of these is an optimal stopping rule and evolves according to a semimartingale process. The number of contracts fluctuates according to a birth-and-death process. Th contracts may be interrelated so that the breaking of one increases (decreases) the probability that another may be terminated. Violation of the no-arbitrage condition induces the firm to transform inputs into the desired output. The production process entails team-formation, purchasing, manufacturing, maintenance, inventory control and marketing. Each of these activities is a stochastic process and can be studied using semimartingale methods. Here the entire production process is a black box with stochastic inputs and stochastic outputs. Each firm's output is a semimartingale. Aggregating over similar firms gives industry output. Finally, the economy's output is the sum of these industry outputs and is also a semimartingale.

Firms within an industry may be closely connected so that they tend to vibrate in unison. Similarly, there may be strong interactions among some industries inducing correlated oscillations.

Overall, the economy may be robust, while at the same time, certain segments are in the midst of mini-depressions and their converse. A prolonged economy-wide depression may be induced by the persistence of strong negative exogenous shocks. These may be the consequence of perverse government policies or the bunching of a series of deleterious random events. It is sometimes difficult to disentangle these two misfortunes.

## 4.5 A Stochastic Theory of the Consumer

The consumer is also assumed to be completely described by a portfolio of stochastic contracts. The acquisition of these agreements or matches is achieved by searching. At any given time, the consumer will be embedded in a network of contracts *and* either implicitly or explicitly searching for new contracts to replace some of the existing, but unsatisfactory matches and to add to his portfolio. Once again he will continue to modify the composition of his portfolio until the no-arbitrage position is reached.

In the one-period certainty model, this equilibrium condition collapses to the simple Fisherian condition:

$$\frac{MV_i}{P_i} = \frac{MV_j}{P_j}, \quad i \neq j, i, j = 1, 2, \ldots, n$$

The multiperiod stochastic model, the overall behaviour of the consumer can be described by a semimartingale process.

Just as the black box containing the 'production function' can be opened and each of its constituents – replacement policy, inventory policy, queueing policy, the composition of teams and the ordering of production processes – analysed, so too the *ceteris paribus* aspects of consumer behaviour can be studied. The effects of changing tastes, the structure of information networks,[39] the social and psychological costs of alternative firm policies can all be studied by applying appropriate aspects of semimartingale theory.

Delving into the production function might be called 'opening economics on the right'. This takes economics into operations research, engineering, artificial intelligence and – as more and more refinements are made – into physics and chemistry. Probing into psychological taste variables, on the other hand, 'opens economics on the left' and leads to the long-neglected social sciences of anthropology, sociology and psychology. Continued pursuit of this 'behavioural theme' eventually encounters neurophysiology, neurobiology, and the hard sciences. Thus both probes meet in some soupy blend of physics-, chemistry- and biology-neuroscience, the next course in this random supper.

## 5  THE ECONOMICS OF NEUROSCIENCE

*Example*  A hungry crayfish has been foraging for some time without success. Finally, it discovers a rich food patch and commences eating. At this point a small predator approaches the crayfish. Under normal circumstances the neuronal response of the crayfish would have surpassed its *escape* threshold and rapid motion would ensue. However, the threshold has been raised by eating. The predator leaves, but is shortly replaced by the distant sound of a dangerous predator. This threat creates sufficient neuronal activity to exceed the escape threshold. The crayfish immediately stops eating, flips its tail and swims to the nearest sanctuary.

The economics of this behaviour is clear. The threshold corresponds to a reservation level. The neurotransmitter is a price which conveys environmental information. Each activity of the crayfish has an opportunity cost, determining the size of the reservation level. This level is high during eating and only high prices (threats or rewards) induce termination (and flight or attack).

This behaviour was observed and is reported in the illuminating review article by Bicker and Menzel (1989). In this elegant experiment, the *signals* (prices) were a combination of transmitters, modulators and hormones.[40] The action of transmitters in promoting information transfer along the synaptic connections among neurons is well-known. These informational transfers are coordinated by modulators at the cell level and also by hormones. The action of the transmitters is rapid and proximate; the modulators operate on a longer time-scale at greater distances; and the hormones act like modulators, but on an even longer time-scale and at greater distances. Hence, the tail flip that initiated the escape of the crayfish was the consequence of the coordinated activity of an information and control system operated by a plethora of spatio-temporal prices. This behaviour corresponds to a decentralised economy's dependence on the coordinated response of numerous agents to information conveyed by prices and interest rates in a stable environment.

The experiments reported by Bickel and Menzel were among the first to observe organisms perform routines in response to the coordinated information transfers among circuits at the cellular level. The experiments are wide-ranging including: the control of hormonal release *over the life cycle* to synchronise the timing of courtship and reproductive behaviour of crickets as well as the division of labour among honeybees.

Learning behaviour is also studied: 'As neuromodulators confer flexibility on neuronal circuits and trigger intracellular biochemical events that outlast the signal, they have been implicated in learning, memory, and the performance of learned tasks in vertebrates and mollusc.'

Marder's summary of this research concludes that it has 'exciting' remifications for computational neuroscience. Using synaptic rules for linking neuro-like components, complex tasks have been performed by network models:

> The challenge is to elucidate how small neuronal network work; how large networks of simple neuronal-like elements work; and how the complexity of neurons (conferred by their shape and ionic currents) and the richness of their connectivity define and constrain the possible functions of a neuronal network. So we need eventually to determine which properties of biological networks are not shared by networks of simple neuronal-like elements. Insights that have been gained from computer-modelled neuronal-like networks and studies of modulation in neuronal networks such as the stomatogastric ganglion should help to understand how large biological networks generate behaviours and process information.

It appears that those chemicals transmitting information among the complex assemblies comprising the brain are the unifying force in neuroscience in the same way that the price mechanism unifies economics. Indeed, our basic hypothesis stipulates an equivalence between the two processes, each of which is equivalent to Brownian motion.

## 5.1 Computer Science-Neuroscience and Economics

Hopfield and Tank (1986) mimic neural networks to construct optimisation algorithms. But how are decisions being made with respect to ranking optimisation problems, designing algorithms, and assembling computers? These are basic *economic* problems. On the other hand, the exciting economic research on organisation theory from decentralised decision-making to conflict resolution can be fortified and stimulated by the network analyses currently used in computer science, information theory, and circuit analysis. These *economic* theories can be tested directly by the structure and behaviour of neural networks as well as by the implied social behaviour.

For example, conflict resolution arises in communication networks whenever congestion occurs.[41] Various algorithms have been devised for resolving these conflicts. Several exhibit both practical wisdom and mathematical ingenuity. Implicit prices and social efficiency are rarely studied. This is an obvious topic for collaboration.

The relevance of *factoring* algorithms for decentralisation of organisation is frequently mentioned by the designers and is well-known to several economists. Thus far, there has been virtually no research on this important topic combining economics and computer science. In game theory, algorithms are certainly as appealing as 'experimental methods' to test alternative conjectures.[42]

Li and Basar (1987), develop a synchronous distributed algorithm for non-cooperative stochastic games, stochastic teams, and stochastic routing in networks which achieves asymptotic agreement. The problem of algorithmic conflict resolution, the collision of information packets in communication networks, are also being studied.

Algorithm network analysis of competition and cooperation has played a key role in several of the major advances in neural network theory. They contain many economic problems and develop methods which may be very useful in economics. For example, several of the articles in Amari and Arbib (1982) possess great potential.

In Korolyuk *et al.* (1988) random walk theory is applied to asymptotic behaviour of *automata* in random environments. This is closely related to the work of Abreu and Rubinstein (1988).

The proposed research might merge the work of Marschak, Radner, Hurwicz, *et al.* with that work by Witsenhausen, Kushner, Tsitsiklis, *et al.*

## 5.2  The Crick Critique

There have been many reservations expressed by distinguished scientists regarding the value of the 'neural network explosion' in artificial intelligence. None is more penetrating nor more constructive than Crick (1989). It has pedagogical value for those who are not specialists in either neurology or artificial intelligence.

The 'units' comprising neural networks resemble neurons in that there are 'exciting' and 'inhibiting' inputs. These are averaged and an output or spike is produced provided the expected input exceeds a critical value – the threshold.[43] Crick acknowledges that since many synapses are plastic, adjusting their strength on a trial-and-error basis, it is important to understand this phenomenon. But this is exactly what the algorithms are attempting as they vary the architecture and strength of the connections.

The back propagation algorithm generalises the Hebb local algorithm by adding a 'teacher' that tells the net how much its 'performance' deviated from the ideal. Roughly speaking, it corresponds to the method of gradient descent. Repeated 'scoldings' by the teacher and small responses by the pupil lead eventually to the desired minimum.

Crick then shows that this ingenious algorithm composed of backdrop nets is 'unrealistic in almost every respect, as indeed some of their inventors have admitted'. He goes on to characterise neural 'models' as existence proofs and not models at all, 'because they do not correspond sufficiently closely to the real things'.[44] Just as some have urged economists to study corporations from the inside, so Crick encourages the computer-oriented brain scientists to '*look inside the brain, both to get new ideas and to test existing ones*'.

Crick is *not* anti-theoretical. He strongly opposes those linguists and psychologists who prefer simple unrealistic models of the brain which are consistent with some of the psychological data. Their position is that the brain is too complex for abstract modelling.

The eloquent arguments of Crick (1989) are relevant to the proposed interdisciplinary research. Just as neuroscience should maintain close contact with empirical brain science, so too this *joint* research should establish close ties with the empirical research in ecology, biology, and economics. The studies by Endler (1986) are superb examples of applied biology. Experimental economics should follow Simon's advice by expanding its methods to study *actual* market behaviour within industries and firms.

## 5.3 The Economics of Routines

Much of what is regarded as civilised behaviour is routine. The common wealth which binds a nation is composed of routines such as a common language, a common ethic, and, in short, a shared patriotism that encompasses a broad range of habitual behaviour. These routines diminish uncertainty: prediction of events contingent on common behaviour are almost always correct. The purpose of this section is to present a methodology explaining the acquisition of habits from economic, neurobiological, and information-theoretic perspectives. The explanation seems compatible with behaviour even though it is based on these three very different disciplines: economics, engineering and neurology.

The methodology – network analysis – is essentially a simple Markov chain – the birth-and-death process. Network analysis has been extremely useful in describing the behaviour of neural networks in neurobiology; the flow of information in computer networks, communication systems, and the reliability of systems composed of graph theory – the so-called fault-tree analysis. Network analysis has potential in economics for explaining hierarchical structures – from the individual to the entire economy. Contractual relations and efficiency are the key economic concepts which compose and regulate these stochastic networks. The resulting behaviour partially explains the genesis of firms. The drive to belong and be recognised accounts for the higher productivity of teams. The manager's primary role is not to control shirking, but to transmit information and coordinate individual effort.

The formation of routines begins in early childhood: speech, walking, and a host of basic functions are learned in the first few years of life. Their acquisition is achieved at random rates, fostered by parents and once learned are performed unconsciously and effortlessly. The child builds on these basic routines to learn other habits fundamental to society. The process is hierarchical and the end-product is a civilised individual. The interactions of these civilised individuals promote a regularity and predictability in society. The selfish instincts are mollified by these habits. They are the source of the trust that while not eliminating does mitigate shirking and cheating and promotes contractual relations, the basic building blocks of an efficient society. Without the common wealth of habitual behaviour which also entails Adam Smith's 'impartial spectator', the monitoring and legal costs of a contractual system would inhibit decentralisaton and coordination, and for all practical purposes, prevent the formation of a viable society.

## 6 THE RATIONALE FOR INTERDISCIPLINARY RESEARCH

The absence of joint research projects by economists, psychologists, neuroscientists and computer scientists reveals the difficulties and perceived rewards of such an enterprise. Recent research has altered the reward structure. If our appraisal is correct, the community of neuroscience and artificial intelligence can learn much from Adam Smith's disciples – modern price theorists who are familiar with the benefits and limitations of the price mechanism. Interpreting neurotransmitters (potentials) as prices, and thresholds as reservation levels, suggest that the accumulated wisdom of microeconomics and its stochastic counterpart is pertinent to the neurosciences.

On the other hand, economic science can also reap substantial gains. For example, the formation of tastes, the foundations of assembly (production functions) and the underpinnings of human capital theory may be fortified. The serendipity characterising many of the revolutionary innovations in computer science via neural network research could accompany this interdisciplinary enterprise.

Combinatorial mathematics is the methodological glue preserving the linkage and in many instances showing the way. Combinatorics is primarily concerned with *flows*. The power of hydrodynamic analysis throughout the sciences testifies to the clear thinking imposed by $H_2O$. The equivalences among hydrodynamics, electric networks, combinatorics, random walks, and the price mechanism have not been exploited by any of the sciences comprising this interdisciplinary enterprise. Indeed, it is in this area that economics may receive immediate rewards.

As we will see, reality is deterministic when viewed from one perspective and stochastic when the focus changes. The nature of the problem coupled with the abilities of the researcher influence his choice between deterministic and probabilistic paths to the solution set. When the analysis is conducted *properly*, the solution set is invariant to the path.

The separation of signal from noise is a serious problem in an economy undergoing a phase transition. In a real economy this might be a period of rapid inflation, while in the neural economy, it might be a period of abnormal transmitter behaviour caused by some organic failure. At any rate, several methods have been devised to isolate the signal.

## 6.1 Applications

The following is a list of applications which could comprise the initial phase of an interdisciplinary research program.[45]

### (a) The Economics of Habit-Formation and Addiction

There is a small but important economic literature on habits, addictions and fluctuating tastes. Several of these articles are related to economic growth and learning-by-doing. As far as I know none of these papers refers to neuroscience research and its relation to Smithian 'psychology'.

Some of the key concepts emerging from this literature include the evolution of preferences: '"Habit forming" means that people learn to consume by consuming and the more they learn the more they enjoy; the evolution of preferences of the consumption level and, of course, the consumption path is itself dependent upon the evolution of preferences'. (Boyer, 1978). Boyer then analyses the effect of habit-formation on economic growth. A sophisticated study of the growth process concludes with a stability analysis of the steady state and its sensitivity to discount rates when habits are endogenous.

Iannaccone (1986) designs a rational model of habit formation and determines when the outcome will be addiction or satiation. 'A commodity is addictive if its current consumption increases as the habits derived from its previous consumption accumulate. It will be called satiating if the opposite occurs'. His discussion attempts to clarify the Stigler–Becker (1977) distinction between 'beneficial' and harmful addiction.

In their recent article Becker and Murphy (1986) include a wide variety of activities in their definition of addiction. They maintain that addictions are usually rational 'in the sense of involuntary forward-looking maximisation with stable preferences'. This rational view provides new insights into addictive behaviour. Their definition is so broad as to include work, music, etc.

They maintain that their model *explains* why abrupt withdrawal is required to terminate strong addictions and 'binge' behaviour, and relate temporary stressful events to permanent addictions. The analysis is insightful but tends to ignore the recent advances in neuroscience regarding addictive behaviour. Their assumption of homogeneity, their description of 'cold turkey', and the inclusion of strong attachments (habits) as *addictions*, which are necessary requirements for civilised behaviour suggest flaws not in their economic analysis, but in their overall perspective.

The economic studies of addiction seem to overlook the effect of addiction on human capital formation, reputation, the importance of parental guidance in the educational process, and the externalities created by the behaviour of addicts. Addiction shocks habits which are essential for civilised behaviour and sometimes the shock is sufficient to unravel these basic traits.

*The Neuroscience of Drug Dependence*   In their recent study Koob and Bloom (1988) try to discern if the 'molecular, cellular, and behavioral data on acute and chronic effects of addictive drugs possess a consistent pattern in which molecular effects influence cellular effects which then alter behavioral phenomena in keeping with the common features of drug dependence'. Three of the most prominent addictive drugs – opiates, psychostimulants and ethanol – are analysed from this triple perspective – molecular, cellular, and behavioural.

They also review a variety of addictive theories. The focus of their study is on:

both the acute initial effects of drugs of abuse on specific neurons and the change in these effects with continued drug exposure. We then seek to link these data into generalizable features of addictive drugs and of the systems on which they product their effects. Finally, we propose a potential role for a specific limbic-estra-pyramidal system that has been implicated in both the reinforcement and adaptive responses to all three drug classes.

They define addiction as follows:

A more recent definition of psychoactive substance dependence used for diagnostic purposes is that dependence 'is a cluster of cognitive, behavioral, and physiologic symptoms that indicate that the person has impaired control of psychoactive substant use and continue use of the substance despite adverse consequences.

They conclude:

> Across all levels of analysis, molecular and cellular mechanisms of the nervous system react to addictive drugs to initiate and maintain patterns of drug-seeking behavior. We hypothesize that these patterns of behavior emerge primarily because the drugs are able to usurp the crucial reinforcement systems and the small finite number of transmitters and response sites that operate normally to shape survival of the organism.
>
> We further hypothesize that the same neurobiological circuits involved in the acute hedonic or 'positive reinforcing' actions of drugs may become modified through chronic use as the self-corrective homeostatic responses of the brain adapt to the drug actions. The opposing process may neutralize reinforcing effects and on withdrawal produce the aversive stimulus effects of the abstinence syndrome. We speculate that these 'negative reinforcing' effects (for example, malaise, dysphoria, and anhedonia) are a major etiological and motivational factor in maintaining drug dependence. Thus in this conceptual framework, physical signs of abstinence *per se* are not necessary or sufficient for dependence but the 'negative reinforcing' effects are necessary and sufficient for dependence.

The notable difference between the neurological and economic studies is the absence of neurological factors in the economic studies *and* the absence of economic factors in the neurological studies. We maintain that neuro-economic analysis of addiction could yield significant new findings.

It is imperative to distinguish between habits that are essential for civilised behaviour and habits or addictions that interfere with civilised behaviour. The fact that these may vary among cultures does not diminish the significance of the distinction. As emphasised by Adam Smith and others, the learning and sustenance of civilising routines coupled with the actions of the 'invisible hand' and 'impartial spectator' are vital to the smooth functioning of those institutions that comprise the free enterprise economy. The disruptive effects of addictions on these civilising habits is their most important *social cost*. More formally, the shock of substances like heroin and cocaine is frequently sufficient to undo the ergodicity of these habits and routines essential for reliable performance in the civilised economy. Whether the source of this disintegration is the addictive substance interacting with environmental and neuronal influences or simply the effect of the substance on neuronal behaviour is irrelevant. The disintegration is prominent and must be included in any analysis of addiction.

### (b)  Learning-by-Doing

This is another area where interdisciplinary research could be valuable. The recent study by Stokey (1988) is a sophisticated economic analysis of learning by doing. This factor is identified as 'the force behind sustained growth'. The effect of learning on growth is analysed in economics with and without a traditional sector where no learning occurs. The analysis reveals the importance of learning in spillover to the production of other goods.

*Learning by Doing in the Neuroscience Literature*  Learning by doing is precisely the manner in which habits and routines are instilled. This activity has received much attention in the neuroscience literature. The attempt to mimic learning includes several strategies. Among the most noteworthy are those inspired by Hebb (1949) the correlation strategies, those inspired by Newton, the gradient descent methods, and those which trace their origin to Darwin, the random mutation and crossover learning algorithms. Routines are formed by repetition. The hypothesis modelled here is the existence of a critical number (threshold) $T$ such that after individual $i$ has repeated the action $T_i$ times, conscious effort becomes negligible in the performance of habitual behaviour.

In their recent study Davies *et al.* (1989) analyse the behaviour of long-term potentiation (LTP). LTP increases synaptic strength markedly with repeated use – a micro version of learning by doing.

Most neurologists consider the induction and maintenance of LTP in the hippocampus as the mechanism fundamental to learning and memory in vertebrates. While the induction of LTP is understood, the causes of its persistence are not well-known. Davies *et al.* show that both pre- and post-synaptic activity appear to influence the maintenance of LTP.

## (c) Conflict and Cooperation[46]

Algorithms have been devised to solve a host of interesting 'agreement/conflict' models on a synchronous and asynchronous system of processes linked by a communications network and conducting distributed computation. Each processor has both private and public information. The public information is acquired from the other processors. For example, $n$ computers may combine to solve a fixed-point problem, where the fixed vector has $n$ components, one calculated on each machine. Synchronous computation is sometimes less efficient than asynchronous because several computers may be much slower than the others and real-time decision-making may be too costly.

Problems studied by Li and Basar (1987) include a variety of cooperative and non-cooperative games, team problems, and stochastic versions of decentralised decision-making. The seminal paper was Aumann (1976).

The transmission of information through a communications network causes 'conflict'. Messages are lost when simultaneous transmission is attempted. The controller of the network must detect these collisions and resubmit lost messages. This type of conflict has received much attention in the past few years.

The general area of convergence theory in an organisational setting is surveyed by Bertsekas and Gallagher (1987). The seminal work is Arrow and Hurwicz in the late 1950s and early 1960s. The Russian school has made considerable progress in applying stochastic automata theory to random walks in random environments. Their analysis of games of infinite automata is quite distinct from classical game theory. Automata select strategies based on the information contained in their inputs. The recent paper by Abreu and Rubinstein (1988) is in this tradition.

The evolutionary strategies devised by the immune system[47] to defeat intruders seem partinent to the recent work on conflict and cooperation by economists. For example, consider an individual who poses as a Swiss citizen with all the necessary papers perfectly forged. He enters easily and remains undetected for $t$ periods. At this point he arouses the suspicion of a co-worker by his ignorance of Swiss history. He is investigated and ejected. Now consider an individual who has just received a heart transplant. His immune system is initially 'convinced' that the heart is the same as the original. Eventually, the constant surveillance by the $T$ cells reveals the truth, and the organ is rejected.[48]

## (d) Game-Theoretic Implications

The question of *common knowledge* has captured the attention of some of the leading game theorists. For example, in Binmore and Brandenberger (1988) the 'Harsanyi doctrine' that priors should be regarded as common knowledge is critiqued along with Aumann's appendage that everyone should know that priors are common. This is interpreted as saying that homogeneity reigns supreme. The key point is that decision-makers do not 'play games' with randomly chosen individuals. If the outcome of the game has serious consequences, the choice of players will be very careful. To use Smith's terminology, only close friends will be chosen. (This assumes that serious games played daily with automobiles, etc., are guided by shared routines; and indeed are not *games*.) Among the group of close friends, it seems reasonable to assume that there is common knowledge relative to the game being played. These games will be fair and predictable in the Doob sense. Of course mistakes will be made and moral hazard remains, but they are being controlled by the *circle of decision-makers one chooses*. The size of the expected losses is determined by the radius of the *circle*[49]

## (e) Neuronal Assembly and Organisation Theory

The formation of assemblies of neurons to perform specific tasks correponds with the cooperative and competitive organisations which characterise a free enterprise society. McCulloch and Pitts (1943) and Hebb (1949) predicted these cell assemblies. Gerstein *et al.* (1989) define neuronal membership in an assembly on the basis of 'correlated' firing, that is, the cooperative timing relations among member-neurons. This associated behaviour has been observed and 'can be used as a defining indicator of neural assembles and assembly processes'.

Palm (1982) applies the assembly method to his circuit arrangements for associative memory.[50] These assembly processes have their economic counterpart in the production processes of the firm. Indeed, all the organisation theory receiving widespread attention by the economics profession is relevant to neuroscience. This is most clearly dramatised by Grossberg *et al.* (1989). This broad-ranging article uses the following terminology: hierarchical resolution of uncertainty; division of labour; cooperative–competitive feedback; discounting; boundary–feature trade-off; a new organisational principle and real-time statistical decision theory and signalling. The pioneering research by Grossberg and his associates at the Center for Adaptive Systems has many implications for the design of economic organisations.

### (f) The Neuroscience of Foraging

The economics of foraging by animals and early man is a well-developed area.[51] The basic model has a threshold structure in that stop and go decisions are determined by optimal stopping rules.

Several neuroscience studies show that foraging has its foundations in neuronal behaviour.[52] Indeed, the learning and competition, cooperation, and threshold phenomena observed at the neuronal level are self-similar with the corresponding activities associated with foraging.

## Concluding Comment

The economics of neuroscience reveals modularity and hierarchy as self-similar phenomena. The brain, the individual, the family, the firm, the industry and the entire economy have evolved modular and hierarchical structures for converting incoming information into decision-making.

## Notes

1. This is a revised version of a paper presented at the International Economic Association Conference, June 1989.
2. It is a pleasure to acknowledge the valuable comments by participants at the IEA Conference, especially those by D. Heymann, J. Jespersen, M. Lippi, H. Brink, J.-P. Fitoussi, E. S. Phelps, R. Goodwin, L. Reichlin, A. Leijonhufvud, E. Prescott, P. Malgrange, B. Rustem, A. Kirman and S. Zambelli. The influence of K. Velupillai permeates the entire piece.
3. For a complete discussion of the relevant computability and complexity literature see Velupillai (1987), Rustem and Velupillai (1990) and McCall and Velupillai (1989).
4. The 'general theory of processes' refers to the probabilistic research initiated by Doob, Meyer and Delacherie. An edifying and inspiring example of this approach is the 'survey' by Aldous (1985).
5. 'Who's on Second??'
6. The most prominent precursor to constructive economics is Adam Smith. See McCall (1989) for details.
7. A penetrating discussion of the early research on business cycles is contained in Lucas (1981).

8. J. Hirshleifer pointed this out. Friedman and Hirshleifer recognised Fisher's brilliance and extended his fundamental ideas via the permanent income hypotheses, adaptive expectations, and investment theory.
9. Goodwin's famous paper is the lead article in the same number.
10. The Koopmans-Hitchcock problem was the linear program discussed by Samuelson. He saw that spatial problems were receiving little attention and that this problem revealed 'the fundamental nature of economic pricing'.
11. A succinct and entertaining portrait of this profound equivalence is Doyle and Snell (1985).
12. Morehouse *et al.* (1950) reference Fisher's hydrodynamic model.
13. The details are spelled out in McCall and Velupillai (forthcoming).
14. In his succinct and profound tribute to Milton Friedman, Sargent (1987) not only gives an insightful glimpse of Friedman's achievements, but also relates them to much of the exciting economic research taking place 'at the frontier'.
15. This research is presented in the *magnus opus* by Abraham and Marsden (1978).
16. See Chapter     of this volume.
17. The leading economists in this 'new' field include: Brock, Day and Grandmont, with the paper by Grandmont having the greatest impact on macroeconomics. The evaluation by Arrow and the survey by Boldrin in the volume edited by Anderson *et al.* (1988) are edifying. The excellent book by Brock and Malliaris (1989) is a comprehensive introduction to dynamical systems for economists.
18. Excellent discussions are contained in Kelly (1979), Pollett (1986).
19. A strong Markov process is stationary with respect to a random time shift.
20. The importance of this interaction is stressed by Arrow and Hahn (1971).
21. Rosen (1985) contains an excellent survey of the conventional implicit contract.
22. These semimartingales are analysed in Cinlar, Jacod, Protter, and Sharpe (1983).
23. For a fine analysis of intertemporal incentives in a stochastic environment, see Holmstrom and Milgrom (1985).
24. The paper by Aase (1985) describes the process we have in mind.
25. The advantages occurring to these customer arrangements are described nicely in Okun (1981). An earlier discussion is contained in Alchian's seminal contribution to the Phelps (1970) volume.
26. Each of the concepts mentioned in this section deserves a deeper and more extensive discussion. The interested reader may wish to consult Elliott (1982).
27. A good discussion of point processes is Bremaud (1981).
28. Potential theory has three physical interpretations: Newtonian gravity, electrostatics, and heat conduction.
29. This aspect of martingale theory is well-known; see Segall (1976).
30. A nice feature of these processes is that they can be controlled. There are essentially three types of control: modification of the process intensity, optimal stopping, and impulse control. Each of these will be studied in

subsequent papers. The reader may wish to consult Bremaud (1981).

31. For additional details the reader may refer to the clear presentation in Hoel *et al.* (1972).
32. For the general case see Metivier (1983).
33. See Karlin and Taylor (1981).
34. The unit length is multiplied by $\varepsilon_n^{-1}$, whereas the unit of time is multiplied by $\alpha_n^{-1}$.
35. The superscript denotes the *i*th coordinate of the vector.
36. See Karlin and Taylor (1981).
37. Metivier shows that this semimartingale property can be derived for many non-Markovian jump processes.
38. See Karlin and Taylor (1981).
39. For example, see Boorman (1975) and Iri (1984).
40. Neuromodulators and neurohormones are controlled by the action of neurotransmitters.
41. See Bertsekis and Gallagher (1987).
42. Abreu and Rubinstein (1988) is an important step in this direction.
43. It should be noted at the outset that *all* the fancy algorithms – simulated annealing, genetic, cellular automata, etc. – are mathematical variations of the McCulloch–Pitts *optimal stopping rule*. This observation in no way diminishes either the remarkable ingenuity or practical significance of these algorithms. Physics, computer science and biology comprise a formidable trio. If economists are familiar with auction and/or search theory which use stopping rules, they need not be intimidated by these 'hard sciences'.
44. His most trenchant comment is: 'I also suspect that within most modelers a frustrated mathematician is trying to unfold his wings.'
45. The current absence of communication is exemplified by the number ($n$) of references to economic research in Logue's (1988) survey of the self-control literature: $n = 0$.
46. Economists have made substantial contributions to understanding the conflict/cooperation perplex. It is impossible to mention these here. The interested reader should consult Hirshleifer (1987) and the references therein.
47. The evolution of the immune system, its ability to distinguish self-from non-self, thereby conferring uniqueness of the individual, Medewar (1957), and the strategies and tactics utilised by intruders and the immune system also are worthy of economic analysis and vice versa. See Langman (1989).
48. This example is not far-fetched. It has been observed that an intruding parasite mimicked the behaviour of the immune system so well that it was incorporated into the system and ceased to be a parasite.
49. When contemplation a particular economic 'game', individuals instinctively partition society into independent subsets with exchangeable members. Decisions are confined to the 'friendliest' subset. The analogy with insurance is compelling.
50. Association and correlation are dependence relations which can be defined precisely. They are then implied by infinitely divisible processes. See McCall (1986).

51. For example, see Stephens and Krebs (1986) and Lippman and McCall (1984).
52. One of the first papers on this topic was 'What the Frog's Eye Tells the Frog's Brain', (reprinted in McCulloch, 1965, by Lettvin *et al*. The recent studies by Deno *et al*. (1989), and Arbib, and Lara *et al*. in Amari and Arbib (1982) completes this title and show how the frog's brain converts incoming information (the presence of a prey) into decision-making behaviour (attack the prey if a threshold criterion is satisfied).

## References

Aase, K. K. (1985) 'R and D-Projects analysed by Semimartingale Methods', *Journal of Applied Probabilities*, 22, pp. 288–99.

Abraham, R. and Marsden, J. E. (1978) *Foundations of Mechanics* (Reading, Massachusetts: Benjamin/Cummings).

Abreu, D. and Rubinstein, A. (1988) 'The Structure of Nash Equilibrium in Repeated Games with Fintie Automata', *Econometrica*, 56, pp. 1259–81.

Alchian, A. A. (1984) 'Specificity, Specialization and Coalitions', *Journal of Institutional and Theoretical Economics*, 140, pp. 34–49.

Aldous, D. J. (1982) 'Some Inequalities for Reversible Markov Chains', *Journal of the London Mathematics Society*, 25, pp. 364–76.

Aldous, D. J. (1985) *Exchangeability and Related Topics* (New York: Springer-Verlag).

Amari, S. and Arbib, M. A. (eds) (1982) *Competition and Cooperation in Neural Nets*, (New York: Springer-Verlag).

Anderson, P. W., Arrow, K. J. and Pines, D. (eds) (1988) *The Economy as an Evolving Complex System* (Wokingham: Addison-Wesley).

Arrow, K. J. (1972) The Economic Implications of Learning by Doing', *Review of Economic Studies*, 29, pp. 155–73.

Arrow, K. J. and Hahn, F. H. (1971) *General Competitive Analysis* (Edinburgh: Holden-Day).

Aumann, R. J. (1976) Agreeing to Disagree', *Annual Statistics*, 4.

Aumann, R. J. (1985) 'What is Game Theory Trying to Accomplish?' in K. J. Arrow and S. Honkapohja (eds) *Frontiers of Economics* (Amsterdam: North-Holland).

Becker, G. S. and Murphy, K. M. (1986) 'A Theory of Rational Addiction', *Journal of Political Economy*, 96, 95–9.

Bertsekas, D. and Gallager, R. (1987) *Data Networks* (Englewood Cliffs, New Jersey: Prentice-Hall).

Bicker, G. and Menzel, R. (1989) 'Chemical Codes for the Control of Behavior in Anthropods', *Nature*, pp. 337–9.

Binmore, K. and Brandenburger, A. (1988) 'Common Knowledge and Game Theory', TE/88/167, London School of Economics and Political Science.

Boorman, S. A. (1975) 'A Combinatorial Optimization Model for Transmission of Job Information Through Contact Networks', *Bell Journal of Economics*, 6, pp. 216–49.

Boyer, M. (1978) 'A Habit-Forming Optimal Growth Model', *International Economic Review*, 19, pp. 585–607.

Bremaud, P. (1981) *Point Processes and Queues* (New York: Springer-Verlag).

Brock, W. A., and Malliaris, A. G. (1989) *Differential Equations, Stability and Chaos in Dynamic Economies* (Amsterdam: North-Holland).

Cinlar, E. and Jacod, J. (1981) 'Representation of Semimartingale Markov Processes in Terms of Wiener Processes and Poisson Random Measures', in Cinlar, Chung, and Getoor (eds) *Seminar on Stochastic Processes, 1981* (Boston: Birkhauser).

Cinlar, E., Jacod, J., Protter, P. and Sharpe, M. J. (1983) 'Semimartingales and Markov Processes', *Z. Wahrscheinlichkeitstheorie verw. Gebiete* 54, pp. 161–219.

Crick, F. (1989) 'The Recent Excitement About Neural Networks', *Nature*, 337, pp. 129–32.

Deno, D. C., Keller, E. L. and Crandall, W. F. (1989) 'Dynamical Neural Network Organization of the Visual Pursuit System', *IEEE Transactions of Biomedical Engineers*, 36, pp. 85–92.

Doyle, P., and Snell, J. L. (1985) *Random Walks and Electric Networks*, (Providence, RI: Mathematical Association of America).

Dubins, L. E. and Savage, L. J. (1965) *How To Gamble If You Must* (New York: McGraw-Hill).

Elliott, R. J. (1982) *Stochastic Calculus and Applications* (New York: Springer-Verlag).

Endler, J. A. (1986) *Natural Selection in the Wild* (Princeton, New Jersey: Princeton University Press).

Enke, S. (1951) 'Equilibrium Among Spatially Separated Markets: Solution by Electric Analogue', *Econometrica*, 19, pp. 40–47.

Feynman, R. (1964) *The Feynman Lectures on Physics* (Reading, Massachusetts: Addison-Wesley).

Feynman, R. (1985) *Q. E. D.* (Princeton, New Jersey: Princeton University Press).

Fisher, I. (1982) *Mathematical Investigations in the Theory of Value and Prices* (New Haven: Yale University Press).

Fogelin, R. J. (1987) *Wittgenstein* (London: Routledge & Kegan Paul).

Gerstein, G. L., Bedenbaugh, P. and Aertsen, H. I. (1989) 'Neuronal Assemblies', *IEEE Transactions of Biomedical Engineers*, 36, pp. 1–14.

Gillespie, J. H. (1989) 'Why Not Use Diffusion Analysis in Population Genetics', in M. W. Feldman (ed.) *Mathematical Evolutionary Theory* (Princeton, New Jersey: Princeton).

Goodwin, R. M. (1951) 'The Non-linear Accelerator and the Persistence of Business Cycles', *Econometrica*, 19, pp. 1–17.

Grandmont, J. M. (1984) 'On Endogenous Competitive Business Cycles', *Institute for Mathematical Studies in Social Sciences*, no 438.

Grossberg, S., Mingolla, E. and Todorovic, D. (1989) 'A Neural Network Architecture for Preattentive Vision', *IEEE Transactions of Biomedical Engineers*, 36, pp. 65–84.

Hammond, J. H., and Magnanti, T. L. (1987), 'Generalized Descent Methods for Asymmetric System of Equations', *Mathematical Operational Research*, 12, pp. 678–99.

Hebb, D. O. (1949) *Organization of Behavior* (New York: John Wiley and Sons).

Hirshleifer, J. (1987) *Economic Behavior in Adversity* (Chicago: University of Chicago Press).

Hoel, P. G., Port, S. C. and Stone, C. J. (1972) *Introduction to Stochastic Processes* (Boston, Massachusetts: Houghton-Mifflin).

Holland, J. H., Holyoak, K. J., Nisbett, R. E. and Thagard, P. R. (1987) *Induction* (Cambridge, Massachusetts: MIT Press).

Holmstrom, B. and Milgrom, P. (1985) 'Aggregation and Linearity in the Provision of Intertemporal Incentives', Report no 466, Economics Series (Stanford, California: Stanford University).

Holyoak, K. J. (1987) 'Review of Rumelhart, D. E. *et al.*', *Parallel Distributed Processing*, vols. 1 and 2, *Science*, pp. 992–6.

Hopenhayn, H. A. and Prescott, E. C. (1987) 'Invariant Distributions for Monotone Markov Processes', Federal Reserve Bank of Minnesota, Working Paper no 299.

Hopfield J. and Tank, D. W. (1986) 'Computing with Neural Circuits: A Model', Science, vol. 233, pp. 625–32.

Iannaccone, L. R. (1986) 'Addiction and Satiation', *Economic Letters*, 21, pp. 95–9.

Iri, M. (1984) 'Structural Theory for the Combinatorial Systems Characterized by Submodular Functions', in  Pulleyblank (ed.) *Progress in Combinatorial Optimization* (New York: Academic Press).

Karlin, S. and Nevo, E. (eds) (1987) *Evolutionary Processes and Theory* (New York: Academic Press).

Karlin, S. and Taylor, H. M. (1981) *A Second Course in Stochastic Processes* (New York: Academic Press).

Kelly, F. P. (1979) *Reversible and Stochastic Networks* (New York: John Wiley and Sons).

Kemeny, J. G., Snell, J. L. and Knapp, A. W. (1976) *Denumerable Markov Chains* (New York: Springer-Verlag).

Koob, G. F., and Bloom, F. E. (1988) 'Cellular and Molecular Mechanisms of Drug Dependence', *Science*, 242 (4 November) pp. 715–23.

Koopmans, T. C. (1949) 'Optimum Utilization of the Transportation System', *Econometrica*, 17, Supplement, pp. 136–46.

Korolyuk, V. S., Pletnev, A. I. and Eidelman, S. D. (1988) 'Automata Walrus Games', *Russian Mathematical Surveys*, vol. 43, pp. 103–47.

Langman, R. E. (1989) *The Immune System* (London: Academic Press, 1989).

Leijonhufvud, A. (1988) 'Notes on "Turbulence" in Economic Systems', unpublished ms., University of California at Los Angeles.

Lettvin, J. Y. Maturvana, H. R., McCulloch, W. S. and Pitts, W. H. (1959) 'What the Frog's Eye Tells the Frog's Brain', reprinted in McCulloch (1965).

Li, S., and Basar, T. (1987) 'Asymptotic Agreement and Convergence of Synchronous Stochastic Algorithms', *IEEE Transactions of*, AC-32, pp. 612–18.

Lippman, S. A. and McCall, J. J. (1984) 'Ecological Decision-making and

Optimal Stopping Rules', unpublished ms. (University of California at Los Angeles).

Llinas, R. R. (1988) 'The Intrinsic Electrophysiological Properties of Mammalian Neurons: Insights Into Central Nervous System Function', *Science*, 242 (December) pp. 1654–64.

Logue, A. W. (1988) 'Research on Self-Control: An Integrating Framework', *Behavioural and Brain Sciences*, vol. 11, pp. 665–709.

Lucas, R. E., Jr. (1981) *Studies in Business Cycle Theory* (Cambridge, Massachusetts: MIT Press).

Lutz, F. and Lutz, V. (1951) *The Theory of Investment of the Firm* (Princeton; Princeton University Press).

McCall, J. J. (1989) 'The Smithian Self and Its Bayesian Brain', University of California, Los Angeles, October.

McCall, J. J. (1989b) 'Exchangeability and the Structure of the Economy: A Preliminary Process Analysis', in H. Brink (ed.) *Advances in Business Cycle Theory* (London: Macmillan).

McCall, J. J. and Velupillai, K. (1989) 'Constructive Foundations For Economics: The Emperor's Old Clothes', submitted to *Economic Journal*, November.

McCulloch, W. S. (1965) *Embodiments of Mind* (Cambridge, Massachusetts: MIT Press).

McCulloch, W. S. (1988) *Embodiments of Mind* (Cambridge, Massachusetts: MIT Press).

McCulloch, W. S. and Pitts, W. (1943) 'A Logical Calculus of the Ideas Immiment in Nervous Activity', *Bulletin of Mathematical Biophysics*, 5, pp. 175–233.

Medawar, P. B. (1957) *The Uniqueness of the Individual* (Dover:).

Metivier, M. (1983) *Weak Convergence of Sequences of Semimartingales*, Tech. Report #49, Center for Stochastic Processes, University of North Carolina.

Morehouse, N. F., Strotz, R. H. and Horwitz, S. J. (1950) 'An Electro-Analog Method for Investigating Problems in Economic Dynamics', *Econometrica*, 18, pp. 313–28.

Nicoll, R. A. (1988) 'The Coupling of Neurotransmitter Receptors to Ion Channels in the Brain', *Science*, 241, pp. 545–51.

Okun, A. M. (1981) *Prices and Quantities* (Washington, DC: Brookings Institution).

Palm, G. (1982) *Neural Assemblies – Studies of Brain Functions*, vol. 7 (New York: Springer-Verlag).

Phelps, E. S. (1970) *Microeconomic Foundations of Employment and Inflation Theory* (New York: Norton).

Pollak, R. A. (1976) 'Habit Formation and Long-Run Utility Functions', *Journal of Economic Theory*, 13, pp. 272–97.

Pollett, P. K. (1986) 'Connecting Reversible Markov Processes', *Advances in Applied Probability* 18, pp. 880–900.

Popper, K. R., and Eccles, J. C. (1977) *The Self and Its Brain: An Argument for Interactionism* (New York: Springer-Verlag).

Prescott, (1987).

Rosen, S. (1985) 'Implicit Contracts', *Journal of Economic Literature*, 23, pp. 1144–75.

Rustem, B., and Velupillai, K. (1990) 'Rationality, Computability and Complexity', *Journal of Economic Dynamics and Control*, vol. 14, pp. 419–32.

Samuelson, P. A. (1952), 'Spatial Price Equilibrium and Linear Programming', *American Economic Review*, 42, pp. 283–303.

Sargent, T. J. (1987) 'Some of Milton Friedman's Scientific Contributions to Macroeconomics', (Stanford, Calif.: Hoover Institution).

Segall, A. (1976) 'Stochastic Processes in Estimation Theory', *IEEE Transactions of Information Theory*, 22, pp. 275–86.

Sims, C. A. (1984) 'Martingale-Like Behavior of Prices and Interest Rates,' Discussion Paper No. 205, Center for Economic Research, University of Minnesota.

Smith, A. (1759) *The Theory of Moral Sentiments* (Liberty Classics, 1759).

Spitzer, F. (1971) 'Markov Random Fields and Gibbs Ensembles', *American Mathematics Monthly*, 78, pp. 142–54.

Stephens, D. W. and Krebs, J. R. (1986) *Foraging Theory* (Princeton, New Jersey: Princeton University Press).

Stigler, G. J., and Becker, G. S. (1977) '*De Gustibus non est Disputandum*', *American Economic Review*, 67, pp. 76–90.

Stokey, N. L. (1988) 'Learning by Doing and the Introduction of New Goods', *Journal of Political Economy*, 96, pp. 701–17.

Strang, G. (1986) *Introduction to Applied Mathematics* (Cambridge, Massachusetts: Wellesley-Cambridge Press).

Takayama, T., and Judge, G. G. (1971) *Spatial and Temporal Price and Allocation Models* (Amsterdam: North-Holland).

Tank, D. W., and Hopfield, J. J. (1987) 'Collective Computation in Neuron-like Circuits', *Scientific American*, pp. 104–14.

Tobin, R. L. (1988) 'A Variable Dimension Solution Approach for the General Spatial Price Equilibrium Problem', *Mathematical Programming* 40, pp. 33–51.

Tucker, A. W. (1950) 'Analogues of Kirchhoff's Laws', unpublished ms. (Stanford: Stanford University).

Velupillai, K. (1987) 'What Have We Learned in the Path From Gödel and Turing to Artificial Intelligence', (University of California at Los Angeles).

Whittle, P. (1982; 1983) *Optimization Over Time*, vols. I and II (New York: John Wiley).

# Part III

# Equilibrium Theories of the Business Cycle

# 5 Hours and Employment Variation in Business-Cycle Theory[1]

Finn E. Kydland  and  Edward C. Prescott
CARNEGIE-MELLON
UNIVERSITY

FEDERAL RESERVE
BANK OF MINNEAPOLIS
AND UNIVERSITY OF
MINNESOTA

## INTRODUCTION

In previous studies (Kydland and Prescott, 1982 and 1988a) we estimate the importance of variations in the Solow technology parameter as a source of aggregate fluctuations. We find that they were a major source accounting for over half of the fluctuations in the output of the American economy in the period immediately after the Korean War. These conclusions are based upon the study of model economies with the property that all workers work the same number of hours in equilibrium and that there is no variation in the number employed. Hansen (1985) studied a growth economy with the Rogerson (1988) labour indivisibilities. In his environment individuals are constrained each period either to work some fixed number of hours or not to work at all. By construction, it is the number employed rather than the hours worked per employed person that varies. In such worlds the aggregate willingness of people to substitute leisure intertemporally is considerably higher than that of the individuals whose behaviour is being aggregated. For the Hansen economy, fluctuations exceeded those experienced by the US economy in the period immediately after the Korean War.

We know that both the hours per worker and the number of workers employed vary. In this paper we present a computable general equilibrium structure in which both the hours a plant is operated and the number of employees who operate it are choice variables. We think that this is a better model to assess the importance of various shocks as a source of aggregate fluctuations. We calibrate the model economy to national income and product account and household survey data and we use it to assess the importance of variations in the Solow (1957) technology parameter. Our estimate is that their contribution is approximately 70 per cent of the total. This is larger than the estimate we previously obtained but it is significantly smaller than that obtained by Hansen (1988). It would be interesting to know whether the findings of Braun (1988), Chang (1988), Christiano and Eichenbaum (1988), and McGratten (1988) regarding the importance of public finance shocks would be altered if they included this structure in their models.

In the spirit of the Hansen economy, ours has a non-convexity in the consumption possibility sets of the households, but the non-convexity is nowhere near as extreme as the Rogerson indivisibility constraint. In our economy agents spend time in commuting to and from work. They can allocate to market activities any number of hours subject only to the time-endowment constraint. Hansen and Sargent (1988) study a similar problem in their straight-time and overtime model. In their economy, agents choose one of three time allocations at each date. These choices are either not to work, to work regular time, or to work regular time plus overtime. In that model, during the overtime period fewer workers use the same capital stock. Consequently, the capital–labour ratio is larger than that during the regular time-period. In our model economy, output of a plant is the product of the number of hours it is operated times a constant-returns-to-scale production function, with capital and the number of workers as inputs operating the plant. Both the number of workers operating the plant and the number of hours which the plant is in operation can be varied. We think that this construction better conforms to micro observations.

In our model economy the utilisation rate of capital is proportional to the number of hours the plants are operated. The capital utilisation rate therefore varies. In this paper we examine whether abstracting from this fact seriously biases the Prescott (1986) estimate of the innovation variance of the Solow technology parameter process. We find the bias is small. Variations in the capital utilisation rate results in the estimated variance of the technology shock being $(0.0079)^2$ when it is in fact $(0.0076)^2$.

An additional feature of our model is that resources are utilised whenever agents move between the household sector and the market sector. The amount of resources used varies across individuals. The nature of the equilibrium is such that those with lower transfer costs are the first to be moved. Total resources used for this purpose turn out to be an increasingly convex function of the number moved. The economy behaves as if there were a stand-in household which experiences costs of adjusting its employment as assumed by Sargent (1979). By being explicit about the microfoundations of these so-called aggregate adjustment costs, there is some hope of deducing their size by examining micro observations. We find that the magnitude of the parameter for which the relative fluctuations in hours per worker and the number of workers of the model economy match those of the post-war American economy is not implausibly large. Given this parameter value, the total costs of moving people between sectors are less than 0.01 per cent of GNP on average.

By introducing heterogeneity of agents we are following Rogerson (1987). A key difference, however, is that in our model resources are used up in changing the level of employment while in his, costs are an increasing function of the number employed. Cho and Cooley (1987) examine the implications of using a modified version of the Rogerson construct to study the empirical elasticity of labour supply responses to temporary changes in the real wage.

The paper is organised as follows: Section 1 specifies the economic environment. Section 2 represents it as an economy in the sense of Arrow–Debreu–McKenzie and carries out the aggregation. In Section 3 we calibrate the economy to the national income and product account and survey data. The experiments based on the model economies are outlined in Section 4. In Section 5, we examine the cyclical behaviour of these model economies. The final section contains summary and conclusions.

## 1 THE ECONOMIC ENVIRONMENT

### Preferences

There are a large number of ex-ante identical agents and these agents have measure one. An agent's utility function is

$$E \sum_{t=0}^{\infty} \beta^t U(c_t, \ell_t)$$

where $c_t$ is consumption at data $t$, $\ell_t$ is leisure and $\beta \in (0, 1)$ is the subjective time discount factor. The function $U$ has the form:

$$U(c, \ell) = \frac{G(c, \ell)^{1-\gamma} - 1}{1 - \gamma}$$

where $\gamma > 0$, $\gamma \neq 1$, and $G$ is a CES function whose parameters will be determined as part of the calibration.

An individual's time-endowment in each period is one. The amount of labour allocated to the market, however, is not $1 - \ell$. Letting $h$ be hours of labour services:

$$\ell(h) = \psi - h \text{ for } 0 < h \leq \psi < 1$$

while

$$\ell(0) = 1$$

The function $\ell(h)$ is discontinuous at zero. The reason for this discontinuity is that time $1 - \psi$ is required for commuting to work in every period that the individual is employed.

Each period, agents are indexed by a parameter $\xi$ which is identically and independently distributed both over time and over agents.[2] Random variables $\xi$ determine the amount of the composite output good that is required to move an individual between the household sector and the market sector. More precisely, if for any individual $h_{t-1} > 0$ and $h_t = 0$ or if $h_{t-1} = 0$ and $h_t > 0$, a cost is incurred. We assume $\xi$ is uniformly distributed on $[0, 1]$. The size of the moving cost is proportional to $\xi$ with a different constant depending upon the direction of the move. The relative size of these constants will be selected in such a way that 'adjustment costs' of changing aggregate employment are symmetric whenever the last-period employment rate is equal to the average employment rate.

## Technology

A given agent working $h$ hours and using $k$ units of capital produces

$$a = zhk^{1-\theta}$$

units of some input. It is an input to a constant returns-to-scale-aggregated CES production function along with inventory services $y$. This production function is denoted $F(a, y)$. Output is used either for consumption $c$, investment $i$, or for moving people between sectors $m$. In particular:

$$m + c + i \leq \left[(1-F)a^{-v} + \sigma y^{-v}\right]^{-1/v} \equiv F(a, y)$$

where $1/(1+v)$ is the elasticity of substitution between $a$ and $y$ and $\sigma$ the share parameter of inventory services.

Investment $i_t$ is the sum of inventory investment $y_{t+1} - y_t$ and investment in plant and equipment. Time is required to build new $k_t$. Letting $s_{jt}$ for $j = 1, \ldots, J$ be the number of units of capital $j$ periods from completion, the laws of motion of the capital stocks are

$$k_{t+1} = (1-\delta)k_t + s_{1t}$$

$$s_{j, t+1} = s_{j+1, t} \text{ for } j = 1, 2, \ldots, J - 1$$

The fraction of value put in place in each stage is denoted $\phi_j$. Consequently, total investment in period $t$ is

$$i_t = (y_{t+1} - y_t) + \sum_{j=1}^{J} \phi_j s_{jt}$$

The number of time-periods required to build new capital and the pattern of value added over the construction period are parameters that must be calibrated.

The shocks to technology are the sum of two independent components:

$$z_{1, t+1} = 0.95\, z_t + \varepsilon_{1t}$$

$$z_{2, t+1} = \varepsilon_{2t}$$

where $z_t = z + z_{1, t+1} + z_{2, t+1}$. The means of $\varepsilon_{1t}$ and $\varepsilon_{2t}$ are zero. Parameter $z$ is the mean of the $\{z_t\}$ process. At the beginning of period $t$, what is observed is $z_t + \varepsilon_{3t}$ where $\varepsilon_{3t}$ is a measurement error. All shocks are normally distributed and independent. For the Kalman filter analysis of this structure see Kydland and Prescott (1982).

## 2 AGGREGATION

At time zero all agents are identical. Using the competitive theory with lotteries of Prescott and Townsend (1984) as extended by Prescott and Rios-Rull (1988), all agents receive the same distribution of date- and event-contingent consumption-leisure pairs but possibly different realisations of the lottery. The competitive equilibrium is the Pareto optimum which maximises the sum of agents' utilities. This fact is exploited in developing our algorithm for computing the equilibrium.

At a given point in time, agents differ in terms of their current moving cost parameter $\xi$ and of their previous-period employment state. Given that the $\xi$ are identically and independently distributed both over time and across individuals, the aggregate state variable must include only the measure of agents employed in the previous period, the value of the technology parameter, a set of sufficient statistics for forecasting future values of this parameter, and the aggregate stocks of capital.

We address two issues in this section: (i) the size of aggregate moving costs, given the number of people to be moved, and (ii) the distribution of consumption and leisure across agents in each period, given the aggregate per capita variables.

**Aggregate Moving Costs**

Current period employment is $n$ and last-period employment is $e$. If $n > e$, some people must be moved from the household sector to the market sector. Agents with the smallest $\xi$ are moved first. We assume that the costs of moving a $\xi$ type from the household sector to the market sector is $\alpha\xi$. If $n < e$, measure $e-n$ must be moved from the market sector to the household sector. The cost of moving a $\xi$ type from the market sector to the household sector is $\alpha\xi$.

The total moving costs when $n > e$ are

$$m = \alpha \int_0^{n-e} \xi \, \frac{f(\xi)d\xi}{(1-e)} \ .$$

Similarly, when $n < e$ aggregate moving costs are

$$m = \alpha \int_0^{e-n} \xi \, \frac{f(\xi)d\xi}{e} \ .$$

The moving-cost function is convex and has value zero if $e = n$. Given this we can locally approximate the function using a quadratic function. We denote quadratic aggregate moving costs as $M(e, n) = \alpha(n - e)^2$.

**Distribution of Consumption and Leisure**

In the remainder of this section we have to make a distinction between population means and individual values. Capital letters denote population means of the corresponding variable.

Let $x(B)$ be the measure of people who consume $c$, work $h$ hours and use $k$ units of capital for $(c, h, k)$ belonging to measurable set $B$. Since we need a linear space for standard competitive analysis, the measures are signed measures. The planner's problem is

$$R(I, K, Y, N) = \max_{x \geq 0} \int U\Big[c, \ell(h)\Big]dx$$

subject to

$$\int c\,dx + I + M(E, N) \leq F\Big(z \int hk^{(1-\theta)}dx, Y\Big)$$

$$\int dx = 1$$

$$\int k\,dx \leq K$$

$$\int I_{\{h>0\}}dx = N$$

For technical reasons we impose the constraint that individual consumption is bounded above by some number as is the amount of capital used by an individual. This results in the space over which $x$ is defined being the Borel sigma algebra of a compact metric space. In equilibrium both these constraints turn out to be non-binding.

For the production functions and utility structure of the CES variety, the solution to this programming problem is to assign people to at most two $(c, h, k)$-triples. One of these points has both $h = 0$ and $k = 0$ and some level of consumption $c = c_0$. The other point is denoted $(c_1, h_1, k_1)$. Letting $n$ be the measure or fraction of people assigned $(c_1, h_1, k_1)$, then $k_1 = K/n$ because it is optimal to assign all caital to workers. Measure or population fraction $1 - n$ are assigned $(c_0, 0, 0)$. For a formal analysis see Hornstein and Prescott (1989).

For some values of the parameters of our CES preference and technology structures, the optimal $n$ is one. But, in the calibration exercise, reasonable values of these parameters result in the average $n$ being 0.75.

This programme has a maximum given that the constraint set is compact and the objective function continuous in the weak* topology. Further, the objective is concave and its constraint set jointly concave in the decision variables $x$ and $N$ and in the constraint variables $E$, $K$, and $I$. Consequently, the value of the program is concave and continuous in $E$, $K$, and $I$.

An implication of this analysis is that the following more restricted social optimum problem can be considered:

$$\max E \sum \beta^t \left[ (1 - n_t)U(c_{0t}, 1) + n_t U(c_{1t}, \psi - h_t) \right]$$

subject to

$$c_t = (1 - n_t)c_{0t} + n_t c_{1t}$$

and to the constraints of Section 1.

## 3   STEADY STATE AND CALIBRATION

By steady state we mean the rest point for the deterministic version of our model economy – that is, the version for which the variances of the shocks are zero. These values are the mean values for the quadratic approximation to the model economy. The calibration exercise is to select values of the parameters for which these values equal the time average values for the US post-war economy.

The *per capita* numbers to which we calibrate our economy are as follows: aggregate output on a quarterly basis is normalised to one. The investment share is one-quarter ($i = 0.25$) and therefore the consumption share is three-quarters ($c = 0.75$). In our economy there is no growth but Hansen (1988) has shown that, provided investment shares are held constant, variations in the average rate of exogenous technological change do not affect business-cycle accounting.

Other numbers to which the model economy is calibrated are the inventory stock to quarterly output ratio ($y = 1.0$), quarterly real interest rate ($r = 0.01$), the fraction of the working-age population who work ($n = 0.75$), and the fraction of productive time that working people work ($h = 0.45$).

The first step in the calibration is to choose elasticities of substitution between inputs in both household and business production. First, consider the households. Over the past several decades, the real wage has increased two to three times, while hours of work per household have remained essentially unchanged. In Kydland (1984) it was formally demonstrated that the special form of a CES utility function that is consistent with this observation is the unitary-elasticity case. Therefore, the form of the current-period utility function is:

$$U(c_t, \ell_t) = \frac{\left[c_t^\mu \ell_t^{1-\mu}\right]^{1-\gamma} - 1}{1 - \gamma}$$

where $0 < \mu < 1$ and $\gamma > 0$ but different from 1. Using a value of $\gamma$ close to 1 corresponds to using a logarithmic utility function.

A technology constraint is

$$m_t + c_t + i_t \leq \left[(1-\sigma)(z_t h_t n_t^\theta k_t^{1-\theta})^{-\upsilon} + \sigma y_t^{-\upsilon}\right]^{-1/\upsilon}$$

where

$$i_t = \sum_{i=1}^{J} \phi_i s_{it} + y_{t+1} - y_t$$

and where $0 < \theta < 1, 0 < \sigma < 1$, and $\upsilon > 0$. Steady state $m_t$ is zero as, in the steady state, no workers are moved between sectors. The fraction $\phi_i$ of total resources put in place at stage $i$ of the project is $1/J$ for all $i$. We let the value of $J$ be 3. Some projects, of course, take more time and some less, but this appears to be a reasonable compromise. There is little evidence that the time to build varies over the cycle.

The fact that factor shares of capital and labour have changed little, in spite of large real-wage increases, is evidence that the elasticity of substitution between the labour and capital inputs is close to 1. On the other hand, our knowledge about the elasticity between the inventory stock and the remaining composite input is much less clear. An event in which the relative price of the two moved considerably would give us a much sharper estimate of its magnitude. Our view is that the substitution elasticity, $1/(\upsilon+1)$, is quite small, and that $\upsilon$ is therefore well above zero, say 3 or 4.

We consider separately the household's and the firm's problem, taking prices as given. Initially, we take hours per period $h$ as a given, and derive the first-order conditions with respect to $n$, $k$, and $y$ for the firm, and with respect to $c_0$, $c_1$, and $n$ for the stand-in household. If the chosen value of $h$ happens to be the equilibrium 1, the marginal product of $h$ must equal the negative of the ratio of marginal utilities with respect to hours and consumption.

The rental price of inventories is

$$u_y = r$$

as inventories do not depreciate. The price of new production capital is

$$q = \sum_{j=1}^{J} \phi_j (1+r)^{j-1}$$

which is the value of resources used to produce one unit of $k$ in terms of the same-date consumption good. Consequently the rental price of capital is

$$u_k = (r+\delta)q$$

The prices of the partially constructed capital goods $s_1$ and $s_2$ are

$$q_1 = \phi_3(1+r)^2 + \phi_2 (1+r)$$

$$q_2 = \phi_3(1+r)$$

Real date $t$ gross investment in plant and equipment using steady state prices is

$$q_1(s_{1,\,t+1} - s_{1,\,t}) + q_2(s_{2,\,t+1} - s_{2t}) + q(k_{t+1} - (1-\delta)k_t)$$

For a steady state allocation, the first two terms are zero and the last simply $q\delta k$. Steady state GNP is therefore $c + q\delta k$.

### The Firm's Problem

The firm rents capital and inventories at rental prices $u_k$ and $u_y$, respectively. These steady-state prices are given by the expressions derived above. Abstracting from growth, the steady-state real interest rate, $r$, equals the rate of time preference, $(1-\beta)/\beta$. The quarterly wage per worker depends on the number of hours $h$ worked in the period. We denote it by $w_h$ to indicate this dependence. Thus, the firm maximises in every period the value of output minus the cost of the inputs:

$$F\left(zhn^\theta k^{1-\theta}, y\right) - u_k\, k - u_y\, y - w_h\, n$$

where we have taken the price of output to be 1. Output is measured in units such that steady-state output is 1. Then:

$$(zhn^\theta k^{1-\theta})^{-v} = 1 - \sigma y^{-v}$$

so that:

$$z = \left[hn^\theta k^{1-\theta}\,(1-\sigma y^{-v})^{1/v}\right]^{-1}$$

From the condition $F_y = u_y$, we get

$$\sigma = u_y\, y^{v+1}$$

Similarly, equating the marginal product of $k$ to $u_k$ implies

$$1 - \theta = u_k\, k/(1-\sigma y^{-v})$$

Finally,

$$w_h = wh = F_a\,(a,\,y)\theta zhk^{(1-\theta)}n^{\theta-1}$$

Wage rate $w$ is a parameter of the household's problem.

To summarise, in this part of the calibration exercise, technology parameters $z$, $\theta$, and $\sigma$, and preference parameter $\beta$, are selected so that steady state $r$, $i$, $y$, and $F(a, y)$ have the specified values. Other evidence is used in selecting $J$, the number of periods required to construct new productive capital, the $\phi_i$, which are the fractions of value added at each of the $J$ stages of production, and $v$, which determines the elasticity of substitution between inventory stocks and the composite of the other inputs.

To be determined are preference parameters $\psi$, $\mu$, and $\gamma$. For this purpose we turn to the household's problem treating parametrically steady state values of prices and capital stocks.

**The Household's Problem**

The maximisation problem facing the stand-in household given steady state prices and capital stocks is

$$\max \sum_{t=0}^{\infty} \beta^t \Big[(1-n_t)U(c_{0t}, 1) + n_t U(c_{1t}, \psi-h_t)\Big]$$

subject to

$$\sum_{t=0}^{\infty} \frac{1}{(1+r)^t}\Big[(1-n_t)c_{0t} + n_t\, c_{1t}\Big] \leqslant \sum_{t=0}^{\infty} \frac{1}{(1+r)^t}\Big[wh_t n_t + ry + rqk\Big]$$

The maximisation is over $\{h_t, n_t, c_{0t}, c_{1t}\}_{t=0}^{\infty}$. Given that $\beta = 1/(1+r)$ and that the first-order conditions have been shown to be necessary for an optimum, the optimal value of the variables have the same value at every date. Consequently, we drop the $t$ subscript.

The problem reduces to:

$$\max_{c_0, c_1, h, n \,\geqslant\, 0} \{(1-n)U(c_0, 1) + nU(c_1, \psi-h)\}$$

subject to

$$(1-n)c_0 + nc_1 \leqslant whn + ry + rqk + rq_1\delta k + rq_2\delta k$$

The period utility function is:

$$U(c,\ell) = \frac{\Big[c^{\mu}\ell^{(1-\mu)}\Big]^{(1-\gamma)} - 1}{1 - \gamma}$$

The value we select for $\gamma$ is 2.0. The value that is used in our previous research is 1.5. The motivation for the larger value is that it results in a greater difference in consumption of those employed and those not employed. With $\gamma = 2.0$ the consumption of the unemployed is about 75 per cent of the consumption of the employed. Smaller values of $\gamma$ resulted in $\psi$ exceeding 1 which is inconsistent with the theory. Larger values of $\gamma$ result in the relative variability of consumption being much less than the figure for the US economy. These are the considerations that led us to choose $\gamma = 2.0$.

With $\gamma$ specified, the parameters $\mu$ and $\psi$ are selected so the optimal $h$ is 0.45 and the optimal $n$ is 0.75. Note that all the remaining variables in the budget constraint are either values of variables to which the economy is calibrated or steady-state prices determined in the calibration. Necessarily, the resulting value of per capita con-

*Table 5.1*  Values used in the experiments

| Parameter values | | Steady states | |
|---|---|---|---|
| *Technology* | | GNP | 1.000 |
| $\theta$ | 0.643 | $c$ | 0.750 |
| $\sigma$ | 0.010 | $c_0$ | 0.588 |
| $\nu$ | 3.000 | $c_1$ | 0.804 |
| $\delta$ | 0.025 | $i$ | 0.750 |
| $\phi_1$ | 0.333 | $k$ | 10.000 |
| $\phi_2$ | 0.333 | $y$ | 1.000 |
| $\phi_3$ | 0.333 | $h$ | 0.450 |
| | | $n$ | 0.750 |
| *Preferences* | | | |
| $\beta$ | 0.990 | | |
| $\mu$ | 0.341 | | |
| $\gamma$ | 2.000 | | |
| $\psi$ | 0.979 | | |
| *Shock variances* | | | |
| $\sigma_1^2$ | $0.0076^2$ | | |
| $\sigma_2^2$ | $0.00154^2$ | | |
| $\sigma_3^2$ | $0.0076^2$ | | |

sumption, $c = (1-n)c_0 + nc_1$, is 0.75, the consumption share of output.

The remaining parameters to be calibrated are the variances, $\sigma_i^2$, for $i = 1, 2, 3$, of the shocks. The variance of the highly persistent shock, $\sigma_1^2$, is set equal to the variance of the Solow residuals for the post-war US economy as estimated by Prescott (1986). This value is $(0.0076)^2$. The ratio of the remaining two variances to the first are set equal to the values used in Kydland and Prescott (1982, 1988a).

Table 5.1 lists the parameter and steady-state values for our model economy.

## 4  EXPERIMENTS

Our model economy is not fully specified until a value for the moving-cost parameter $\alpha$ is specified. In the first experiment the value chosen is $\alpha = 0$. This value corresponds to no costs of moving a person into or out of the market sector. We find that for this economy virtually all the variation in the aggregate hours of labour is in the number of workers employed and none in the hours per employed person. The economy behaves very much like the Hansen (1985) economy with fluctuations in output being approximately as large as those for the US economy in the period 1954–88. One difference is that the amount of fluctuations induced by a given variation in the Solow technology parameter is not as large as for the Hansen economy. The reason for this difference is that we have a greater degree of risk aversion than does Hansen (our $\gamma$ is 2.0 while his is 1.0). Like the Hansen economy, the aggregate willingness of agents to substitute leisure intertemporally is very high.

Our assessment is that this economy, like the Hansen economy, overestimates the amount of fluctuations induced by Solow technology shocks. This failure of hours per worker to vary led us to introduce costs of moving people between the household and the market sector. An issue is what value to choose for the moving-cost parameter $\alpha$. The criterion for our selection of $\alpha = 0.5$ is that this value results in the relative variations in employment and in hours per employee being approximately the same as for the US economy. With $\alpha = 0.5$, the average aggregate moving costs are less than 0.01 per cent of average GNP. This is not a large number. At the microlevel, if the increase in employment is 2 per cent in a quarter, then the moving cost of moving one additional person to the market sector is $100. We do not view this figure as being unreasonable.

To summarise, Economy I has no moving costs ($\alpha=0$). Economy II has what we consider reasonable moving costs with $\alpha = 0.5$ and is the one that will be used to estimate the importance of Solow technology shocks. For comparison purposes, a third economy is also examined. For it, the moving costs are so large ($\alpha=500$) that virtually all the variation is in hours per worker and none in the number of workers. Our view is that this economy underestimates fluctuations induced by shocks to the economy.

## 5    CYCLICAL BEHAVIOUR OF THE MODEL ECONOMIES

Lucas (1981, p. 215) defines the business-cycle phenomenon as being the statistical properties of the co-movements of the cyclical components of aggregate time-series. This definition is not complete until the method for calculating the cyclical component of a time-series is specified. The method we use is to subject each time-series to a common linear transformation. This transformation filters out low-frequency movements in the data. Consequently, the statistics that we are labelling the cyclical components, change little if some slowly varying function is added to the time-series being transformed. If the added component is a linear trend, the cyclical component series does not change at all. For details of the method, see Kydland and Prescott (1982, fn. 15).

The particular time-series that we examine are dictated by the augmented neoclassical growth model with both the consumption-savings decision and the market-time allocation decision endogenised. They are autocorrelations of output, percentage standard deviations for all the variables and their correlations with GNP, including leads and lags. They capture well the strength of the co-movements with output, the phase shifts in the co-movements and relative amplitude of fluctuation. The auto-correlations of real output capture persistence of fluctuations.

This we found to be a very useful summary organisation of data from the point of view of the theory. These statistics are not highly sensitive to the very low-frequency movements which can arise from any number of sources. From the point of view of the theory, it is natural to think in terms of levels rather than rates of change.

For purposes of comparison, we present in Table 5.2 statistics for the cyclical components of US aggregate time-series for the 138-quarter period 1954:1–1988:2. The cyclical component is defined in exactly the same way for the US data as for the model economies.

For each of the three values of $\alpha$, twenty independent samples were drawn. In each sample, which is 138 quarters long, the cyclical components are calculated and the same set of statistics computed as for the US data. Based on the twenty samples, then, averages and standard deviations are reported for each of these statistics. They provided an indication of the sampling distributions of the statistics for the model economies and can be compared with the statistics for the US economy in Table 5.2. The results of the three experiments are reported in Tables 5.3–5.5 inclusive.

**The Major Finding**

The key question motivating this and our previous studies is what fraction of US post-war business cycles can be accounted for by technological shocks, also commonly described as Solow residuals.

*Table 5.2*   Cyclical behaviour of the US economy: deviations from trend of key variables, 1954:1–1988:2.[a]

| Variables x | Std dev. % | Cross-correlation of output with | | | | |
|---|---|---|---|---|---|---|
| | | x(t−2) | x(t−1) | x(t) | x(t+1) | x(t+2) |
| Gross national product | 1.74 | 0.63 | 0.85 | 1.00 | 0.85 | 0.63 |
| Consumption expenditures | 1.27 | 0.71 | 0.81 | 0.81 | 0.66 | 0.45 |
| Services and non-durable goods | 0.86 | 0.67 | 0.76 | 0.76 | 0.63 | 0.47 |
| Durable goods | 5.08 | 0.65 | 0.74 | 0.77 | 0.60 | 0.37 |
| Fixed investment expenditures | 5.51 | 0.65 | 0.83 | 0.90 | 0.81 | 0.60 |
| Total non-farm inventories | 1.68 | −0.06 | 0.18 | 0.49 | 0.72 | 0.82 |
| Hours (household survey) | 1.50 | 0.44 | 0.68 | 0.86 | 0.86 | 0.75 |
| Civilian employment | 1.08 | 0.36 | 0.61 | 0.82 | 0.89 | 0.82 |
| Hours per worker | 0.56 | 0.48 | 0.64 | 0.69 | 0.58 | 0.43 |
| Hours (establishment survey) | 1.69 | 0.39 | 0.67 | 0.88 | 0.92 | 0.81 |
| Output/hours, business sector | 1.04 | 0.68 | 0.65 | 0.55 | 0.23 | −0.05 |

[a]*Data Source*: *Citibase*

*Table 5.3*   Cyclical behaviour of economy with no moving costs[a]

| Variables x | Std dev. % | Cross-correlation of output with | | | | |
|---|---|---|---|---|---|---|
| | | x(t−2) | x(t−1) | x(t) | x(t+1) | x(t+2) |
| Output | 1.69 | 0.45 | 0.71 | 1.00 | 0.71 | 0.45 |
| | (0.18) | (0.09) | (0.06) | (0.00) | (0.06) | (0.09) |
| Consumption | 0.70 | 0.36 | 0.65 | 0.97 | 0.78 | 0.56 |
| | (0.08) | (0.08) | (0.05) | (0.01) | (0.05) | (0.09) |
| Fixed investment | 4.59 | 0.41 | 0.60 | 0.90 | 0.83 | 0.51 |
| | (0.47) | (0.10) | (0.07) | (0.03) | (0.02) | (0.06) |
| Inventory stock | 1.17 | 0.30 | 0.48 | 0.78 | 0.66 | 0.22 |
| | (0.09) | (0.07) | (0.08) | (0.04) | (0.05) | (0.12) |
| Capital stock | 0.44 | −0.36 | −0.21 | −0.08 | 0.16 | 0.52 |
| | (0.06) | (0.07) | (0.06) | (0.06) | (0.05) | (0.03) |
| Hours | 1.28 | 0.42 | 0.64 | 0.95 | 0.72 | 0.42 |
| | (0.13) | (0.10) | (0.07) | (0.01) | (0.05) | (0.08) |
| Employment | 1.28 | 0.42 | 0.64 | 0.95 | 0.72 | 0.42 |
| | (0.13) | (0.10) | (0.07) | (0.01) | (0.05) | (0.08) |
| Hours per worker | 0.00 | | | | | |
| Productivity (output/hours) | 0.61 | 0.35 | 0.64 | 0.77 | 0.46 | 0.36 |
| | (0.04) | (0.08) | (0.06) | (0.04) | (0.10) | (0.13) |

[a] These are the means of 20 simulations, each of which was 138 periods long. The numbers in parentheses are standard errors.

*Table 5.4* Cyclical behaviour of economy with moving costs[a]

| Variables x | Std dev. % | Cross-correlation of output with | | | | |
|---|---|---|---|---|---|---|
| | | $x(t-2)$ | $x(t-1)$ | $x(t)$ | $x(t+1)$ | $x(t+2)$ |
| Output | 1.53 | 0.51 | 0.76 | 1.00 | 0.76 | 0.51 |
| | (0.17) | (0.09) | (0.05) | (0.00) | (0.05) | (0.09) |
| Consumption | 0.64 | 0.42 | 0.69 | 0.97 | 0.82 | 0.62 |
| | (0.08) | (0.08) | (0.04) | (0.01) | (0.04) | (0.09) |
| Fixed investment | 4.21 | 0.46 | 0.65 | 0.89 | 0.85 | 0.55 |
| | (0.45) | (0.10) | (0.07) | (0.03) | (0.02) | (0.06) |
| Inventory stock | 1.01 | 0.36 | 0.55 | 0.80 | 0.69 | 0.32 |
| | (0.08) | (0.07) | (0.07) | (0.04) | (0.05) | (0.12) |
| Capital stock | 0.41 | −0.36 | −0.22 | −0.05 | 0.19 | 0.51 |
| | (0.06) | (0.08) | (0.07) | (0.06) | (0.05) | (0.03) |
| Hours | 0.93 | 0.46 | 0.67 | 0.93 | 0.88 | 0.66 |
| | (0.12) | (0.11) | (0.07) | (0.02) | (0.03) | (0.06) |
| Employment | 0.83 | 0.40 | 0.61 | 0.87 | 0.93 | 0.80 |
| | (0.11) | (0.13) | (0.09) | (0.03) | (0.02) | (0.04) |
| Hours per worker | 0.23 | 0.42 | 0.51 | 0.65 | 0.23 | −0.17 |
| | (0.02) | (0.07) | (0.06) | (0.05) | (0.03) | (0.04) |
| Productivity (output/hours) | 0.79 | 0.48 | 0.71 | 0.89 | 0.46 | 0.22 |
| | (0.06) | (0.08) | (0.06) | (0.02) | (0.08) | (0.12) |

[a] These are the means of 20 simulations, each of which was 138 periods long. The numbers in parentheses are standard errors.

For the experiment with no moving cost (see Table 5.3) and the variance of the highly persistent technology shock calibrated to correspond in size to Solow residuals for the US economy, the standard deviation of cyclical GNP is almost as large as that for the USA. For the case of reasonable moving cost, (see Table 5.4) so that both employment and hours per worker vary, with only technology shocks the standard deviation of cyclical output is nearly seven-eighths as large as in the data.

The correlation between output and labour productivity is 0.89 for the model economy and only 0.55 for the US data. If Solow technology shocks accounted for virtually all of the fluctuations, this would be bothersome. This, however is not our finding. We find that the Solow technology shocks account for about 70 per cent of post-war business cycles. If this correlation for the US data were near 1, there would be a problem for the theory. Our estimate of the importance of technology shocks implies that at least 25 per cent of the cycle is accounted for by other factors for which hours vary more than GNP.

*Table 5.5*  Cyclical behaviour of economy with very large moving costs[a]

| Variables x | Std dev. % | Cross-correlation of output with | | | | |
| | | x(t−2) | x(t−1) | x(t) | x(t+1) | x(t+2) |
| --- | --- | --- | --- | --- | --- | --- |
| Output | 1.31 | 0.45 | 0.71 | 1.00 | 0.71 | 0.45 |
| | (0.14) | (0.09) | (0.06) | (0.00) | (0.06) | (0.09) |
| Consumption | 0.52 | 0.35 | 0.64 | 0.97 | 0.78 | 0.57 |
| | (0.06) | (0.08) | (0.05) | (0.01) | (0.05) | (0.09) |
| Fixed investment | 3.76 | 0.39 | 0.58 | 0.85 | 0.85 | 0.52 |
| | (0.38) | (0.10) | (0.07) | (0.04) | (0.02) | (0.06) |
| Inventory stock | 0.93 | 0.31 | 0.51 | 0.79 | 0.66 | 0.25 |
| | (0.07) | (0.07) | (0.08) | (0.04) | (0.05) | (0.12) |
| Capital stock | 0.35 | −0.35 | −0.22 | −0.07 | 0.16 | 0.50 |
| | (0.05) | (0.08) | (0.07) | (0.06) | (0.05) | (0.03) |
| Hours | 0.41 | 0.42 | 0.63 | 0.92 | 0.76 | 0.45 |
| | (0.04) | (0.11) | (0.07) | (0.02) | (0.04) | (0.07) |
| Employment | 0.01 | | | | | |
| Hours per worker | 0.41 | 0.43 | 0.63 | 0.92 | 0.75 | 0.44 |
| | (0.04) | (0.11) | (0.07) | (0.02) | (0.04) | (0.07) |
| Productivity (output/hours) | 0.94 | 0.44 | 0.72 | 0.99 | 0.66 | 0.43 |
| | (0.09) | (0.09) | (0.06) | (0.003) | (0.07) | (0.11) |

[a] These are the means of 20 simulations, each of which was 138 periods long. The numbers in parentheses are standard errors.

Furthermore, Kydland and Prescott (1988b) found that, cyclically, aggregate number of hours varies more than the labour input.

**Hours and Employment Behaviour**

With no moving cost, all the aggregate hours variation is the result of changes in the number of workers. There are no fluctuations in hours per worker. For the economy with $\alpha = 0.5$, hours per worker varies considerably. The total number of hours varies about 60 per cent as much as output, which is somewhat less than in the US data. It would be bothersome if this were not the case. There is considerable temporal aggregation even when only a quarter of a year is the time period. With temporal aggregation some of hours per worker variation over the period reflects variation in employment over the subperiods.

An important finding is that employment lags the cycle while hours per worker lead slightly. This is the case for the US data (see Table

5.2). Compared with the no-moving-cost case, there is a stronger tendency for productivity to lead the cycle.

## 6 SUMMARY AND CONCLUSIONS

We have developed a computable general equilibrium structure in which both the hours for which a plant is operated and the number of employees can be varied. This we think is a better structure for assessing the contribution of shocks, whether they be technology, terms of trade, monetary or public finance shocks, to aggregate fluctuations.[3] We used this theory to estimate the importance of Solow technology shocks and find that they are a major contributor. If they were the only source of shocks, the variance of aggregate fluctuations would be about 70 per cent as large as our finding.

In the aggregate, leisure is more substitutable than at the individual level. In this sense, the economy behaves as if there were indivisibilities. It has been suggested that the indivisibilities of Hansen (1985) and Rogerson (1988) were *ad hoc*. Our framework provides a theoretical foundation for their approach.

Another innovation is a microbased theory of aggregate workforce adjustment costs. Without modest costs associated with individuals moving into and out of the market sector, there are virtually no variations in hours per worker. With these adjustment or moving costs, hours per worker leads output as is the case for aggregate US time-series.

### Notes

1. The views expressed herein are those of the authors and not necessarily those of the Federal Reserve Bank of Minneapolis or the Federal Reserve System. This paper is preliminary and is circulated to stimulate discussion. It is not to be quoted without the authors' permission.
2. We will be using the Uhlig (1987) law of large numbers for a continuum of identical and independent random variables.
3. Cooley and Hansen (1988) introduce money via a cash-in-advance constraint. Greenwald, Hercowitz, and Huffman (1988) permit the utilisation rate of capital to vary. Hansen (1988) introduces positive growth. Danthine and Donaldson (1989) introduce an efficiency-wage construct. In all these cases, the quantitative nature of fluctuations induced by technology shocks changed little.

## References

Braun, R. A. (1988) 'The Dynamic Interaction of Distortionary Taxes and Aggregate Variables in Post-war US Data, North-western University Working Paper.

Chang, L. J. (1988) 'Corporate Taxes, Disaggregated Capital Markets and business cycles', Carnegie-Mellon University Working Paper.

Cho, J. and Cooley, T. F. (1987) 'Employment and Hours over the Business Cycle', University of Rochester Working Paper.

Christiano, L. J. and Eichenbaum, M. (1988) 'Is Theory Really Ahead of Measurement? Current Real Business Cycle Theory and Aggregate Labor Market Fluctuations', Federal Reserve Bank of Minneapolis Working Paper no 412.

Cooley, T. F. and Hansen, G. D. (1988) 'The Inflation Tax and the Business Cycle', University of California at Los Angeles, Working Paper.

Danthine, J. P. and Donaldson, J. B. (1989) 'Efficiency Wages and the Business Cycle Puzzle', Columbia Graduate School of Business Working Paper.

Greenwald, J., Hercowitz, Z., and Huffman, G. W. (1988) 'Investment, Capacity Utilization and the Business Cycle', *American Economic Review*, vol. 78, pp. 402–18.

Hall, R. E. (1988) 'Substitution over Time in Work and Consumption', NBER Working Paper.

Hansen, G. D. (1985) 'Indivisible Labor and the Business Cycle', *Journal of Monetary Economics*, vol. 16, pp. 309–28.

Hansen, G. D. (1988) 'Technical Progress and Aggregate Fluctuations', manuscript, University of California, Los Angeles.

Hansen, G. D. and Sargent, T. J. (1988) 'Straight Time and Overtime in Equilibrium', *Journal of Monetary Economics*, vol. 21, pp. 281–308.

Hornstein, A. and Prescott, E. C. (1989) 'The Plant and the Firm in General Equilibrium', manuscript, University of Minnesota.

Kydland, F. E. (1984) 'Labor-force Heterogeneity and the Business Cycle', Carnegie–Rochester Conference Series on Public Policy, vol. 21, pp. 173–208.

Kydland, F. E. and Prescott, E. C. (1982) 'Time to Build and Aggregate Fluctuations', *Econometrica*, vol. 50, pp. 1345–70.

Kydland, F. E. and Prescott, E. C. (1988a) 'The Work Week of Capital and its Cyclical Implications', *Journal of Monetary Economics*, vol. 21, pp. 343–60.

Lucas, R. E. (1981) *Studies in Business Cycle Theory* (Cambridge, Massachusetts: MIT Press).

McGratten, E. R. (1988) 'The Macroeconomic Effects of Tax Policy in an Equilibrium Model', Stanford University Working Paper.

Prescott, E. C. (1986) 'Theory Ahead of Business Cycle Measurement', Carnegie–Rochester Conference Series on Public Policy, vol. 25, pp. 11–44.

Prescott, E. C. and Rios-Rull, J. V. (1988) 'Classical Competitive Analysis in a Growth Economy with Search', Federal Reserve Bank of Minneapolis Working Paper no 329.

Prescott, E. C. and Townsend, R. M. (1984) 'Pareto Optima and Competitive Equilibria with Adverse Selection and Moral Hazard', *Econometrics*, vol. 52, pp. 21–45.
Rogerson, R. (1987) 'Indivisible Labor and the Business Cycle: the Case of Heterogeneous Households', manuscript, University of Rochester and Southern Illinois University.
Rogerson, R. (1988) 'Indivisible Labor, Lotteries, and Equilibrium', *Journal of Monetary Economics*, vol. 21, pp. 3–16.
Sargent, T. J. (1979) *Macroeconomic Theory* (New York: Academic Press) pp. 370–9.
Solow, R. M. (1957) 'Technical Change and the Aggregate Production Function', *Review of Economics and Statistics*, vol. 39, pp. 312–20.
Uhlig, H. (1987) 'A Law of Large Numbers for Large Economies', Federal Reserve Bank of Minneapolis Working Paper no 342.

# Comment

## Jean-Paul Fitoussi
OFCE, PARIS, FRANCE

First of all I have to say this is a brilliant paper which accomplishes the implementation of the research programme enunciated by Lucas in building mechanical analogs of the economy able to generate time-series which mimic the behaviour of actual series – a kind of Turing machine as Velupillai and I have said in a review article about a book of Lucas.

Here in this paper the exercise is very brilliant and the theoretical technology is very impressive, building a computable general equilibrium structure in which the hours of plant operations and the numbers of employees can be varied. But I got the impression that the theory behind this theoretical structure is much less impressive and gives a strong impression of '*déjà vu*', already seen.

There is a well-defined optimisation problem for the consumer. This problem is the constant elasticity of substitution utility function, a well-defined technology which is captured by a constant elasticity of substitution production function between two factors. One is a composite factor – that is, output obtained out of hours of work and capital – and the other is inventories and this is a Cobb-Douglas production function between output and capital with unit elasticity of substitution which captures the constant share property of the US economy.

In this setting persistent stochastic technology shocks drive the system. This is an expression of what is now called in the USA the 'unit root revolution' and the persistence is also included in the fact that it takes time to build.

So, out of this model the typical question is why are large movements in the time allocated to market activity? Why are the large movements in the time allocated to market activity and little associated movements in the real wage?

Phrased differently, the question is the Keynesian problem: why are there such huge variations in employment with so little variation in the real wage?

The neoclassical answer relies on the strong intertemporal substitu-

128

tion effect, the Keynesian one on some sort of price inflexibility, but both are able to explain the same set of facts. That is the observational equivalence proposition.

So the fact that the data generated by the model mimic the actual data is not impressive – especially as both explanations need *ad hoc* assumptions. I have nothing against *ad hoc* assumptions. I think that one cannot have any model of the economy without *ad hoc* assumptions. And we know from general equilibrium theory and the Sonnenschein–Debreu results, that you cannot have well-defined aggregate functions out of microeconomics foundation.

So they must have some *ad hoc* assumptions in their models.

But now what we have to decide is: what *ad hoc*ery is more acceptable than the other?

In this approach the propagation mechanism is intertemporal substitution in employment. To get large efficient movements in labour input in response to such small changes in technology requires easy substitutability of labour over time.

The macromodel requires an elasticity of at least 1 or 2, but the elasticity estimated from microdata is extremely low.

How to reconcile that is the main attempt of the paper.

There has been an earlier attempt by Rogerson and Hansen which starts with the observation that there may be important non-convexities, such as transportation cost, in the labour-supply decision.

The paper by Kydland and Prescott starts with an objection to the former attempt – they introduce heterogeneity in the individual cost of going to work, in the form of a randomly distributed variable both over time and over agents.

But notice here that if the distribution is not random hysteresis effects will result.

A second objection comes to mind: fixed costs of moving between sectors should equally affect both micro and macro estimates of labour-supply elasticity.

It is not correct to say that by micro evidence there are two preference parameters since microestimates are also affected by fixed costs.

Although non-convexity might be part of the explanation of elastic labour supply Kydland and Prescott do not reconcile micro and macro evidence. This point may be unfair.

I am not sure I have really understood Kydland and Prescott's explanation, but I do not see how these particular amendments reconcile the two different sets of evidence.

Another point linked to that is the fact that in Kydland and Prescott's steady state the cost of moving people is zero, because employment does not change. So you have a very peculiar labour market where the turnover rate is zero. Otherwise, if the turnover rate is not zero you would have a sizeable cost of moving people, whatever the state.

The second question to link to the particular technology Kydland and Prescott are using is the distinction between hours and men. The hours worked correspond to the operating hours of the plant. What if they are different – i.e. what if you have shift work; what also if the cost of operating a plant increases with the time a plant is operated? For example you can have quicker depreciation of fixed capital because the capital is used more intensively.

The second broad point is connected with calibration. The theory is supposed to be more persuasive if the model economy is not constructed to fit cyclical fact, that is parametrised on the basis of microeconomic information and the economy long-run property. If I understood well it seems to me that there is a lot of tautology in the way the exercise is implemented because the authors have very few microinformations and the calibration is made mainly out of the long-run property of the actual time-series.

If the microeconomic informations were correct the aggregation problem remains.

I do not see how the authors can deduce such behaviour from a microeconomic foundation without having *ad hoc* assumptions.

Having said that, I have to confess that I am full of admiration of the model that has been presented.

I have no strong inside criticism, just an outside one because I am puzzled by the moral implications of this kind of model which denies the fact of, say, 'involuntary unemployment', and which seems to be devised to fit the US data but does not seem at all able to fit the European data on unemployment where you have much less variability in output and in unemployment and long persistence of a high rate of unemployment which by all means seems to be involuntary.

# Comment

Edmund Phelps
COLUMBIA UNIVERSITY, NEW YORK

Well! It is always a pleasure to read and discuss a paper by Kydland and Prescott. This paper seems an especially helpful one for understanding the theory that it depends upon.

The last time I discussed a paper theirs was the Lucas and Prescott paper on the island paradigm. I was fortunate enough to find a mistake so I would have something to say. This time I did not find a mistake.

What I would like to discuss is the critical business of the merits and demerits of the broad theory that the paper employes and seeks to support. That theory, of course, is what may be called the neoclassical non-monetary theory of employment fluctuations. I think it is justly credited to people in Minnesota and Rochester.

It is neoclassical since it postulates full or complete information on the part of the agents as well as correct expectations.

By contrast the new-classical theory, which derives from some rather Keynesian models in the microeconomic foundations volume, postulated un-shared information, asymmetric information. And of course that new-classical theory was also largely monetary in emphasis.

This non-monetary theory is accurately called neo-neoclassical I suppose, since it is stochastic. That is important, but not crucial, for one reason, namely that some disturbances are potentiated by the agents' beliefs, or understanding, that these disturbances are random and therefore temporary. If they were thought to be permanent they would lose some or all of their punch.

The stochastic feature is crucial, of course, if we want to regard the problem for analysis as one of accounting for certain moments of some theoretical and empirical probability distributions.

I must say this is one respect in which my own thinking differs a little bit from the neoclassical way of thinking: that the problem is to explain the different moments of a probability distribution. I seem to find myself thinking more in historical terms, maybe I am getting old.

The basic *Gestalt* of the theory is that fluctuations of the real wage, of the real interest rate, and of real wealth around their trend paths drive the economy left and right along its labour-supply function.

Now, the labour market clears so that employment is equal to the amount of the labour supplied, and rational expectations prevail so that the economy is driven by fundamentals rather than by fads and bubbles, and so forth.

I want to make three points now about this kind of non-monetary theory – this neoclassical and neo-neoclassical non-monetary theory.

First, I am sceptical about all the three features of that *Gestalt*. I do not think that the labour supply is very sensitive to those incentives: real wages, real interest rates, etc. I also do not think that the labour market clears in any interesting or relevant sense. Of course I know that you can always sell out, but that seems to me to be somehow beside the point. I do not think that the economy is only driven by the fundamentals. But I am not the only one, Fitoussi is another one. There are a lot of us who do not believe in those kinds of things and there are a lot of other perfectly respectable and admirable economists, such as Kydland and Prescott, who do believe in those things. So the question arises, on whom falls the burden of proof? I guess that one goes into conferences just to see where the burden of proof is moving. I hope it is not moving in my direction, but I sometimes have the feeling that it is!

The second point I want to make needs a little bit of development. When Kydland and Prescott say that 70 per cent of the fluctuations in employment or hours, I am not sure which, are due to fluctuations in the Solow technology level they are referring of course to a theoretical economy of their devising in which the numerical parameters have been chosen to make it fit the American economy as well as it can. We do not know that this theory is even close to being the best theory for the American economy. There is, for example, another sort of non-monetary theory, I call it the structuralist non-monetary theory.

This structuralist non-monetary theory embraces at least two different kinds of models. One of them is the incentive wage theory of employment (or the efficiency wage theory of employment).

The efficiency wage model, under certain restrictions, can be illustrated by Figure 5.1.

We have a labour-supply function of the Walrasian Marshallian type which I take to be rather inelastic with respect to anything which is going to come up this morning. And then there is this interesting thing which goes by many names which I usually call the equilibrium locus: it is the locus of potential equilibrium points.

Oswald and Blanchflower called it the wage locus. This apparatus,

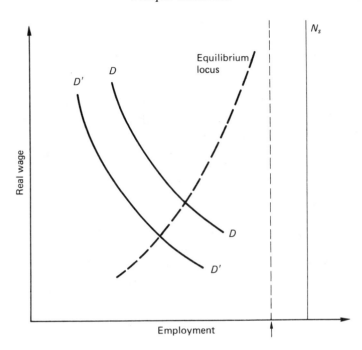

*Figure 5.1* Efficiency wage model

of course, has many fathers. Without realising it I suppose that the paper I wrote in 1968 was about a point on that locus. I did not entertain the possibility of real shocks that would possibly have moved the natural rate around. You might say that this is the locus of possible natural rates. Which one is the actual natural rate depends upon the demand – real demand price for labour.

If there is a downward shift in the real demand price for labour due, for instance, to a productivity shock, the result is a fall in the real wage and an important fall in employment while the amount of labour supply does not necessarily change at all – and may change very little.

Now it seems to me that if we take this model as a model for discussion we find that Kydland and Prescott's theory misunderstands the equilibrium motion to be the supply curve.

The data in the real world are data drawn up by the demand curve and equilibrium locus, but in their theory there is no equilibrium locus. There is only the supply curve and the authors impute to the supply curve this big slope which rightly belongs to the equilibrium locus and not to the supply curve.

I do want to emphasise that that is only one model within the family of the structuralist non-monetary theory of employment fluctuations.

I come now briefly to my third point. The sort of structuralist theory that I have in mind suggests that there are myriads of sources of fluctuations in labour demand: budgetary deficits, government purchases, consumer time preference, overseas events, as well as technical change. All of these can shift the aggregate demand for labour curve. While in their admirably stripped-down model it is hard for anything but the technology level, the Solow parameter, to shift that.

The message of their paper seems to be, and maybe it is not intended to be in this way, that we can forget most of these factors that I just mentioned (current spending, time preference, terms of trade, etc.) because 70 per cent or so of the fluctuation in which we are interested is attributable to fluctuations in these mysterious Solow parameters.

I have not completely understood it but I am troubled by it and my mind keeps on taking up an image of a scientist – an acoustical engineer let's say – who sets up his instruments in Carnegie Hall and after a year or so of reading the output of his instruments he reports that 70 per cent of the variation in the decibel reading is due to the animals outside on Seventh Avenue and to the airplanes overhead and to the subway train.

That may be so, it may be that 70 per cent of the fluctuations in Carnegie Hall are due to those outside factors. But I am not interested in those exogenous outside factors. I want to know about the disturbances to the decibel readings that are caused by the physical performances going on in the hall. Why is that?

One reason. I suppose, is that the most dramatic disturbances are those going on inside the hall. The performances going on in Carnegie Hall are man-made; we can control those disturbances. Likewise we can do something about fiscal policy, government expenditure, etc.

So it is particularly that sort of disturbance in which I am interested. Therefore I want a theory that is good at capturing the effects of disturbances, etc. For that reason I still feel quite frustrated or dissatisfied with the neoclassical non-monetary theory.

Like Jean-Paul Fitoussi I am full of admiration for the capital work which it implies.

# 6 Cycles and Non-Stationary Equilibrium Search[1]

Chaim Fershtman   and   Arthur Fishman
TEL AVIV UNIVERSITY     TEL AVIV UNIVERSITY
ISRAEL                  ISRAEL

## INTRODUCTION

There has never been agreement among economists regarding the causes of cycles and fluctuations in economic activity. There can be little doubt that extraneous shocks to the economy are a major source of such fluctuations. Nevertheless, in our view, it is important to have models in which cyclic activity arises as an inherent property of the equilibrium interaction between economic agents at the micro level. More specifically, we would like to know if it is possible that despite the absence of any shocks, a stationary environment exhibits a non-stationary time-path as a consequence of the dynamic strategic interaction between the economic actors.

The persistence of endogenously determined oscillations in one market creates a non-stationary environment in related markets which may, in principle, respond by exhibiting cyclic behaviour of their own. Moreover, the transmission of fluctuation from one market to another may generate cyclic behaviour of the second market which persists long after the initial stimulus is gone, as has been shown, for example, by Rotemberg and Saloner (1986). Thus, using McCall's terminology (this volume), once one market 'vibrates' endogenously, the interrelationship between markets may transmit this vibration across the economy, leading to cyclical activity at the aggregate level. This line of reasoning is particularly appealing when the oscillation originates in a market whose effect on and ability to transmit vibrations to other markets is especially significant. An obvious candidate is the labour market.

Previous modelling efforts aimed at achieving endogenous fluctuations of the type discussed above have emphasised the role of self-fulfilling prophecies. A brief and highly selective discussion of this literature is presented in section 2. Our focus in the remainder of the paper will be to present an example of an explicitly dynamic search equilibrium in an imperfect labour market in which workers search for profitable employment over time. The equilibrium displays cyclic patterns in both wage offers and the acceptance rate of workers (i.e. the incidence of unemployment). As will be shown, depending on the parameters of the model, in many cases the only equilibria consistent with wage dispersion in the model are cyclical. Thus the incidence of wage and employment cycles in our model are an inherent feature of the intertemporal optimisation of agents and not a mere consequence of arbitrary, self-fulfilling expectations.

The remainder of the paper is organised as follows. Section 2 presents a brief and non-comprehensive look at a class of models exhibiting endogenous cyclical patterns as a consequence of self-fulfilling beliefs. Section 3 discusses the general properties of non-stationary search equilibrium models. In section 4 we discuss a simple example of a cyclic search equilibrium in which cyclic behaviour is a consequence of arbitrary, self-fulfilling beliefs. In section 5 we demonstrate our main claim by deriving a cyclical search equilibrium in which the periodic fluctuations in wages and employment are a necessary and inherent feature of the dynamic interaction between firms and workers.

## 2   CYCLES WITH SELF-FULFILLING PROPHECIES

In this section we discuss models of endogenous business cycles which are a consequence of self-fulfilling expectations. In models of this type, agents maintain essentially arbitrary but commonly shared expectations about the future course of the economy and, based on these expectations, take individually rational actions which in the aggregate serve to fulfil these expectations. Azariadis (1981), Cass and Shell (1983), Grandmont (1983) and Farmer and Woodford (1984), among others, demonstrate the existence of such equilibria in overlapping generations models.

Diamond (1982) derives such equilibria in the context of a matching model. Production opportunities arrive stochastically and are distinguished by different production costs. Potential trading partners arrive stochastically at a rate which is positively related to aggregate production in the economy. A successful trade is concluded only if one's partner has output in inventory. As the profitability of any particular project increases the more quickly a trade can be successfully completed, it follows that actual aggregate activity is determined by expectations about its extent. Diamond and Fudenberg (1986) have shown that this scheme can be extended to generate cyclic activity when traders correctly anticipate that the economy will alternate between optimistic ('boom') and pessimistic ('decline') phases. In a related vein, Schleifer (1986) analyses a model in which technological improvements arrive at a constant rate but in some equilibria are only implemented cyclically. The inventor of a new technology can earn temporary excess profit from its implementation but the entry of imitators eventually eliminates excess profits. For this reason, owners of new technologies would like to receive their profits when they are the highest, i.e., when aggregate activity is at its peak. Expectations about the arrival of booms therefore help to determine whether firms are willing to postpone innovation until the arrival of a boom. If all potential innovators expect a boom only in the distant future, they may choose to delay implementation until the expected date of the boom. The economy then stays in a slump until all inventors innovate simultaneously and fulfil their expectation of a boom.

## 3 GENERAL ATTRIBUTES OF NON-STATIONARY SEARCH EQUILIBRIA

Consider a market in which consumers are imperfectly informed about the prices firms charge and thus engage in costly search. Given a search technology $Z$ and the information they have regarding the current and future distributions of prices they decide on the optimal search rule. This search rule can determine the type or intensity of search they adopt at each period and the optimal stopping rule. In equilibrium the distribution of prices at every period is a result of profit maximisation by firms given the consumers' search rule.

The search technology, $Z$, can, for example, be sequential, in which case only one price quotation can be bought at each period (e.g. McCall, 1970); noisy (Burdett, and Judd, 1983), in which case there is an exogenously given probability that a sample contains more than one price quotation; or a combination of FSS and sequential search such that consumers decide at each period on the number of price quotations they would like to buy (Morgan and Manning, 1982, 1985).

The standard approach of equilibrium search theory (e.g. Mac-Minn, 1980; Reinganum, 1979; Rob, 1985; Burdett and Judd, 1983) is to derive a stationary (possibly degenerate) price or wage distribution which represents an optimal response by sellers (employers) and is consistent with the optimal search of buyers (workers), given the search technology. In general, however, there is no reason to believe that sellers are committed to prices they have posted in the past. Firms can change prices over time which, in principle, may lead to non-stationary price distributions. Once the assumption of stationarity is dropped, the consumers' decision problem is much more complex because the optimal search rule now account for future changes in the distribution of prices.

For example, consider the case in which risk-neutral consumers search sequentially, sampling a single price at each period. At period $t$, they anticipate that the average market price at $t+1$ is $Ep_{t+1}$. This information helps determine their reservation price at $t$. Specifically, they will reject a price exceeding:

$$(Ep_{t+1} + c)(1 + r)$$

where $r \geq 0$ is the rate of time preference and $c > 0$ is the cost of observing a price. If the price distribution is stationary, $Ep_t$ is constant so that the reservation price is constant as well. In a non-stationary environment, however, consumers need to consider not just period $t + 1$ but also the price distribution at all future periods. Thus the reservation price at period $t$, denoted $\bar{p}_t$, satisfies the following condition:

$$\bar{p}_t \leq \min_{\tau > t} (Ep_\tau + c)(1 + r)^{\tau - t} \tag{1}$$

If this condition does not hold there is a period $\tau$ such that instead of paying $\bar{p}_t$ at period $t$ the consumer, will, on the average, be better off by deferring search until period $\tau$.

When the search technology allows consumers determine the number of price quotations they purchase every period, their reaction to a non-stationary price distribution can be even more complex. Specifically, they might wish to intensify their search in particular periods when future price distributions are likely to be less favourable. In this case, firms must account for the changes in consumers' reservation prices and search intensities along time when determining prices at each period.

We now provide two examples of cyclical search equilibria. The first is a simple example in which the cycles are a result of non-stationary consumers' expectations. In the second example we will analyse a job market in which cycles are determined endogenously as a result of the dynamic interaction between workers and firms.

## 4  AN EXAMPLE OF A SIMPLE CYCLIC SEARCH EQUILIBRIUM

A cyclic search equilibrium can be obtained very easily in the sequential search setting. Consider, for example, the problem examined by Diamond (1971). He showed that if all consumers have a positive search cost, and the search technology is sequential, the only equilibrium is that in which all firms charge the monopoly price. By allowing for non-stationarity, however, we can easily construct cyclic equilibria in a dynamic setting.

Consider a market consisting of a continuum of identical, infinitely lived risk-neutral consumers and a continuum of infinitely lived, identical, profit-maximising firms.

At each period a new cohort of consumers enters the market, each of whom wishes to buy exactly one unit at a price not exceeding $p^*$. In each period, a consumer in the market may solicit at most one price from a randomly selected firm at a cost of $c > 0$. Upon purchasing his unit, he leaves the market forever. Consumers minimise the expected cost of purchasing a unit, including the price paid and search costs (for simplicity, ignore discounting). We claim that the following dynamic price path is an equilibrium.

At each even period $t$ all firms charge the monopolistic price $p^*$ and at every odd period, all firms charge $\hat{p} > p^*$. Consumers adopt the following search rule. They search only in even periods in which their reservation price is $p^*$. At odd periods they are out of the market. Thus consumers entering at even periods solicit a price and buy immediately. Consumers entering at odd periods only solicit a price in the following period, at which time they buy at $p^*$.

The above is an equilibrium as no firm or consumer can benefit by changing its behaviour. The proof of this claim is based on our assumption of an infinite number of firms and agents; as no firm can on its own cause a change in the price distribution, it cannot induce consumers to search at odd periods. Thus lowering the price at that period will not increase profits.

The preceding equilibrium is cyclic and exhibits non-stationary patterns both in prices and in the quantity sold. It is clear from our construction that we can construct other cycles in a similar fashion.

This type of cyclic equilibrium is similar to the type of cycles described in section 2. If all consumers expect that at odd periods all firms charge $\hat{p}$, then it is indeed equilibrium behaviour on the part of firms to charge this price. Moreover, non-cyclical equilibria exist as well. If all consumers expect $p^*$ at each period, this stationary price path is an equilibrium. Thus the driving force behind these cyclic equilibria is the essentially arbitrary expectations of consumers. This however, is not the only way to achieve cycles in a search equilibrium. Our objective in the next section is to illustrate cyclic equilibria in which the price distribution at two consecutive periods *cannot* be identical, i.e. given an equilibrium price distribution at period $t$, this price distribution is never an equilibrium at period $t-1$. Thus in this case, non-stationarity is an inherent feature of the model and not just an outcome of choosing expectations in a particular way.

## 5 A MODEL OF CYCLICAL JOB SEARCH

In this section we present a simple model of job search which is based on our previous paper (Fershtman and Fishman, 1989).

In each period a new cohort of identical, infinitely lived workers enters the labour market. The reservation wage of each worker is $w^*$ such that no one accepts a job that pays less than $w^*$. There is an infinite number of firms who all have the same technology. By employing a worker for one period, $\lambda$ units of a product x are produced which can be sold at a price $P_x$. Thus the per-period profits of the firm from hiring a worker at a salary $w$ is $\pi(w) = \lambda P_x - w$.

Firms may offer different wages and we assume that workers are imperfectly informed. They know the distribution of wages but do not know the wage offered by each firm. Once a worker accepts a job offer with a wage of $w$ he continues to receive this wage throughout his life. Thus, we exclude on-the-job search and moreover do not allow the worker to resign his job and search for another job. Letting $r > 0$ be the common discount factor, the worker's life time income is

$I(w) = w/r(1 + r)^t$ where $t$ is the period in which the worker accepts the employment.

We assume that workers wish to maximise their discounted lifetime income such that they are indifferent between accepting an offer of $\delta w$ today and an offer of $w$ in the next period when $\delta = \dfrac{1}{1+r}$.

We let $\alpha > 0$ denote the measure of new workers per firm entering the market at every period. Since workers do not necessarily accept an offer in their first period in the market, the unemployed might accumulate. Thus, let $\alpha_t \geq \alpha$ be the measure of workers per firm at period $t$. Since all workers are identical, there is no difference between a worker who just entered the market and one who entered several periods ago.

Let $G_t(w)$ be the – possibly degenerate – distribution of wages at period $t$. Workers know this sequence of distributions and search over time so as to find the wage that maximises their discounted lifetime income.

We assume that the search technology is a combination of FSS and sequential technologies. The model is essentially a dynamic extension of the model studied by Burdett and Judd (1983). At every period each worker may solicit any number of job offers at a constant cost of $c > 0$ per offer. All the job offers demanded at period $t$ are received simultaneously. Workers observe these job offers and then decide whether to accept one of them or to continue to search at the next period.

Firms are not committed to any job offer for more than one period. In particular we allow firms to change the wage they offer every period.

For convenience of the exposition, we will assume there is a terminal period $T > 1$ at which employment may be accepted (but jobs accepted prior to or at $T$ pay $w$ forever). Our analysis obtains without change for an infinite horizon as well, however.

We let $q_t^n$ be the probability that a randomly selected worker observes $n$ wage quotations at period $t$. The workers' behaviour at period $t$ is thus summarised by

$$(< q_t^n > \overset{\infty}{n}=0, \bar{w}_t^n )$$

where $\bar{w}_t^n$ is the reservation price of a worker who observes $n$ wage offers at period $t$.

Note especially, that we do not exclude the possibility that $n = 0$.

That is to say, workers may decide not to search at all at any period. Clearly, when the wage distribution is stationary such behaviour cannot occur in equilibrium as workers are impatient. When the wage distribution is non-stationary, however, one can imagine a situation in which workers defer costly search in anticipation of more favourable wage offers in future periods.

We define equilibrium as the following tuple:

$$< \alpha_t, < q_t^n > n \overset{\infty}{=} 0, \bar{w}_t, G_t(w) > \underset{t=1}{T}$$

such that:

(i) At every period $t$, given $(\alpha_t, < q_t^n > n \overset{\infty}{=} 0, \bar{w}_t)$ each firm maximises its profits by offering a wage in the support of $G_t(w)$. Moreover every wage in the support of $G_t(w)$ yields the same pay-off and firms cannot gain by deviating and offering a wage outside the support of $G_t(w)$.

(ii) For every $t$, given the sequence of distributions, $G_t(w)$, $G_{t+1}(w)$, . . ., $(< q^n > n \overset{\infty}{=} 0, \bar{w}_t)$ is consistent with optimal search behaviour of workers.

A *non-stationary dynamic search equilibrium* is an equilibrium that has the property: $G_{t_1}(w) \neq G_{t_2}(w)$ for some $t_1$, $t_2 \leqslant T$.

A *cyclical dynamic search equilibrium* is a non-stationary equilibrium for which $G_t(w) = G_{t+z}(w)$ for some given integer $z$.

Note that the above definitions are given in terms of the wage distributions. One can, however, also think in terms of employment cycles. In the analysis that follows we show how the two types of non-stationarities are related.

We analyse the model by backward induction, i.e. analysing the terminal period, $T$, and then continuing backwards. The analysis of the last period is identical to the analysis of single period non-sequential search which was solved by Burdett and Judd (1983).[2] They showed that there are one, two or three market equilibria; one monopoly wage equilibrium and zero, one or two dispersed wage equilibria. In any dispersed price equilibrium, a proportion $1 > q > 0$ of buyers observe only one price while the proportion $1 - q$ observe two prices.

Since firms are indifferent between offering $w^*$ or any other wage in the support of $G_T(w)$, the equal profit condition is:

$$(P_x \lambda - w^*)q = (P_x \lambda - w)[q + 2(1 - q)G_T(w)] \quad (2)$$

Therefore

$$G_T(w) = \begin{cases} 0 & \text{if } w \leq w^* \\ \dfrac{q(w - w^*)}{(P_x \lambda - w)2(1 - q)} & \text{if } w^* < w < \bar{w} \\ 1 & \text{if } w \geq \bar{w} \end{cases} \quad (3)$$

where

$$\bar{w} = \frac{qw^* + P_x \lambda 2(1 - q)}{2 - q} \quad (4)$$

Let $v(w^*, q)$ be the expected difference between the income of a worker who searches once and a consumer who searches twice. At the last period, workers simply wish to maximise their wage. Thus:

$$V(w^*, q) = 2 \int_{w^*}^{\bar{w}} wG_T(w) \, dG_T(w) - \int_{w^*}^{\bar{w}} wdG_T(w) \quad (5)$$

In equilibrium, workers are indifferent between sampling once and sampling twice. Thus at equilibrium

$$V(w^*, q) = c \quad (6)$$

Substituting (3) in (5), integrating by parts and solving the integrals gives:

$$\begin{aligned} V(q, w^*) = \tau \cdot \{w^* - \bar{w} &+ (\ln(r - \bar{w}) - \ln(r - w^*)) \\ &(w^* - r + 2\tau r - 2\tau w^*) \\ &+ \frac{\tau}{r - \bar{w}} (\bar{w}^2 + 2w^*r + w^{2*}) - \frac{2\tau w^* r}{r - w^*} \\ &+ 2\tau w^* - 2\tau\bar{w}\} \end{aligned} \quad (7)$$

where $\tau = \dfrac{q}{2(1 - q)}$.

Numerical analysis reveals that $V(q, w^*)$ is a bell-shaped function of $q$, attaining a unique maximum at some $q^*$, $0 < q^* < 1$, and that

$V(q, w^*) \to 0$ as $q \to 1$ and as $q \to 0$. Thus there exists $c^* > 0$ such that:

1. If $c < c^*$, there exist two wage dispersion equilibria corresponding to the two values of $q$ for which $V(q, w^*) = c$.
2. If $c = c^*$, $G_T^*(w)$ is uniquely determined.
3. If $c > c^*$, no wage dispersion equilibrium exists. In this case the unique equilibrium is the single wage (Diamond) equilibrium, $w^*$.

It can also be shown that $V(q, w^*)$ is shifted down by an increase in $w^*$. This important property of $V(q, w^*)$ will be subsequently exploited to derive the cyclical equilibrium.

Let $E_T$ denote the mean of $G_T$. If $c < c^*$, there will exist two values of $E_T$, one corresponding to each equilibrium value of $q$. Our analysis will not be based on a specific choice between these two equilibria.

Now consider a worker in the market at $T-1$. As discussed in section 3, his reservation wage is not exogenous but must account for the possibility of further search in the last period. Specifically, his expected pay-off from searching again in the following period is $\delta\left\{\dfrac{E_T}{r} c\right\}$. Thus a wage $w$ is accepted at $T-1$ if and only if $\dfrac{w}{r} \geq \delta\left\{\dfrac{E_T}{r} - c\right\}$, i.e. iff $w \geq \delta\{E_T - cr\}$. This yields the reservation wage at period $T - 1$:

$$\bar{w}_{T-1} = \max\left\{w^*, \delta(E_T - cr)\right\} \tag{8}$$

There are three possibilities: First, if $\delta(E_T - cr) \leq w^*$, $\bar{w}_{T-1} = w^*$. In this case, wages are distributed identically at $T - 1$ and $T$. In fact, in this case prices are distributed identically at each period and the equilibrium is stationary.

A second possibility is that $w^* < \delta(E_T - cr)$. In this case, $\bar{w}_{T-1} > w^*$ and $G_{T-1} \neq G_T$. $G_{T-1}$ is non-degenerate if there exists $q_{T-1}$ such that $V(\bar{w}_{T-1}, q_{T-1}) \geq 0$. $G_{T-1}$ is constructed analogously to $G_T$ by substituting $\bar{w}_{T-1}$ for $w^*$. It is obvious that in this case the expected wage at $T - 1$, $E_{T-1} > E_T$; wages decline from $T - 1$ to $T$. However, it is also possible that $G_{T-1}$ is degenerate although $G^*$ is not.

To see why, recall that an increase in the reservation price shifts the function $V(w, q)$ down. Thus it is possible that there exist $q_T$ such that $V(w^*, q_T) \geq c$ but $V(\bar{w}_{T-1}, q) < c$ for all $q \in [0, 1]$. When this is the case, what is the equilibrium wage configuration at $T - 1$? Clearly each employer offers $\tilde{w}_{T-1}$. None will offer more than this because every worker receiving this offer accepts it. It would then seem that all workers in the labour market at $T - 1$ accept work at the wage $\tilde{w}_{T-1}$. This is not the case, however. It is true that a worker who receives an offer of $\tilde{w}_{T-1}$ accepts it. However, he can increase his expected pay-off by not looking for work at $T - 1$. The expected return from soliciting a wage at $T - 1$ is $\dfrac{\tilde{w}_{T-1}}{r} - c$. The expected return of a worker who is 'voluntarily unemployed' at $T - 1$ and seeks employment at $T$ is $\dfrac{\tilde{w}_{T-1}}{r}$. Thus all workers in the market at $T - 1$ remain unemployed and only accept a job in the following period; there is unemployment at $T - 1$ and a 'boom' in hiring and production at $T$.

To summarise, if there is wage dispersion at $T$ the following possibilities exist at $T - 1$:

1. Wages are identically distributed at $T - 1$ and $T$ and there is full employment at each period.
2. Wages are distributed differently at $T - 1$ and $T$, the mean wage is greater at $T - 1$ and there is full employment at each period.
3. At $T - 1$ all employers offer the same wage, all unemployed workers in the market at $T - 1$ remain unemployed and there is a boom in hiring and production at $T$.

It is clear that the different wage and employment patterns described above are not confined to the last two periods but will in general occur throughout the market's horizon. This suggests the existence of cyclic equilibria. Such an equilibrium is presented in Table 6.1.

The patterns of equilibrium wages and unemployment specified in Table 6.1 are illustrated in Figures 6.1, 6.2 and 6.3

Hiring occurs only at periods 1, 7, 12 and 17. These are the cyclic boom periods at which all unemployed workers in the market seek and accept jobs. During boom periods, wages are dispersed across employers. Boom periods are separated by spells of unemployment which endure for five periods. At each of these periods, unemployed workers in the market do not engage in costly job search and hence remain unemployed. All employers offer the same wage which is the

*Table 6.1*  Simulation of cycles in the labour market ($w^* = 0.0$   $c = 5.0$   $r = 0.2$)

| t | 1 | 2 | 3 | 4 | 5 | 6 | 7 | 8 | 9 | 10 | 11 | 12 | 13 | 14 | 15 | 16 | 17 |
|---|---|---|---|---|---|---|---|---|---|----|----|----|----|----|----|----|----|
| $Ew$ | 1.98 | 0.40 | 0.48 | 0.58 | 0.70 | 0.83 | 2.0 | 0.46 | 0.55 | 0.66 | 0.79 | 1.95 | 0.41 | 0.49 | 0.59 | 0.70 | 1.85 |
| $\bar{w}$ | 7.94 | 0.4 | 0.48 | 0.58 | 0.70 | 0.83 | 7.86 | 0.46 | 0.55 | 0.66 | 0.79 | 8.07 | 0.41 | 0.49 | 0.59 | 0.70 | 8.5 |
| $\tilde{w}$ | 0.33 | 0.4 | 0.48 | 0.58 | 0.70 | 0.83 | 0.38 | 0.46 | 0.55 | 0.66 | 0.79 | 0.34 | 0.41 | 0.49 | 0.59 | 0.70 | 0.0 |
| $U$ | 0.0 | $\alpha$ | $2\alpha$ | $3\alpha$ | $4\alpha$ | $5\alpha$ | 0.0 | $\alpha$ | $2\alpha$ | $3\alpha$ | $4\alpha$ | 0.0 | $\alpha$ | $2\alpha$ | $3\alpha$ | $4\alpha$ | 0.0 |

*Notes*:

$Ew$ -  Average wage

$\bar{w}$  -  Maximum wage offered in the market

$\tilde{w}$  -  Reservation wage

$U$  -  Unemployment

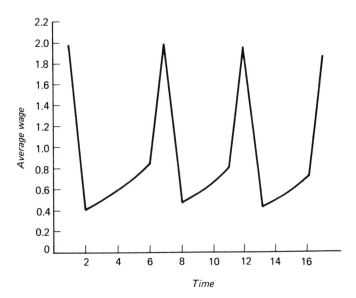

*Figure 6.1*   Equilibrium wage cycle

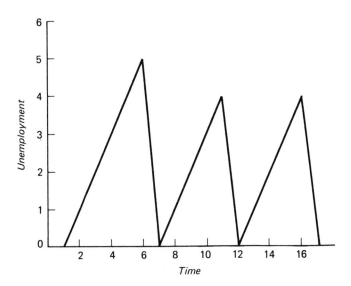

*Figure 6.2*   Unemployment wage cycle

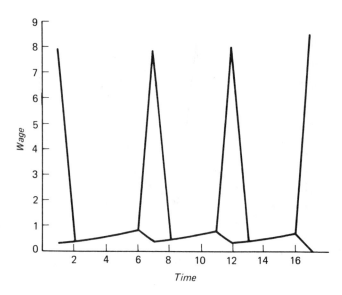

*Figure 6.3* Equilibrium wage range

reservation price of a worker whose search cost is sunk. That is, if an unemployed worker were to seek employment, s/he would be guaranteed to find an acceptable wage. In equilibrium, however, the time-pattern of wages is such that it is unprofitable for her to invest in job search at any time other than a boom. It is especially interesting that the lowest wages are charged at boom periods, during which the reservation wage is at a minimum. This is because the average wage is at its peak; workers invest in search costs in anticipation of a high wage but are willing to settle for a very low wage once this cost has been sunk.

In fact, it is precisely because the reservation wage is 'too high' during the unemployment spell that wage dispersion is absent; when $\bar{w}$ is too high, the peak of the $V(\ )$ function lies below $c$. The level of the reservation wage is determined by the proximity to the next boom period. Thus $\bar{w}$ is at its peak one period preceding the boom and at its minimum during the boom period, at which time the arrival of the next boom is furthest away. The interval between booms (the duration of the unemployment spell) is determined so that the reservation wage at the boom periods is small enough to support dispersion and, as a consequence, a high average wage.

It should be clear from the preceding discussion that the existence of the cyclic equilibrium is not limited to a finite horizon but may continue to cycle for ever. The cyclic pattern is not a consequence of an arbitrary, self-fulfilling expectation but is determined solely by the parameters of the model: the discount rate, the search cost, the reservation wage, $w^*$, and the technology.

### Notes

1. This paper was prepared for the IEA Conference on 'Recent Developments in Business Cycles Theory – Methods and Empirical Applications' 7–11 June 1989, Copenhagen.
2. The following formulae differ slightly from those of Burdett and Judd since they study price, rather than wage dispersion.

### References

Azariadis, Costas (1981) 'Self-Fulfilling Prophesies', *Journal of Economic Theory*, vol. 25, pp. 380–96.

Burdett, K. and Judd, K. (1983) 'Equilibrium Price Dispersion', *Econometrica*, vol. 51, pp. 955–69.

Cass, David and Shell, Karl (1983) 'Do Sunspots Matter?', *Journal of Political Economy*, vol. 91, pp. 193–227.

Diamond, Peter A. (1971) 'A Model of Price Adjustment', *Journal of Economic Theory*, vol. 3, pp. 156–168.

Diamond, Peter A. (1982) 'Aggregate Demand Management in Search Equilibrium', *Journal of Political Economy*, vol. 90, pp. 881–94.

Diamond, Peter A. and Fudenberg, Drew (1986) 'Rational Expectations Business Cycles in Search Equilibrium', mimeo.

Farmer, Roger and Woodford, Michael (1984) 'Self-Fulfilling Prophecies and the Business Cycle', University of Pennsylvania, unpublished (April).

Fershtman, C. and Fishman, A. (1989) 'Price Cycles and Booms: Dynamic Search Equilibrium', mimeo.

Grandmont, J. M. (1983) 'Endogenous Competitive Business Cycles', Discussion Paper no 8316, CEPREMAP.

Manning, R. and Morgan, P. (1982) 'Search and Consumer Theory', *Review of Economic Studies*, vol. 49, pp. 203–16.

McCall, J. J. (1970) 'Economics of Information and Job Search', *Quarterly Journal of Economics*, vol. 84, pp. 113–26.

MacMinn, R. D. (1980) 'Search and Market Equilibrium', *Journal of Political Economy*, vol. 88, pp. 308–15.

Morgan, P. and Manning, R. (1985) 'Optimal Search', *Econometrica*, vol. 53, pp. 923–44.

Reinganum, J. F. (1979) 'A Simple Model of Equilibrium Price Dispersion', *Journal of Political Economy*, vol. 87, pp. 851–8.

Rob, R. (1985) 'Equilibrium Price Distribution', *Review of Economic Studies* pp. 487–504.

Rotemberg, J. J. and Saloner, G. (1986) 'A Supergame – Theoretic Model of Price Wars During Booms', *American Economic Review*, vol. 76, no 2, pp. 390–407.

Shleifer, Andrei (1986) 'Implementation Cycles' *Journal of Political Economy*, vol. 94, pp. 1163–89.

# Comment

Alan Kirman
EUI, FLORENCE

This paper deals with a problem which has recently provoked considerable interest among economists: can we find cyclical behaviour in economies which are not subject to exogenous shocks? Besides giving us a review and discussion of the properties of models in which this is the case, they provide a simple example in which such behaviour occurs. Finally they develop a model in which they suggest that periodic fluctuations in wages and employment are a necessary and inherent feature of the dynamic interaction between firms and workers.

The important feature of this paper is that it concentrates on situations in which the cyclical nature of the equilibrium does not depend on some exogenously given signal. The sunspot equilibrium discussed briefly by the authors depends on the fact that the agents hold the 'arbitrary' belief that the evolution of the economy is related to the behaviour of some 'irrelevant' variable such as sunspots. As Spear (1989) has pointed out, in a situation in which there are two groups of agents trading on two islands, the prices of one island can serve as the sunspots of the other.

In the present case the same sort of feature appears in the sense that at a Nash equilibrium it is the interaction between agents currently anticipating each others' actions that leads to cycles.

A complete formal analysis or a search model which allows for dispersion and would permit cyclical behaviours is given by Hormendi (1979) in an article which, although having some technical problems, has unfortunately been largely overlooked.

Two points should be made clearly at the outset. First, a clear distinction has to be made between a stationary equilibrium and a stationary environment. Although, at first sight, the distinction might seem clear, it should be remembered that it is the interaction between agents which generates non-stationarity here. Hence for each agent the behaviour of the other agents constitutes part of his environment. Thus although collectively there is no 'external' interference, individually such interference is indeed present.

Second, in what sense are beliefs 'arbitrary'? The objection to the sunspot type of equilibrium is that the belief that the economy is related to sunspots only has a foundation when it is held but there is no special reason for the belief being held. However, when there are several equilibria each depending on different beliefs, which of these beliefs is held is also arbitrary?

This said, let us briefly examine the particular examples of the paper. The structure of the first model is simple and standard in the search literature. That cycles can appear in an equilibrium here is due to the nature of the Nash equilibrium and the assumption of a continuum of players. Indeed, one might ask what the sense is of a Nash equilibrium in such a case since no individual alone can change the characteristics of the situation and deviation in consequence has very limited significance. It is clear that any number of strange equilibria can be constructed in this way. This observation is of importance in what follows.

The model which constitutes the heart of the paper is intriguing but nevertheless has features which might trouble the average economist. There is a continuum of firms and a continuum of workers per firm. The workers are infinitely lived and more of them appear at each point in time. The arriving workers all know the sequence of wage distributions with which they will be faced over time. For reasons of convenience there is a terminal period $T$ after which all workers who have accepted a job at $w$ are paid $w$ for ever. This terminal date plays a crucial role in the argument often although we are told that it could be dropped. At least for me this is far from intuitively clear and perhaps the authors might have given some indication or reference as to why this might be so. Another problem of a technical nature is the sense to be made of the 'probability that an agent receives $n$ offers at date $t$'. These are simple technical questions, and ones which apply no doubt to other literature in this area. More important is to what extent the rather frightening image of a world in which more and more individuals arrive at each period and then work for ever from $T$ onwards is plausible or necessary to the analysis?

It may help to understand how the cyclical equilibrium in which agents work at some period and not at others is constructed.

First, the argument is based on backward induction from $T$ thus the existence of this terminal point plays a vital role.

Then, depending on the cost of searching, different types of equilibria can exist. If costs of search are high enough a certain proportion of workers $q$ will search once and the rest search twice; they will all be indifferent between the two. Two objections can be raised here: if workers are indifferent how can we be sure that precisely $q$ will search once and $1-q$ twice? Even if this question could be answered it should be noted that there are two solutions for $q$ and therefore there is no way of knowing which may occur. Note that this is, of course, a criticism which always applies whenever one only shows the existence of multiple equilibria.

This said it is interesting to look at the equilibria described. Note first that one possible equilibrium is a permanent recession in which no one is employed but no one can do anything about this. This points up the problem of using Nash equilibria in such an analysis.

Second, how plausible is it that reservation wages are lowest in a boom? Not all economists, I think, would regard this as realistic.

Third, as the authors point out, there are many different types of equilibria characterised by periods of inactivity and activity and the presence of so many equilibria seems almost too generous a reply to the original questions.

Last, given that we have questioned the nature of the equilibrium notion, it seems that one avenue might be to reflect on the fact that a firm never loses by offering $W^*$, the reservation wage, and this would be plausible since any perturbation of the situation could make such behaviour profitable. This consideration would eliminate many equilibria.

In conclusion, the authors have done us the service of presenting a simple example in which many types of endogenous cyclical equilibria are present. However, in so doing they have opened a Pandora's box of technical problems and more fundamental questions about the nature of the equilibrium employed, and have no doubt provided a fertile field for further research on this type of problem.

**References**

Hormendi, R. C. (1979) 'Dispersed Transactions Prices in a Model of Decentralized Pure Exchange', chapter 4 in S. A. Lippman and J. J. McCall (eds) *Studies in the Economics of Search* (Amsterdam: North-Holland).

Spear, S. (1989) 'Are Sunspots Necessary?', *Journal of Political Economy*, vol. 97, August, pp. 965–73.

# Part IV

# Non-equilibrium Macrodynamics of Fluctuation

# 7 Rationality and Cycles in the Multiplier-Accelerator Model[1]

J. P. Laffargue        and        P. Malgrange
UNIVERSITY OF PARIS                   CNRS and
and CEPREMAP                          CEPREMAP

## INTRODUCTION

Most large-scale macroeconometric models used by policy-makers for economic forecasting and policy evaluation rest on a common theoretical structure, often called *neo-Keynesian theory*. More precisely, they consist in an implementation of the IS–LM scheme, enlarged in a dynamic fashion by the inclusion of capital accumulation combined with progressive adjustment mechanisms and anticipations. However the understanding of their working is obscured by the fact that dynamic adjustment equations are reduced forms, mixing true adjustment mechanisms and expectations formation. The analysis of the role of anticipations alone is then impossible. In order to handle this problem it is necessary to build a model in which agents' behaviour is rigorously derived. In such a model, the anticipated future values of relevant variables will appear explicitly. The aim of this paper is to reappraise of the theoretical foundations of the real block of macroeconometric models. Indeed it is well-known that this block, an elaboration of the famous multiplier–accelerator model, plays a fundamental role in the short- and medium-run working of these models.

The following model supposes that households' consumption and firms' factor-demand derive from an intertemporal optimisation in an infinite horizon. Factor prices are set rigidly at a level implying an excess supply of the labour and commodity markets. Then different expectations schemes are introduced in order to evaluate their dynamic implications. The present study is very close in spirit to Blanchard and Sachs (1982). It can be viewed as a simplified implementation consistent with standard macroeconometric models.

157

158     *Non-Equilibrium Macrodynamics of Fluctuation*

The main conclusion emerging from this paper is not surprising and meets some very well-known results:

1. In the case of adaptive, backward expectations, our model may easily be calibrated to describe the reaction of macroeconometric models to shocks on Government expenditures, at least up to the medium run.
2. By contrast, introducing rational expectations leads to much quicker adjustments, starting as soon as the policy is announced and dependent on the time evolution of this policy.

Another lesson which can be drawn from this exercise is that *the rationalisation of the multiplier–accelerator mechanism imposes a degree of sophistication without relation to the simplicity of the Samuelsonian oscillator.*

The paper is organised as follows: Section 1 is devoted to the presentation of a closed economy dynamic model. The equilibrium steady-state properties are examined in Section 2. It is shown that this steady state is undetermined, revealing that some fundamental piece of the model is missing. The dynamic evolution of the system around the equilibrium is finally studied in Sections 3 and 4, assuming adaptive and rational expectations respectively.

## 1   GENERAL STRUCTURE OF THE MODEL

Our objective is to build a discrete time-dynamical model embodying intertemporal consumption and accumulation mechanisms as well as government intervention, but as simple and close to the macroeconometric practice as possible. We thus consider a closed economy involving three types of representative agents (firms, consumers, government) and four types of commodities (labour, all-purpose goods, operative capital, government bonds). There is no money. The all-purpose good is taken as *numéraire*. The (real) wage rate $\omega$ and the (real) interest rate $r$ on bonds are supposed exogenously given at levels consistent with positive profits. Because of arbitrage condition between capital and bonds, the stock market value, $q$, of one unit of operative capital is the only flexible price. In this section we consider the intertemporal programme of the consumer.

**Households' Consumption**

The representative consumer is supposed to be in excess labour supply. His planned consumption results from the following infinite horizon standard programme:

$$\text{Max} \sum_{t=0}^{\infty} (1 + \delta)^{-t} u(C_t), \quad \text{with:} \sum_{t=0}^{\infty} (1 + r)^{-t-1} C_t = W_0. \quad (1.1)$$

In the following we suppose: $r = \delta$ so that consumption is planned constant through time and equal to consumers permanent income $RP_0 = r W_0$. The consumer wealth $W_0$ consists of his human capital net of taxes, and his two assets, bonds $B_0$ and real asset $q_0 K_0$:

$$W_0 = B_0 + q_0 K_0 + \sum_{t=0}^{\infty} (1 + r)^{-t-1} [\omega L_t^e - T_t^e] \quad (1.2)$$

with $L_t^e$ and $T_t^e$, respectively labour and taxes anticipated for date $t$.

The stock market value $q_0$ is itself determined by:

$$q_0 = \sum_{t=0}^{\infty} (1 + r)^{-t-1} (\pi/K)_t \quad (1.3)$$

with $(\pi/K)_t$ profit rate for period $t$.[2]

**Firms' Investment**

The factor demand by firms is also standard: it results from the adjustment cost model under demand constraint (see, e.g., Grossman, 1972):

$$\text{Min} \sum_{t=0}^{\infty} (1 + r)^{-t-1} [\omega L_t + \Phi (I_t/K_t)I_t]$$

$$Q_t^e = f(K_t, L_t) \quad (1.4)$$

$$I_t = K_{t+1} - K_t$$

$$K_0, Q_t^e \text{ given}$$

where $\Phi(.)$ represents the unit cost of purchasing and installing investment $I_t$, $f(K_t, L_t)$ is the production function, and $Q_t^e$, the demand expected at period 0 for period $t$.[3] Denoting by $(1+r)^{-t} q_t'$ and $(1+r)^{-t} \lambda_t$ the Lagrange multipliers associated with the two constraints, we get:

$$q_t' = \Phi(I_t/K_t) + I_t/K_t \Phi' (I_t/K_t) \quad (1.5a)$$

$$\lambda_t = \omega/f'_L(K_t, L_t) \tag{1.5b}$$

$$(1 + r)\, q'_t = q'_{t+1} + \lambda_{t+1} f'_K(K_{t+1}, L_{t+1})$$
$$+ (I_{t+1}/K_{t+1})^2\, \Phi'(I_{t+1}/K_{t+1}) \tag{1.5c}$$

$$Q^e_t = f(K_t, L_t) \tag{1.5d}$$

$$I_t = K_{t+1} - K_t \tag{1.5e}$$

$$\lim_{t \to \infty} (1+r)^{-t}\, q'_t\, K_t = 0 \qquad K_0,\, Q^e_t \text{ given} \tag{1.5f}$$

The system can be rewritten in a more compact way through elimination of $I_t$ by (1.5e), $L_t$ by inversion of the production function (1.5d), $\lambda_t$ by (1.5b), and by taking into account the homogeneity of $f$:

$$\Psi(K_{t+1}/K_t) = q'_t \tag{1.6a}$$

$$(1 + r)q'_t = q'_{t+1} + \omega\, \xi(Q^e_{t+1}/K_{t+1}) + \eta(K_{t+2}/K_{t+1}) \tag{1.6b}$$

$$\lim_{t \to \infty} (1+r)^{-t}\, q'_t\, K_t = 0 \tag{1.6c}$$

$K_0,\, Q^e_t$ given

where the functions $\Psi(.)$, $\xi(.)$ and $\eta(.)$ result almost immediately from (1.5a) and (1.5c).

Let us remark that we end up with a conventional order-two system, characterised by one initial condition and one terminal condition. As a consequence, this system cannot be solved recursively through time. The usual, recursive form of the accelerator model rests on *a linear approximation and formal resolution of (1.6) around the steady state*. This point is well-known since Lucas (1967).

Firms profits $\pi$ take into account the expected stock market capital gain on new equipments:

$$\pi_0 = Q_0 - \omega L_0 + [q^e_1 - \Phi\,(I_0/K_0)]I_0 \tag{1.7}$$

We recall that $\omega$ is supposed sufficiently low to make it profitable for firms to satisfy the demand:

$$\omega \leqslant f'_L\,(K_t, L_t) \tag{1.8}$$

**Fiscal Policy and Equilibrium**

Government sets discretionary present and future spendings and taxes, $G_t$ and $T_t$. Public debt is financed by issuing bonds $B_t$ yielding an interest rate $r$. These bonds are held by households. The government budget constraint is thus:

$$B_{t+1} = (1+r)B_t + G_t - T_t \quad t \geq 0, \text{with:} \quad \lim_{t \to \infty} (1+r)^{-t} B_t = 0 \ (1.9)$$

The two last equations formalise the accounting identity on the goods market, integrating installation costs as intermediate consumption, and the hypothesis that notional labour supply $N^*$ exceeds labour demand by firms $L_0$, respectively:

$$Q_0 = C_0 + G_0 + \Phi (I_0/K_0)I_0 \tag{1.10}$$

$$L_0 \leq N^* \tag{1.11}$$

## 2 STATIONARY STATE

The perfect foresight stationary state corresponding to (1.1)–(1.11) is:

$$C^* = r \, W^* \tag{2.1}$$

$$W^* = B^* + q^*K^* + (\omega L^* - T^*)/r \tag{2.2}$$

$$r \, q^* = \pi^*/K^* \tag{2.3}$$

$$Q^* = f(K^*, L^*) \tag{2.4}$$

$$q'^* = 1 \tag{2.5}$$

$$r \, q'^*/\omega = f'_K /f'_L \tag{2.6}$$

$$\pi^* = Q^* - \omega L^* \tag{2.7}$$

$$\omega \leq f'_L \tag{2.8}$$

$$r^* B^* = T^* - G^* \tag{2.9}$$

$$Q^* = C^* + G^* \qquad (2.10)$$

$$L^* \leq N^* \qquad (2.11)$$

**Factor Costs, Tobin's $q$ and Marginal Productivity**

The linear homogeneity of the production function implies:

$$Q^* = f'_L \, L^* = f'_K \, K^*$$

On the other side, combining (2.3) and (2.7) yields:

$$Q^* = \omega L^* + r \, q^* \, K^*$$

Then, using firms' equilibrium equations (2.5) and (2.6), we get:

$$\frac{\omega}{f'_L} = \frac{r}{f'_K} = \frac{\omega L^* + r \, K^*}{f'_L \, L^* + f'_K \, K^*} = \frac{\omega L^* + r \, K^*}{\omega L^* + r \, q^* \, K^*}$$

It is easy to show that the 'excess demand' condition (2.8) amounts to an interior position of $(\omega, r)$ with respect to the factor-price frontier. Equivalently the stock market value of the operative capital $q^*$ must exceed 1. Indeed this extra value of capital is explained by the presence of an extra income after the payment of the two factors.

**Indetermination of the Equilibrium**

(2.2) shows that the disposable income of households $r \, W^*$ is the sum of labour, capital and public debt incomes minus taxes:

$$rW^* = \omega L^* + r \, q^* \, K^* + r \, B^* - T^*$$

The sum of the two first terms is the income created by firms $Q^*$ in equation (2.3) and (2.7). The sum of the two last, amounts to the opposite of government spendings – (2.9). It follows that by accounting identities, the consumer's income is, equal to the output net of government demand – that is, equal to households' consumption. It then results that the *ex-ante* consumption function (2.1) is redundant. This indeterminacy comes from the fact that consumers do not plan any savings in the steady state and thus consume nothing other than what is left by the other agents. It is beyond the scope of this paper to elucidate the roots of this apparent indeterminacy which refers to an open question: it seems impossible to generate 'truly Keynesian' phenomena in a real, non-monetary economy, where Say's law should occur, nominal rigidities are needed but there is up to now no satisfactory way to introduce them – see for instance Grandmont (1989).

## 3  DYNAMICS WITH ADAPTIVE EXPECTATIONS

In this section we suppose that expectations of future values for relevant variables are based on a simple, backward treatment of information, independently of the model. More precisely, in order to keep close to conventional macroeconometric models, the partial adjustment model of expectations is selected.

### Consumption

Households entirely consume their – expected – permanent income $RP$. This last is computed from a partial adjustment to their actual disposable income $R$:

$$RP = \lambda_1 RP_{-1} + (1 - \lambda_1)R \qquad 0 < \lambda_1 < 1 \tag{3.1}$$

with $R$ defined by:

$$R = \omega L + \pi + r B - T \tag{3.2}$$

the profit $\pi$ itself being written as:

$$\pi = Q - \omega L + [q^e_{+1} - \Phi(I/K)]I \tag{3.3}$$

We observe that the appreciation of the value of new investment creates an unobserved element, the future stock-market value of capital. It is not in the tradition of a multiplier–accelerator type model to take this element into account explicitly. However we cannot postulate the equality between $q^e_{+1}$ and $\Phi(I/K)$ as an approximation, because, in the stationary state, $\Phi(I^*/K^*) = \Phi(0) = 1$ while $q^*$ is generally greater than 1 as we saw in previous section. We then postulate static expectation for $q$ at its long-run value $q^*$ and write the consumption function as:

$$C(= RP) = \lambda_1 C_{-1} + (1 - \lambda_1)[Q + (q^* - \Phi(I/K)) I + r B - T] \quad (3.4)$$

Using accounting identities of government and of good market, this expression may be rewritten as:

$$C = \lambda_1 C_{-1} + (1 - \lambda_1)[C + q^* (K_{+1} - K) + B_{+1} - B] \quad (3.5)$$

From (3.5) we infer that:

$$(1 - \lambda_1)[q^* K_{+1} + B_{+1}] - \lambda_1 C = (1 - \lambda_1)Z^*$$

where $Z^*$ is an 'historical constant' given by initial conditions:

$$Z^* = q^* K(0) + B(0) - \lambda_1/(1 - \lambda_1) C(-1) \quad (3.6)$$

**Investment**

As we saw in the first section, the intertemporal programme faced by firms leads to a non-recursive dynamic system. Let us suppose that the expected future demands $Q^e_{+i}$ lie around a constant steady-state level $Q_{ss}$, and that the initial capital $K_0$ is close enough to its long-run value $k\, Q_{ss}$, where $k$ is the long-run capital–output ratio – see (2.4) and (2.6). We then get the familiar linear recursive approximation of (1.6) as the following accelerator model:

$$K_{+i+1} = \lambda_2 K_{+i} + (1 - \lambda_2)K^0_{+i}$$

$$K^0_{+i} = k\, Q^0_{+i}$$

$$Q^0_{+i} = (\mu_2 - 1) \sum_{j=0}^{\infty} \mu_2 - j - 1\, Q^e_{+i+j+1} \qquad i \geqslant 0,\ K \text{ and } Q^e_{+i+1}$$

given.

$\lambda_2$ and $\mu_2$ are the eigenvalues of the linear approximation of system (1.6). They verify:

$$0 < \lambda_2 < 1 < 1 + r < \mu_2$$

$K^0_{+i}$ is understood as the optimal capital and $Q^0_{+i}$ as a permanent expected demand, at period $t$ for period $t + i$.

It results from a well-known general property of adaptive processes that expectations made at a given date do not depend on the horizon. More especially, here $Q^e_{+i}$ is equal to $Q^e_{+1}$, which is itself given by a geometric filter of past values of $Q$. The same is true for the $Q^0_{+i}$s and we have:

$$Q^0_{+i} = Q^0 = (1 - \lambda_3) \sum_{j=0}^{\infty} \lambda_3 j \, Q_{-j} \qquad 0 < \lambda_3 < 1 \qquad (3.7)$$

Let us call $Q^0_{-1}$ – resp $Q^0(-1)$ – the permanent demand expected at period $t - 1$ – resp $(-1)$ – for period $t$ – resp $0$ –, we can rewrite (3.7) as:

$$Q^0_{+i} = Q^0 = (1 - \lambda_3) \, Q + \lambda_3 \, Q^0_{-1}, \qquad (3.8)$$

with $Q^0(-1)$ given by:

$$Q^0(-1) = (1 - \lambda_3) \sum_{j=0}^{\infty} \lambda_3 \, j \, Q(-j) \qquad (3.9)$$

### The Dynamics of the Adaptive System

We first note that the linear approximation of the accounting identity (1.10) around every steady state reads simply:

$$Q = C + I + G \qquad (3.10)$$

With the notation $\lambda'_i = 1 - \lambda_i$, the linearised dynamic system with adaptive expectations may be written:

$$\lambda_1 \, C = \lambda_1 \, C_{-1} + \lambda'_1 [q^* \, (K_{+1} - K) + B_{+1} - B] \qquad (3.11)$$

$$K_{+1} = \lambda_2 \, K + \lambda'_2 \, k \, Q^0 \qquad (3.12)$$

$$Q^0 = \lambda_3 \, Q^0_{-1} + \lambda'_3 \, Q \qquad (3.13)$$

$$B_{+1} = (1+r) \, B + G - T \qquad (3.14)$$

$$Q = C + K_{+1} - K + G \qquad (3.15)$$

The dynamic evolution of this four-order system is set by the four initial conditions $K(0)$, $B(0)$, $Q^*(-1)$, $C(-1)$ and the evolution of the exogenous variables $G(t)$ and $T(t)$ for $t \geq 0$. It can be seen that the dynamics of this system are largely decomposable. First, the government budget constraint (3.14) imposes the evolution of public debt, given $G(t)$ and $T(t)$, and delivers one eigenvalue of $1 + r$. However, the solvability constraint, $\lim_{t \to \infty} (1+r)^{-t} B(t) = 0$, imposes that taxes cannot be choosen independently, but must be set so as to prevent $B$ from increasing at a rate greater than $r$. The consumption function is itself responsible for an eigenvalue of 1. Initial conditions give the value of the historical constant $Z^* - (3.6) -$ and thus solve the indetermination of the steady state delivering the missing long-run consumption function:

$$C^* = \lambda_1' / \lambda_1 \, (q^* \, K^* + B^* - Z^*)$$

It is easy to see that this relation together with (2.1)–(2.11) uniquely determines the unique realisable steady state equilibrium. But it is also worth noting that a shock on initial conditions and/or adjustment parameters have permanent effects and alter the steady state.

The remaining two equations describing the dynamics of anticipated permanent demand $Q^0$ and the capital $K_{+1}$ may be then written as follows:

$$\begin{pmatrix} Q^0 \\ K_{+1} \end{pmatrix} = \lambda_1 m \begin{bmatrix} \lambda_3 & \lambda_3' \mu \\ \lambda_1' \lambda_3 k & \lambda_2 - \lambda_2' \lambda_3' k \end{bmatrix} \begin{pmatrix} Q^0_{-1} \\ K \end{pmatrix} + \begin{bmatrix} \lambda_3' m \\ k \lambda_2 \lambda_3' m \end{bmatrix} H$$

with

$$m = [1 - \lambda_1' \, (1 + (q^* - 1) \, \lambda_2' \lambda_3' k - \lambda_2' \lambda_3' k]^{-1}$$
$$\mu = \lambda_2 \, (1 + q^* \, \lambda_1' / \lambda_1) - 1$$
$$H = G + \lambda_1' \, (1 + r) \, B - \lambda_1' \, T - \lambda_1 Z^*$$

$m$, short-run public-expenditure multiplier on output, is conventionally given by the inverse of the gap to 1 of the sum of the short-run propensity to consume and to invest. If this last sum is smaller than 1, then $m$ *is* positive and greater than 1 and diminishes as the adjustment-lag parameters $\lambda_1$, $\lambda_2$ and $\lambda_3$ increase.

The computation of the eigenvalues of this system leads to the conclusion that, as in the usual multiplier–accelerator model, all kinds of dynamics are possible depending on the numerical values of the parameters (see, for instance, Deleau *et al.*, 1984, for an analysis of the dynamical behaviour of the real blocks of macroeconometric models).

## 4 DYNAMICS WITH RATIONAL EXPECTATIONS

Now we will assume that agents hold rational expectations. As there is no uncertainty in the model these expectations amount to perfect foresight.[4]

### Consumption

Households know the future values of employment $L_{+i}$, of taxes $T_{+i}$ and of the stock market value of capital $q_{+i}$. Relations (1.3) and (1.7) yield:

$$qK = \sum_{i=0}^{\infty} (1 + r)^{-i-1} [Q_{+i} - \omega L_{+i} + \Phi(I_{+i}) / K_{+i}) I_{+i}]$$

The government budget constraint (1.9) may be written:

$$B = \sum_{i=0}^{\infty} (1 + r)^{-i-1} [T_{+i} - G_{+i}]$$

The consumption function becomes:

$$C = rW = r \sum_{i=0}^{\infty} (1 + r)^{-i-1} [Q_{+i} - L_{+i} - \Phi(I_{+i} / K_{+i}) I_{+i}]$$

Taking into account the equilibrium of the good market (1.10), we finally obtain:

$$C = r \sum_{i=0}^{\infty} (1 + r)^{-i-1} C_{+i}, \quad \text{or equivalently:} \quad C = C_{+i}, \ \forall\, i > 0$$

The consumption function only states that consumption stays constant through time and hence does not solve the indeterminacy of the steady state. Thus we get a different result from the adaptive expectations case. To solve the indeterminacy, we will add now the assumption that *agents expect a precise unemployment level in the long run*, hence a given steady state level $L^*$ of employment. Equilibrium conditions for firms (2.4) to (2.6) then uniquely determine $Q^*$ and $K^*$. (2.10) gives the consumption level $C^*$.

## Investment

The same strategy of analyzing the linearized system around the steady state leads to the same equations as in the adaptive case except for the fact that now the expected demand $Q^0_{+1}$ has to be identified with $Q_i$.

## The Dynamics of the Perfect Foresight System

The linearised dynamical system with perfect foresight becomes:

$$C = C_{+1} \tag{4.1}$$

$$K_{+1} = \lambda_2 K + \lambda'_2 k \, Q^0 \tag{4.2}$$

$$Q^0 = 1/\mu_2 \, Q^0_{+1} + (1 - 1/\mu_2) \, Q_{+1} \tag{4.3}$$

$$B_{+1} = (1 + r) B + G - T \tag{4.4}$$

$$Q = C + K_{+1} - K + G \tag{4.5}$$

Now we have two initial conditions: $K(0)$ and $B(0)$, one terminal condition: $L_\infty = L^*$ and the condition that $Q^0$ $(= Q)$ is bounded. Furthermore we need to set the exogenous variables $G(t)$ and $T(t)$ consistently with the government solvency constraint.

The system is still decomposable. The government budget constraint is responsible for an eigenvalue of $1 + r$. The solvency condition constrains public intervention in order to prevent the public debt to diverge at a rate greater than $1 + r$. This eigenvalue has no impact on the rest of the model. The consumption function is responsible for a unit root: households smooth their consumption flow which is equal to its stationary level: $C^* = Q^* - G^*$. The rest of the system may be written as in the adaptive case by the following backward looking two state variables system:

$$(1 - \lambda'_2 \mu'_2 k) \begin{pmatrix} Q^0 \\ K_{+1} \end{pmatrix} = \begin{bmatrix} \mu_2 & -\lambda'_2 \mu'_2 \\ \lambda'_2 \mu_2 k & \lambda_2 - \lambda'_2 \mu'_2 k \end{bmatrix} \begin{pmatrix} Q^0_{-1} \\ K \end{pmatrix}$$

$$+ \begin{bmatrix} \mu'_2 \\ -\lambda'_2 \mu'_2 k \end{bmatrix} (G - G^* + Q)$$

with $K(0)$ given and $Q^0$ bounded.

This two-points boundary problem has been studied by Blanchard and Kahn (1980). They show that if the number of roots less than 1 in modulus is equal to the number of predetermined variables, the system has a unique solution.

Here one characteristic root $\varrho_1$ is smaller than 1. The other, $\varrho_2$, is greater than $1 + r$. The proof of this result rests on the fact that $rk$ is smaller than 1, which holds true here because the factor prices are inside their frontier.

Let us define:

$$Z = -\frac{\lambda_2' \mu_2' k}{1 - \lambda_2' \mu_2' k} (G - G^* + Q^*) \tag{4.6}$$

The application of the Blanchard–Kahn formulae yields the following expression for the path of capital:

$$K_{+1} = \varrho_1^j K(0) + \sum_{j=0}^{t} \varrho_1^j \sum_{k=0}^{\infty} \varrho_2^{-k-1} Z_{+1-j+k} \tag{4.7}$$

Hence the value of output:

$$Q = (Q^* - G^*) + (K_{+1} - K) + G$$

We will now suppose that a time 0 the capital is at its reference steady-state level and we will examine the effect of variations of government spendings expressed in difference, denoted by a 'hat', with respect to this reference.

### (a) Permanent and Constant Increase of Government Spendings from Time 0

Let us suppose that $G(t) = G^* + \hat{G}$, for $t \geq 0$. The 100 per cent crowding-out of private consumption by public spendings in the steady state and the constancy through time of households' expenditures, imply that these expenditures decrease by $\hat{G}$ from the beginning. In other words, $\hat{Z}(t) = 0$ for $t \geq 0$ and capital, output and employment stay at their stationary reference level.

### (b) Transitory Increase of Public Spendings Expected at Date 0

We now suppose $\quad G(t) = G^* + \hat{G}, \quad$ for $0 \leq t \leq \theta - 1$
and $\quad\quad\quad G(t) = G^*, \quad\quad\quad$ for $t \geq \theta$.

The fiscal expansion being transitory and households keeping constant through time their consumption, this last stays as its reference level:

$$\hat{C}(t) = 0, \quad t \geq 0$$

Formulae (4.6) and (4.7) then give the dynamics of the capital:

$$\hat{K}(t) = \frac{\lambda_2' \mu_2' k}{\lambda_2' \mu_2' k - 1} \frac{1}{\varrho_2 - 1} \left[ \frac{1 - \varrho_1^t}{1 - \varrho_1} - \varrho_2^{-\theta + 1} \frac{\varrho_2^t - \varrho_1^t}{\varrho_2 - \varrho_1} \right] \hat{G}, \text{ for } 0 \leq t \leq \theta - 1$$

$$= \varrho_1^{t - \theta + 1} \hat{K}(\theta - 1), \qquad\qquad\qquad\qquad \text{for } t \geq \theta$$

The dynamics of production follows by:

$$\hat{Q}(t) = \hat{K}(t + 1) - \hat{K}(t) + \hat{G}, \quad \text{for } 0 \leq t \leq \theta - 1$$

$$= \hat{K}(t + 1) - \hat{K}(t), \qquad \text{for } t \geq \theta$$

Figure 7.1 illustrates the variation of the level of production associated with a transitory unitary expansion of fiscal policy $-\hat{G} = 1-$, between periods 1 and $\theta$, with $\theta = 1, 2, 10$, and 20, respectively. The structural parameters are calibrated on those of a macro-model by Deleau *et al.* (1984), leading to the values: $k = 1.66$, $\lambda_2 = 0.5$ and $\mu_2 = 2.1$, and hence to eigenvalues; $\varrho_1 = 0.38$ and $\varrho_2 = 1.46$.

When facing a transitory demand shift, firms find it profitable to expand their capacities temporarily. This acceleration mechanism reinforces the increase in effective demand. Initial investment $\hat{I}(0) = k(1 - \varrho_2^{-\theta + 1})(1 - \varrho_1)\hat{G}$ and initial production: $\hat{Q}(0) = \hat{I}(0) + \hat{G}$, are the greater, the longer the duration of the shift.[5] As period $\theta$ comes nearer, firms plan a progressive backward shift in capital toward its long-run reference level, with adjustment speed $\varrho_1$. This generates after $\theta$ a production level slightly lower than the reference. In the intermediary period, the level of capital is roughly adjusted to increased autonomous demand and firms make no investment yielding an excess production w.r.t. the reference of exactly $\hat{G}$. The monotonicity and the speed of the response appear in sharp contrast with the previous adaptive case, and the strength has a limit substantially lower.

We also observe that the effect of permanent shock – case (*a*) – is not the limit of that of a longer and longer transitory shock – case (*b*).

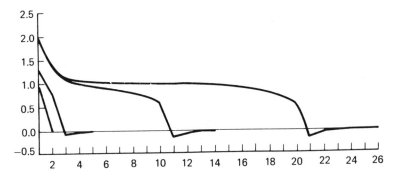

*Figure 7.1* Government spending multipliers

An 'adaptive' intuitive analogy is the fact that the *present effect* of a *present shock* is not the limit of the *present effect* of a nearer and nearer *future shock*. Indeed here, the expectations 'start' from the asymptotic equilibrium steady state and go backward to the present period.

*(c) Permanent Increase of Public Spendings from Period θ and Anticipated from Period 0*

We suppose: $G(t) = G^*$     for $0 \leqslant t \leqslant \theta - 1$
and: $G(t) = G^* + \hat{G}$   for $t \geqslant \theta$

This policy experiment is nothing but the sum of a permanent fiscal expansion from period 0 and the opposite of case (*b*). The expectation of future increase in public spendings has thus a strong depressive effect on output, because consumers immediately adjust their consumption to its long-run value, lower by exactly $\hat{G}$.

It is worth stressing that this highly counter-intuitive result as well as the previous one rests crucially on the – *ad hoc* – hypothesis added to the model in order to solve the indeterminacy that *agents agree to forecast a given long-run level of unemployment.*

CONCLUSION

The macroeconomic model which has been presented is very simple but close to the macroeconometric tradition. In this model the behaviour of agents (households' consumption and firms' factor

demand) has been derived from intertemporal optimisation programmes. Furthermore factor prices have been supposed rigidly fixed
at levels generating excess supply on both labour and goods markets.
The dynamic consequences of different schemes of anticipations have
then been analysed.

Two main conclusions emerge from this study:

1. *In the long run* households' consumption function is not distinct
   from their budget constraint and disappears as an independent
   relation. The resulting lack of determination reveals that the
   system is incomplete, a hidden phenomenon in macroeconometric
   models because of their dynamically recursive working.
2. *The dynamic working* of our model appears highly contrasted
   according to the way expectations are formed. In the case of
   adaptive expectations, backward oriented, its dynamic evolution
   is quite similar to that of usual macroeconometric models, at least
   in the medium run. Furthermore, the evolution of output and
   employment is entirely determined by initial conditions – with a
   permanent influence – and by economic policy. By contrast, the
   introducton of rational expectations leads to a much quicker
   adjustment, instantaneous for consumption and progressive for
   investment because of adjustment costs. This type of adjustment,
   acting as soon as economic policy is announced and resting crucially on its expected duration, is totally absent from traditional
   macroeconometric models.

**Notes**

1. This paper is a revised version of Laffargue and Malgrange (1987). We are
   grateful to J. Jespersen and B. Thalberg for their very stimulating comments.
2. We suppose that the discounted values of relevant anticipations of agents
   converge to 0.
3. The function $I \Phi(I/K)$ is supposed $C^2$, increasing and convex with respect
   to $I$. The unit installation cost verifies: $\Phi \geq 1$, $\Phi(0) = 1$. The production
   function $f(K, L)$ is $C^2$, linear homogeneous, increasing and concave.
4. Up to now we have just assumed that expectations do not diverge 'too
   quickly'. But now we can easily see that expectations are actually
   bounded, because there is no feasible unbounded path.
5. As there is one period of gestation for investment, a one-period increase

in public spendings produces no effect on capital variation, i.e. the short-run multiplier is equal to 1.

## References

Blanchard, O. J. and Kahn, C. M. (1980) 'The Solution of Linear Difference Models under Rational Expectations', *Econometrica*, vol. 48, pp. 1305–11.
Blanchard, O. J. and Sachs, J. (1982) 'Anticipations, Recessions and Policy: an Intertemporal Disequilibrium Model', *Annales de l'INSEE*, vol. 47–8, pp. 117–44.
Deleau, M., Malgrange, P. and Muet, P. A. (1984) 'A Study of Short-Run and Long-Run Properties of Macroeconometric Models by Means of an Aggregative Core Model', in P. Malgrange and P. A. Muet (Eds) *Contemporary Macroeconomic Modelling*, (Oxford: Basil Blackwell).
Giavazzi, F. and Wyplosz, C. (1986) 'The Zero Root Problem: A Note on the Dynamic Determination of the Stationary Equilibrium in Linear Models', *Review of Economic Studies*, vol. 52, pp. 353–7.
Grandmont, J. M. (1989) 'Keynesian Issues and Economic Theory', CEPREMAP Working Paper no 8907, March 1989.
Grossman, H. (1972) 'A Choice-Theoretic Model of an Income-Investment Accelerator', *American Economic Review*, vol. 62, pp. 630–41.
Laffargue, J. P. and Malgrange P. (1987) 'Rationalité des comportements et des anticipations dans les blocs réels des modèles macroéconomiques', *Recherches Economiques de Louvain*, vol. 53, pp. 203–22.
Lucas, R. E. (1967) 'Adjustment Costs and the Theory of Supply', *Journal of Political Economy*, vol. 75, pp. 321–34.

# Comment

Bjørn Thalberg
UNIVERSITY OF LUND
SWEDEN

My first comment is of a general nature. This is a microfoundation type of study where the authors specify a disaggregated multiplier–accelerator type of model. Their model builds explicitly on the dec:sions of representative agents, and represents on the whole a more basic specification of the theory than the corresponding macro model. It should therefore be useful to shed light on various properties of the macromodel. However, since in this case the macro model is so familiar, intuitively understandable, and fairly well-known empirically, and since the micro model is not very transparent (in fact it contains as the authors note, 'a degree of sophistication without relation with the simple Samuelsonian oscillator') I think the reader is – at least in the first place – tempted to use the macromodel to evaluate the micro model. Hence, when I came to the result of the section 'The Dynamics of the Adaptive System', it strengthened my belief in the relevance and realism of the authors' micromodel that its public-expenditures multiplier is shown to be comparable and similar to the conventional multiplier derived from the macroeconomic model. However, coming to the results of the following section. 'The Dynamics of the Perfect Foresight System', I was confused as the results of this section do not seem reasonable (cf. below). Consequently it seems to me that one may ask whether the micro model is misspecified in some part, or whether the assumption of perfect foresight is so extreme and unrealistic in the case studied that the results are very implausible, or whether the authors and/or the discussant have rendered themselves guilty of some calculation or interpretation error.

My second comment concerns the price-variables of the model. Four prices enter the model – i.e. the price of the all-purpose good, the wage rate, the interest rate, and the stock-market value $q$, of one unit of operative (installed) capital. Three of the prices are assumed to be constant, only $q$ is allowed to vary. Why, in a disaggregated multiplier–accelerator model, is it first and foremost important to

174

account for variations in $q$? There may be some good reasons for this choice, but I miss the authors' critical discussions on these matters.

Third, in the case of perfect foresight, and in a state of disequilibrium and Keynesian unemployment, a permanent and constant increase in government spending is found to have no effect on total output. From the very beginning private consumption would decrease by the same amount. The possible existence of such a new steady state may be understandable from a purely formal point of view, but a possible jump to it seems highly unrealistic in a demand-constrained system, and it strongly contradicts conventional analyses by means of macro-level multiplier–accelerator models. Moreover, in the case of perfect foresight, but assuming that the increase in public spending is transitory (lasting $x$ time units), the result is different. Now there is an effect on output. For example, when $x$ is 20, output is found to exceed its reference level for about 22 time units. We may increase $x$ to say 100 or more and find that there is a substantial effect on output for a long time; only when $x$ is increased to infinity there is no effect. It seems strange.

Regarding the authors' discussion on the relevance of nonlinearities for business-cycle theory I would like to ask whether it is in principle impossible to account for any degree of asymmetry between up – and down-swings by means of linear models; and further I may ask whether the author would comment on Blatt's (1980) claim that this class of model should be rejected on the sole reason that it cannot explain the fact that the length of the downturn is generally shorter than that of the upturn.

**Reference**

Blatt, J. M. (1980) 'On the Frisch Model of Business Cycles', *Oxford Economic Papers*, vol. 32, no 3, p. 3.

# Comment[1]

Jesper Jespersen
COPENHAGEN SCHOOL OF BUSINESS, FREDERIKSBERG,
DENMARK

## 1  RATIONALITY AND CYCLES IN THE MULTIPLIER-ACCELERATOR MODEL

Professors Laffargue and Malgrange have presented a theoretical framework which they claim could shed some light on the working of the real sector of a conventional macroeconometric model based on the IS–LM scheme. What they, in fact, offer us is a non-monetary neoclassical fix-price model with utility-maximising consumer(s) and cost-minimising producer(s). All prices except 'Tobins "$q$"' are 'set rigidly at a level implying an excess supply in the labour and commodity markets'.[2]

The cyclical features of the model are mainly derived from the investment function. Here we find the accelerator principle employed and extended with an instalment cost assumption which delays the adjustment process.

In these comments I shall discuss, first, the statement that 'the equilibrium steady state is undetermined' and second the assumptions behind the rather peculiar simulation results reached at the end of the paper.

## 2  INDETERMINATION OF THE EQUILIBRIUM

It is well-known from the simple real-sector Keynes model that without any exogenous demand components *and* a consumption function being parallel to the 45-degree line there is no unique equilibrium solution. Production could be anything between zero and full employment.

That cannot be the case within the neoclassical model that Professor Malgrange offers us. There are an explicit production function (1.4) and cost-minimising firms. We are told that the production function has a conventional shape with decreasing marginal factor

176

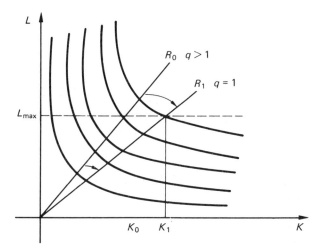

*Figure 7.2* Capital–labour isoquant

output and constant returns to scale. Hence the level of production in the short run is either determined by demand (when $q < 1$) and supply (when $q > 1$). Both cases may imply unemployment.

In the long run (the steady state) will be determined from the supply side. When the growth rate of the economy becomes similar to the real interest rate we have the equilibrium solution, where the rate of profit is equal to the given rate of interest. Depending on the parameters of the model *and* the given factor and output prices there is only one unique solution to the model. Of course, the planned output may be constrained by full employment, but that is not the case in this paper. When $q$ exceeds 1, the sum of investments and consumption, given the assumption of fixed prices, leads to suppressed inflation. There is no steady state unless $q = 1$. With $(q^*r > r)$ we will get a Wicksellian inflationary process – without inflation due to the fixed prices. This point can be demonstrated. Figure 7.2 shows the familiar capital ($K$) – labour ($L$) isoquant diagram. Investment has to be enlarged for a certain period to turn the factor ray from $R_0$ to $R_1$. In this transitory period private consumption is suppressed until $q$ becomes equal to 1.

In the stationary state the entire production is consumed. The model does not explicitly tell us how the production is divided between private and government consumption. But even in this case there can be only one level of government consumption, $G$ that matches equation (2.9), $G = T - rB$, (where $T$ is taxes and $rB$ is interest paid on government bonds) *and* utility maximisation of private consumers.

Therefore, it is not correct to claim (p. 162) that the equilibrium is indeterminate. Quite the opposite, I should say: equilibrium is unambiguously determined by (*i*) the (*ad hoc?*) fixed prices and (ii) the assumed micro-foundation of the model. In a world without uncertainty live-cycle-optimising consumers do consume their entire expected income. In that respect the traditional Keynesian macro-consumption function becomes redundant. That is perfect in accordance with the assumptions underlying the authors' model. Hence the conclusion reached at the end of the paragraph on 'Indetermination of the Equilibrium' is correct, but the heading is somewhat misleading. Indeterminacy normally indicates that there is an extra degree of freedom, which is not the case in this model. That is in fact also the way the paragraph is terminated: *'it seems impossible to generate "truly Keynesian" phenomena in a real, non-monetary economy, where Say's law should occur'* (p. 163) which is quite contrary to the postulate that the equilibrium is indeterminate.

## 3    RATIONALITY AND CYCLES

### 3.1    Rationality

The authors take up the discussion of the lack of microeconomic foundations in the conventional macroeconomic models. The justification for putting the word 'rationality' into the title of the paper is that an explicit utility-maximising and cost-minimising behaviour is introduced.

This comment is probably not the right place to discuss this interpretation of rationality. But one may wonder to what extent it makes the theoretical foundation of a *macro*econometric model more (or less?) rational to constrain the employed equations for the *aggregate* private consumption and investment by the assumption that they are similar to the behaviour of one (micro) utility-maximising consumer,[3] and one (micro) cost-minimising firm. How do we know that this simplified formulation catches at the macrolevel a more rational behaviour by the agents than the conventional *ad hoc* specification? Let me with specific reference to the fix-price model add: what, in this context, is the 'rationality' behind the assumption of fixed prices?[4]

These questions, of course, go well beyond the purpose and tradition behind the paper, but the applicability of the conclusions seems to depend on the answers.

## 3.2 Cycles

The introduction of the two 'rational' agents is claimed to help in analysing the dynamic structure mirroring the 'true adjustment mechanisms and expectation formation'. Before proceeding into the discussion of the formation of expectations it should be emphasised that an important part of the dynamic structure in macromodels can be referred to the *aggregation* of the microbehaviour.[5] This aspect is absent in the paper and may explain why cycles also are nearly absent in the simulations reported.

On the other hand it is a correct observation that quite often econometric models are presented without any explicit specification about the derivation of the lags. The behavioural foundation of the dynamic structure is hidden behind a (semi)reduced structure.

When the representative household is assumed to have *adaptive* expectations the model generates the old-fashioned multiplier–accelerator results. The shape of the 'business cycle' depends on the numerical values of the parameters. Accordingly the introduction of 'rationality' (maximising representative agents) by itself seems not to have made substantial change to the properties of the model.

However, the assumption of *rational* expectations changes the model in one important respect. The permanent income consumption function (3.1) is substituted by (4.1) $C = C(t + 1)$. This, of course, changes the dynamic properties of the model.

Three policy experiments with 'rational expectations' are analysed:

1. a 'permanent and constant increase of government spending from time 0'. Here we get full crowding-out and no change in the level of output, only in the composition. This emphasises that the steady-state output is uniquely determined and by that private consumption, cf. my discussion above;
2. a 'transitory increase of public spendings expected at date 0';
3. a 'permanent increase of public spendings from period $Q$ and anticipated from period 0'. The second experiment has a temporary expensive effect reinforced by the accelerator mechanism, whereas the third experiment has *the opposite effect!*

In the third case the consumers start to adjust their demand downward anticipating the higher taxes in the future! That creates (transitory) unemployment and is due to the Keynesian flavour of the model, where $q < 1$ in the short run. One may ask whether it is 'rational' for agents and government to act so myopically. For instance, why does not a rational government counteract the reaction of the agents? When prices are fixed and resources underutilised, is it then rational not to expect economic policy to stimulate the economy?

What I am questioning is, whether it really makes sense to assume agents to have perfect foresight and the economic policy to be so narrow-minded.

In any case the simulation results must be very sensitive to the way rationality is interpreted. If, for instance, equation (4.1) was substituted by $C + G = C(+1) + G(+1)$, meaning that consumers within the assumption of the 'rational' model are optimising not only private consumption, but private *and* government consumption, which is just another kind of rational behaviour and expectations. Then the overall budget-constraint would change. The simulation results of this changed optimisation behaviour would be quite different. For instance, there would be no drop in activity in anticipation of the government expenditure.

The heading of this subsection reporting on simulations with rational expectations is called 'The Dynamics of the Perfect Foresight System'. I have some difficulty seeing how the referred results are compatible with 'perfect foresight' or 'rational expectations'. This rather mechanical treatment of the formation of expectations may be of limited relevance for macroeconometric modelling. In that respect I would much prefer the more pragmatic (but probably more realistic) approach put forward, *inter alia*, by Wren–Lewis (1985). Here expectations are modelled separately for each market and type of agent.

CONCLUSION

The authors raise a number of interesting questions concerning the dynamics of macro-econom(etr)ic models. The dynamic properties are extremely dependent on the way expectations is specified. The paper has given a clear-cut demonstration of how a rather innocent assumption of rational expectations and fixed prices may lead to obscure results.

In other words the novelty of the model which Laffargue and Malgrange offer us, compared with conventional macroeconometric models, is the indication of how 'rationality' (the microeconomic foundation) can be integrated into a conventional macromodel without leaving the demand side (the short run) entirely aside. This approach is very much in accordance with the recommendation of *inter alia*, Klein (1978), but the assumption of fixed (relative) factor prices undermines the usefulness of the conclusions arrived at in the medium/long run.

**Notes**

1. This comment has benefited from enlightening discussions with Pierre Malgrange, Marco Lippi, and K. Velupillai. None of them, of course, are responsible in any respect for my interpretation. Let me add that this comment is also influenced by my own experiences from more than 15 years of practical work with a large-scale econometric model of the Danish economy.
2. It is unclear how the cost-minimising firms behave to end up with excess supply of goods?
3. This point is debated rather intensely outside the traditional neoclassical literature. Even Arrow seems to have second thoughts about the meaning of 'rational choice'. Just to cut a few of his worries: 'In the case of consumer demand, the budget constraint must be satisfied, but many theories can easily be devised that are quite different from utility maximisation' (Arrow, 1987, p. 202) and, further, 'The attainment of equilibrium requires a disequilibrium process. What does rational behaviour mean in the presence of disequilibrium?' (ibid, p. 203).
4. 'The price- and wage-ridigity elements of Keynesian theory are hard to fit into a rational framework, though some valiant efforts have been made' (Arrow, 1987, p. 202).
5. Lippi (1988) has a very illuminating discussion of these points related to a simple multiplier–accelerator model, pp. 17–19. One may add, that even an aggregation of purely identical agents may lead to complicated dynamics unless they are assumed to behave independently.

**References**

Arrow, K. J. (1987) 'Rationality of Self and Others in an Economic System', in R. M. Hogarth and Melvin W. Reder (eds) *Rational Choice: The*

*Contrast between Economics and Psychology* (Chicago, Illinois: University of Chicago Press).

Klein, L. (1978; 1985) 'The Supply Side', *American Economic Review*, vol. 68, March 1978, pp. 1–7; reprinted in J. Marquez (ed.) *Economic Theory and Econometrics – Lawrence Klein* (Oxford: Oxford University Press) ch. 26.

Lippi, M. (1988) 'On the Dynamics of Aggregate Macroequations: From Simple Microbehaviour to Complex Macrorelationships', in G. Dosi, C. Freeman, R. Nelson, G. Silverberg, L. Soete (eds) *Technical Change and Economic Theory* (London and New York: Pinter) ch. 8.

Wren-Lewis, S. (1985) 'Expectations in Keynesian Econometric Models', in T. Lawson and H. Pesaran (eds) *Keynes's Economics: Methodological Issues* (Beckenham: Croom Helm) ch. 4.

# 8 Strange Attractors and Endogenous Business Cycle Theory

## Hans-Walter Lorenz
### GEORG-AUGUST-UNIVERSITÄT GÖTTINGEN

## 1 INTRODUCTION

Dynamical systems theory in the 1970s and 1980s has been dominated by research on non-linear systems and so-called chaotic motion. As economic time-series are obviously characterised by irregularities, it has been presumed that these irregularities can be modelled by the help of chaotic dynamical systems.

While there exist several alternative mathematical definitions of chaotic motion, a rather heuristic and eclectic definition will be used in this paper.

**Definition**

A dynamical system $\dot{x} = f(x)$, $x \in \mathbf{R}^n$, is called *chaotic* when the following properties are satisfied:

(i) There exists an attracting set $\mathbf{A} \subset \mathbf{R}^n$, i.e., there exists an $n$-dimensional neighbourhood $U \subset \mathbf{A}$ such that for $x(0) \in U$, all $x(t)$ stay in $U$ $\forall t$ and $x(t) \rightarrow \mathbf{A}$,

(ii) there exists a sensitive dependence on initial conditions, and

(iii) the attracting set $\mathbf{A}$ is indecomposable.

When the set $\mathbf{A}$ fulfils all three conditions (i)–(iii), it will be called a *strange attractor* in the following. After appropriate modifications this definition of chaotic motion can also be applied to discrete-time maps but is not equivalent with the Li/Yorke definition of chaos, i.e., the mere existence of periodic motion of arbitrary length and aperiodic behaviour is not sufficient for encountering the sensitive dependence on initial conditions.

The literature on economic examples of chaotic motion has concentrated mainly on the investigation of low-dimensional, discrete-time maps basically for two reasons. First, the mathematics of one-dimensional unimodal maps seems to be more or less completely understood, and convenient tools for establishing chaotic motion are available.[1] Second, many established business-cycle models are formulated in discrete-time because this time-concept seems to be adequate when the economic decision process is reduced to a single (or representative) optimising agent in the neoclassical tradition. However, when more than a single agent is involved, a continuous time-concept represents the more adequate framework for studying dynamical phenomena because (optimal or non-optimal) individual decision processes and appropriate actions overlap and do not take place in periods with identical lengths and starting-points. In addition, when stocks and flows are to be distinguished, a continuous time-concept is actually mandatory. The usual objection that empirical data has a discrete character seems to be irrelevant because this fact can also be taken into account in continuous-time econometrics.[2]

The paper attempts to survey recent developments in modelling chaotic, continuous-time, dynamical systems in economics. Section 2 reviews forced oscillator systems and coupled oscillator systems which can be called *simply structured* chaotic systems. Section 3 contains an economic example of a three-dimensional dynamical system that is compatible with the Shil'nikov scenario. Some reflexions on the relevance of non-linearities in business-cycle models can be found in the concluding section.

## 2  CHAOTIC MOTION IN NON-LINEAR DYNAMICAL SYSTEMS – A BRIEF SURVEY OF ECONOMIC APPLICATIONS

This section concentrates on simply structured, chaotic dynamical systems. As the emphasis is placed on continuous-time systems, dynamical systems relying on the notion of discrete periods will only be recalled in passing.

### Discrete-Time Systems

One-dimensional discrete-time maps belong to the best-understood dynamical systems. When a map $f: J \to J, J \subset \mathbf{R}$, has a single critical

*Table 8.1* Economic examples of chaotic motion in discrete time

| Dimension | Economic application |
|---|---|
| $n = 1$ | Neoclassical growth, Day (1982);<br>Growth cycles, Pohjola (1981), Stutzer (1980);<br>Keynesian macromodel, Day/Shafer (1986)<br>Optimal growth, Boldrin/Montrucchio (1986);<br>Financial intermediation, Woodford (1989); |
| $n = 2$ | Kaldor's business-cycle model, Dana/Malgrange<br>(1984), Herrmann (1986);<br>Non-Walrasian macromodel, Hommes (1989). |

point $x_c \in J$ with $f'(x_c) = 0$ and $f'(x) > 0$ $(< 0)$ $\forall$ $x < x_c$ $(x > x_c)$ i.e. when it is a unimodal map, then a series of flip bifurcations can occur for changing values of a parameter such that period-doubling behaviour exists. For parameter values beyond a specific threshold value, periods of arbitrary order and aperiodic behaviour emerges.[3] When several additional requirements are fulfilled, the map can be chaotic in the sense of the definition given above.[4]

While the non-invertibility of the map $f$ is essential in one-dimensional dynamical systems, discrete-time systems with $n \geqslant 2$ must be invertible in order to allow for chaotic motion. For example, chaotic motion can be established in diffeomorphisms with the help of theorems of Diamond (1976) and Marotto (1978).[5] Analytical difficulties usually restrict applications of the theorems to two-dimensional dynamical systems. In addition, Marotto's concept of *snap-back repellers* requires numerical support in most non-trivial examples. An example of an application of Marotto's technique can be found in Herrmann (1985) who demonstrated that a discrete-time version of the familiar Kaldor model (Kaldor, 1940) possesses a strange attractor. Hommes (1989) established chaos in a non-Walrasian macromodel by reducing the system dynamics to a circle map.

Table 8.1 contains a list of chaotic economic models which can be interpreted as business-cycle models in a broader sense. In the face of the rapidly growing literature, the list cannot claim to be complete. Furthermore, microeconomic chaotic models are not included in this list.

**Simply Structured Continuous-Time Systems**

Chaotic motion in continuous-time dynamical systems requires at least a three-dimensional state space. However, there does not exist a common structural form of all known dynamical systems with chaotic properties. In addition to the simply structured dynamical systems to be discussed in the following, a variety of prototype equations exist whose potential irregular behaviour cannot always be immediately suspected.[6]

Two simple families of dynamical systems deserve particular attention because they emerge in several economic models. *Forced oscillators* and *coupled oscillators* constitute variations of the basic notion of a non-linear oscillator. A dynamical system

$$\dot{\mathbf{x}} = \mathbf{f}(\mathbf{x}, \mu), \mathbf{x} \in \mathbf{R}^n, n \geqslant 2, \mu \in \mathbf{R} \tag{1}$$

with $\mu$ as a parameter is called an oscillator if the specific form of $\mathbf{f}$ allows for endogenous fluctuations in the vector of state variables.[7] Equation (1) can be written as a second-order differential equation when $n = 2$:

$$\ddot{x} + g_1(x)\dot{x} + g_2(x) = 0, \quad x \in \mathbf{R} \tag{2}$$

The Equation constitutes an oscillator when the expressions $g_1(x)$ and $g_2(x)$ fulfil certain requirements. For example, when $g_1$ is a parabolic expression with $g_1(0) < 0$ and $g_1'(0) > 0$, and when $g_2(x)$ is an odd function with $g_2'(x) > 0 \ \forall x$, then every trajectory approaches a unique limit cycle.[8]

The first family of simply structured dynamical systems that allow for chaotic motion is represented by *coupled oscillator systems*. Two dynamical systems (1) are coupled when the evolution of the endogenous variables $x_i$, $i = 1, 2$, in system $i$ is not only determined by the magnitude of these variables but when it is also influenced by the motion of the variables in other systems, i.e.

$$\begin{aligned} \dot{\mathbf{x}}_1 &= \mathbf{f}_1(\mathbf{x}_1, \mathbf{x}_2), \quad \mathbf{x}_1 \in \mathbf{R}^n, \quad n \geqslant 2 \\ \dot{\mathbf{x}}_2 &= \mathbf{f}_2(\mathbf{x}_1, \mathbf{x}_2), \quad \mathbf{x}_2 \in \mathbf{R}^m, \quad m \geqslant 2 \end{aligned} \tag{3}$$

When at least three two-dimensional oscillators are coupled, it follows from a theorem of Newhouse/Ruelle/Takens that the motion can be chaotic.[9]

Equation (2) can be interpreted as a special form of the more general non-autonomous equation

$$\ddot{x} + g_1(x)\dot{x} + g_2(x) = h(t), \quad x \in \mathbf{R} \tag{4}$$

where $h(t)$ is a function of time. When $h(t)$ is periodic, equation (4) is called a *forced oscillator*. When the (exogenous) forcing is strong as compared with the amplitude of the endogenous variable $x$, the dynamic behaviour of (4) can be chaotic.[10]

The emergence of both families in economics will be illustrated by the help of an extremely simple example from international trade theory.[11] Assume that the dynamic behaviour of $n$ economies is precisely described by the set of two-dimensional differential equation systems:

$$\dot{Y}_i = \alpha_i[I_i(Y_i, K_i) - S_i(Y_i) + EX_i(Y_j) - IM_i(Y_i)]$$
$$i = 1, \ldots, n \; i \neq j \tag{5}$$
$$\dot{K}_i = I_i(Y_i, K_i) - \delta_i K_i$$

with the usual meaning of the symbols. Consider first the autarkic case without any international trade activities, i.e. $EX_i(\cdot) = IM_i(\cdot) = 0 \; \forall i$. Assume that all $n$ autarkic economies are endogenously oscillating due to non-linearities in the investment functions $I_i(\cdot)$ and/or the savings functions $S_i(\cdot)$. The entire dynamical system consisting of $n$ economies represents a system of $n$ uncoupled two-dimensional oscillators. The introduction of international trade in the way of equations (5) represents a dynamic coupling of the $n$ economies. When $n \geq 3$, international trade can result in chaotic motion of $(Y_i, K_i) \; \forall i$.

Coupled oscillator systems can emerge in economic models in two different ways. The first one is trivial and includes the example mentioned above. The variables of several economic units are assumed to oscillate. The different units are constructed by considering either a multitude of essentially identical units like international economies or qualitatively different units like sectors of an economy. The question of how to couple the units is a subordinate problem because there will always exist a large number of possible ways to link economic decisions, production processes, etc. The construction of economically convincing, preferably low-dimensional examples of endogenously oscillating economies or its subsystems constitutes the essential problem. The question of whether coupled oscillator systems with potentially chaotic behaviour exist is therefore actually identical with the question of whether non-linear, endogenous cycle models are economically meaningful.

The second possibility to encounter these systems consists in considering a dynamical system of arbitrary dimension ($n \geq 6$) from the beginning and attempting to decouple the system into single autarkic oscillators. This procedure may be more convincing from a methodological point of view because it is not necessary any more to construct simply structured endogenously oscillating economic units. However, the analytical difficulties in separating a high-dimensional system into (perhaps economically meaningless) low-dimensional oscillators can be considerable.

The international trade example can also be used as a demonstration of the emergence of a forced oscillator.[12] Let $n = 2$ in (5) and assume that the trade flow is unidirectional in the sense that country 1 is exporting goods to country 2 but does not import goods from that country. In that case, the entire dynamical system consists of the four equations

$$
\begin{aligned}
\dot{Y_1} &= \alpha_1 \left[ I_1(Y_1, K_1) - S_1(Y_1) + EX_1(Y_2) \right] \\
\dot{K_1} &= I_1(Y_1, K_1) - \delta_1 K_1 \\
\dot{Y_2} &= \alpha_2 \left[ I_2(Y_2, K_2) - S_2(Y_2) - IM_2(Y_2) \right] \\
\dot{K_2} &= I_2(Y_2, K_2) - \delta_2 K_2
\end{aligned}
\tag{6}
$$

i.e. the change in the variables $Y_2$ and $K_2$ in country 2 depends only on internal variables.

It may be possible to solve the differential equation system of country 2 explicitly. Suppose that such a solution is available, i.e.

$$
\begin{aligned}
Y_2(t) &= Y[Y_2(0), K_2(0), t] \\
K_2(t) &= K[Y_2(0), K_2(0), t]
\end{aligned}
\tag{7}
$$

and that $Y_2(t)$ and $K_2(t)$ are both oscillating with a constant amplitude.[13]

With an oscillating income in country 2, the export of country 1 will be oscillating as well. The motion of $Y_1$ and $K_1$ in country 1 is described by

$$\dot{Y}_1 = \alpha_1 \{I_1(Y_1, K_1) - S_1(Y_1) + EX_1[Y_2(t)]\}$$
$$\dot{K}_1 = I_1(Y_1, K_1) - \delta_1 K_1 \tag{8}$$

or, written as a second-order differential equation:

$$\ddot{Y}_1 + f(Y_1)\dot{Y}_1 + g(Y_1) = \alpha_1 EX_1[Y_2(t)] \tag{9}$$

Depending on the structural forms of the terms $f(Y_1)$ and $g(Y_1)$ and the magnitude of the forcing term, equation (9) may constitute a forced oscillator such that chaotic motion prevails in country 1.

Other economic examples of strongly forced oscillators can be found in a variety of business-cycle models like a version of Goodwin's (1951) non-linear accelerator model (Lorenz, 1987c) and a Keynesian stabilisation model (Lorenz, 1989). One of the first investigations of exogenous, periodic forcing can be found in Goodwin (1946) in a study of Schumpeterian innovation swarms. All these models are charactrised by the assumption that exogenous influences which are usually considered constant are themselves periodic.

It was demonstrated above that a variety of economic examples can be provided for simply structured, chaotic dynamical systems such as one-dimensional discrete-time maps or forced and coupled oscillators. This is not really surprising because most dynamic economic models are constructed in the same deterministic way as traditional models in the natural sciences where investigations of chaotic dynamics originated.

The above-mentioned dynamical systems, for which economic examples exist, are summarised in Table 8.2. These systems constitute only a part of the spectrum of dynamical systems with chaotic properties. The majority of intensively investigated systems do not seem to possess much relevance to economics. It is, for example, possible to construct examples of the emergence of the well-known Lorenz attractor in models of urban evolution, but the models are highly structurally unstable and the results depend crucially on the numerical specification of the models. A family of dynamical systems that allows for a broader spectrum of possible applications will be outlined in Section 3 together with an economic example from standard business-cycle theory.

*Table 8.2*   Examples of families of chaotic dynamical systems

| Dimension | Discrete time | Continuous time |
|-----------|---------------|-----------------|
| $n = 1$ | unimodal maps (non-invertible) | impossible |
| $n = 2$ | diffeomorphisms (snap-back repellers, horseshoe maps, transversal homoclinic orbits) | impossible |
| $n = 3$ | ditto | forced oscillators Shil'nikov scenario (homoclinic orbits) |
| $n > 3$ | ditto | coupled oscillators ($n = 6$) |

## 3   THE SHIL'NIKOV SCENARIO AND SPIRAL-TYPE CHAOTIC ATTRACTORS

It has been observed that almost all chaotic dynamical systems in higher-dimensional state space possess so-called *homoclinic orbits*. A homoclinic orbit or a *saddle loop* is a trajectory that leaves a saddle point on the unstable manifold and returns to it on the stable manifold. One of the few theorems that refer to the existence of such homoclinic orbits in establishing chaotic motion is due to Shil'nikov (1965).[14] The Shil'nikov theorem deals with a specific homoclinic orbit which is depicted in Figure 8.1. The homoclinic orbit approaches the fixed point in a spiralling fashion on the stable manifold.

It is difficult to apply the Shil'nikov theorem directly to a specific dynamical system but it was demonstrated by Arneodo, Coullet and Tresser (1981, 1982) that the third-order differential equation

$$\dddot{x} + a\ddot{x} + \dot{x} = f_\mu(x), \quad a > 0 \tag{10}$$

is compatible with the Shil'nikov theorem for several members of the one-parameter family of functions $f_\mu(x)$, including

$$f_\mu(x) = \begin{cases} 1 + bx \text{ if } x < 0 \\ 1 - \mu x \text{ if } x \geq 0 \end{cases} \quad \text{and} \quad f_\mu = \mu x(1 - x)$$

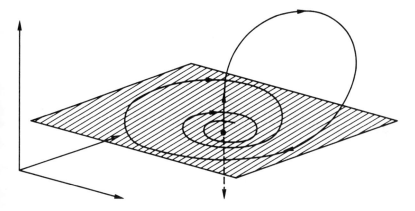

*Figure 8.1*   A Shil'nikov-type homoclinic orbit

i.e. a linear tent function and the logistic function, respectively, for appropriate values of the parameter $\mu$. The essential property of the function $f_\mu(x)$ is that an interval $J \subset \mathbf{R}$ is mapped to itself and that the function is unimodal. In contrast to unimodal chaotic maps in one-dimensional, discrete-time systems, rather flat shapes of the function are sufficient to encounter chaotic motion in (10) in many cases.

In the following, a pedagogical economic example of the emergence of equation (10) will be presented that constitutes a minor modification to Metzler's (1941) cycle model with inventories.[15]

Let $Y$ denote the national product and assume that output adjusts according to discrepancies between the desired and actual inventory stock, i.e.

$$\dot{Y} = \alpha[B^d(t) - B(t)], \quad \alpha > 0 \tag{11}$$

with $B^d(t)$ as the desired and $B(t)$ as the actual inventory stock at $t$. The actual inventory stock changes if disequilibria prevail on the goods market, i.e.

$$\dot{B}(t) = S(Y) - I(Y) \tag{12}$$

with $S$ and $I$ as savings and investment, respectively. The desired inventory stock is assumed to depend linearly on expected output, $Y^e(t)$, in $t$:

$$B^d(t) = kY^e(t), \quad k > 0 \tag{13}$$

Expected output is determined according to a modified extrapolative expectation hypothesis which considers not only the rate of change of current output but which also includes the changes in this rate:

$$Y^e(t) = Y + a_1 \dot{Y}(t) + a_2 \ddot{Y}(t) \tag{14}$$

Combining (14) and the differentiated forms of (11)–(13) yields the third-order differential equation

$$\dddot{Y} + \frac{\alpha k a_1 - 1}{\alpha k a_2} \ddot{Y} + \frac{1}{a_2} \dot{Y} = \frac{S(Y) - I(Y)}{k a_2} \tag{15}$$

or, abbreviated:

$$\dddot{Y} + A_1 \ddot{Y} + A_2 \dot{Y} = A_3[S(Y) - I(Y)] \tag{16}$$

In terms of deviations from the stationary equilibrium, (16) can be written as

$$\dddot{y} + A_1 \ddot{y} + A_2 \dot{y} = A_3(s(y) - i(y)) \tag{17}$$

Gandolfo (1983) demonstrated that (17) is globally unstable when savings is a linear function of output, when investment is constant, and when $A_1 < 0$ and $A_2 > 0$. Suppose on the contrary that $s(y)$ and $i(y)$ be non-linear but monotone functions of output, and assume that the difference $s(y) - i(y)$ is a unimodal function of $y$ with critical value $y_c > 0$. The steepness of the function can be controlled by the parameter $A_3$. When $A_1 > 0$ and $A_2$ close to 1, equation (17) is qualitatively identical with equation (10) with a logistic form of $f_\mu(\cdot)$. Figure 8.2 shows a plot of a numerically calculated trajectory of (17).[16] The largest Lyapunov exponent for the chosen parameter constellation is slightly positive, the sum of all exponents is negative. The set of points in the figure therefore represents a chaotic attracting set.

The example presented above is not very robust with respect to structural changes. In fact, adding numerically small higher-order time derivatives on the left-hand side of (17) does not guarantee that the dynamical behaviour is still characterised by attractors like the one in Figure 8.2. However, small variations in the parameters or replacing the constant coefficients by slightly non-linear functions do not immediately destroy the chaotic behaviour in these systems.

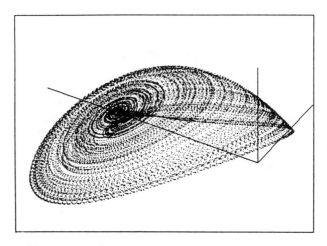

*Figure 8.2*   The Shil'nikov-type attractor of (17)

The example shows that it is relatively easy to transform a traditional model into a dynamical system that is compatible with the Shil'nikov scenario.[17] The modification is certainly arbitrary, but it should be kept in mind that the original model does not dwell on the only meaningful assumptions. In fact, the standard result in the original Metzler models can only be found when a subset of all possible assumptions on the structure of the r.h.s. expression in (17) is considered.

## 4   THE RELEVANCE OF NON-LINEARITIES FOR BUSINESS-CYCLE THEORY

All examples of non-linear, endogenous-cycle models mentioned above are extremely simple models with respect to their economic content. No single model can claim to explain more than one or two items in the list of so-called stylised facts. Genuinely non-linear, traditional business-cycle models or modifications of linear models should therefore be considered as classroom models.

It can be argued that linear business-cycle models represent a more adequate approach to an explanation of observable fluctuations in empirical time series because considerably more stylised facts can be modelled with this approach. At least two objections can be made at this point:

- Whether or not a phenomenon is called a stylised fact depends to some degree on the dominating paradigm. An example is the discussion on the symmetry or asymmetry of up- and down-swings over a cycle. Only rarely can this (empirically actually ambiguous) phenomenon be found in the list of stylised facts in the rational expectations literature, while non-linear time-series analysts usually consider this phenomenon as their starting-point.
- How many stylised facts can be explained by a model depends mainly on the dimension of the model. It cannot be expected that a simple non-linear model whose dynamic behaviour is determined by a two-dimensional or three-dimensional difference or differential equation system can generate motions in its variables that are completely satisfactory from an empirical point of view. The advantage of the linear approach consists in the fact that higher-dimensional systems of difference equations can be solved more easily. The model economy can then be more complex than its non-linear counterpart.

The dynamic complexity of non-linear dynamical systems does not provide much hope that large-scale non-linear economic models can be investigated by purely analytical methods. In most cases numerical simulations will constitute the only way to derive information on the dynamical behaviour of a model economy. It should be noted, however, that numerical simulations are also required in the linear case when permanent exogenous shocks are superimposed on the endogenous system dynamics, i.e., when irregularities are to be modelled. Thus, the analytical advantage of linear models vanishes in the really interesting case. In addition to the standard objections to the usage of simulation experiments, another objection emerges when the dynamical system is non-linear. While a simulation can nicely demonstrate the dynamical behaviour of a system when, e.g. parameters are changed, it usually cannot determine the origin of a particular type of motion. The interaction of the elements of a dynamical system which are actually responsible for the onset of, e.g., chaotic motion, can be hidden for an experimenter though he may know precise parameter values for the onset of turbulence.[18]

Linear business cycle models represent an artificial subset of all possible structural forms of dynamical systems in economics. Nevertheless, when exogenous, stochastic terms are superimposed on these models, they can fit empirical time-series amazingly well. However, from a theoretical point of view it is rather unsatisfactory when non-economic forces are finally responsible for the persistence of economic cycles. On the other hand, recent work in non-linear time-series analysis has (tentatively) demonstrated that non-linearities probably play a dominant role in the generation of empirical time-series. Linear stochastic models can be very good statistical approximations to non-linear time-series, but they might not reflect the true dynamical structure of the economy.

Non-linear models represent an alternative to the linear approach only when these models generate endogenous and persistent fluctuations. Endogenous fluctuations in a model usually imply that the fixed point of the dynamic process, i.e., the stationary equilibrium, is unstable.[19] However, it should be stressed that an unstable stationary equilibrium in a non-linear model does not mean that the economy is globally unstable. For example, when a non-linear system possesses an attracting closed orbit, the notion of fixed-point stability simply has to be replaced by the notion of orbital stability. When a model economy has an attracting set in the form of a fixed-point attractor, a limit cycle, or a strange attractor, the motion is bounded in a neighbourhood of this set, and the paradigm of a stable economy is actually not violated. This does not conflict with the assumption of temporary equilibrium on single markets, i.e., that supply always equals demand, because examples of oscillating equilibria exist.

In the dynamical-systems literature, oscillating behaviour in a dynamical system is synonymous with the presence of non-linearities. When a non-linear dynamical system allows for endogenous oscillations, the onset of chaotic motion can be expected in a variety of models with a sufficiently high dimension. If the task of business-cycle theory consists in providing theoretical descriptions of those economic forces which imply an irregular oscillating behaviour of an economy, non-linearities should be natural ingredients in cycle models. The analytical problems mentioned above will prevent the construction of large-scale models, and non-linear business cycle models can therefore serve only as pedagogical examples of the onset of complex cyclical motion.

This pedagogical character also follows from another consideration. Chaotic dynamical systems emerge in completely deterministic environments. The assumption of deterministic relations fixed one-to-one laws of motion is an unrealistic hypothesis that can be dated back to early neoclassical economist who were inspired by the mechanistic world-view. The best that can be done in many if not most descriptions of actual behaviour is to provide upper and lower bounds to the change in a variable. Modelling stochastic dynamical systems or differential inclusions might be considered the only satisfactory way to depict the evolution of actual economies.[20] However, an analytical treatment of chaotic dynamical systems with stochastic components involves severe mathematical difficulties, implying that numerical simulations will once again be necessary for an illustration of the system dynamics.

Summarising, the following conclusions might be drawn for economic dynamics and business-cycle theory.

- Business-cycle theory deals with analytical explanations of observable irregular fluctuations. Economic theory should therefore disregard exogenous influences when they are mainly responsible for the onset and persistence of cycles. It follows that business-cycle models should be non-linear models that allow for chaotic motion.
- Non-linear business-cycle models are naturally low-dimensional dynamical systems. There is not much hope to gain economic insight into numerically simulated high-dimensional systems.
- When low-dimensional systems are the appropriate objects in studying non-linear economic systems, traditional business-cycle models like the ones presented above should be revived. The linear character of most models can usually be overcome by assuming economically plausible non-linearities. Most elements of modern business-cycle models like accelerators, production lags, inventory holdings, expectations, etc., which are responsible for the onset of oscillations can be found in traditional models.
- Non-linear business-cycle theory will probably never be able to offer models that can explain a considerable list of stylised facts because the dimension of the models is too low.
- Deterministic, non-linear, chaotic business-cycle models have a classroom character because they do not take stochastic elements in economic relations into account.

**Notes**

1. Cf. Grandmont (1988), Nusse (1987), Whitley (1983), or Lorenz (1989) for surveys of mathematical results on one-dimensional unimodal maps.
2. Cf. Gandolfo/Martinengo/Padoan (1981) for a detailed discussion of discrete-time versus continuous-time concepts in economic dynamics and an introduction to continuous-time econometrics.

3. Cf. Baumhol/Benhabib (1989) and Kelsey (1988) for surveys of the period-doubling route to chaos and economic examples.
4. For example, when the Schwarzian derivative is negative, when the origin is a repeller, and when the critical point is mapped to the origin, the map is chaotic with sensitive dependence on initial conditions. Cf. Whitley (1983) for details.
5. A map $f$ is called a $C^k$-diffeomorphism if it is one-to-one, onto, and $f$ and its inverse are $k$-times differentiable.
6. Extensive lists of established, chaotic, dynamical systems can be found in Garrido – Simó (1983) and the multivolume book by Abraham and Shaw (1983) with many graphical illustrations.
7. The Poincaré-Bendixson theorem or the Hopf bifurcation theorem can be appropriate tools for establishing the emergence of endogenous fluctuations in these systems. Cf. Lorenz (1989) for a survey.
8. Cf. Levinson and Smith (1942) for details.
9. Cf. Lorenz (1989) pp. 147f.
10. Cf. Guckenheimer and Holmes (1983) pp. 67ff. for details.
11. Cf. Puu (1987) for a similar example. Other examples can easily be constructed, cf. Lorenz (1987b) for a model of a multisector economy. The pioneering paper is Goodwin (1947) who investigated spill-over effects between markets.
12. The following example is inspired by Puu (1987).
13. Note that this is a strong assumption. A dynamical system can be solved only in very particular cases, e.g., when only linearities are involved. In addition, a specific parameter constellation is required for permanent oscillations in the linear case.
14. Compare, e.g., Guckenheimer – Holmes (1983) for a discussion of a particular version of the theorem that makes use of the notion of Smale's (1963) horseshoes (cf. Grandmont, 1988 for the construction of these maps).
15. A more detailed discussion of the following model can be found in Lorenz (1988). The original Metzler model is formulated in discrete time. The continuous-time version is due to Gandolfo (1983) and is better suited for modelling stocks and flows.
16. The simulated equation is $\ddot{Y} + 0.4\dot{Y} + 0.95Y = 0.6Y(1.3 - Y)$.
17. Another economic example of the Shil'nikov scenario can be found in Lorenz (1988) in a reconsideration of Phillips's (1954) multiplier–accelerator.
18. As an example consider the well-known two-dimensional Henon map. It still does not seem to be entirely clear whether the map generates a strange attractor or whether the standard graph reflects a motion in the neighbourhood of the unstable manifold.
19. An exception to this rule can be found in systems with multiple, competing attractors.
20. This uncertainty can be incorporated into dynamic economic models in the same qualitative way as in stochastic linear models, but it is not required that stochastic elements have a dominating influence.

## References

Abraham, R. H. and Shaw, C. D. (1983) *Dynamics, the Geometry of Behavior* (Santa Cruz: Aerial).

Arneodo, A., Coullet, P. and Tresser, C. (1981) 'Possible New Strange Attractors with Spiral Structure', *Communications in Mathematical Physics*, vol. 79, pp. 573–9.

Arneodo, A., Coullet, P. and Tresser, C. (1982) 'Oscillations with Chaotic Behavior: An Illustration of a Theorem by Shil'nikov', *Journal of Statistical Physics* 27, pp. 171–82.

Baumol, W. J. and Benhabib, J. (1989) 'Chaos: Significance, Mechanism, and Economic Applications', *Journal of Economic Perspective*, vol. 3, pp. 77–105.

Boldrin, M. and Montrucchio, L. (1986) 'On the Indeterminacy of Capital Accumulation Paths', *Journal of Economic Theory*, vol. 40, pp. 26–39.

Dana, R. A. and Malgrange, P. (1984) 'The Dynamics of a Discrete Version of a Growth Cycle Model', in J. P. Ancot (ed.) *Analysing the Structure of Economic Models* (The Hague: Martinus Nijhoff) pp. 205–22.

Day, R. H. (1982) 'Irregular Growth Cycles', *American Economic Review*, vol. 72, pp. 406–14.

Day, R. H. and Shafer, W. (1986) 'Keynesian Chaos', *Journal of Macroeconomics*, vol. 7, pp. 277–95.

Diamond, P. (1976) 'Chaotic Behaviour of Systems of Difference Equations', *International Journal of Systems Science*, vol. 7, pp. 953–6.

Gandolfo, G. (1983) *Economic Dynamics: Methods and Models* (Amsterdam: North-Holland) 2nd edn.

Gandolfo, G., Martinengo, G. and Padoan, P. C. (1981) *Qualitative Analysis and Econometric Estimation of Continuous Time Dynamic Models* (Amsterdam: North-Holland).

Garrido, L. and Simó, C. (1983) 'Prolog: Some Ideas About Strange Attractors' in L. Garrido (ed.) *Dynamical Systems and Chaos* (Berlin–Heidelberg–New York: Springer).

Goodwin, R. M. (1946) 'Innovations and the Irregularity of Economic Cycles', *Review of Economics and Statistics*, vol. 28.

Goodwin, R. M. (1947) 'Dynamical Coupling with Especial Reference to Markets Having Production Lags', *Econometrica*, vol. 15, pp. 181–204.

Goodwin, R. M. (1951) 'The Non-linear Accelerator and the Persistence of Business Cycles', *Econometrica*, vol. 19, pp. 1–17.

Grandmont, J.-M. (1988) 'Non-linear Difference Equations, Bifurcations, and Chaos', CEPREMAP # 8811, forthcoming in *Market Psychology and Business Cycles*.

Guckenheimer, J. and Holmes, P. (1983) *Non-linear Oscillations, Dynamical Systems and Bifurcations of Vector Fields* (New York–Berlin–Heidelberg: Springer).

Herrmann, R. (1985) 'Stability and Chaos in a Kaldor-type Model', DP 22, Department of Economics, University of Göttingen.

Hommes, C. (1989) 'Periodic, Quasi-Periodic and Chaotic Dynamics in a Simple Piece-wise Linear Non-Walrasian Macromodel', mimeo, University of Groningen.

Kaldor, N. (1940) 'A Model of the Trade Cycle', *Economic Journal*, vol. 50, pp. 78–92.

Kelsey, D. (1988) 'The Economics of Chaos or the Chaos of Economics', *Oxford Economic Papers*, vol. 40, pp. 1–31.

Levinson, N. and Smith, O. K. (1942) 'A General Equation for Relaxation Oscillations', *Duke Mathematical Journal*, vol. 9, pp. 382–403.

Lorenz, H.-W. (1987a) 'International Trade and the Possible Occurrence of Chaos', *Economics Letters*, vol. 23, pp. 135–8.

Lorenz, H.-W. (1987b) 'Strange Attractors in a Multisector Business Cycle Model', *Journal of Economic Behavior and Organization*, vol. 8, pp. 397–411.

Lorenz, H.-W. (1987c) 'Goodwin's Non-linear Accelerator and Chaotic Motion', *Zeitschrift für Nationalökonomie – Journal of Economics*, vol. 47, pp. 413–18.

Lorenz, H.-W. (1988) 'Spiral-Type Chaotic Attractors in Low-Dimensional Continuous-Time Business Cycle Models', mimeo, University of Göttingen.

Lorenz, H.-W. (1989) *Non-linear Dynamical Economics and Chaotic Motion* (Berlin–Heidelberg–New York: Springer).

Marotto, F. R. (1978) 'Snap-Back Repellers Imply Chaos in $R^n$', *Journal of Mathematical Analysis and Applications*, vol. 72, pp. 199–223.

Metzler, L. A. (1941) 'The Nature and Stability of Inventory Cycles', *Review of Economics and Statistics*, vol. 23, pp. 113–29.

Nusse, H. E. (1987) 'Asymptotically Periodic Behavior in the Dynamics of Chaotic Mappings', *SIAM Journal of Applied Mathematics*, vol. 47, pp. 498–515.

Phillips, A. W. (1954) 'Stabilisation Policy in a Closed Economy', *Economic Journal*, vol. 64, pp. 290–323.

Pohjola, M. J. (1981) 'Stable and Chaotic Growth: the Dynamics of a Discrete Version of Goodwin's Growth Cycle Model', *Zeitschrift für Nationalökonomie*, vol. 41, pp. 27–38.

Puu, T. (1987) 'Complex Dynamics in Continuous Models of the Business Cycle', in D. Batten, J. Casti, and B. Johansson (eds) *Economic Evolution and Structural Change* (Berlin–Heidelberg–New York: Springer).

Shil'nikov, L. P. (1965) 'A Case of the Existence of a Countable Number of Periodic Motions', *Soviet Math. Dokl.* vol. 6, pp. 163–6.

Smale, S. (1963) 'Diffeomorphisms with Many Periodic Points', in S. S. Cairns, (ed.) *Differential and Combinatorical Topology* (Princeton: Princeton University Press) pp. 63–80.

Stutzer, M. (1980) 'Chaotic Dynamics and Bifurcation in a Macro-Model', *Journal of Economic Dynamics and Control*, vol. 2, pp. 253–76.

Whitley, D. (1983) 'Discrete Dynamical Systems in Dimensions One and Two', *Bulletin of the London Mathematical Society*, vol. 15, pp. 177–217.

Woodford, M. (1989) 'Imperfect Financial Intermediation and Complex Dynamics', in W. Barnett, J. Geweke, and K. Shell (eds) *Chaos, Sunspots, Bubbles, and Non-linearity* (Cambridge: Cambridge University Press).

# Comment

Christian Groth
UNIVERSITY OF COPENHAGEN

Until recently, and perhaps still, investigators of dynamic economic problems have been inclined to reject models not containing asymptotically stable steady states or limit cycles. However, the mathematical theory of non-linear dynamics and 'chaotic attractors' has opened our eyes to the possibility of irregular, fluctuating and *yet bounded* motion arising from a deterministic dynamic system. This gives new ways of interpreting the seemingly random character of economic time-series. It also throws new light (or 'darkness' if you want) on the theory of expectations and forecasting because small errors or uncertainties in the initial conditions can give rise to evolutions which are completely different after some time. If a dynamic system is chaotic – i.e. contains bounded trajectories that are neither asymptotically periodic nor asymptotically stationary – then knowledge of the state of the system for an arbitrarily long time does not in practice enable one to predict the subsequent evolution past a limited time range.

The recent literature has shown several examples of chaotic motion generated by discrete-time dynamics based on economic first principles. In continuous-time systems, which in order to generate chaos must be of dimension three at least, such examples seem, by now, rare (if we disregard coupled oscillators and forced oscillators).

The paper by Lorenz has drawn our attention to an interesting application by the physicists Arneodo, Coullet and Tresser,[1] of a theorem by Shil'nikov on existence of a 'strange attractor' (an attractor which is neither a sink nor a limit cycle) in a third-order differential equation. Lorenz provides a model which is, as far as I know, the first attempt to utilise the Arneodo *et al.* conditions in economics. Although I have my reservations as to the particular model proposed by Lorenz, I find this attempt very useful as an inspiration for further research.

Now to the specific model offered by Lorenz as an economic example of the Shil'nikov–Arneodo *et al.* scenario. The model is claimed to constitute a minor modification of Metzler's (1941) inventory cycle model with extrapolative expectations. There is no doubt that it is modification, though it is possible to question whether it is minor. The first step in the modification consists in a transformation to continuous time of the original discrete-time version by Metzler, a transformation which corresponds to a model in Gandolfo (1983). The second step in the modification is to change the linear savings and constant fixed investment hypotheses proposed by Gandolfo.

The model with which Lorenz ends up can be written:

$$\dot{Y} = \alpha(B^d - B) \qquad\qquad \alpha > 0 \qquad\qquad (1)$$

$$B^d = kY^e \qquad\qquad k > 0 \qquad\qquad (2)$$

$$Y^e = Y + \theta\dot{Y} + \frac{\theta^2}{2}\ddot{Y} \qquad \theta > 0 \qquad\qquad (3)$$

$$\dot{B} = Y - (C + I) \qquad\qquad\qquad (4)$$

$$C = C(Y) \qquad\qquad\qquad (5)$$

$$I = I(Y) \qquad\qquad\qquad (6)$$

with $Y$, $B^d$, $B$, $Y^e$, $C$ and $I$, i.e. output, desired inventories $\theta$ time units ahead, actual inventories, expected output $\theta$ time units ahead, consumption, and investment in fixed capital, as the endogenous variables. The expectations in (3) are extrapolative in the sense of following a second-order Taylor approximation.

In order to make this example fulfil the Arneodo *et al.* conditions for a strange attractor Lorenz assumes:

(i) $\theta \approx \sqrt{2}$;

(ii) $\alpha > \frac{1}{k\theta}$; and

(iii) the function $f_k(Y) \equiv \frac{2}{k\theta^2}[Y - C(Y) - I(Y)]$ has a hump, cf. Figure 8.2.

Presupposing the marginal propensity to consume to be non-increasing, it is a weakness of this example that it depends crucially on investment in fixed capital being a strictly convex function of the output level. Making investment a function of the expected rate of change of output or of the gap between actual and desired fixed

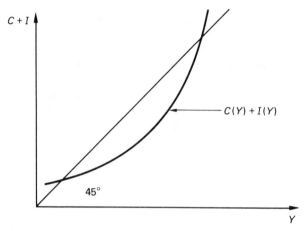

*Figure 8.3*

capital, as it should rather be, destroys the example.

Furthermore, the model seems susceptible to the following criticisms:

(a) output should adjust not only to a discrepancy between actual and desired inventories, but also to a gap between current production and sales (equation 1));
(b) desired inventories should be related to expected sales rather than expected activity level (equation 2).

One might therefore ask whether remedying these two points would help making the Shil'nikov – Arneodo conditions more plausible. At least the following model which, albeit still *ad hoc*, is more in line both with the old Metzlerian ideas and with empirical research on inventories, leads to the tentative answer: No!

$$J^d = \lambda(B^d - B) \qquad\qquad \lambda > 0 \qquad\qquad (7)$$

$$\dot{Y}_c = \gamma(J^d + C - Y_c) \qquad \gamma > 0 \qquad\qquad (8)$$

$$B^d = kC^e \qquad\qquad k > 0 \qquad\qquad (9)$$

$$C^e = C + \theta\dot{C} + \frac{\theta^2}{2}\ddot{C} \qquad \theta > 0 \qquad\qquad (10)$$

$$\dot{B} = Y_c - C \tag{11}$$

$$C = C(Y) \tag{12}$$

$$Y = Y_c + I_0 \qquad\qquad I_0 > 0 \tag{13}$$

where $J^d$ is desired inventory investment, $Y_c$ is production of consumption goods, and $C^e$ is expected sales of consumption goods $\theta$ time units ahead. We assume investment in fixed capital, $I_0$, constant, because entering a proper investment function would result in a *fourth* order dynamical system.[2]

Now, this model gives a third-order differential equation in $Y$ containing the multiplicative terms $\dot{Y}\ddot{Y}$ and $\dot{Y}^2$ (if $C'''(Y) \neq 0$, also $\dot{Y}^3$), i.e. the proposition of Arneodo et al. cannot be used. Replacing extrapolative expectations by adaptive expectations still leaves us with the term $\dot{Y}^2$. To get rid of these multiplicative terms we need $C''(Y) \equiv 0$, but then we just have a linear (and instable) system.

What all this amounts to is first that it appears hard to base the needed hill-shaped function $f_u(x)$ on excess supply as a function of the activity level. But other candidates for a hill-shaped function, usable in other theoretical contexts, are possible.[3] Second, it seems difficult to maintain that 'traditional models in business-cycle theory can exhibit chaotic motion when economically irrelevant modifications to the structural relations are undertaken' as claimed in Lorenz's introduction. Indeed, one might call into question this project, because of the *ad hoc* character of traditional business-cycle models. They seem more in need of economically *relevant* modifications.

This leads to my final remark. I see no reason to favour the non-linear business-cycle approach as compared with the linear-with-exogenous-stochastic-shocks-approach on the grounds that 'from a theoretical point of view it is rather unsatisfactory when non-economic forces are finally responsible for the persistence of economic cycles', as Lorenz says towards the end of his paper. Random disturbances to the economy from the environment (weather, nature, biology, science, politics etc.) seem inevitable. And – to speak in the language of Frisch – even if the *impulses* are external shocks, the *propagation* mechanism is of an economic character. Which of the approaches is the better, remains, I suppose, a question of their ability to explain the empirical regularities we observe.

**Notes**

1. For references, see Lorenz's paper.
2. This is so, even if the second derivative in the Taylor expansion (10) is ignored, or if we use adaptive expectations instead of extrapolative expectations.
3. The evolution and diffusion of new technology is an example, cf. Goodwin's paper (Chapter 16).

# Part V

# 'Golden Age' Fluctuations and Inter-war Regimes: Two Empirical Studies

# 9 Money and Business Cycles in Britain, 1870–1913

Forrest Capie
CITY UNIVERSITY, LONDON

## INTRODUCTION

Friedman and Schwartz's work on the monetary history of the USA, especially the evidence presented in 'Money and Business Cycles' (1963) had a profound impact on our views on the American economy. Their work drew attention to the need for similar studies of other countries. But surprisingly no long-period study of the cycle after 1870 was ever carried out for Britain. Even more surprisingly in the latest and avowedly quantitative economic history textbook on Britain (Floud and McCloskey, 1981) there is no chapter on money. There is a brief dismissal of the role of money in the cycle.

The empirical case for money and economic activity, particularly the fluctuations in activity, has never been set out for Britain in this period. Only in recent years have sufficiently robust data on money and income allowed serious study and in that period interest in the subject appears to have waned. I therefore unabashedly set out to examine the case, to see if there are the kinds of regularities that would allow formulation or adoption of hypotheses, and the testing of them. One of the founders of business cycle analysis, Wesley Mitchell was accused of measurement without theory. But as Friedman paraphrased Mitchell in an eloquent defence:

> In the study of any class of phenomena it is necessary first to examine the phenomena themselves, and to find empirical regularities, in order to provide a basis for generalization and abstraction; and at this stage the orderly organization of empirical data is more important than the elaboration and refinement of abstract hypotheses. (*Journal of Political Economy*, 1950, p. 469).

There seems to have been a return to an approach that historians generally feel happier with, that of setting out as surely as possible what happened, before going on to attempt to say how and why. In a recent NBER conference volume (Gordon, 1986) there was, as one reviewer put it, 'a commendable return to National Bureau traditions, most authors [being] concerned mainly to document what happened, rather than skipping immediately to the question why' (Eichengreen, 1987, p. 581).

Of course if the empirical regularities are not found it may simply be that the data or the measuring devices are at fault. But until regularities are found there is little point in pursuing the hypotheses. I proceed in that tradition by examining the pattern of the variables and where possible indicating the nature of the relationship. Economic historians were all, after all, brought up on that distinguished economic historian, J. H. Clapham, who wrote, 'Every economic historian should . . . have acquired what might be called the statistical sense, the habit of asking . . . how large? how long? how often? and how representative?' I think we have now, even if we have changed the words to amplitude, periodicity, frequency and significance.

It is virtually impossible though, to work without some implicit hypothesis, however subconsciously it is lodged. Dangers can arise when a hypothesis is believed in too passionately for all the evidence can be made to support the hypothesis if the belief in it is strong enough. W. S. Jevons was one of the first serious investigators of business cycles. According to a recent assessment, 'he searched avidly for evidence of crisis where there appeared to be ones [*sic*] missing . . . and even for evidence which would make the cycles come at exactly equal intervals'. (Morgan, 1989) Incidentally Jevons's evidence was essentially on timing. He was thoroughly seduced by his 'treacherous', 'entrancing' and 'beautiful coincidence' (Morgan, 1989, ch. 1, line 5).

In this paper I set out a brief historiography of the subject and follow that with an outline of the theory that supplies our basic hypotheses and directs us to the variables and measurement required. Then follow a number of different measures of the series and some tentative conclusions on the relationship, or in this case mostly the absence of relationship. We are led to conclude that there is no clear relationship between money and the business cycle in Britain over this period at least. Indeed there may be little or no cyclicality in the monetary data. A brief attempt at explaining this contrast with the USA follows. It rests upon the nature of the banking system and the role of the Bank of England.

**Historiography**

Fluctuations in the British economy once received a great deal of attention in the literature on British economic history. The view that came to dominate was that exports were the principal initiating factor in economic fluctuations. This was so for all periods almost since the beginning of industrialisation. This is a remarkable position to have reached for it is surely extraordinary that over two centuries, fluctuations that have invariably been described as cycles with regular periodicity, should be explained by activity abroad. Insistence on regular periodicity has disappeared from much of the cycle literature, but even if regular periodicity were not insisted on for the British experience, it would still be surprising for exports to be the principal source of shocks.

In an early, meticulous, and subsequently influential, study Gayer, Rostow, and Schwartz (1953) argued that for the years 1790–1850 exports were the essential trigger in expansionary phases of the cycle. They then gave a highly eclectic view of the cyclical process in which investment also played a part.

For the inter-war years in Britain leading economists of the time attributed the source of cycles to exports. Exports 'lead the way in time both into depression and out of depression' (Beveridge, 1939). The view that Britain's recessions were imported became the accepted one. Corner (1956) added evidence on the great depression. Matthews, too, concluded that exports were of major significance in inter-war cycles. Even though after 1945 the nature of cycles had clearly changed, the view that exports could again have been responsible, has been advanced by Britton (1986).

But for no other period has the view been put more strongly than for the years 1870–1914. Ford (1963) (and in a subsequent series of publications) has argued that the key element in fluctuations was exports: 'the proximate cause of cyclical fluctuations in the United Kingdom from 1860 to 1914 lay in the behaviour of exports of goods and services, aided sometimes by home investment . . .'. Investment is seldom left out of these accounts and the multiplier–accelerator model applied. Ford has reiterated these views in a distinguished economic history textbook in the 1980s (about to go into a second edition in the 1990s). This role for exports has been given further support in a recent study by Hatton (1987) who concluded that 'exports were an important determinant of economic fluctuations between 1870 and 1913' (Hatton, 1987, p. 15).

Most of this explanation begs the question about the genuine origin of business cycles. It is not of course logically impossible that the source of fluctuations is exogenous. Among the earliest explanations of fluctuations was that of sunspots and that was certainly exogenous. But the export argument for Britain rests in large part on the openness of the British economy where for much of the period exports have been in excess of 25 per cent of output. With this degree of openness, irregular shocks could certainly buffet the economy and could be capable via the multiplier model of initiating sharp movements in total output. It would remain rather unsatisfactory evidence in the search for understanding of business cycles in general. An attempted endogenous link has been postulated. It is that British exports in their turn depended on British overseas investment. The argument is that the scale and path of British overseas investment determined the demand for British goods. Ford demonstrated that foreign lending led exports by one or two years. These arguments depended greatly on timing relationships.

A different version of this view for the late nineteenth century has been advanced by Matthews (1959). For Matthews investment was central to the explanation but it was a special view on investment and depended on the special place of Britain and the nature of the world economy. Britain's large overseas investment tended to alternate with large movements in domestic investment. In fact there is the appearance of something close to 15-to-20-year cycles in both these series. When the two are added together they produce a variable that peaks every seven to ten years in a way that coincided with peaks in national income. Matthews concluded (Matthews, 1959, p. 220) that 'the seven-to-ten-year periodicity of fluctuations in national income derived mainly from the existence of two unsynchronised waves . . . in home and foreign investment respectively'.

There has never therefore been much room for a monetary explanation – indeed it has recently been specifically rejected. Ford stated 'monetary influences were not a significant internal cyclical factor in the United Kingdom' (in Floud and McCloskey, 1981, p. 48). It is true that Hawtrey regarded the cycle as 'a purely monetary phenomenon' and he wrote extensively on the subject, drawing on British experience in the late nineteenth century without the benefit of robust data. One interpretation of Hawtrey (Haberler) is that depression came when demand fell after a shrinkage in the quantity of money. The solution lay in stabilising the flow of money. A shrinkage in the money stock led directly to a fall in consumer spending and recession followed since producers could not dispose of their output at anticipated prices. Stocks rose, production fell, unemployment rose and wages fell. In the upswing the opposite happened. But what lay behind changes in the money supply?

In the 1960s following the work of Friedman and Schwartz on the USA, Walters (1969) examined the role of money in Britain over the period 1880–1960s, in a statistical way. Specifically he attempted to test the competing monetary and Keynesian explanations. The results were not strong, though for the years 1880–1914 the monetary model performed better – changes in the money stock gave rise to almost equal-sized changes in nominal income, roughly half of which occurred in the current year and the remainder in the following year.

Recently, Eichengreen in questioning the usefulness of available structural models, turned to time-series methods. In using vector autoregression techniques that are in essence tests of antecedence he was careful to emphasise the limitations of the tests and to stress that they merely provided guidance for specifying reasonable structural relationships. But the results were sufficiently strong for him to conclude that 'for the late Victorian period (1869–1901) fluctuations in the monetary base emerge as the single most important determinant of the trade cycle'.

## SOME THEORETICAL CONSIDERATIONS

In approaching a problem such as this the economic historian takes up the available theoretical framework and endeavours to apply the elements that can be applied. The theory is invariably quite well-established – probably sufficiently established to be set out in recent textbooks; that is to say, quite widely agreed upon. It will often also be available in summary form in collections of studies by more strictly defined applied economists. However, this is less true for money and the cycle. The fact is that there is no widely agreed position on the role of money in the cycle. Just as that may have been about to emerge in the 1970s other developments in macroeconomics meant that business-cycle research took different turns and the 1980s have seen the growing consensus of the 1970s on money become another minority view. We have to go to Friedman and Schwartz (1963) for the essence of the monetary model.

This section, in preparing the way for an examination of the role of money in Britain in the late nineteenth century, outlines the monetary theory of the cycle that does seem to be reasonably settled.

We noted above that an early view on the role of money was that of Hawtrey. Hawtrey is sometimes accredited with having a monetary theory of the cycle. He certainly had a stronger view on money than most economists of the 1920s and 1930s who would mostly have agreed that the monetary theory of the cycle was the dominant explanation. But what would they have meant by that? Were they endorsing the view that changes in the money supply were the key source of business cycles? The answer is probably, 'no'. They simply believed that cyclical fluctuations would only occur in a developed monetary economy. Most economists of their time would have felt that money was essentially permissive or could on occasions be exacerbatory.

We really have to look to the USA for the precursor of the Friedman and Schwartz model – to Irving Fisher (1911). Fisher dealt with a cyclical process that was brought about by changes in the quantity of money, and that process was also affected by the changes brought about in other monetary variables such as inflationary expectations and nominal interest rates. Friedman and Schwartz worked within that quantity theory framework. When they distilled the results of their study of money in the USA, (Friedman and Schwartz, 1963) a study informed by the modern quantity theory, their focus was deliberately narrow: their attention was on the money stock and changes in that in relation to a business-cycle chronology defined by the National Bureau.

Their examination was in the first place a statistical one, primarily establishing some empirical relationships. The principal conclusion was that changes in the money stock conformed to the *major* movements in the reference cycle chronology with a long lead. And the question then was, which way was the influence running – was it from money to income? Their position was a cautious one: 'If the answer is affirmative, then one can speak of a monetary theory of business cycles or – more precisely – of the need to assign money an important role in a full theory of business cycles' (Friedman and Schwartz, 1963, p. 50).

The statistical evidence was then supported by detailed historical studies of some major movements, and following that they outlined a 'tentative sketch of the mechanism transmitting monetary changes'. The core of this was that unexpected rises in the rate of change of money growth – from, say, a Bank purchase of bonds – led the sellers of the bonds to rearrange their portfolios, first buying similar securities. But as they bid the price of these up, they made a switch to other securities and as their prices rose moved on to non-financial assets. The latter's price was at that stage relatively lower than financial assets. The rise that then came in the price of final goods tended to correct portfolios by making the real value of monetary assets less than they would otherwise be. An important point is that the process tends to overshoot because at the higher rate of price-rise the amount of money demanded will be less in real terms than initially, relative to wealth and income. In the early stages of the process holders overestimate the extent of monetary redundancy, having overvalued money stocks at unduly low levels of prices.

Initially there is a greater rise in monetary base than in broad money so there follows a period when the latter must for a while grow faster to catch up, for the relationship between the two is basically stable. But it is the tendency to overshoot that produces a cyclical adjustment process.

Friedman and Schwartz added that another feature of cyclical experience that could be accounted for by their material was the behaviour of the currency–deposit ratio. Following the bond purchase the initial redundant real balances are in the hands of holders of financial assets and are then diffused, so they are first in the hands of those with a low currency–deposit ratio. As redundant balances are diffused the currency–deposit ratio falls early in the contraction, reaches a trough around mid-expansion and then declines to mid contraction.

Slightly different stories would be told according to the source of money stock change. And the monetary interpretation leaves open the reasons for the change in the rate of growth of the money stock. There have been many different reasons in different historical situations. In the end though the core of the Friedman and Schwartz model is that a discrepancy can arise between desired and actual money balances.

Such a discrepancy is not allowed under the perfectly clearing markets of new classical models or of interest-rate equilibrating Keynesian models. And yet there is a connection with the new classical. For Lucas the cycle can come about from a confusion on the producer's part between relative and general prices. And he incorporates the Brunner and Meltzer distinction between transitory and permanent changes. There is a highly elastic response to a small change in price if it is regarded as transitory (rather than permanent). A small change in price thus brings about large changes in output which is what is observed in the cycle. Thus a change in the general price level that was mistaken for a change in a producer's own price and thought to be transitory would set cyclical forces in motion. The link with the monetary theory is that movements in prices are explained by movements in the quantity of money. This fact as Lucas says, 'is as well-established as any we know in aggregative economics, and is not sensitive to how one measures either prices or the quantity of money'. He goes on to say 'Everything points to a monetary shock as the force triggering the real business cycle.' (Lucas, 1981, p. 233).

These then are the bare elements of the monetary theory that we might consider as the starting-point in the investigation of money in late nineteenth-century Britain.

**Data**

A great deal of effort was devoted to data collection and improvement. A debate has run since the late nineteenth century on the role that money played in the economy in the period 1870–1914. Unfortunately, the monetary data used initially were seriously deficient and even the best efforts of Sheppard and others in the 1970s still left room for improvement. All our revisions and explanations and sources are presented in Capie and Webber (1985). The new series have been quite widely accepted as the improvements they purport to be and have found their way into the British bible of statistics, Mitchell's *British Historical Statistics* (1988).

These new monetary data have been collected in such a way as to allow the construction of a number of series whose behaviour is of interest in an investigation of the cycle – series such as the reserve–deposit ratio, the currency–deposit ratio and different definitions of money.

**The Reference-cycle Chronology**

There is one accepted monthly and annual chronology of the business cycle for Britain, that set out by Burns and Mitchell (1946). Friedman and Schwartz revised some of their turning points (see Table 9.1).

*Why did Friedman and Schwartz Modify Reference Cycle Phases?*

Friedman and Schwartz revised the NBER chronology up to 1938, and extended it through to 1975 by examining a small collection of

*Table 9.1*   Reference-cycle Chronology: Peaks and Troughs

| Burns and Mitchell Peak | Trough | Friedman and Schwartz Peak | Trough |
|---|---|---|---|
| 1872 Sep. | 1879 June | 1874 | 1879 |
| 1882 Dec. | 1886 June | 1883 | 1886 |
| 1890 Sep. | 1895 Feb. | 1890 | 1893 |
| 1903 June | 1904 Nov. | 1900 | 1904 |
| 1907 June | 1908 Nov. | 1907 | 1908 |
| 1912 Dec. | 1914 Sep. | 1913 | 1914 |

*Sources*: Burns and Mitchell (1946); Friedman and Schwartz (1982).

economic indicators. These revisions omit the 1901 trough and 1903 peak as well as shifting the peak for 1917 to 1918 (ibid, p. 74). There is one other difference: Friedman and Schwartz give a year only and not a month.

Friedman and Schwartz point out (ibid, p. 308, fn) that Burns and Mitchell did a far more exhaustive study of US than of UK data and had far more US data available. Friedman and Schwartz's own examination left them always inclined to recognise more turning-points the broader the range of data to examine, and they felt that the concentration of extra turning-points in the pre-1914 US data (25 compared with 13 in the UK, 1866–1914) might be artificial. Not only were there more US data but the UK data were given a less critical examination than the post-1914 statistics, where there are 28 US turning-points and 26 UK turning-points. Friedman and Schwartz postulate that the role of the UK was changed so drastically by the First World War that her cyclical pattern may also have changed and that Britain's financial pre-eminence in the world before the war may have enabled it to ride out fluctuations that would have left echoes at home after the war. Cycle phases were of shorter duration after the war, in the USA as well as in the UK, although it was more marked in the case of the UK.

However, if in the pre-war period cycles were transmitted internationally, and Britain was at the heart of the gold standard, it would seem strange that the UK should not have experienced all the cycles to some degree, and it may be that Burns and Mitchell's analysis, instead of affording the USA too many cycles pre-1914, did not award the UK enough (see Bordo, 1986).

**Trend and Cycle**

One means of removing trend from the data is that used by Friedman and Schwartz – to take the logarithm of first differences. This is a measure of the percentage rate of change from one time-period to the next. Figure 9.1 illustrates the result of this for the monetary base and output for Britain for the period 1870–1914, from which it can be seen there is no clear demonstration of unambiguous precedence either way. It could be argued that under the gold standard the direction of causation should run from income (output) to money but there is no evidence for that either in these series.

This result was broadly found for another series on the rate of change of the broad money measure and output, no case could be pushed very far on the strength of the evidence. A year by year tracing of the path of $M_3$ against real GDP would lend support to a lead of one or two years of money over output. (Again this could be perverse for the expected relationship under a gold standard.) However, it should be stressed that it is almost as easy to read the evidence the other way around with output leading money.

Equally there was no clear lead of money over prices, and no clear lag, and no other close correspondence. The series move together at times, are at odds at times and on occasions one leads while at another the other does. This same basic lack of obvious correspondence seems to be true of the broad money measure and prices.

The lack of clear correspondence between money and the business cycle holds irrespecive of the cycle chronology that is used.

**Amplitude of Movements in Rate of Change of Money Stock**

Friedman and Schwartz stressed that it was in major movements that money was important, and some account should therefore be taken of amplitude. One approach to this would be to measure amplitude in the NBER way and compare and possibly correlate the amplitude of the two series. But another perhaps more satisfactory approach – that of the Friedman-and-Schwartz study – is to compare the moving standard deviation of the annual percentage rate of change in the series. These standard deviations provide a measure of the variability of the respective rates of change of money and income. The objective is to see how the amplitude of cycles in the rate of change in the money stock is related to the severity of business cycles. The latter are now proxied by the measure of real output.

217

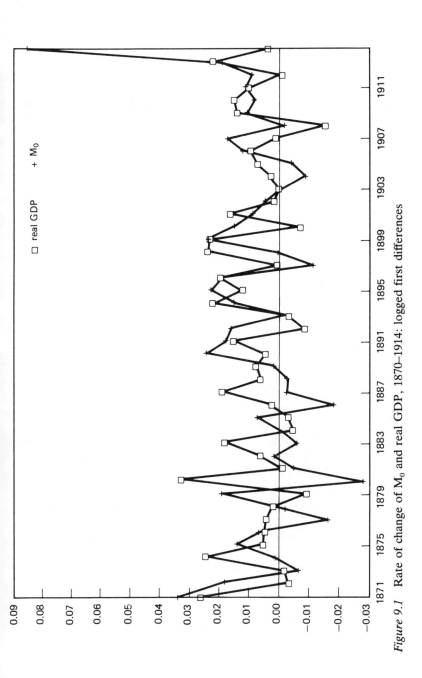

*Figure 9.1*  Rate of change of M₀ and real GDP, 1870–1914: logged first differences

Moving averages of four-year periods and seven-year periods were taken. The first allows a direct comparison with Friedman and Schwartz for the USA. They used a number of terms but the average length of the cycles there was four years. The second is used since the average length of the cycle over this period in Britain was seven years. Figure 9.2 plots the seven-year moving standard deviation for money ($M_3$) and output (GDP). The chart shows a moderately close relation between the variability of money and of output, but only from 1880 to 1900. In the 1870s there is apparently no correspondence and from 1900 to 1914 there is little. What stands out is that income is more variable than money throughout. This latter was a finding of Friedman and Schwartz and fits too with the Lucas story. The pattern for all the series was this general lack of correspondence. From this evidence there do not appear to be clear and unambiguous cycles and certainly none for income that correspond to the NBER's dating.

**Real and Nominal Variables**

Where the early discussion focused on accelerating and decelerating money growth, current discussion would substitute unanticipated money growth; it is alleged that only the unanticipated portion of the change in the money stock affects real variables. Barro (1977; 1978) pioneered a methodology that separated anticipated from unanticipated change. The methods used have been criticised on various counts and Barro himself resorted to a much simpler approach in his recently revised textbook. The approach is to take a proxy of recent trend in the variable and call that the normal path, then to extend that to the year being considered with the difference between actual and extended being taken to represent the unexpected.

Following Barro (1984) we carry out this exercise here to illustrate the movements and interactions between nominal and real variables. The focus is on shocks or surprises in money and prices in order to find interesting relationships with real variables. Table 9.2 does this for 1870–1914.

The table provides the shortfall of each variable in each recession across the period. The shortfall is calculated in the following way. The trough year of recession is taken. The previous peak year is the base year. The average rate of growth of the variable over the five years prior to the peak (which will usually include some downswing and upswing and hence approximate trend) is taken to represent

219

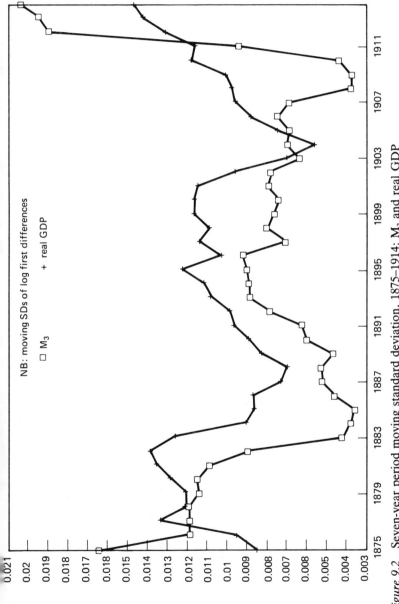

*Figure 9.2* Seven-year period moving standard deviation, 1875–1914: $M_3$ and real GDP

*Table 9.2*     Real and nominal variables during recessions 1870–1914

| Final year of recession:<br>Base year for comparison: | 1879<br>1874 | 1886<br>1883 | 1893<br>1890 | 1904<br>1900 | 1908<br>1907 | 1914<br>1913 |
|---|---|---|---|---|---|---|
| *Real Income* | | | | | | |
| $Y$ | 1239 | 1399 | 1547 | 2031 | 2041 | 2359 |
| $Y°$ | 1371 | 1477 | 1594 | 2144 | 2140 | 2403 |
| $Y° - Y$ as % shortfall | 10.7 | 5.6 | 3.1 | 5.6 | 4.9 | 1.9 |
| *Prices* | | | | | | |
| $P$ | 87 | 82 | 84 | 87 | 90 | 95 |
| $P°$ | 113 | 91 | 87 | 100 | 91 | 103 |
| $P° - P$ as % shortfall | 30.5 | 10.4 | 4.0 | 14.9 | 0.9 | 8.1 |
| *Money* (1) | | | | | | |
| $B$ | 15.6 | 14.0 | 16.0 | 19.7 | 20.8 | 28.8 |
| $B°$ | 16.8 | 13.5 | 15.3 | 20.9 | 21.1 | 24.3 |
| $B° - B$ as % shortfall | 7.6 | –3.7 | –3.9 | 6.0 | 1.4 | –15.6 |
| *Money* (2) | | | | | | |
| $M$ | 56.4 | 61.5 | 72.2 | 89.8 | 96.7 | 119.8 |
| $M°$ | 67.9 | 61.8 | 72.0 | 101.8 | 97.6 | 113.9 |
| $M° - M$ as % shortfall | 20.4 | 0.4 | –0.3 | 13.3 | –0.9 | –4.9 |

*Note*: $Y$ is real GDP, $P$ is the GNP deflator, $B$ the monetary base and $M$ broad money ($M_3$ equivalent).

normal. The 'normal' growth is then projected from the base year to show what a normal or expected figure would be in the year of deepest recession. The difference between the actual and the projected is the shortfall. Thus real GDP in 1908 was £2041m. In the previous peak (1907) it had been £2140m. Had income continued to grow at its normal rate it would have been greater – by 4.9 per cent. The shortfall is therefore 4.9 per cent. Therefore any negative shortfall is evidence of a higher figure in recession than expected.

The data on real income show recessions of roughly similar size in the nineteenth century except for the first which was twice normal severity and the last which was rather feeble.

Turning to the behaviour of the monetary base ($B$). For the first recession there is a 7.6 per cent shortfall. In the following two recessions there is an excess of base money – i.e. base money is larger than would have been provided, had previous trend growth continued. The next two are unremarkable and the final one should be treated with caution this being the 1914 financial crisis when war broke out and the gold standard abandoned and the monetary base hugely expanded by the monetary authorities. So over these six recessions before the First World War there is no clear relationship between contractions in output and shortfalls in the monetary base. The broader definition of money yields no clearer picture of any relationship. In three of five recessions there is virtually no shortfall, while in the other two it is rather substantial.

Finally prices. Here we find quite substantial shortfalls – by over 30 per cent in the first recession and by more than 8 per cent in three others. Given that there are no banking panics in the British economy over these years, there should be no abnormal change in the real demand for base money. In the two largest recessions there is a close correspondence between prices and broad money.

**Recent Time-series Techniques**

The exercise so far has proceeded within the conventional framework of measurement and reference-cycle chronology. But there have been serious challenges to these approaches. While it is obvious that modern industrial economies move unevenly through time, and the up- and down-movements have been seen as fluctuations about a trend it is possible to regard the movements as the result of a series of shocks that simply leave the impression of a cyclical pattern. The conventional approach to trend-cycle analysis has been to use *ad hoc* filters to detrend series using techniques such as moving averages (many of the results discussed above use just such a technique.) But recent research effort has focused on the nature of the movement in the series, in the jargon to discover whether the data are generated by a trend-stationary or a difference-stationary process and to see whether oscillations are transitory or persistent. Most of the work done has been on US data but some work on UK data (e.g. Mills and Taylor, 1989) reports a difference-stationary process for the period immediately after the Second World War but a trend-stationary process for the period 1860–1914 (Crafts, Leybourne and Mills, 1989, on a industrial-production series).

In this section I report briefly on some work in progress (Capie and Mills, 1989) that employs structural time-series models to establish the path of the trend growth of money and output and hence the extent and timing of fluctuations around the trend. The Kalman filter is used to decompose our respective series on income and money into their trend and cycle components. The technique allows such decomposition to estimate not on an *ad hoc* moving average but rather by an optimal linear filter derived by signal extraction techniques from the actual stochastic process generating the data. What the technique reveals is that there is indeed a cycle in British income data over this period. However, the cycle does not agree closely with the conventional (NBER) dating of the business cycle. There is occasional coincidence in the turning-points in the two chronologies, and at other points quite close correspondence. But there are also some large differences, the most extreme being that the revised series shows 1874 as a trough whereas it is a peak in the conventional dating.

The most interesting result though is that the monetary data do not show any cyclicality at all. This result is confirmation of a kind of our inability to detect cyclical relationship by other means. If we accept this result we would conclude that it was not monetary shocks that produced fluctuations in income in this period.

When the relationship is pursued more rigorously this result is confirmed – a weak or non-existent relationship between money and the cycle in real output.

**Some Explanation**

This section explores the possibility that it is the absence of financial crises in Britain that provides much of the explanation for the lack of movement in the monetary series. The monetarist approach to the question identifies financial crises with banking panics and regards these as exacerbatory for monetary contractions and therefore for the consequences of that contraction. (By implication if banking panics were removed a major source of monetary movements would be removed.) Where there is a loss of confidence in institutions, that leads the public to convert bank deposits into currency and results in a large contraction of deposits. The currency–deposit ratio rises sharply as does the reserve–deposit ratio. That behaviour in turn damages economic activity.

The other main strain in the literature sees financial crises 'as an essential part of the upper turning-point of the business cycle – as a necessary consequence of the previous boom' (Bordo, 1986). The mechanism at work in this view is different from the monetarist, but what is important (and similar) for our purposes is that at some point there is a huge shift from real assets into cash and the consequences are similar, a contraction in the broad measure of money supply.

There is also a downturn in activity though of course in this explanation the connection between money and output is viewed differently.

There were no financial crises, no banking panics in Britain in this period. The principal reasons for stability are to be found in the behaviour of the Bank of England as a lender of last resort, and in the structure of the commercial banking system and allied to the latter, the banks' freedom to locate and hence diversify their portfolios.

To assert that there were no financial crises in this period may seem provocative and requires some substantiation. Schwartz (1986) has provided what seems to me a very useful definition and distinction. The distinction is between what she calls real and pseudo crises. A real crisis is one that threatens the financial system, one that involves a banking panic and widespread banking failure. Banks like other firms will fail but such a failure, however large, should not be seen as a crisis unless it threatens to lead to a collapse of the system. A panic occurs only when the demand by depositors to convert deposits into currency exceeds the capacity of the *system* to supply. And with that definition in view she concludes that there had been no financial crisis in Britain since 1866 and none in the USA since 1933.

## Lender of Last Resort

There had been financial crises in England in the nineteenth century. Indeed if we look at the period immediately prior to 1870 there is evidence broadly consistent with the results for the USA.

In a recent article Collins (1988) took up the Friedman-and-Schwartz framework and applied it to mid-nineteenth century Britain. This was a period of regular financial crises, crises appearing at the peak of the cycle, and there is a different behaviour found than in the later part of the century when financial crises disappear.

After placing great emphasis on the extreme fragility of the data, Collins carried out a detailed historical study of the three mid-century cycles. In particular he examined the behaviour of the commercial banking sector through the course of quite sharp oscillations in banking conditions. He points out that there was a pattern of a rise in the cash ratio at the peak of the cycle. He also noted the sharp fall in a measure of banks' 'liquidity' as an economic upswing petered out. In his examination of the individual cycles of the 1850s, 1860s and 1870s a fairly close correspondence was found between the monetary series, economic activity and prices. But Collins concludes

tentatively; whether the banks 'were initiators of change, and the
more general question of the direction of causation may not have
been resolved'.

But these experiences coupled with Bagehot's exhortations and
changing opinion led eventually to the Bank of England, around
1870, accepting its role of lender of last resort ready to provide
liquidity to the market in times of difficulty. The Bank had for a long
time acted in the last resort to supply the system with funds but
Bagehot's particular contribution was to insist that the Bank should
commit itself in advance to that position. His emphasis on precommitment was to assure the market that sound banks would always find
sufficient liquidity (at a price) even when unsound banks were failing.
From the fact that there were no crises of the kind defined it does not
of course automatically follow that the Bank's behaviour was responsible. But in a recent interesting investigation of the issue Ogden
(1988) examined the period in detail (much of it on daily data from
the Bank's archives) particularly periods of pressure – that is, where
there seemed to be 'excessive' discounting – and found evidence that
the Bank responded quickly and adequately to ease liquidity needs of
the market. This undoubtedly contributed to avoiding any pressure
developing into widespread fear of and actual failure.

**Banking Structure**

There was another important institutional aspect that undoubtedly
promoted stability in British banking and perhaps in the economy too
and it is one that contrasts with the USA. It is the structure of the
banking system. By 1870 British banking had evolved to its modern
form, with a number of commercial banks the larger of which had
many branches throughout the country. This structure continued to
develop as the summary in Table 9.3 shows.

As early as 1870 there were more than 3000 bank offices in the
country (0.73 offices per 10 000 of the population). Although the
total number of banks in all categories fell fairly steadily throughout
the period there were still over 100 banks in 1914 and there were
around 8000 bank offices at that point (1.63 per 10 000 of the
population). The fall in total number of banks was in part a consequence of the contemporary concern with size associated as it was
with security and prestige, and so of the mergers/acquisitions that
took place as an accelerating pace in the 1890s. But the main point to
make is that there was a great growth from an already substantial

*Table 9.3*  British branch banking, 1870–1910

|      | London Banks | | Provincial Banks | | All UK Banks | |
|------|-------|--------|-------|----------|-------|--------|
|      | Banks | Branch | Banks | Branches | Banks | Branch |
| 1870 | 56    | 84     | 299   | 1092     | 387   | 2728   |
| 1880 | 65    | 109    | 258   | 1396     | 358   | 3454   |
| 1890 | 65    | 149    | 200   | 1795     | 303   | 4347   |
| 1900 | 39    | 135    | 108   | 1875     | 188   | 5922   |
| 1910 | 27    | 36     | 47    | 1516     | 112   | 7565   |

*Source*: Capie and Webber (1985).

base in 1870 of this branching network. This meant that any one bank, usually with headquarters in London, had loans and sources of funds in most if not all parts of the country covering the whole spectrum of industry, agriculture and services. This branch network meant that if a branch (or even several branches) were in trouble in an area adversely affected by a fall in demand for its product, the resources of the bank could readily be diverted to ease the pressure. This could be done without any indication being given to a wider public and so could remove an important potential source of apprehension for the depositor.

This structure of course contrasts starkly with the structure in the USA where branch banking or certainly inter-state branching was prohibited. A small bank failure could therefore lead to another and so on to a run, particularly in the absence of a clearly recognised lender of last resort.

There continued to be many banks in Britain without branches and there were fairly frequent bank failures as Table 9.4 shows, and there were also regular new entrants to the system every year. But these failures did not result in runs, they were simply accepted as part of the pattern of business enterprise. There were even occasionally quite large bank failures such as that of the City of Glasgow bank in 1878. This was a badly run bank, with corrupt practices, which was clearly insolvent and allowed to fail. It had close connections with a number of other banks all of which were affected. But there was no run on banks, no banking panic, no financial crisis, no significant rise in C/D or R/D ratios.

*Table 9.4*   Number of bank failures in Britain, 1870–1914

| 1870 | 0 | 1890 | 1 | 1910 | 4 |
|------|----|------|---|------|---|
| 1 | 2 | 1 | 4 | 11 | 4 |
| 2 | 6 | 2 | 1 | 19 | 1 |
| 3 | 1 | 3 | 0 | 13 | 0 |
| 4 | 2 | 4 | 8 | 14 | 5 |
| 5 | 2 | 5 | 5 | | |
| 6 | 3 | 6 | 1 | | |
| 7 | 4 | 7 | 2 | | |
| 8 | 10 | 8 | 2 | | |
| 9 | 10 | 9 | 2 | | |
| 1880 | 3 | 1900 | 0 | | |
| 1 | 4 | 1 | 5 | | |
| 2 | 2 | 2 | 0 | | |
| 3 | 1 | 3 | 3 | | |
| 4 | 6 | 4 | 1 | | |
| 5 | 1 | 5 | 4 | | |
| 6 | 0 | 6 | 0 | | |
| 7 | 4 | 7 | 1 | | |
| 8 | 3 | 8 | 1 | | |
| 9 | 0 | 9 | 0 | | |

## CONCLUSION

In brief summary this exercise in measurement has shown that the relationship between money and the business cycle in Britain is far from unambiguous. A variety of measures fails to reveal the kind of correspondence that has been found for the USA. The question then becomes, how can this contrast with the USA be explained. But it is worth stressing that the contrast should not be overdrawn since Friedman–Schwartz's position was a cautious one and one that relied not only on average statistical results but in good part on evidence from *major* downturns. There were no major downturns of the kind found in the USA in this period in the United Kingdom and no banking panics or financial crises. The suggested explanation for this essential difference may lie in the facts that there was in Britain an accepted lender of last resort by the start of this period; there was also a well-established and expanding branch banking system that operated without restrictive regulation. The result of these elements was that there were no threats to the financial system, little volatility in the monetary series. Some of the movement in monetary series in the USA undoubtedly arises from the recurrent financial crises that were an essential part of the business cycle.

# References

Aldcroft, D. and Fearon, P. (1972) *British Economic Fluctuations, 1790–1939* (London: Macmillan).

Barro, Robert J. (1977) 'Unanticipated Money Growth and Unemployment in the United States', *American Economic Review*, pp. 101–15.

Barro, Robert J. (1978) 'Unanticipated Money, Output and the Price Level in the United States', *Journal of Political Economy*, pp. 549–80.

Barro, Robert J. (1984) *Macroeconomics* (Chichester: Wiley).

Beveridge, W. H. (1939) 'Unemployment and the Trade Cycle', *Economic Journal*, vol. XLIX.

Bordo, Michael D. (1986) 'Explorations in Monetary History: A Survey of the Literature', *Explorations in Economic History*, vol. 23.

Britton, Andrew (1986) *The Trade Cycle in Britain, 1958–82* (Cambridge: Cambridge University Press).

Capie, Forrest and Mills, T. C. (1989) 'Money and Business Cycles in the US and UK, 1870–1913' (mimeo).

Capie, Forrest and Webber, Alan (1985) *A Monetary History of the United Kingdom, 1870–1982: Data Sources and Methods* (London: Allen & Unwin).

Capie, Forrest and Wood, Geoffrey (eds) (1986) *Financial Crises and the World Banking System* (London: Macmillan).

Collins, Michael (1988) English Banks and Business Cycles, 1848–80' in Cottrell and Moggridge (1988).

Coppock, D. J. (1972) 'The Causes of Business Fluctuations' in Aldcroft and Fearon (1972).

Corner, D. C. (1956) 'Exports and the British Trade Cycle, 1929', *Manchester School*, vol. XXIV.

Cottrell, P. and Moggridge, D. (1988) *Money and Power* (London: Macmillan).

Crafts, N. F. R., Leybourne, S. J. and Mills, T. C. (1989) 'Trends and Cycles in British Industrial Production, 1700–1913', *Journal of the Royal Statistical Society*, series A 152.

Eichengreen, B. J. (1983) 'The Causes of British Business Cycles', *Journal of European Economic History*, vol. 12, no 1.

Eichengreen, B. J. (1987) Review of Robert Gordon (1986) *Journal of Economic History*, vol. XLVII.

Feinstein, C. H. (1972) *National Income, Expenditure and Output of the United Kingdom, 1855–1965* (Cambridge: Cambridge University Press).

Fisher, Irving (1911) *The Purchasing Power of Money* (New York: Macmillan).

Floud, Roderick and McCloskey, Donald (1981) *The Economic History of Britain since 1700: vol. 2, 1860 to the 1970s* (Cambridge: Cambridge University Press).

Ford, A. G. (1963) 'Notes on the Role of Exports in British Economic Fluctuations, 1870–1914', *Economic History Review*, 2nd series vol. 1b.

Ford, A. G. (1981) 'The Trade Cycle in Britain, 1870–1914' in Floud and McCloskey (1981).

Friedman, Milton (1950) 'Wesley C. Mitchell as an Economic Theorist', *Journal of Political Economy*, vol. 58.

Friedman, Milton and Schwartz, Anna J. (1963) 'Money and Business Cycles', *Review of Economics and Statistics*, vol. 45.

Gayer, A. D., Rostow, W. W. and Schwartz, A. J. (1953) *The Growth of the British Economy, 1790–1850* (Oxford: Clarendon).
Gordon, Robert A. (1964) *Business Fluctuations* (London: Harper & Row).
Gordon, Robert J. (ed.) (1986) *The American Business Cycle* (Chicago: University of Chicago Press).
Greasley, David (1986) 'British Economic Growth: the Paradox of the 1880s are the Timing of the Climates in', *Explorations in Economic History*, vol. 23.
Haberler, Gottfried (1964) *Prosperity and Depression* (London: Allen & Unwin) 5th edn.
Hawtrey, R. G. (1913) *Good and Bad Trade* (London: Macmillan).
Jevons, W. S. (1874) *The Principles of Science* (London: Macmillan).
Kyun, Kim (1988) *Equilibrium Business Cycle Theory in Historical Perspective* (Cambridge: Cambridge University Press).
Lewis, W. A. (1978) *Growth and Fluctuations, 1870–1913* (London: Allen & Unwin).
Lucas, R. (1981) *Studies in Business Cycle Theory* (Oxford: Blackwell).
Matthews, R. C. O (1959) *The Trade Cycle* (Cambridge: Cambridge University Press).
Matthews, R. C. O, Feinstein, C. H. and Oddling-Smee, J. C. (1982) *British Economic Growth, 1856–1973* (Oxford: Oxford University Press).
Mills, T. C. and Taylor, M. P. (1989) 'Random Walls Components in Output and Exchange Rates: Some Robust Tests on UK Data', *Bulletin of Economic Research*, vol.
Mitchell, B. (1988) *British Historical Statistics* (Cambridge: Cambridge University Press).
Mitchell, W. C. and Burns, A. F. (1946) *Measuring Business Cycles* (New York: National Bureau of Economic Research).
Morgan, Mary (1989) *The History of Economic Ideas* (Cambridge: Cambridge University Press).
Nelson, C. R. and Plosser, C. I. (1982) 'Trends and Random Walks in Macroeconomic Time-series: Some Evidence and Implications', *Journal of Monetary Economics*, vol. 10.
Nishimura, S. (1973) 'The Growth of the Stock of Money in the UK, 1870–1913', unpublished paper, Hosei University, Tokyo.
Nishimura, Shizayu (1988) 'The Mechanism of the Supply of Money in the United Kingdom, 1873–1913' in Cottrell and Moggridge (1988).
Ogden, E. M. (1988) 'The Bank of England as Lender of Last Resort', unpublished Ph.D. thesis, City University, London.
Rostow, W. W. (1948) *British Economy of the Nineteenth Century* (Oxford: Oxford University Press).
Sheppard, D. K. (1971) *The Growth and Role of UK Financial Institutions, 1880–1962* (London: Methuen).
Tinbergen, J. (1951) *The Business Cycle in the UK, 1870–1914* (Amsterdam: North-Holland).
Walters, A. A. (1969) *Money in Boom and Slump* (IEA) Hobart Paper 44.

# 10 The Comparative Performance of Fixed and Flexible Exchange-Rate Regimes: Inter-war Evidence*

Barry Eichengreen
UNIVERSITY OF CALIFORNIA AT BERKELEY

## 1 INTRODUCTION

The behaviour of floating exchange rates over the past 15 years has surprised and dismayed the proponents of flexibility. Nominal exchange rates have displayed a strikingly high degree of variability. The rise in nominal exchange-rate variability has been accompanied by a rise in real exchange-rate variability. Many observers believe that the connection is causal: that nominal exchange-rate movements have been a source of costly swings in relative prices. Exchange-rate flexibility does not seem to have provided the insulation from foreign disturbances or the autonomy for domestic policy predicted by early models. The implication is that exchange-rate flexibility may have larger costs and smaller benefits than forecast in 1973.

Proponents of flexibility would counter that the performance of floating rates over the past 15 years has been dominated by destabilising policies and exceptional disturbances. Exchange rates have been perturbed by two oil shocks, a productivity slowdown, an OECD-wide disinflation, and eight years of US budget deficits. Instead of permitting exchange rates to float freely, policy-makers have intervened in the foreign-exchange market in an attempt to limit fluctuations. Since their exchange-rate targets are not consistent with other policies, these support operations are not sustainable. The result is alternating periods of stability and volatility and even greater risks to market participants.

Resolution of this debate requires more analysis but also more data, drawn ideally from periods when both shocks and policies differed from those of recent decades. Data from the inter-war period have obvious appeal. The 1920s and 1930s witnessed an unusual variety of international monetary arrangements. Three exchange-rate regimes can be distinguished: free floating to 1926, fixed rates from 1927 to 1931, and managed floating from 1932. It is possible to compare the performance of fixed and flexible rates in a period subject to very different disturbances than those of recent decades. It is conceivable, of course, that differences in performance, for the inter-war period as for the 1970s and 1980s, are attributable to particular disturbances rather than to the properties of exchange-rate regimes. But if the same patterns are found in data for a variety of periods, it becomes increasingly implausible to blame a peculiar conjuncture of exogenous shocks.

A further attraction of inter-war experience is that the performance of free and managed floating can be compared. In the first half of the 1920s, there were only a handful of isolated instances of government intervention in the foreign-exchange market. In the first half of the 1930s, in contrast, intervention was systematic and continuous. If efforts to manage their fluctuation account for the peculiar behaviour of floating rates, then this should be evident in a comparison of the two inter-war regimes.

A final reason to focus on this period is its enduring influence on exchange-rate policy. The classic account of inter-war currency experience by Nurkse (1944) remains the *locus classicus* of arguments against floating. Nurkse concluded that freely floating rates are rendered excessively volatile by speculative capital movements. To this day the view that exchange-rate instability in the 1920s and 1930s disrupted international trade and economic activity, with dire political consequences, remains a source of support for exchange-rate stability in Europe (as described by Giavazzi and Giovannini, 1988). Refuting this characterisation of inter-war experience is essential, therefore, for advocates of floating rates (Friedman, 1953, p. 176). Unfortunately, neither Nurkse's nor Friedman's viewpoint is buttressed by much in the way of empirical evidence. This paper provides a first instalment of the evidence needed for a comparative assessment of the three inter-war exchange-rate regimes.

## 2 THE STRUCTURE OF THE THREE REGIMES

The fixed exchange rates of the gold standard quickly fell into abeyance with the outbreak of the First World War.[1] During the war, exchange-rate movements were limited by exchange control, by the dangers of transferring assets between countries, and by the support operations of the USA. In March 1919, US intervention on behalf of the British pound and French franc was withdrawn, marking the transition to generalised floating. Exchange rates continued to float until the middle of the 1920s, when they were pegged to gold and, *de facto*, stabilised against one another.

A dominant characteristic of this regime was the freedom of the float. With few exceptions, governments refrained from intervening directly in the foreign-exchange market. The Bank of France intervened briefly in April 1924 to inflict losses on speculators who had sold francs short. It intervened again in the spring and summer of 1925 in an effort to stem the franc's depreciation. Belgian and German authorities also intervened sporadically. But these episodes were exceptions to the rule. Exchange rates were driven by market forces in the presence of minimal government intervention. This is not to imply that governments never adjusted policies in response to foreign-exchange-market trends, only that they rarely intervened in that market directly. Indeed, the desire to place upward pressure on the exchange rate so as to permit stabilisation at the old gold parity was an overriding goal of European policy. Where inflation ran out of control, the goal became stabilisation pure and simple.

The transition to fixed rates took place in the middle of the 1920s. Sweden stabilised in 1924, Britain in 1925, France (*de facto*) in 1926, Italy in 1927. The sequencing of stabilisations makes it difficult to attach a date to the start of the fixed rate regime. But by 1927, reconstruction of the fixed rate system was largely complete. Bilateral rates were fixed indirectly, since countries declared parities against gold rather than foreign currencies. But with domestic currency convertible into gold and specie imports and exports unrestricted, arbitrage in the international gold market constrained the fluctuation of bilateral rates. Exchange rates could rise or fall only to the gold points (given by the costs of shipping, insurance and short-term credit), at which it became profitable to engage in gold market arbitrage. This limited bilateral rates to narrow bands.

The fixed rate regime of the 1920s operated only for a couple of years before doubts began to surface about its sustainability. Large, persistent payments imbalances threatened to exhaust the reserves of deficit countries. The reason for these difficulties remains a subject of debate.[2] Some observers emphasised the tendency of central banks to impede the balance of payments adjustment mechanism by sterilising reserve flows. Others argued that the adjustment mechanism was in fact permitted to operate but, given the limited flexibility of wages and prices, proved insufficiently powerful to counteract the massive shock of the Great Depression.

In 1929 the fixed rate system began to crumble around the edges. Argentina and Uruguay suspended gold payments in December. Canada introduced new monetary restrictions tantamount to devaluation. Brazil, Chile, Paraguay, Peru, Venezuela, Australia and New Zealand, without officially suspending gold convertibility, permitted their currencies to slip below par. Exchange rates in the industrial centre also came under pressure but were successfully maintained.

In the spring and summer of 1931, Germany and Austria, faced with domestic banking panics and runs on central bank reserves, suspended gold convertibility and imposed exchange controls. Next to experience a run was the Bank of England. The devaluation of sterling in September 1931 induced two dozen other countries to follow suit. These events are conventionally taken to mark the demise of the fixed rate system. In fact fixed rates lingered, though on a diminished and steadily shrinking scale. The USA floated the dollar in 1933. Czechoslovakia devalued in 1934, Belgium in 1935, France, the Netherlands and Switzerland in 1936. Like the transition from flexible to fixed rates, the transition back is difficult to date with precision.

A distinguishing feature of this episode was pervasive government intervention in the foreign-exchange market. In contrast to the first half of the 1920s, governments intervened systematically to influence the fluctuation of exchange rates. They established special Treasury or central bank accounts (known as exchange equalisation funds) to limit exchange-rate fluctuations. Historians debate whether these funds intervened symmetrically, buying foreign exchange when the domestic currency rose and selling it when the domestic currency fell, or intervened asymmetrically, only purchasing foreign exchange when the currency rose. A related debate is whether or not the impact on the money supply was sterilised.[3] Whatever the answer, observers agree that, compared with the early 1920s, intervention in the foreign-exchange market was systematic and sustained.

Some countries employed intervention to peg to their trading partners. By 1932, the outlines of a group of sterling-area countries could be discerned. Countries such as Portugal, Sweden and the rest of Scandinavia, which traded heavily with Britain, joined the British Commonwealth in pegging to the pound. A second group of countries, centred on Germany, adopted exchange controls, which permitted them to pursue more expansionary policies and allowed a black-market discount on their currencies to emerge. A third group, including the USA, France, Belgium, the Netherlands, Switzerland, Czechoslovakia and Poland, continued to peg to gold and therefore to maintain stable rates *vis-à-vis* one another.

The next round of devaluations occurred in 1933, when Roosevelt chose to take the USA off gold. Over the succeeding nine months, the dollar depreciated by nearly 70 per cent against the French franc and other gold currencies. Cuba, Guatemala, Panama and the Philippines followed the USA off gold. Many South American countries depreciated further to maintain their competitiveness in the US market, creating an informal dollar area. But this quasi-dollar area never achieved the cohesiveness of its sterling counterpart. With France, Belgium, Switzerland, the Netherlands, Czechoslovakia and Poland still maintaining gold convertibility and the Sterling Area countries tightening their pegs, the world was increasingly splintered into distinct currency areas.

France's devaluation in September 1936 marked another change in regime. The devaluation was accompanied by a Tripartite Agreement issued simultaneously by France, Britain and the USA, in which they affirmed their desire to cooperate in minimising the fluctuation of exchange rates. Switzerland and Holland devalued immediately thereafter, and other countries endorsed the principles of the Tripartite Pact.[4]

## 3 DATA AND CONVENTIONS

To analyse exchange-rate behaviour under these regimes, I assembled weekly data on exchange rates and ancillary variables. For the years 1921–36, Einzig (1937) provides continuous end-of-week observations on spot and forward foreign-exchange rates for eight industrial countries. For other countries, spot rates were drawn from the *Monthly Statistical Bulletins* of the League of Nations. Einzig also provides 30-day market rates of discount on a monthly average basis. These can be combined with the exchange-rate data by generating appropriately-weighted averages of the weekly observations of the latter.

Partitioning the period into regimes is inevitably arbitrary. The three periods I distinguish are January 1922–August 1926 (free floating), January 1927–August 1931 (fixed rates) and January 1932–August 1936 (managed floating). Although continuous forward exchange-rate quotations become available in January 1921, consistent series for several other variables start only in 1922. It is convenient, therefore, to begin the analysis with January 1922. Few of my conclusions hinge on this starting-date. I choose January 1927 to mark the start of the fixed-exchange-rate period, since the French franc was stabilised in December 1926. Most of the other currencies considered were stabilised at earlier dates. The choice of January 1927 should therefore highlight the distinguishing features of the fixed-rate period.

Britain floated the pound on 19 September 1931, with Sweden, Norway and Denmark following at the end of September, Finland in October, and Japan in December. But policies designed to manage the fluctuation of these exchange rates were widely adopted only in 1932. For this reason (and for symmetry with January 1921 and January 1927) I choose January 1932 to mark the start of managed floating. I end the analysis in August 1936, the month before France, the Netherlands and Switzerland devalued and the international monetary system was again transformed. The two periods of transition (September–December 1926 and September–December 1931), being difficult to assign to a particular period, are omitted.

I follow Einzig by using the pound sterling as the reference currency. It is possible to use other reference currencies, computing the relevant bilateral rates from triangular arbitrage. But direct market quotations are likely to be cleaner than those computed assuming triangular arbitrage, or for that matter than calculations of effective exchange rates. The choice of reference currency in fact makes little difference for most of the conclusions that follow.[5] It only matters for rankings of exchange-rate stability across countries within periods. Countries which pegged to sterling obviously appear to have enjoyed the greatest exchange-rate stability when sterling is used as the reference currency, while countries which pegged to the dollar appear to have enjoyed the greatest stability when the dollar is used. But the average volatility of exchange rates under free floating compared with managed floating is unaffected by the choice. And it is with the comparative performance of the successive regimes, rather than the comparative performance of countries, that this paper is concerned.

Here even more than in other periods, conclusions are heavily influenced by outliers. The extreme behaviour of exchange rates, interest rates and prices during the German hyperinflation dominates the international averages even when a relatively large cross-section of countries is considered. I consequently calculate most summary statistics omitting German data.

## 4  EXCHANGE RATE VARIABILITY

A standard indictment of flexible exchange rates is that they give rise to costly variability. The assertion can be broken into two parts: that there is an association between flexibility and variability, and that variability is costly. I focus here on the first of these propositions.

Tables 10.1 and 10.2 display measures of the nominal exchange rate changes at weekly and monthly intervals. The exchange rate is defined as the foreign-currency price of the domestic currency, an increase signifying appreciation. The predominance of negative means for 1922–6 indicates that the reference currency, the pound sterling, was appreciating on average. The preponderance of positive values for 1932–6 indicates that sterling was weakening relative to the currencies of the gold bloc, while the negative values for the USA and Belgium remind us that some countries opted for large depreciations against sterling.

The standard deviations of exchange rate changes are considerably larger during the period of freely floating exchange rates at the beginning of the 1920s than under managed floating in the 1930s or under pegged rates from 1927 to 1931.[6] On average, the standard deviation of weekly changes is about four times as large under free floating (excluding Germany) as under managed floating. For monthly changes, the standard deviation is 50 per cent larger under free floating (again excluding Germany) than under managed floating. Clearly, exchange-rate variability was positively associated with the freedom of the float.

The behaviour of exchange rates in the gold-standard period (1927–31) was of course very different. The standard deviations of average percentage changes at both weekly and monthly intervals are small compared with either floating-rate period. The anomalous behaviour of the Italian lira reinforces the point: the lira was stabilised

*Table 10.1*  Weekly holding period returns
$(e - e_{-1})/e_{-1}$ where e = £/foreign currency
(Mean and Standard Deviation are in per cent)

| Period | Country | # of Obs | Mean | Standard Deviation | Kurtosis | Skewness |
|--------|---------|---------|------|--------------------|----------|----------|
| *Free floating* | USA | 243 | −0.0582 | 0.5659 | 4.41263 | −0.50525 |
| *Jan. 1922 to* | France | 243 | −0.4056 | 3.7334 | 26.61692 | 3.20364 |
| *August 1926* | Belgium | 243 | −0.4246 | 3.3176 | 6.95342 | 0.83557 |
| | Netherlands | 243 | −0.0225 | 0.3305 | 2.85755 | 0.00995 |
| | Italy | 243 | −0.1008 | 2.1120 | 10.03896 | 1.06194 |
| | Switzerland | 243 | −0.0588 | 0.5632 | 8.68960 | −1.27418 |
| | Germany | 243 | −5.8580 | 19.2724 | 7.69773 | −1.24616 |
| | Group w/Ger. | 1701 | −0.9898 | 4.2707 | N/A | N/A |
| | | | | | | |
| 1/22–6/23 | Germany | 79 | −7.1176 | 18.1959 | 5.19578 | 1.33889 |
| 12/23–8/26 | Germany | 143 | −0.0845 | 2.0930 | 18.26350 | −1.32898 |
| | Group w/o German hyper- inflation | 1680 | −0.4967 | 4.5059 | N/A | N/A |
| | | | | | | |
| *Fixed rates* | USA | 245 | −0.0006 | 0.0634 | 4.95476 | 0.79697 |
| *Jan. 1927 to* | France | 245 | −0.0041 | 0.0791 | 18.09449 | 0.54552 |
| *August 1931* | Belgium | 245 | −0.0007 | 0.0532 | 0.98735 | −0.20406 |
| | Netherlands | 245 | 0.0031 | 0.0750 | 3.69021 | 0.62432 |
| | Italy | 245 | 0.0637 | 0.8240 | 42.12113 | 4.09295 |
| | Switzerland | 245 | 0.0031 | 8.4500 | 8.54001 | 0.30155 |
| | Germany | 245 | −0.0045 | 0.0995 | 9.85131 | 0.01692 |
| | Group | 1715 | 0.0087 | 0.3199 | N/A | N/A |
| | | | | | | |
| *Managed* | USA[a] | 242 | −0.1512 | 1.3941 | 13.55535 | −2.49615 |
| *floating* | France | 244 | 0.0557 | 0.9118 | 3.34139 | 0.34173 |
| *Jan. 1932 to* | Belgium | 244 | −0.0672 | 1.6159 | 62.90761 | −6.28143 |
| *August 1936* | Netherlands | 244 | 0.0065 | 0.5973 | 11.90388 | 0.12467 |
| | Italy[b] | 239 | 0.0288 | 0.9863 | 4.31911 | 0.92046 |
| | Switzerland[c] | 242 | 0.0698 | 1.1178 | 10.93090 | 0.47981 |
| | Germany | 244 | 0.0603 | 1.0507 | 5.75554 | 0.02627 |
| | Group | 1689 | 0.0004 | 1.1417 | N/A | N/A |

*Notes*:  [a] Missing 3/4/33 and 3/11/33.
          [b] Missing 11/30/35 and 12/21/35.
          [c] Missing 12/3/32 and 12/10/32.

Kurtosis is calculated as $K = \dfrac{\displaystyle\sum_{i=1}^{N} \left( \dfrac{x_i - \bar{x}}{S} \right)^4}{N} - 3$ where

$$S = \left( \sum_{i=1}^{N} (x_i - \bar{x})^2/(N-1) \right)^{1/2}$$

Skewness is calculated as $SK = \dfrac{\displaystyle\sum_{i=1}^{N} \left( \dfrac{x_i - \bar{x}}{S} \right)^3}{N}$

*Source*: See text.

only midway through 1927 and shows exceptional volatility due to its movement over the first part of that year.

Tables 10.1 and 10.2 also report the kurtosis and skewness of the distribution of exchange-rate changes. Kurtosis measures the 'fatness' of the tails of the exchange-rate distribution, indicating whether an unusual proportion of changes was relatively large. Positive values of the statistic computed signify a disproportionate share of observations in the tails relative to the normal distribution. Studies of the post-1973 period have suggested that kurtosis is a common feature of floating rates. Tables 10.1 and 10.2 indicate that this is also a feature of inter-war experience. Kurtosis is often large for those currencies for which the mean percentage change is large (France and Italy in the first half of the 1920s, Italy in the second half). Although there are cases where average percentage changes are very large but kurtosis is not so pronounced (Germany from 1922 to 1926), the dominant association of large movements with kurtosis suggests that exchange-rate variability was episodic, a conclusion consistent with studies of recent decades.

Interestingly, kurtosis is common to all three inter-war regimes; it is not obvious that it increases with the degree of exchange-rate variability.[7]

Skewness measures the symmetry of distribution of exchange-rate changes. Negative values for the USA and Belgium in the 1930s confirm that dollar and franc movements were skewed by discrete devaluations (by the USA in 1933 and Belgium in 1935). A large positive value for Italy in 1927–31 (Table 10.1) confirms that the

*Table 10.2*  Monthly holding period returns

| Period | Country | # of Obs | Mean | Standard Deviation | Kurtosis | Skewness |
|---|---|---|---|---|---|---|
| *Free floating* | U.S. | 56 | −0.2398 | 1.2788 | 3.45619 | −0.82206 |
| 1922.01–1926.08 | France | 56 | −1.8976 | 6.5612 | 10.26536 | 2.44108 |
| | Belgium | 56 | −1.8640 | 7.1690 | 8.80784 | 2.00190 |
| | Netherlands | 56 | −0.0880 | 0.6199 | 0.28450 | −0.62054 |
| | Italy | 56 | −0.4794 | 4.1122 | 1.05382 | 0.92705 |
| | Switzerland | 56 | −0.2534 | 1.1138 | 1.94649 | 0.34462 |
| | Group w/o Ger | 336 | −0.8046 | 3.4758 | N/A | N/A |
| 1/22 to 6/23 | Germany | 18 | −30.0477 | 26.7688 | −1.19338 | 0.12987 |
| 12/23 to 8/26 | Germany | 33 | −0.1523 | 1.6409 | 2.65800 | 0.80723 |
| | Group w/ Ger | 387 | −2.1091 | 4.4028 | N/A | N/A |
| *Fixed rates* | U.S. | 56 | 0.1055 | 0.8202 | 44.35583 | 6.57578 |
| 1927.01–1931.08 | France | 56 | 0.0917 | 0.8435 | 46.15152 | 6.75524 |
| | Belgium | 56 | 0.1138 | 0.8373 | 47.75379 | 6.94352 |
| | Netherlands | 56 | 0.0132 | 0.1246 | −0.28132 | 0.04062 |
| | Italy | 56 | 0.4322 | 2.1429 | 11.79899 | 3.33032 |
| | Switzerland | 56 | 0.1311 | 0.8682 | 45.35807 | 6.69467 |
| | Germany | 56 | 0.0945 | 0.7553 | 46.00722 | 6.75890 |
| | Group | 392 | 0.1403 | 0.9127 | N/A | N/A |
| *Managed floating* | U.S. | 56 | −0.6474 | 2.6895 | 4.22938 | −1.90477 |
| 1932.01–1936.08 | France | 56 | 0.2502 | 1.6847 | 4.20390 | 0.18375 |
| | Belgium | 56 | −0.2559 | 3.7077 | 30.15620 | −4.93156 |
| | Netherlands | 56 | 0.2617 | 1.6931 | 0.94489 | 0.06340 |
| | Italy[a] | 54 | 0.1580 | 1.8646 | 0.19169 | 0.12881 |
| | Switzerland | 56 | 0.2246 | 1.7293 | 1.06710 | 0.39773 |
| | Germany | 56 | 0.2742 | 1.8559 | 0.51436 | 0.42678 |
| | Group | 390 | 0.0402 | 2.1943 | N/A | N/A |

*Notes*: [a] Missing 1935.11 and 1935.12.
$(e - e_{-1})/e_{-1}$ where $e$ = £/foreign currency (mean and standard deviation are in per cent)
*Source*: See text.

distribution of lira movement was skewed by the series of unusually large weekly appreciations preceding Italy's stabilisation.[8] Finally, the distribution of French franc movements in the first half of the 1920s is positively skewed, especially the weekly data, by a small number of unusually large *appreciations* in a period when the franc was depreciating on average. This points to the 'bear squeeze' of early 1924, when the authorities engineered a sudden appreciation of the franc, rather than the 'runs' on the franc in 1923, 1925 and 1926 as the unusual period. The monthly data in Table 10.2 suggest the same behaviour by the Belgian franc, which followed its French counter-part for much of the floating period.

Table 10.3 displays comparable statistics for holding period re-turns. The percentage change in the exchange rate is adjusted for the differential between domestic and foreign interest rates. This statistic provides another measure of the implications for international inves-tors of exchange rate variability. Holding period returns show much the same pattern as nominal exchange rate chages. On average, holding period returns were larger and more variable under free floating than under managed floating and under managed floating than under fixed rates. Interest rate differentials did not render investors indifferent to exchange rate changes.

## 5  EXCHANGE RATE PREDICTABILITY

Exchange rate variability is different from exchange rate uncertainty. Table 10.4 therefore reports a measure of the magnitude of the residuals from a standard exchange rate forecasting equation. The log spot rate is regressed on a constant term and its own lagged value, a slight generalisation of the assumption of a random walk with no drift in previous studies.[9] The forecasting equations are reported in Table 10.A1. The standard deviation of the forecast errors is shown in the top panel of Table 10.4. Monthly data are used to facilitate comparisons with the behaviour of real exchange rates (Section 6 below). Since no forward data are used, it is possible to expand the sample of countries.

Though the standard deviations of the residuals from the exchange-rate forecasts are larger under the managed float of the 1930s than the free float of the 1920s for five of the eleven countries, on average (excluding Germany) this measure of exchange-rate unpredictability falls by about 15 per cent when moving from the free to the managed float. This is smaller than the concurrent fall in the variability of spot rates. An interpretation is that government policy succeeded in damping fluctuations in spot-exchange rates on average but was subject to changes that were difficult to predict.

To explore whether these results are robust to alternative forecasting

*Table 10.3* Monthly holding period returns, interest-rate adjusted

| Period | Country | # of obs | Mean | Standard deviation | Kurtosis | Skewness |
|---|---|---|---|---|---|---|
| *Free floating* | USA | 56 | −0.1907 | 1.8164 | 1.78684 | −0.50992 |
| 1922.01–1926.08 | France | 56 | −0.3655 | 6.6760 | 10.46026 | 2.46421 |
| | Belgium | 56 | 0.1135 | 7.1185 | 9.18542 | 2.11209 |
| | Netherlands | 56 | −0.0250 | 1.3673 | −1.14055 | 0.05452 |
| | Italy | 56 | 2.4348 | 4.1428 | 1.36201 | 1.07691 |
| | Switzerland | 56 | −1.1690 | 1.5148 | 0.07059 | 0.80897 |
| | Group | 336 | 0.1330 | 3.7726 | N/A | N/A |
| | | | | | | |
| 1/22–6/23 | Germany | 18 | −23.0243 | 26.7536 | 0.08716 | 0.72006 |
| 2/24–8/26 | Germany | 31 | 8.2150 | 11.2455 | 3.23597 | 1.95435 |
| | Group w/ Ger | 385 | −0.2989 | 5.4488 | N/A | N/A |
| | | | | | | |
| *Fixed rates* | USA | 55 | −0.4095 | 0.6597 | −0.68482 | −0.03105 |
| 1927.01–1931.07 | France | 55 | −1.1742 | 0.7410 | −0.77282 | −0.03148 |
| | Belgium | 55 | −0.2397 | 0.5865 | −0.45596 | −0.11543 |
| | Netherlands | 55 | −0.4392 | 0.6006 | −0.46389 | 0.06922 |
| | Italy | 55 | 2.8321 | 2.6597 | 9.47487 | 2.93389 |
| | Switzerland | 55 | −1.0791 | 0.6712 | −0.39798 | −0.10824 |
| | Germany[a] | 54 | 1.8514 | 0.8162 | −0.12928 | −0.39212 |
| | Group | 384 | 0.1873 | 1.1885 | N/A | N/A |
| | | | | | | |
| *Managed floating* | USA | 56 | −1.0587 | 2.5961 | 3.67211 | −1.70672 |
| 1932.01–1936.08 | France | 56 | 1.6707 | 2.4830 | 3.15543 | −1.36501 |
| | Belgium | 56 | 1.0988 | 3.8725 | 23.19736 | −4.16349 |
| | Netherlands | 56 | 0.7501 | 2.4673 | 1.65155 | −0.77240 |
| | Italy[b] | 54 | 3.4895 | 2.1208 | 0.59755 | −0.10645 |
| | Switzerland[c] | 55 | 1.0557 | 2.2713 | 5.58014 | −1.76080 |
| | Germany | 56 | 3.1415 | 2.1132 | 0.71507 | 0.39411 |
| | Group | 389 | 1.4402 | 2.6248 | N/A | N/A |

*Notes*: [a] To 1931.06.
 [b] Missing 1935.11 and 1935.12.
 [c] To 1936.07.
 (Mean and standard deviation are in per cent)
 $i^* - i + (e - e_{-1})/e_{-1}$ where $e$ = £/foreign currency
*Source*: See text.

equations, I fit a simple (ARMA) model of the exchange rate (the results of which are reported in the Appendix, Table A2). In each case (except for Denmark in the fixed-rate period, when the ARMA model did not solve) one autoregressive and one moving-average term were the preferred time-series representation of the data. The corresponding standard errors of the residuals are shown in the bottom panel of Table 10.4. The results are essentially identical to the AR(1) forecasts described above.

## 6   REAL EXCHANGE RATES

Table 10.5 summarises the variability of real exchange rates under the three regimes. The real exchange rate is computed as the ratio of domestic to foreign wholesale price indices, converted to foreign currency using the nominal exchange rate. The standard deviation of the first difference in the log real rate is on average 15 per cent larger in the period of free floating than under managed floating.[10] The cross-country correlation of the standard deviation of the first differences of (log) nominal and real rates exceeds 0.8 for both the early 1920s and the early 1930s. This suggests that nominal exchange-rate variability in periods of relatively free floating translated into a comparable, if not proportionate, increase in the variability of relative prices.

Table 10.6 reports the standard deviation of real-exchange-rate-forecast errors analogous to those for the nominal exchange rate in Table 10.4. In the top panel, the unweighted average of this measure of the forecast error is nearly 10 per cent larger under managed floating in the 1930s than under free floating in the 1920s (again excluding Germany). The notable exceptions are the high inflation countries: France, Belgium and Italy (and of course Germany) in the early 1920s. There is a positive relationship between the predictability of nominal exchange rates and the predictability of real exchange rates in both periods of floating.[11] That relationship is in fact stronger under free floating: the correlation coefficient for the real and nominal exchange rate forecast errors is 0.89 under free floating (ten countries, excluding Germany) and 0.74 under managed floating.

The bottom panel of Table 10.6 confirms that more general forecasting equations do not alter the implications of the analysis.

*Table 10.4*  Nominal exchange rate predictability (standard deviation of residuals from exchange rate forecasts)

| | Period 1 1922–6 | Period 2 1927–31 | Period 3 1932–6 |
|---|---|---|---|
| *AR(1) Forecasts* | | | |
| Denmark | 0.03264 | 0.00151 | 0.03070 |
| Finland | 0.02621 | 0.00168 | 0.02985 |
| Norway | 0.03252 | 0.00311 | 0.02808 |
| Sweden | 0.01061 | 0.00178 | 0.02995 |
| Switzerland | 0.00994 | 0.00157 | 0.01729 |
| USA | 0.01050 | 0.00168 | 0.02781 |
| France | 0.06329 | 0.00088 | 0.01689 |
| Netherlands | 0.00626 | 0.00120 | 0.01694 |
| Belgium | 0.06998 | 0.00093 | 0.04190 |
| Italy[e] | 0.03654 | 0.01361 | 0.01953 |
| Germany[a] | 0.35800 | 0.00129 | 0.01851 |
| Germany[b] | 0.01460 | | |
| Average excluding Germany | 0.02985 | 0.00280 | 0.02590 |
| *ARMA(1.1) Forecasts* | | | |
| Denmark | 0.02785 | na | 0.03070 |
| Finland | 0.02607 | 0.00167 | 0.02969 |
| Norway | 0.03170 | 0.00299 | 0.02783 |
| Sweden | 0.01020 | 0.00158 | 0.02862 |
| Switzerland | 0.00991 | 0.00139 | 0.01624 |
| USA | 0.01013 | 0.00167 | 0.02716 |
| France | 0.06301 | 0.00082 | 0.01516 |
| Netherlands | 0.00572 | 0.00108 | 0.01554 |
| Belgium | 0.06930 | 0.00091 | 0.04109 |
| Italy[e] | 0.00390 | 0.00855 | 0.01839 |
| Germany | 0.33438[c] | 0.00117 | 0.01756 |
| Germany | 0.01434[d] | | |
| Average excluding Germany | 0.02578 | 0.00230 | 0.02782 |

*Notes*: Monthly data are used. Precise definitions of periods are described in
Section 3.
  [a] 1922.01–1923.07 and 1923.12–1926.08.
  [b] 1922.01–1922.05 and 1924.01–1926.08.
  [c] 1922.01–1923.07 and 1924.01–1926.08.
  [d] 1924.02–1926.08.
  [e] 1935.12–1936.02 omitted due to missing data.
  na not available
*Source*: See text.

*Table 10.5*  Standard deviations of real exchange rates: monthly rates
(£ as reference currency)

|  | Period 1 1922–6 | Period 2 1927–31 | Period 3 1932–6 |
|---|---|---|---|
| Belgium | 0.0480 | 0.0105 | 0.0330 |
| Germany | 0.1380[a] | 0.0077 | 0.0212 |
| Netherlands | 0.0148 | 0.0109 | 0.0231 |
| Italy | 0.0371 | 0.0156 | 0.0204 |
| USA | 0.0153 | 0.0102 | 0.0358 |
| France | 0.0395 | 0.0129 | 0.0194 |
| Switzerland | 0.0173 | 0.0113 | 0.0205 |
| mean w/o Germany | 0.0292 | 0.0121 | 0.0254 |
| mean w/Germany | 0.0584 | 0.0114 | 0.0248 |

*Notes*: Monthly data are used. Precise definitions of periods are described in
Section 3.
[a] Missing 1923.09–1923.12 due to break in wholesale price index.
Real exchange rate: $\log R_t - \log R_{t-1}$
*Source*: See text.

Table 10.4 confirmed that the greater stability of spot rates in the
gold-exchange-standard period enhanced the predictability of the
spot rate. According to Table 10.6, it also enhanced the predictability
of the real rate. For all but two countries, the real rate was easier to
predict in the fixed-rate period than in either period of floating rates.
This is especially impressive given the major terms of trade shocks to
which the world economy was subjected between 1929 and 1931.

## 7  INTERNATIONAL CAPITAL MOVEMENTS

A common criticism of flexible exchange rates is that the risks to
which they give rise interfere with international capital mobility
(McKinnon, 1987). Exchange-rate uncertainty discourages investors
from arbitraging international interest-rate differentials, preventing
real-interest-rate convergence across countries and limiting the integration of national financial markets. Frankel and MacArthur (1988)
present evidence for the period since 1960 consistent with the hypothesis. They report an increase in the variability of international real-
interest-rate differentials since 1973, which, in light of the concurrent
decline in political barriers to international capital movements, they
attribute to currency risk.

*Table 10.6* Real exchange rate predictability (standard deviation of residuals from real exchange rate forecasts)

|  | Period 1 1922–6 | Period 2 1927–31 | Period 3 1932–6 |
|---|---|---|---|
| *AR(1) Forecasts* | | | |
| Denmark | 0.02090 | 0.01055 | 0.02956 |
| Finland | 0.01819[e] | 0.01193 | 0.0309 |
| Norway | 0.02938 | 0.01226 | 0.0323 |
| Sweden | 0.01384 | 0.00930 | 0.0303 |
| Switzerland | 0.01553 | 0.01084 | 0.01863 |
| USA | 0.01333 | 0.01019 | 0.02633 |
| France | 0.03661 | 0.01323 | 0.01614 |
| Netherlands | 0.01456 | 0.01078 | 0.02203 |
| Belgium | 0.03589 | 0.01007 | 0.02685 |
| Italy | 0.03655 | 0.01361 | 0.01953[d] |
| Germany | 0.10836[a] | 0.00755 | 0.0207 |
| Germany | 0.01760[b] | | |
| Average excluding Germany | 0.02348 | 0.01128 | 0.02526 |
| *ARMA(1.1) Forecasts* | | | |
| Denmark | 0.02090 | 0.01054 | 0.02890 |
| Finland | 0.01815 | 0.01186 | 0.03040 |
| Norway | 0.02930 | 0.01220 | 0.03170 |
| Sweden | 0.01350 | 0.00926 | 0.02930 |
| Switzerland | 0.01553 | 0.01072 | 0.01861 |
| USA | 0.01318 | 0.00945 | 0.02534 |
| France | 0.03598 | 0.01323 | 0.01593 |
| Netherlands | 0.01416 | 0.01070 | 0.02120 |
| Belgium | 0.03518 | 0.01007 | 0.02676 |
| Italy | 0.03391 | 0.00855 | 0.01839[d] |
| Germany | na | 0.00750 | 0.02040 |
| Germany | 0.01716[c] | | |
| Average excluding Germany | 0.02298 | 0.01066 | 0.02465 |

*Notes*: Monthly data are used. Precise definitions of periods are described in Section 3.
[a] 1922.01–1923.07 and 1923.12–1926.08.
[b] 1922.01–1922.05 and 1924.01–1926.08.
[c] 1924.02–1926.08.
[d] 1932.02–1935.10 only.
[e] 1923.01–1926.08.
*Source*: See text.

*Table 10.7*  International capital movements under three exchange-rate regimes, 1924–36 (sum of absolute value of balances on capital account) (Millions of US$)

|  | *Freely floating rates (1922–26)* | *Fixed rates (1927–31)* | *Managed floating (1932–6)* |
|---|---|---|---|
| Eight creditor countries | 6967 | 8722 | 9525 |
| Fourteen developed or semi-developed debtor countries | 4853 | 6695 | 2223 |
| Twelve underdeveloped debtor countries | 1312 | 2035 | 1138 |
| Total | 13132 | 17452 | 12886 |

*Source*: Computed from United Nations (1949).

Inter-war experience provides another opportunity to consider this question. Table 10.7 displays the volume of international capital flows. These estimates, calculated by the United Nations as the inverse of the balance of trade in goods, services and gold (the current account plus net gold flows), vary in reliability and coverage.[12] They imply that capital movements were most extensive during the fixed-rate period. But there is no direct correspondence between the degree of exchange-rate flexibility and the volume of capital flows. Capital movements were larger in the early 1920s, when exchange rates floated freely and were most variable, than in the early 1930s, when managed floating gave rise to somewhat less nominal variability. Of course, other factors besides exchange-rate variability surely influenced the volume of capital flows. The debt defaults of the 1930s may have depressed the volume of capital flows by discouraging long-term foreign lending. That capital flows to the debtors fall with the shift from free to managed floating, whereas capital flows among the creditors do not, suggests that an association between the freedom of the float and the volume of capital movements may re-emerge if one controls for the risk of default.

Differences among periods become more evident if capital movements are scaled by national income.[13] Figures 10.1 and 10.2 contrast these measures of the magnitude of capital flows under the three international monetary regimes for all countries for which the requisite

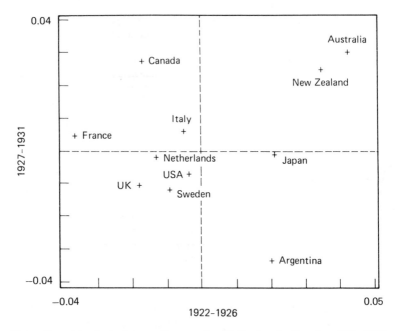

*Note*: Countries included are France, the Netherlands, Sweden, UK, USA,
    Argentina, Australia, Canada, Italy, Japan and New Zealand.
*Source*: See text.

*Figure 10.1*   Capital flows as percentage of GNP 1922–6

data are available. Figure 10.1 contrasts the periods 1922–6 and
1927–31, Figure 10.2 the periods 1927–31 and 1932–6. The figures
reinforce the implications of Table 10.7, but render the extent of
capital movements in the first half of the 1920s even more impressive.
The standard deviation of the capital-flows–national-income ratio is
larger in the free-floating period 1922–6 than in the fixed-rate period
1927–31 that followed. (For the data underlying Figure 10.1, the
standard deviations are 0.025 for 1922–6 and 0.019 for 1927–31.) The
standard deviation for 1932–6 is considerably smaller (0.016) despite
the presence of the Finnish outlier. These measures indicate no
obvious association between the flexibility of nominal exchange rates
and the magnitude of international capital movements.

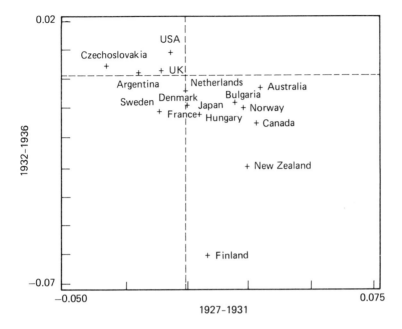

*Note*: Countries included are France, Netherlands, Sweden, UK, USA, Argentina, Australia, Czechoslovakia, Canada, Denmark, Finland, Japan, New Zealand, Norway, Bulgaria and Hungary.
*Source*: See text.

*Figure 10.2* Capital flows as percentage of GNP 1927–31

## 8  REAL INTEREST DIFFERENTIALS

The problem with basing inferences about the extent of international capital mobility on direct measures of capital flows is that the magnitude of capital movements depends not only on the integration of international capital markets but also on national economic conditions. One can visualise a situation in which capital is highly mobile but, because economic policies minimise the savings-investment gap in each country, few if any capital movements are observed.

These problems have led authors to consider the question using data on asset returns, notably real-interest-rate differentials, rather than asset flows.[14] Table 10.8 reports real interest differentials (the nominal differential less the inflation differential, in per cent per

*Table 10.8*   Real interest differential (Interest differential less inflation differential, in per cent)

| Period | Country | # of obs | Sample mean | S.E. of mean | Sample stand dev | Root MSE | 95% band |
|---|---|---|---|---|---|---|---|
| *Free floating* | USA | 56 | 0.2536 | 0.4305 | 0.01860 | 0.01843 | 0.0338 |
| 1922.01–1926.08 | France | 56 | 0.2605 | 0.8764 | 0.03786 | 0.03752 | 0.0911 |
| | Belgium | 56 | –0.3066 | 0.9130 | 0.03944 | 0.03909 | 0.0764 |
| | Netherlands | 56 | –0.1872 | 0.4459 | 0.01926 | 0.01909 | 0.0337 |
| | Italy | 56 | –2.3994 | 0.4884 | 0.02110 | 0.02091 | 0.0498 |
| | Switzerland | 56 | 0.7722 | 0.4121 | 0.01780 | 0.01764 | 0.0332 |
| | Group w/o Ger. | 336 | –0.303 | 0.2579 | 0.02729 | 0.02704 | 0.0551 |
| 1922.01–1923.10 | Germany | 22 | –70.2884 | 136.8874 | 3.70693 | 3.62170 | –10.3358 |
| 1924.02–1926.08 | Germany | 31 | –8.0963 | 3.3788 | 0.10862 | 0.10685 | 0.2837 |
| | Group w/ Ger. | 389 | –4.8821 | 7.7496 | 0.88246 | 0.86218 | 0.2800 |
| *Fixed rates* | USA | 56 | 0.5702 | 0.2638 | 0.01140 | 0.01129 | 0.0221 |
| 1927.01–1931.08 | France | 56 | 1.1687 | 0.3218 | 0.01390 | 0.01378 | 0.0311 |
| | Germany | 56 | –1.7795 | 0.2663 | 0.01150 | 0.01482 | 0.0384 |
| | Belgium | 56 | 0.2796 | 0.2703 | 0.01168 | 0.01157 | 0.0250 |
| | Netherlands | 56 | 0.3167 | 0.2606 | 0.01126 | 0.01115 | 0.0219 |
| | Italy | 56 | –2.8919 | 0.5088 | 0.02198 | 0.02178 | 0.0679 |
| | Switzerland | 56 | 1.2052 | 0.2819 | 0.01218 | 0.01207 | 0.0280 |
| | Group | 392 | 0.6614 | 0.1215 | 0.01389 | 0.01422 | 0.0380 |
| *Managed floating* | USA | 56 | 0.6254 | 0.3092 | 0.01336 | 0.01324 | 0.0225 |
| 1932.01–1936.08 | France | 56 | –1.5809 | 0.5461 | 0.02359 | 0.03006 | 0.0573 |
| | Germany | 56 | –2.9204 | 0.2663 | 0.01150 | 0.01140 | 0.0471 |
| | Belgium | 56 | –1.3697 | 0.4768 | 0.02060 | 0.02042 | 0.0329 |
| | Netherlands | 56 | –0.8568 | 0.4903 | 0.02118 | 0.02099 | 0.0418 |
| | Italy | 56 | –3.4499 | 0.3709 | 0.01603 | 0.01588 | 0.0536 |
| | Switzerland | 56 | –1.0151 | 0.3566 | 0.01541 | 0.01527 | 0.0345 |
| | Group | 392 | –1.5096 | 0.1593 | 0.01821 | 0.01909 | 0.0480 |

*Source*: See text.

annum) for the three inter-war exchange-rate regimes. Given the extremity of German experience in the early 1920s, I again compute averages for free-floating period both including and excluding Germany.

The real-interest differentials (and other statistics calculated below) are constructed as the British rate minus the rate for other countries.[15] Positive sample means for the USA and France in the early 1920s show that real-interest rates for these countries were 25 basis points lower than British rates. Positive UK–US differentials reflect tight British monetary policy designed to induce the deflation required for a return to the pre-war sterling parity. Positive UK–French differentials reflect the loose monetary policy associated with French inflation and depreciation of the franc. Similar stories can be told for the other periods. For example, in the 1930s the preponderance of negative sample means indicates that, except in comparison with the USA, the Bank of England's policy of cheap money succeeded in lowering real interest rates relative to those of other countries.

The group averages indicate that real-interest differentials were larger in the two floating periods than under fixed rates (1927–31). Again, however, there is no direct correspondence between the degree of exchange-rate variability and the magnitude of the differential. Real-interest differentials were on average five times as large under managed floating as under free floating. Here for once we have a case where direct evidence on capital flows and indirect evidence from asset returns point to the same conclusion. Note that the contrast between periods is not due to a subgroup of countries: for every country in the sample (except Germany) the differentials were larger under managed than under free floating. As in the estimates of real and nominal exchange rate predictability above, the decline in nominal exchange-rate variability with the move from free to managed floating did not deliver a comparable reduction in real-interest differentials.[16]

The story must be modified slightly when one considers the level of the differentials rather than their variability. The sample standard errors of the real interest differentials are consistent with the hypothesis that the extent of financial market integration (as measured by the variability of the real-interest differential) is directly correlated with the degree of exchange-rate stability. Real-interest differentials were half again as variable under free floating as under managed floating, and half again as variable under managed floating as under fixed rates. (I refer to results for 1922–6 excluding Germany.) The root mean squared error, an alternative measure of variability, provides the same picture. If the average level of the real-interest differential was larger in the early 1930s than in the early 1920s, its variability was larger under the 1920s float than the 1930s float. This suggests, plausibly, that political factors such as capital controls, actual or anticipated, may have been responsible for the larger average differentials in the 1930s, while exchange-rate volatility may have been responsible for their greater variability in the 1920s.

Variations across countries within each period are consistent with the interpretation. Under the early 1920s float, countries with relatively stable exchange rates (the USA, whose currency was pegged to gold and relatively stable against sterling, along with the Netherlands and Switzerland) have small sample standard deviations compared with countries with more volatile exchange rates (France, Belgium and Italy). Within this group of volatile exchange-rate countries, there is a direct correspondence between the degree of nominal exchange-rate variability and the variability of the real-interest differential (with Belgium and France exhibiting larger differentials than Italy). The very large variability of the Anglo-German real-interest differential drives home the point.

Under fixed rates (1927–31) there is relatively little difference across countries in the average level or variability of the real interest differential. Since this was the period not only with least exchange-rate variability but also with least risk of capital controls and fewest political impediments to capital mobility, it is difficult to determine whether the degree of exchange-rate flexibility or other factors were responsible for the contrast.

For managed floating (1932–6), real-interest differentials against London were both larger and more variable for gold-bloc countries such as France, Belgium and the Netherlands than for countries such as Germany and Italy which suspended at least some provisions of the gold standard and imposed exchange controls of varying degrees of severity. One would think that exchange controls would be inconsistent with international financial-market integration and real-interest convergence, but 1930s experience is not clearly consistent with this view. The relatively low average level and variability of the US and Swiss real-interest-rate differentials are difficult to reconcile with any explanation that would contrast gold-bloc and exchange-control countries. One would think that Switzerland in particular should be grouped with the gold bloc, where in fact the variability of its real-interest differential more closely resembles those of Germany and Italy.

## 9    DECOMPOSING REAL INTEREST DIFFERENTIALS

Shedding light on these patterns requires digging deeper into the composition of the differentials. I follow Frankel and MacArthur

(1988) in decomposing the real interest differential into three components. Defining the real differential as:

$$r - r^* = (i-\pi) - (i^*-\pi^*) \tag{1}$$

where $r$ is the real interest rate, $i$ is the nominal interest rate, $\pi$ is the expected rate of inflation and asterisks denote foreign variables, we can add and subtract the forward discount $f_d$ and the expected rate of depreciation of the domestic currency $\Delta s^e$:

$$r - r^* = (i-i^*-f_d) + (f_d-\Delta s^e) + (\Delta s^e\pi+\pi^*) \tag{2}$$

The first term is the covered-interest differential. In the absence of transactions costs, information costs, capital controls, risk of future capital controls and default risk, the mean and variability of this component of the real-interest differential should be negligible. If capital controls and like factors were significant impediments to real-interest-rate convergence, they should be picked up by this term. Following Aliber (1973) and Frankel and MacArthur (1988), I refer to $i-i^*-f_d$ as the 'political risk' premium to highlight the political dimension of adoption of capital controls.

The second term is the exchange-risk premium. The forward discount on foreign exchange need not equal the expected rate of depreciation of the foreign currency if investors demand compensation for the risks of exchange-rate changes. A large literature documents the existence of an exchange-risk premium for the 1980s. The question is how its magnitude compares in the 1920s and 1930s, and the extent to which it contributes to real-interest differentials.

The third term is expected real depreciation. Only if the expected rate of depreciation of the nominal exchange rate equals the expected inflation-differential will purchasing-power parity hold in an expectational sense. But if, for example, the rate of depreciation of the domestic currency is expected to exceed the difference between domestic and foreign inflation rates, the real exchange rate of the home country is expected to depreciate. The purchasing power of domestic goods over foreign goods is expected to decline; to induce investors to hold assets that yield a return denominated in domestic goods, they must be compensated by a higher real-interest rate.

Table 10.9 displays the first component of the real-interest differential – the political-risk premium. The results reveal the greater magnitude of political risk in the early 1930s than in the early 1920s,

*Table 10.9*   Covered interest differential (interest differential less forward discount, in per cent)

| Period | Country | # of obs | Sample mean | S.E. of mean | Sample stand dev | Root MSE | 95% band |
|---|---|---|---|---|---|---|---|
| *Free floating* | USA | 56 | −0.1733 | 0.308 | 0.01331 | 0.01319 | 0.0230 |
| 1922.01– | France | 56 | −2.4928 | 0.4414 | 0.01907 | 0.01890 | 0.0427 |
| 1926.08 | Belgium | 56 | −2.2103 | 0.2491 | 0.01076 | 0.01066 | 0.0369 |
| | Netherlands | 56 | −0.2050 | 0.3404 | 0.01471 | 0.01458 | 0.0239 |
| | Italy | 56 | −3.2402 | 0.4740 | 0.02048 | 0.02029 | 0.0829 |
| | Switzerland | 56 | 0.9022 | 0.2644 | 0.01142 | 0.01132 | 0.0246 |
| | Group w/o Ger. | 336 | −0.9032 | 0.1455 | 0.01540 | 0.01526 | 0.0372 |
| 1922.01–1923.01 | Germany | 13 | −9.3530 | 4.6581 | 0.09697 | 0.09316 | 0.1364 |
| 1924.12–1926.08 | Germany | 21 | −2.9399 | 0.8131 | 0.02151 | 0.02100 | 0.0450 |
| | Group w/Ger. | 370 | −1.3157 | 0.2153 | 0.02392 | 0.02327 | 0.0460 |
| *Fixed rates* | USA | 56 | 0.4805 | 0.1911 | 0.00825 | 0.00818 | 0.0134 |
| 1927.01– | France | 56 | 1.2056 | 0.2427 | 0.01048 | 0.01039 | 0.0275 |
| 1931.08 | Germany | 55 | −2.2164 | 0.2497 | 0.01069 | 0.01059 | 0.0318 |
| | Belgium | 56 | 0.2620 | 0.1503 | 0.00649 | 0.00643 | 0.0131 |
| | Netherlands | 56 | 0.5146 | 0.1777 | 0.00768 | 0.00761 | 0.0157 |
| | Italy | 56 | −2.7894 | 0.3066 | 0.01324 | 0.01312 | 0.0503 |
| | Switzerland | 56 | 1.0024 | 0.3165 | 0.01367 | 0.01355 | 0.0226 |
| | Group | 391 | −0.2150 | 0.0910 | 0.01039 | 0.01035 | 0.0360 |
| *Managed floating* | USA | 56 | 0.1933 | 0.2221 | 0.00960 | 0.00970 | 0.0220 |
| 1932.01– | France | 56 | −2.4627 | 0.7529 | 0.03253 | 0.03224 | 0.0864 |
| 1936.08 | Germany | N/A | N/A | N/A | N/A | N/A | N/A |
| | Belgium | 56 | −1.6589 | 0.3331 | 0.01439 | 0.01426 | 0.0327 |
| | Netherlands | 56 | −1.1805 | 0.572 | 0.02471 | 0.02449 | 0.0594 |
| | Italy | 47 | −5.2501 | 0.5416 | 0.02340 | 0.02315 | 0.1007 |
| | Switzerland | 56 | −1.4404 | 0.5911 | 0.01946 | 0.01929 | 0.0453 |
| | Group | 327 | −1.8762 | 0.2100 | 0.02192 | 0.02173 | 0.0640 |

*Source*:   See text.

and in the early 1920s than in the gold-exchange-standard period 1927–31. (Unless stated to the contrary, I refer to the results excluding Germany in the early 1920s.) This is quantitative confirmation of the prevalence of exchange controls in the 1930s.

Controls were also utilised by countries in the 1920s to combat inflation and exchange-rate depreciation, as well as by some countries seeking to strengthen their currencies and return to par. *A priori*, it is not obvious that they represented a more serious impediment to international capital mobility in the 1920s or the 1930s. Actual controls may have been more prevalent in the 1930s, but investors might hesitate to transfer capital across national borders because of a perceived danger of future controls as well as because of their actual presence. Table 10.9 suggests that political risk was a more serious impediment in the 1930s. The sample mean of our measure of political risk is twice as large in the 1930s as in the 1920s. The contrast between the 1930s and early 1920s is all the more striking in view of the fact that data limitations prevent the inclusion of Germany in the 1930s.

The contrast between the two periods of floating on the one hand and the fixed-rate years on the other is even more striking. Political risk is four times as large in the early 1920s as in 1927–31, nine times as large in the early 1930s as in 1927–31. The same ranking emerges when one considers the variability of the covered-interest differential (as measured by either the sample standard deviation or the root-mean-squared error) rather than its average level.

Which countries account for the rise in political risk? The rise is quite general: the sample mean rises in absolute value for all countries except Belgium. The largest increase is that of Italy, presumably reflecting a combination of capital controls and default risk due to political developments.

Alternative measures of the variability of the covered-interest differential tell a consistent story. Judged by the standard deviations, political risk under the managed float of the 1930s was greater than under the free float of the 1920s, and greater under the free float than under fixed rates. Interestingly, however, the USA is an exception to the rule that political risk was greater in the 1930s than in the early 1920s. Both the sample standard deviation and the root-mean-squared error are larger in 1922–6 than in 1932–6. This difference could be due to an unusually high perceived risk of exchange control in the 1920s, or an unusually low risk in the 1930s. The second explanation is more plausible than the first. It is hard to imagine why fears of the imposition of capital controls by the USA in the early 1920s would have been greater or more variable than comparable fears in the 1930s. And neither the root-mean-squared error nor the sample standard deviation for the USA in 1922–6 are much different from the comparable statistics for other countries such as the Netherlands and Switzerland, where fears of exchange control were

minimal. For the 1930s, the USA covered-interest differential behaves very differently from those of these other countries. It remains
an open question why investors in dollars should have been so
sanguine about political risk in a period when the Roosevelt Administration felt free to experiment with the exchange rate and to make
radical changes in other economic arrangements.

This evidence of political risk under floating rates is difficult to
reconcile with the argument of Stockman (1988) and Giovannini
(1989) that capital controls tend to be associated with fixed exchange
rates. According to this argument, policy-makers habitually adopt
nominal exchange-rate targets that are incompatible with domestic
policies. They turn to controls to alleviate the conflict. As Giovannini
points out, capital controls were a prominent feature of the European
Monetary System (EMS) throughout its first decade of operation.
They were used to reconcile the relatively inflationary policies pursued by the weak currency countries with sustained periods of nominal
exchange-rate stability. Under the Bretton Woods System, exchange
controls were prevalent as late as 1958, at which time the external
convertibility of the European currencies was finally restored. There
were also subsequent instances, such as the US Exchange Equalization
Tax of the 1960s, when countries with fixed exchange rates sought to tax
and control capital movements.

But in the inter-war period, capital controls were more prevalent
under floating than under fixed rates. The inter-war system of fixed
rates provides a counter-example to the general proposition.

Was political risk solely responsible for deviations from covered
interest parity in the 1930s, or did other factors play a role? Table 10.10
displays the sum of the other two components of the real-interest
differential: exchange risk plus expected real depreciation. Estimating
these components separately requires an assumption about how investors formed expectations of depreciation. Given the difficulty of
constructing such forecasts and the controversial nature of any empirical proxy, I first circumvent the problem entirely, considering the
two components together, which eliminates the expected depreciation term. The sum of the two components $(f_d - \pi + \pi^*)$ is denoted the
real forward discount or 'currency risk', since it encompasses both
the exchange-risk premium and expected real depreciation due to
divergent movements anticipated in the exchange rate and the international inflation differential.

Table 10.10 shows that currency risk was greatest in the early
1920s, not in the early 1930s when real-interest differentials were

*Table 10.10*  Real forward discount (forward discount less inflation differential, as per cent)

| Period | Country | # of obs | Sample mean | S.E. of mean | Sample stand dev | Root MSE | 95% band |
|--------|---------|----------|-------------|--------------|------------------|----------|----------|
| *Free* | | | | | | | |
| *floating* | USA | 56 | 0.4269 | 0.3045 | 0.01315 | 0.01304 | 0.0294 |
| 1922.01– | France | 56 | 2.7533 | 0.7185 | 0.03104 | 0.03076 | 0.0780 |
| 1926.08 | Belgium | 56 | 1.9037 | 0.9511 | 0.04109 | 0.04072 | 0.0903 |
| | Netherlands | 56 | 0.0178 | 0.3178 | 0.01373 | 0.01361 | 0.0284 |
| | Italy | 56 | 0.8407 | 0.6171 | 0.02666 | 0.02642 | 0.0511 |
| | Switzerland | 56 | –0.1300 | 0.3212 | 0.01388 | 0.01375 | 0.0268 |
| | Group w/o Ger. | 336 | 0.9687 | 0.7375 | 0.02555 | 0.02532 | 0.0625 |
| 1922.01– | | | | | | | |
| 1923.01 | Germany | 13 | 44.5546 | 14.7277 | 0.30658 | 0.29455 | 0.8061 |
| | Germany | 21 | 0.6561 | 0.4676 | 0.01237 | 0.01208 | 0.0199 |
| | Group w/Ger. | 380 | 2.4170 | 0.5478 | 0.06165 | 0.05952 | 0.0830 |
| | | | | | | | |
| *Fixed rates* | USA | 56 | 0.0897 | 0.2285 | 0.00987 | 0.01268 | 0.0176 |
| 1927.01– | France | 56 | –0.0370 | 0.3966 | 0.01713 | 0.01698 | 0.0415 |
| 1931.07 | Germany | 55 | 0.5572 | 0.1645 | 0.00704 | 0.00698 | 0.0174 |
| | Belgium | 56 | 0.0176 | 0.2576 | 0.01113 | 0.01103 | 0.0209 |
| | Netherlands | 56 | –0.1978 | 0.2717 | 0.01174 | 0.01163 | 0.0191 |
| | Italy | 56 | –0.1184 | 0.3216 | 0.01389 | 0.01355 | 0.0264 |
| | Switzerland | 56 | 0.0325 | 0.2576 | 0.01113 | 0.01103 | 0.0180 |
| | Group | 392 | 0.1644 | 0.1055 | 0.01206 | 0.01230 | 0.0216 |
| | | | | | | | |
| *Managed* | | | | | | | |
| *floating* | USA | 56 | 0.4321 | 0.3425 | 0.01480 | 0.01466 | 0.0252 |
| 1932.01– | France | 56 | 0.8818 | 0.5989 | 0.02587 | 0.02564 | 0.0598 |
| 1936.08 | Germany | N/A | N/A | N/A | N/A | N/A | N/A |
| | Belgium | 56 | 0.2892 | 0.6153 | 0.02658 | 0.02634 | 0.0247 |
| | Netherlands | 56 | 0.3238 | 0.3620 | 0.01564 | 0.01550 | 0.0260 |
| | Italy | 47 | 1.9678 | 0.7350 | 0.02909 | 0.02878 | 0.0836 |
| | Switzerland | 56 | 0.4252 | 0.3965 | 0.01713 | 0.01697 | 0.0417 |
| | Group | 327 | 0.6856 | 0.2114 | 0.02207 | 0.02186 | 0.0485 |

*Source*:  See text.

largest. The sample mean of the real-forward discount is early 150 per cent as large under the free float as under the managed float. Equally striking is the contrast between the currency risk in the two floating periods and the fixed-exchange-rate years. By this measure, currency risk was four times as great under managed floating as under fixed rates, and six times as great under free floating as under fixed rates.

Alternative measures (standard deviations, root-mean-squared errors) yield the same ranking. Currency risk was greater under free than managed floating, and greater under managed floating than fixed rates. But by these alternative measures, which focus on the variability of the real forward discount rather than its level, the contrast between the two floating-rate regimes is less impressive.

The differences across regimes in currency risk are quite general. They apply to all countries in the sample. The mean real-forward discount, for example, is smaller for every country under fixed rates than under either floating-rate regime.

In contrast, within each exchange-rate regime there are dramatic differences across countries in the magnitude of currency risk. Under the free float of the 1920s, currency risk was by the greatest for France and Belgium, followed at a distance by Italy. France and Belgium are the high inflation countries in the sample, while Italy experienced moderate inflation.

Under the managed float of the 1930s, cross-country variations in currency risk were moderate in size. Under fixed rates, in contrast, cross-country variations were small. Currency risk was greatest for Germany and Italy, the two countries for whom convertibility was most in doubt.

Table 10.11 and 10.12 decompose currency risk into the exchange-risk premium (the forward discount less expected nominal depreciation) and expected real depreciation (expected nominal depreciation net of the expected inflation differential). Actual depreciation of the currency over the period is used as a proxy for expected depreciation, actual inflation as a proxy for expected inflation.[17] Both components contribute to the greater magnitude of the currency-risk premium under free rather than managed floating. The mean exchange-risk premium was nearly four times as large under free floating as under managed floating; in turn, mean exchange risk was nearly four times as great under managed floating as under fixed rates. Apparently, investors demanded more compensation for the risks associated with uncertain exchange-rate fluctuations under freely floating rates than under managed floating, and under managed floating than under fixed rates. The same pattern is evident in the sample standard deviation: it is nearly twice as large in 1922–6 as in 1932–6, and nearly twice as large in 1932–6 as in 1927–31.

Cross-country variations in the exchange-risk premium support the notion that investors required a premium to hold highly variable currencies. In the early 1920s the largest and most variable risk premia are, in descending order, those of Germany, Belgium, France,

*Table 10.11*   Exchange risk premium (forward discount less exchange depreciation, in per cent)

| Period | Country | # of obs | Sample mean | S.E. of mean | Sample stand dev | Root MSE | 95% band |
|---|---|---|---|---|---|---|---|
| *Free* | | | | | | | |
| *floating* | USA | 56 | −0.4858 | 0.5683 | 0.02455 | 0.02433 | 0.0524 |
| 1922.01– | France | 56 | −5.3667 | 2.8122 | 0.12149 | 0.12040 | 0.2421 |
| 1926.08 | Belgium | 55 | −6.4902 | 3.1355 | 0.13425 | 0.13303 | 0.2704 |
| | Netherlands | 56 | −0.1239 | 0.3018 | 0.01304 | 0.01292 | 0.0237 |
| | Italy | 56 | −1.2938 | 2.1777 | 0.09408 | 0.09323 | 0.1624 |
| | Switzerland | 56 | −0.6490 | 0.5255 | 0.02270 | 0.02250 | 0.0397 |
| | Group w/o Ger. | 336 | −2.3822 | 0.7956 | 0.08420 | 0.08350 | 0.2030 |
| 1922.01– | | | | | | | |
| 1923.01 | Germany | 13 | −99.7031 | 28.7729 | 0.5990 | 0.57546 | −1.8039 |
| 1924.12– | Germany | 21 | 0.1758 | 0.3694 | 0.00977 | 0.00954 | 0.0110 |
| 1926.08 | Group w/Ger. | 370 | −5.654 | 1.2428 | 0.13802 | 0.13406 | 0.2470 |
| | | | | | | | |
| *Fixed rates* | USA | 54 | −0.0124 | 0.0576 | 0.00244 | 0.00242 | 0.0053 |
| 1927.01– | France | 54 | −0.0450 | 0.0675 | 0.00286 | 0.00284 | 0.0057 |
| 1931.06 | Germany | 54 | 0.2484 | 0.0740 | 0.00314 | 0.00311 | 0.0060 |
| | Belgium | 54 | 0.0175 | 0.0675 | 0.00174 | 0.00172 | 0.0033 |
| | Netherlands | 54 | 0.0275 | 0.0530 | 0.00225 | 0.00223 | 0.0037 |
| | Italy | 54 | 1.2966 | 1.1717 | 0.04971 | 0.04925 | 0.1115 |
| | Switzerland | 54 | 0.0101 | 0.0852 | 0.00362 | 0.00358 | 0.0075 |
| | Group | 378 | 0.2204 | 0.1689 | 0.01896 | 0.01878 | 0.0070 |
| | | | | | | | |
| *Managed* | | | | | | | |
| *floating* | USA | 54 | −1.7480 | 1.5602 | 0.06620 | 0.06558 | 0.1361 |
| 1932.01– | France | 54 | 1.8187 | 0.7438 | 0.03156 | 0.03127 | 0.0648 |
| 1936.06 | Belgium | 54 | −0.6088 | 1.8729 | 0.07946 | 0.07872 | 0.0766 |
| | Netherlands | 54 | 1.5978 | 0.7164 | 0.03039 | 0.03011 | 0.0717 |
| | Italy[a] | 47 | 2.6985 | 0.8494 | 0.03362 | 0.03326 | 0.0696 |
| | Switzerland | 54 | 1.4983 | 0.7314 | 0.03103 | 0.03074 | 0.0643 |
| | Group | 317 | 0.8358 | 0.4845 | 0.04981 | 0.04934 | 0.0770 |

*Notes*:   [a] January 1932 to November 1935.
*Source*:   See text.

and Italy, corresponding to their ranking in order of exchange-rate volatility (as measured by standard deviations of holding period returns in Table 10.2). Smaller risk-premia were demanded of countries with relatively stable currencies such the USA, Switzerland and the Netherlands.

It is not clearly why the USA, whose currency was pegged to gold throughout the 1920s, should have had a larger risk-premium than Switzerland and Holland. But while the dollar was pegged *vis-à-vis*

*Table 10.12*   Real exchange depreciation (exchange depreciation less inflation, in per cent)

| Period | Country | # of obs | Sample mean | S.E. of mean | Sample stand dev | Root MSE | 95% band |
|---|---|---|---|---|---|---|---|
| *Free* | | | | | | | |
| *floating* | USA | 56 | 0.9127 | 0.7009 | 0.03028 | 0.03001 | 0.0581 |
| 1922.01– | France | 56 | 8.1200 | 3.1119 | 0.13443 | 0.13323 | 0.2615 |
| 1926.07 | Belgium | 55 | 8.3198 | 3.7342 | 0.15989 | 0.15843 | 0.3118 |
| | Netherlands | 56 | 0.1417 | 0.4551 | 0.01966 | 0.01949 | 0.0383 |
| | Italy[a] | 54 | 3.0154 | 1.9845 | 0.08419 | 0.08341 | 0.1604 |
| | Switzerland | 56 | 0.519 | 0.6740 | 0.02912 | 0.02869 | 0.0602 |
| | Group w/o Ger. | 333 | 3.4934 | 0.8890 | 0.09366 | 0.09280 | 0.2143 |
| 1922.01– | | | | | | | |
| 1923.11 | Germany | 22 | 414.9204 | 186.7499 | 5.17087 | 5.05705 | 11.4914 |
| 1924.02– | Germany | 31 | 0.9248 | 0.9452 | 0.03031 | 0.02989 | 0.0504 |
| 1926.08 | Group w/Ger. | 386 | 26.7363 | 10.9102 | 1.23756 | 1.21040 | 0.6310 |
| *Fixed rates* | USA | 54 | 0.1004 | 0.2100 | 0.00891 | 0.00883 | 0.0149 |
| 1927.01– | France | 54 | 0.0939 | 0.3656 | 0.01550 | 0.01536 | 0.0256 |
| 1931.06 | Germany | 54 | 0.307 | 0.1869 | 0.00793 | 0.00786 | 0.0157 |
| | Belgium | 54 | 0.0818 | 0.2442 | 0.01036 | 0.01026 | 0.0201 |
| | Netherlands | 54 | –0.1457 | 2.2599 | 0.01103 | 0.01092 | 0.0191 |
| | Italy | 54 | –2.6842 | 1.8990 | 0.08057 | 0.08000 | 0.2297 |
| | Switzerland | 54 | 0.0414 | 0.2730 | 0.01158 | 0.01148 | 0.0201 |
| | Group | 378 | –0.3151 | 0.2864 | 0.03215 | 0.03192 | 0.0194 |
| *Managed* | | | | | | | |
| *floating* | USA | 54 | 2.2267 | 1.7331 | 0.07353 | 0.07285 | 0.1655 |
| 1932.01– | France | 54 | –1.0865 | 0.9167 | 0.03889 | 0.03853 | 0.0749 |
| 1936.06 | Germany | 54 | –0.9442 | 0.8644 | 0.03667 | 0.03633 | 0.0671 |
| | Belgium | 54 | 0.9074 | 2.2802 | 0.09674 | 0.09584 | 0.0892 |
| | Netherlands | 54 | –1.2651 | 0.7623 | 0.03234 | 0.03204 | 0.0653 |
| | Italy | 54 | –0.4682 | 0.9767 | 0.04143 | 0.04105 | 0.0670 |
| | Switzerland | 54 | –1.1218 | 0.7873 | 0.03340 | 0.03309 | 0.0689 |
| | Group | 378 | –0.2503 | 0.4932 | 0.05536 | 0.05491 | 0.0845 |

*Notes*:   [a] 1922.01–1926.06.
*Source*:   See text.

gold, it was not pegged against other currencies, such as sterling. Table 10.2 shows that the sterling–dollar rate was more volatile between 1922 and 1926 than either the British–Swiss or British–Dutch exchange rates. The premium on dollars is thus consistent with the hypothesis linking exchange-rate variability, via uncertainty, to the exchange-risk premium.

For the managed float, cross-country differences are more difficult to interpret. The largest exchange-risk premia were demanded of Italy, France and the USA, in descending order. But the sample standard deviation and the root-mean-squared error indicate that the exchange-risk premium was most variable in Belgium and the USA. Belgium and the USA are the two countries in the sample which moved from the pegging their exchange rates to gold to managed floating midway through the period. Apparently, the exchange-risk premium rose significantly when countries departed from the gold standard.

For the fixed-rate regime, there is little systematic cross-country variation in exchange-risk premia. One suggestive fact is that the means and sample standard deviations are larger for Germany and Italy than for the other countries. Germany and Italy were the two countries in the sample whose gold-standard parities were in most serious doubt, which may explain the relatively large risk-premia attached to their currencies.

Expected real depreciation, the final component of the real interest differential, was also greater under free than managed floating.[18] Average real depreciation was 3.5 per cent per month between 1922 and 1926, but only 0.3 per cent per month between 1932 and 1936. Similarly, the sample standard deviation of the rate of real depreciation was almost twice as large under free as under managed floating. Not all countries conform to the pattern: for Switzerland, the Netherlands and the USA, the average rate of real depreciation is larger in the early 1930s than in the early 1920s. The correlation dominates where the variability of the nominal rate was especially pronounced: in France, Belgium and Italy in the 1920s. This suggests that even if there existed a positive association between the freedom of the float and the variability of the expected change in the real exchange rate, where the correlation was weak it could be overwhelmed by other influences.

The importance of other factors in determining expected real depreciation is underscored by the fact that the variability of expected real depreciation was actually greater under fixed rates between 1927 and 1931 than under the subsequent managed-floating regime. The fixed-rate period coincided with the Great Depression and the collapse of commodity prices, which wreaked havoc with real exchange rates.[19] This points up the inability of fixed nominal rates to guarantee real exchange-rate stability.

To summarise, currency risk was greater under free floating in the

1920s than under managed floating in the 1930s, because both the exchange-risk premium and the variability of the real exchange-rate were greater. The variability of freely floating rates appears to have rendered financial assets denominated in different currencies increasingly poor substitutes. In conjunction with imperfectly flexible domestic-currency prices, the variability of nominal rates under free floating led to large real-exchange-rate changes, limiting the integration of international commodity markets. Yet despite the greater magnitude of currency risk in the 1930s real-interest differentials were smaller in the early 1920s because capital controls and other forms of government intervention in international financial markets were more extensive under managed floating.

The evidence from asset returns suggests that capital mobility was lower in the 1930s than the 1920s due to the fact and threat of capital controls. Exchange-risk premia and real-exchange-rate variability were in fact greater in the early 1920s, but these were insufficient to swamp the effect of controls. Only if one wishes to argue that the capital controls of the 1930s were a legacy of dissatisfaction with the 'hot money' flows experienced under free floating in the 1920s is it possible to assert that the degree of exchange-rate flexibility bears a direct relationship to the degree of international financial-market integration.

## 10   THE CREDIBILITY OF FIXED EXCHANGE RATES

The preceding analysis reveals the most interest rate convergence and international financial market integration under fixed rates. This section considers whether the decision to peg the exchange rate delivered those benefits immediately or only after a period of transition.

Pegging nominal rates did not equalize real interest rates across countries. But as Tables 7–11 show, insofar as real interest differentials remained, they were attributable to terms of trade shocks creating expectations of real exchange rate changes. If exchange rates were credibly fixed, however, these terms of trade shocks should not have produced *nominal* interest rate differentials. Equation (2) above, reproduced here for clarity,

$$r - r^* = (i - i^* - f_d) + (f_d - \Delta s^e) + (\Delta s^e - \pi + \pi^*)$$

can be rewritten (bringing the inflation terms to the left-hand side) as:

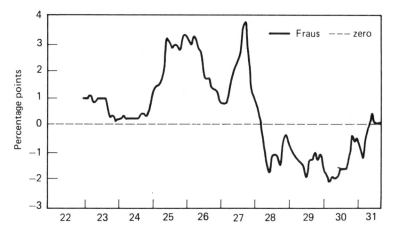

*Figure 10.3*   French–US interest differential

$$i - i^* = (i-i^*-f_d) + (f_d-\Delta s^e) + (\Delta s^e) \tag{3}$$

The nominal interest-differential will be negligible under fixed rates if

(i) deviations from covered interest parity are negligible;
(ii) risk-premia are negligible;
(iii) expectations of nominal exchange rate changes are zero.

Table 10.9 confirms that deviations from covered-interest parity $(i-i^*-f_d)$ were negligible between 1927 and 1931. Table 10.11 confirms that risk-premia $(f_d-\Delta s^e)$ were small. So nominal interest-differentials in this period predominantly reflect doubts about the credibility of the commitment to fix the nominal exchange rate.[20]

Figures 10.3–10.5 show the nominal interest-differential against the USA for France, Belgium and Italy, three of the last industrial countries to stabilise. The interest rates are 90-day market discount rates. The figures suggest that fixed nominal rates did not instantaneously deliver nominal interest-rate convergence and financial-market integration.

Figure 10.3 for France shows that fully a year following the franc's *de facto* stabilisation was required before even short-term interest rates fell to US levels. Nominal rates declined over the second half of the 1926, following Poincaré's accession to power in the summer.

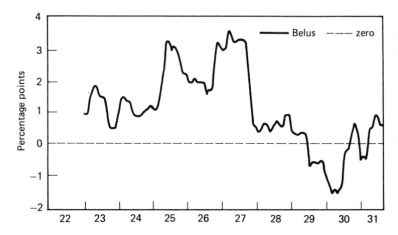

*Figure 10.4*   Belgian–US interest differential

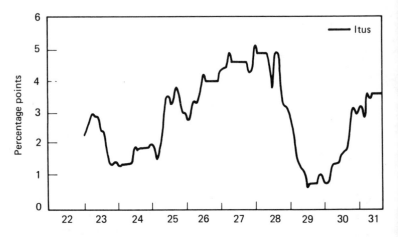

*Figure 10.5*   Italian–US interest differential

The fall in nominal rates reflects rapid deflation associated with the recovery of the exchange rate. But once the exchange rate and prices were stabilised in December 1926, the nominal interest-differential rose, presumably reflecting continued doubts about the government's commitment to peg the nominal rate.

Interpretation of French experience is complicated by the 18-month lag between *de facto* and *de jure* stabilisation. The nominal interest-

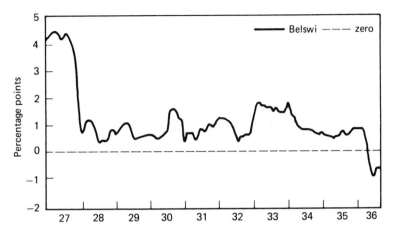

*Figure 10.6* Belgian–Swiss interest differential

differential is consistent with instantaneous credibility if one believes that the government's commitment to fixed rates was only complete following *de jure* stabilisation. But Figure 10.4 for Belgium buttresses the view that credibility was not acquired instantaneously. Legal stabilisation in Belgium took place abruptly in October 1926. In contrast to Poincaré, Franqui moved immediately from *de facto* to *de jure* stabilisation. Yet Figure 10.4 shows that, as in France, a year passed before the credibility of this commitment to a fixed nominal rate was accepted by the market. There had been a previous attempt to stabilise the Belgian franc (the Janssen Plan of October 1925–March 1926). On that previous occasion, like the current one, *de facto* stabilisation had been accompanied by tax increases sufficient to balance the budget and foreign loan negotiations.[21] Yet the Janssen stabilisation had failed. This helps us to understand why the market remained sceptical of the Franqui stabilisation for much of 1927.

The same pattern is evident in Figure 10.5 for Italy. Stabilisation took place in 1927, yet a significant interest differential *vis-à-vis* the USA remained until 1929.

Figures 10.6 and 10.7, which show Belgian and French interest differentials against Switzerland, make two further points. First, our conclusions about the gradual nature of the transition to credibly fixed exchange rates are not affected by choice of reference currency. Second, the credibility of the commitment to a fixed rate appears to have depended more on individual national policies than on the gold

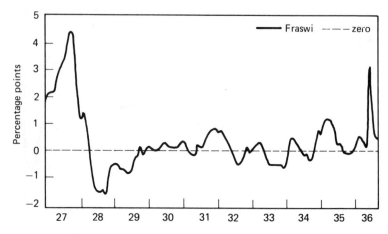

*Figure 10.7*  French–Swiss interest differential

standard system as a whole. There was little question about the stability of the Swiss franc, at least until the second half of 1935. The Belgian–Swiss nominal interest differential remained roughly constant throughout 1931–4, even after Britain and the USA had devalued. There is only the slightest indication of a larger nominal interest differential in the early 1930s than in the late 1920s. The same is true of France. Until the election that brought the Popular Front to power in the spring of 1936, there was little sign of growing scepticism about the credibility of the official commitment to maintain the nominal peg.

## 11  SUMMARY

This paper has reported evidence on the characteristics of fixed and flexible exchange rate regimes. Using inter-war evidence, it has uncovered important differences across regimes, encompassing both nominal and real variables and both policy inputs and performance outputs.

The variability of the nominal exchange rate was found to be positively associated with the freedom of the float. Nominal rates were considerably more variable under free than under managed floating. The kurtosis in the distribution of exchange-rate changes suggests that such variability was episodic: that free floating rates

*Figure 10.8* Standard deviation of change in $M_1$ for thirty countries

were highly variable mainly because of a few periods of exceptional volatility.

Yet the reduction in nominal exchange-rate variability achieved with the move from free to managed floating was not accompanied by a commensurate fall in exchange-rate uncertainty. Alternative forecasting equations suggest that the spot rate was almost as difficult to predict in the early 1930s as in the early 1920s. While government policy succeeded in damping spot-rate fluctuations, it seems to have been subject to periodic shifts that heightened risk. If this interpretation is correct, then the decline in exchange-rate variability between the early 1920s and early 1930s did not necessarily imply an improvement in welfare.

This point is reinforced by the observation that there was a strong association between nominal exchange-rate predictability and real exchange-rate predictability in both periods of floating. It appears that intervention to stabilise nominal exchange rates did not guarantee a commensurate reduction in either real or nominal exchange-rate uncertainty.

Policies which stabilised exchange rates might, in principle, have encouraged international capital mobility. But there is no direct correspondence between the degree of exchange-rate stability and the volume of capital flows, because there is no direct correspondence between exchange-rate stability and exchange-rate risk, or between exchange-rate stability and the real interest-rate differentials in response to which capital movements take place. For many countries, real-interest differentials were larger under the managed float of the 1930s than under the free float of the 1920s. This is because capital controls which posed a barrier to international capital mobility were more pervasive in the 1930s. The question is whether exchange controls are a necessary concomitant of attempts to limit exchange rate flexibility; evidence from 1927–31 suggests a negative answer. The fixed-rate regime operated without the presence or prospect of significant exchange controls. It delivered reductions in nominal exchange-rate uncertainty, real exchange-rate uncertainty and real-interest differentials.

This suggests that whether a reduction in exchange-rate variability confers economic benefits depends on how that reduction is achieved. In the 1930s, exchange-rate flexibility was limited through government intervention in the markets, using instruments including but not restricted to exchange control. There was only limited international policy coordination to minimise exchange-rate swings. Conflicts therefore arose between domestic policies and exchange-rate stability, causing intervention to be subject to changes whose timing was difficult to predict. In the second half of the 1920s, nominal exchange rates were fixed instead through the systematic adaptation of monetary and fiscal policies. This permitted fixed nominal rates to deliver many of the benefits anticipated by their advocates.

## APPENDIX

*Table 10A.1*    Alternative forecasting equations for nominal exchange rates

|  | AR(1) Equations | | ARMA(1,1) Equations | | |
|---|---|---|---|---|---|
|  | α | β | α | β | MA(1) |
| *Floating rates* | | | | | |
| Denmark | 2.6771 | 0.9940 | 2.7740 | 0.9903 | 0.6117 |
| Finland | 5.1989 | 0.9038 | 5.2014 | 0.8913 | 0.1166 |
| Norway | 3.0515 | 0.9883 | 3.0780 | 0.9839 | 0.2249 |
| Sweden | 2.8902 | 0.9592 | 2.8777 | 0.9382 | 0.2880 |
| Switzerland | 3.2204 | 0.8865 | 3.2200 | 0.8809 | 0.0790 |
| USA | 1.5878 | 0.9674 | 1.5708 | 0.9540 | 0.2790 |
| France | 7.3377 | 0.9923 | 7.2800 | 0.9922 | 0.1035 |
| Netherlands | 2.4924 | 0.9719 | 2.4787 | 0.9415 | 0.4551 |
| Belgium | 5.5270 | 0.9787 | 5.5178 | 0.9780 | 0.1467 |
| Italy | 7.1783 | 0.9963 | 7.1582 | 0.9962 | 0.4016 |

*Table 10A.1* continued

| | AR(1) Equations | | ARMA(1,1) Equations | | |
|---|---|---|---|---|---|
| | α | β | α | β | MA(1) |
| Germany (1) | 20.7137 | 0.9697 | 21.8430 | 0.9720 | 0.1295 |
| Germany (2) | 30.6420 | 0.9280 | 30.6370 | 0.9022 | 0.2015 |
| *Fixed rates* | | | | | |
| Denmark | 2.9003 | 0.3709 | | na | |
| Finland | 5.2634 | 0.7220 | 5.2630 | 0.7572 | –0.0858 |
| Norway | 2.9004 | 0.8865 | 2.8991 | 0.9116 | –0.2965 |
| Sweden | 2.8975 | 0.4464 | 2.8975 | 0.5974 | –0.1946 |
| Switzerland | 3.2148 | 0.9810 | 3.2179 | 0.9637 | 0.5609 |
| USA | 1.5813 | 0.7241 | 1.5813 | 0.7399 | –0.0338 |
| France | 4.8205 | 0.7229 | 4.8204 | 0.5730 | 0.4581 |
| Netherlands | 2.4924 | 0.7750 | 2.4926 | 0.5643 | 0.6003 |
| Belgium | 3.5523 | 0.7976 | 3.5523 | 0.7021 | 0.2509 |
| Italy | 4.5221 | 0.6203 | 4.5234 | 0.3410 | 0.9910 |
| Germany | 30.6473 | 0.8404 | 30.6470 | 0.6806 | 0.5390 |
| *Managed floating* | | | | | |
| Denmark | 3.8186 | 0.9669 | 3.8321 | 0.9675 | 0.0403 |
| Finland | 6.1390 | 0.9751 | 6.1330 | 0.9743 | 0.1053 |
| Norway | 3.6474 | 0.9654 | 3.6464 | 0.9646 | 0.1317 |
| Sweden | 3.6172 | 0.9649 | 3.6125 | 0.9637 | 0.1478 |
| Switzerland | 2.7155 | 0.9644 | 2.7339 | 0.9475 | 0.3706 |
| USA | 1.6827 | 0.9642 | 1.6619 | 0.9591 | 0.2203 |
| France | 4.3103 | 0.9650 | 4.3248 | 0.9480 | 0.4855 |
| Netherlands | 1.9786 | 0.9648 | 1.9927 | 0.9492 | 0.4375 |
| Belgium | 3.2988 | 0.9601 | 3.2738 | 0.9380 | 0.2112 |
| Italy | 4.0926 | 0.9500 | 4.1014 | 0.9251 | 0.3688 |
| Germany | 30.1390 | 0.9620 | 30.1468 | 0.9497 | 0.3387 |

*Source*: See text.

*Table 10A.2* Alternative forecasting equations for real exchange rates

| | AR(1) Equations | | ARMA(1,1) Equations | | |
|---|---|---|---|---|---|
| | α | β | α | β | MA(1) |
| *Floating rates* | | | | | |
| Denmark | 2.8799 | 0.8986 | 2.8789 | 0.9074 | –0.0396 |
| Finland[a] | 5.6648 | 0.8873 | 5.6670 | 0.9009 | –0.0723 |
| Norway | 2.9240 | 0.9192 | 2.9227 | 0.9103 | 0.0689 |
| Sweden | 2.8789 | 0.9299 | 2.8777 | 0.9213 | 0.2293 |

*continued on p. 268*

*Table 10A.2     continued*

|  | AR(1) Equations | | ARMA(1,1) Equations | | |
|---|---|---|---|---|---|
|  | α | β | α | β | MA(1) |
| Switzerland | 3.2270 | 0.9586 | 3.2340 | 0.9619 | −0.0272 |
| USA | 1.9811 | 0.9143 | 1.9828 | 0.8913 | 0.1613 |
| France | 3.3702 | 0.9698 | 3.4001 | 0.9318 | −0.2220 |
| Netherlands | 2.5296 | 0.9313 | 2.5234 | 0.9048 | 0.2551 |
| Belgium | 3.3599 | 0.8418 | 3.3811 | 0.9012 | −0.2365 |
| Italy | 7.1780 | 0.9963 | 7.1582 | 0.9963 | 0.4016 |
| Germany (1) | 8.1914 | 0.1575 | na | na | na |
| Germany (2) | 30.7520 | 0.7373 | 30.753 | 0.6303 | 0.2883 |
| *Fixed rates* | | | | | |
| Denmark | 2.8149 | 0.3950 | 2.8149 | 0.3240 | 0.0843 |
| Finland | 5.1060 | 0.9947 | 5.1041 | 0.9947 | 0.1108 |
| Norway | 2.7560 | 0.9584 | 2.7580 | 0.9473 | 0.1054 |
| Sweden | 2.8424 | 0.9320 | 2.8407 | 0.9375 | −0.0263 |
| Switzerland | 3.1766 | 0.8575 | 3.1718 | 0.9148 | −0.1815 |
| USA | 1.9238 | 0.9245 | 1.9275 | 0.8830 | 0.4401 |
| France | 3.3087 | 0.8083 | 3.3087 | 0.8086 | −0.0023 |
| Netherlands | 7.5370 | 0.9997 | 7.5855 | 0.9997 | 0.1193 |
| Belgium | 1.7363 | 0.8680 | 1.7359 | 0.8769 | −0.0390 |
| Italy | 4.5221 | 0.6203 | 4.5234 | 0.3410 | 0.9910 |
| Germany | 30.4990 | 0.9799 | 30.4946 | 0.9800 | 0.1253 |
| *Managed floating* | | | | | |
| Denmark | 3.5708 | 0.9691 | 3.5664 | 0.9675 | 0.2149 |
| Finland | 6.4406 | 0.9791 | 6.4230 | 0.9779 | 0.1876 |
| Norway | 3.4890 | 0.9683 | 3.4707 | 0.9658 | 0.1987 |
| Sweden | 3.5627 | 0.9677 | 3.5426 | 0.9648 | 0.2623 |
| Switzerland | 2.9196 | 0.8629 | 2.9196 | 0.8485 | 0.0572 |
| USA | 1.9415 | 0.9474 | 1.9343 | 0.9352 | 0.2859 |
| France | 3.1006 | 0.6647 | 3.1006 | 0.5307 | 0.2416 |
| Netherlands | 2.3933 | 0.9117 | 2.3907 | 0.8627 | 0.3020 |
| Belgium | 1.6938 | 0.9533 | 1.6901 | 0.9467 | 0.0863 |
| Italy[b] | 4.0926 | 0.9500 | 4.1013 | 0.9251 | 0.3688 |
| Germany | 30.2056 | 0.9651 | 30.2105 | 0.9579 | 0.1854 |

*Notes*:  [a] 1923.01–1926.08
         [b] 1932.02–1935.10
*Source*: See text.

**Notes**

* This research is supported in part by grants from the National Science Foundation, German Marshall Fund, and Institute of Business and Economic Research of the University of California at Berkeley. Carolyn Werley provided superb research assistance.

1. This statement is too sweeping to be entirely accurate. The pound sterling remained officially convertible into gold throughout the war, although bureaucratic impediments and the special difficulties of gold export permitted substantial depreciation. The US dollar remained officially convertible into gold throughout the war, although moral suasion discouraged citizens from attempting to acquire gold from the authorities. In the interest of brevity, I omit such qualifications for the rest of this section. A more detailed summary of interwar exchange rate experience is in Eichengreen (1989).

2. Notable contributions to this literature include Viner (1932), Gayer (1939), Brown (1940), Nurkse (1944), and Kindleberger (1973).

3. On these debates see Nurkse (1944, ch. VI), Hall (1935) and Howson (1980).

4. Whether meaningful action accompanied these words remains a matter for debate. Three references to this literature are Beyen (1949), Clarke (1977) and Eichengreen (1985).

5. The problem with conducting tests of market efficiency using effective rates is that the results depend on choice of weights. In fact, however, very similar conclusions emerge from an analysis of effective rates, as I will show in a forthcoming paper.

6. Mean changes are also reported but are more difficult to interpret than global measures of variability, since they reflect mainly the movement of the reference currency.

7. The average value of the statistic is larger for the early 1930s than for the early 1920s, although the difference is due to entirely the experience of one country, Belgium. Belgium floated against sterling throughout the period, but pegged against the gold bloc until the spring of 1935. At that point Belgium devalued and repegged to France at a lower level, which accounts for the kurtosis.

8. This episode was limited to such a short period that there is little evidence of it in the monthly data used to construct Table 10.2.

9. See, for example, Artis (1987).

10. Here I report only a select few summary statistics on the behaviour of real rates. Below I provide more information on the distribution of real rate changes. The analysis here differs from that in Eichengreen (1988) by analysing the log real rate in first difference form.

11. In Eichengreen (1988) I documented the strong positive correlation between the variability of real and nominal exchange rates within both periods. The present result, for the correlation between the variability of real and nominal exchange rate forecasts within both periods, is suggestive of stronger welfare implications.

12. They are especially incomplete at the beginning of the 1920s, when

newly-established governments had not yet set up reliable recording systems, and in the second half of the 1930s, when various governments are suspected, for political reasons, of having window-dressed their accounts. To the extent that this leads to underreporting of the volume of capital flows during the two floating-rate periods, comparisons should be treated with caution.

13. Data on GNP and GDP for this period are fragile and must be treated gingerly. To prevent any one annual estimate from dominating the analysis, in the text I generally rely on five-year averages. Sources of national income estimates are as in Eichengreen and Portes (1986).

14. A recent survey is Hodrick (1987).

15. Since I use monthly observations of 90-day forward exchange rates and, where possible, interest rates, the standard deviations of these means are calculated assuming $N/3$ independent observations, where $N$ is the number of months.

16. International real interest differentials reached such high levels during the German hyperinflation that their inclusion is sufficient to raise the average interest differential for 1922–6 to some three times that for 1932–6.

17. In future work I plan to construct alternative measures of expected exchange-rate changes by projecting actual changes on variables proxying for currently available information. Since here I use actual depreciation as a proxy for expected depreciation, for the remainder of this section I do not distinguish the two.

18. Two accounts which emphasise the impact of the Depression on real exchange rates are Lewis (1949) and Diaz-Alejandro (1983).

19. This is a result that may be driven by the use of actual depreciation as a proxy for expected depreciation. In the future work described note 17, I plan to reconsider this question.

20. One cannot extract information on this question from Tables 10.9–10.12, since they are constructed under the assumption that the expected change in the nominal rate is the same as the observed change over the period.

21. An account of the failed Janssen stabilisation is Shepherd (1936).

## References

Aliber, Robert (1973) 'The Interest Rate Parity Theorem: A Reinterpretation', *Journal of Political Economy*, vol. 81, pp. 1451–9.

Artis, M. J. (1987) 'The European Monetary System: An Evaluation', *Journal of Policy Modeling*, vol. 9, pp. 175–98.

Beyen, J. W. (1949) *Money in a Maelstrom* (London: Macmillan).

Brown, William Adams (1940) *The International Gold Standard Reinterpreted, 1914–1934* (New York: National Bureau of Economic Research).

Clarke, S. V. O. (1977) 'Exchange-Rate Stabilization in the mid-1930s:

Negotiating the Tripartite Agreement', *Princeton Studies in International Finance*, no 41 (Princeton: Princeton University Press).

Diaz-Alejandro, Carlos (1983) 'Stories of the 1930s for the 1980s', in Pedro Aspe Armella, Rudiger Dornbusch and Maurice Obstfeld (eds) *Financial Policies and the World Capital Market* (Chicago: University of Chicago Press).

Eichengreen, Barry (1985) 'International Policy Coordination in Historical Perspective: A View from the Interwar Years', in Willem Buiter and Richard Marston (eds) *International Economic Policy Coordination* (Cambridge: Cambridge University Press) pp. 139–78.

Eichengreen, Barry (1988) 'Real Exchange Rate Behavior under Alternative International Monetary Regimes: Inter-war Evidence', *European Economic Review*, vol. 32, pp. 363–71.

Eichengreen, Barry (1989) 'International Monetary Instability Between the Wars: Structural Flaws or Misguided Policies?', prepared for the Fourth International Conference of the Institute for Monetary and Economic Studies of the Bank of Japan, 30 May–1 June.

Eichengreen, Barry and Portes, Richard (1986) 'Debt and Default in the 1930s: Causes and Consequences', *European Economic Review*, vol. 30, pp. 599–640.

Einzig, Paul (1937) *The Theory of Forward Exchange* (London: Macmillan).

Frankel, Jeffrey A. and MacArthur, Alan T. (1988) 'Political vs. Currency Premia in International Real Interest Rate Differentials: A Study of Forward Rates for 24 Countries', *European Economic Review*, vol. 32, pp. 1083–1114.

Friedman, Milton (1953) 'The Case for Flexible Exchange Rates', in *Essays in Positive Economics* (Chicago: University of Chicago Press).

Giavazzi, Francesco and Giovannini, Alberto (1988) 'Can the European Monetary System Be Copied Outside Europe? Lessons from Ten Years of Monetary Policy Coordination in Europe', NBER Working Paper no 2786 (December).

Giovannini, Alberto (1989) 'How Fixed Exchange Rate Regimes Work: Evidence from the Gold Standard, Bretton Woods and the EMS', in Marcus Miller, Barry Eichengreen and Richard Portes (eds) *Blueprints for Exchange Rate Management* (New York: Academic Press).

Hall, N. F. (1935) *The Exchange Equalisation Account* (London: Macmillan).

Hodrick, Robert (1987) *The Empirical Evidence on the Efficiency of Forward and Futures Foreign Exchange Markets* (Chur, Switzerland: Harwood Academic Publishers).

Howson, Susan (1980) 'Sterling's Managed Float: The Operation of the Exchange Equalisation Account', *Princeton Studies in International Finance*, no 46 (Princeton: Princeton University Press).

Kindleberger, Charles (1973) *The World in Depression, 1929–1939* (Berkeley: University of California Press).

League of Nations (various issues) *Monthly Statistical Bulletin* (Geneva: League of Nations).

Lewis, W. A. (1949) *Economic Survey, 1919–1939* (London: Allen & Unwin).

McKinnon, Ronald (1987) 'Monetary and Exchange Rate Policies for International Financial Stability: A Proposal', unpublished manuscript, Stanford University.

Nurkse, Ragnar (1944) *International Currency Experience* (Geneva: League of Nations).

Shepherd, Henry L. (1936) *The Monetary Experience of Belgium, 1914–1936* (Princeton: Princeton University Press).

Stockman, Alan (1988) Exchange Rate Volatility Under Alternative Exchange Rate Regimes: An Equilibrium Model', *Journal of Monetary Economics* (forthcoming).

United Nations (1949) *International Capital Movements During the Inter-War Period* (Lake Success, New York: United Nations).

# Comment

Axel Leijonhufvud
UNIVERSITY OF CALIFORNIA, USA

This is a good paper that repays close study. Eichengreen has mar-
shalled a lot of useful data and his analysis is very helpful. The paper,
I believe, is part of a larger research effort on international monetary
relations between the wars and it is not really possible properly to
evaluate this piece until we see its place, and how much weight it is
asked to carry, in the larger structure that Barry Eichengreen is
building.

From the 21 inter-war years, Eichengreen selects three periods,
each approximately 4½ years long. The first one, ending with the
stabilisations of the mid-1920s, had fully *flexible* exchange rates; the
second, ending in the Great Depression, had *fixed* rates and the third
had *managed flexibility*. The paper is a comparative study of these
three samples that involves no formal modelling or fancy econometrics. It is, however, a very good example of how much can be
learned from the intelligent and historically informed use of simple
descriptive statistics.

One example will suffice to illustrate. Eichengreen finds that 'the
cross-country correlation of the standard deviation of the first differences of [log] nominal and real rates is at least 0.8' for the first and
third periods. Purchasing power parity theory had a great revival with
the breakdown of Bretton Woods in the 1970s. By now, most of us
may have unlearned it yet again. But, lest you take it as a 'good
approximation', it is useful to have the antidote 'that nominal exchange rate variability in periods of relatively free floating translated
into a comparable . . . increase in the variability of relative prices'.
Also of interest is the (probably less robust) finding that, although
the flexible rate period had considerably greater variability of exchange rates than the managed float period, the *predictability* of
exchange rates was apparently somewhat better in the absence of
'management'. The paper yields quite a number of informative
observations of this sort.

But Eichengreen is also out after bigger game – namely, to learn
something about the performance characteristics of exchange

273

regimes in general from the particulars of the inter-war period. If possible, he would like to draw lessons from the period that could inform our choices of regime half a century later.

Is it possible? The difficulty is, of course, that 1919–39 presents us with a series of rather pathological cases. The flex-rate period ha, hyperinflations, ordinary inflations, and conflicts over reparations. The fixed rate system unravelled into the Great Disaster. The relative stability of exchange rates 'managed' in the third period was a minor blessing bestowed on a world infected by 'beggar thy neighbour' policies all around and with world trade in deep depression.

Of all this, Eichengreen is well aware, of course. He tries to find samples of more or less 'normal' experience by cutting out transition periods, by excluding Germany up through its hyperinflation, and so on. How far is it possible, in this way to separate out the 'technical performance characteristics' of each regime from those particular upheavals of the world that were coincident with it?

The conceptual difficulties involved may be made clearer (and the substantive conclusions thereby murkier) by considering some counterfactual experiments, such as: suppose we had had fixed rates in 1922–6 and flexible rates in 1927–31 – what then? The first of these – fixed rates already from 1922 onwards – seems an all but impossible notion. The second prompts somewhat more interesting conjectures: (a) Flexible rates from 1927 on might have shown better 'performance characteristics' than in 1922–6, given the relatively compatible actual national macro-policies of 1927–31. But, then, does this *ceteris paribus* clause make sense in the context of our counterfactual experiment? (b) A system of flexible rates, without central banks obliged to defend their reserves, need not have transmitted the Great Depression epidemic with the torrential force of 1931. But, then, does it make sense to suppose that policy-makers might have responded free of the inflationary fears so very recently inculcated?

Suppose we conclude, on the one hand (with Eichengreen), that the fixed rate system 'worked well' in 1927–31 but, on the other, that it played an important role in the plunge into world-wide depression in 1931. How then do we size it up ? Eichengreen's line on this is that it worked well as long as we had policy coordination but failed when such coordination was no longer forthcoming to the extent required. A fair enough conclusion, I think, although with a high degree of policy coordination *any* exchange rate system should work pretty well.

The conclusion that the proper functioning of the fixed rate system requires policy coordination is ironic. The traditional line on this (older than the Currency School and surely older also than David Hume) has been that a commodity standard is a 'natural' system having the virtue of functioning automatically. It allows the merchant to operate in a world of warring princes – a virtue still demonstrated (even if spottily and probably for the last time) during the first few months of the First World War. The supposed automaticity of the gold standard has not been recaptured in this century. Instead, we end up with fixed rates arrangements that require perpetual negotiations among the participating countries to be kept going.

The incentives to economise on reserves may work slowly but they work surely. They cause banking systems to centralise reserves and are thus behind the creation of central banks to begin with. To make it possible for central banks to get along on minimal reserves, national monetary authorities monopolise the note issue and restrict the rights of private sector agents to redeem notes or even to hold gold altogether. But even insulated from private sector demand for the ultimate liquidity medium, the central banks of the world eventually end up short of liquidity themselves. Even a slight assymetry of credit policies over the cycle – doing more to accommodate private sector credit demand on the upswing than to ensure the 'reflux' of reserves on the downswing – will create a long-run inflationary trend that, even if slight, gradually reduces the stock of international reserves in relation to world GNP and world trade. (Note that this process will operate faster the more surplus countries obey what many think to be the 'rules of the gold standard' and inflate when they gain reserves so as to 'share the adjustment burden'). The next step then becomes swap arrangements, SDRs and *hoc genus omne* – and, when cooperation eventually fails, the final step is flexible rates.

In order to be able to choose between exchange rate regimes on the basis of their performance characteristics, we would first have to find institutional arrangements that eliminate or compensate for the externalities and time-consistency problems of this underlying historical process. Not a simple matter!

# Part VI

# The Political Economy of Long Waves

# 11 Long Cycles: Preview and Current Issues

Revold M. Entov and
Andrey V. Poletayev

INSTITUTE FOR WORLD ECONOMY AND
INTERNATIONAL RELATIONS MOSCOW, USSR

In this paper we are going to make an attempt to trace some main lines of the development of the long-cycles concepts in a historical perspective. Given the diversity and number of publications which have appeared since the concept was first introduced over 100 years ago, as well as the existence of several fundamental reviews (Weinstock, 1964; Barr, 1979; Delbeke, 1981; Van Duijn, 1983; Goldstein, 1988; and others), we do not intend to provide a comprehensive and detailed analysis of all the literature in the field. This task is beyond the limited scope of the present paper. Our purpose is to accentuate several controversial problems which seem to be crucial for the future development of long-cycles studies.

## 1 EMPIRICAL BACKGROUND

Before turning to the analysis of the theoretical issues, it may be worth remembering that the very formation of the operational concept of long economic cycles is largely due to empirical analysis. This point seems to be all the more significant since (as will be shown later) the modern theory of long cycles has somewhat lost that direct link with its empirical basis, and consequently it is the empirical verification which seems to arouse the most controversy.

One of the first references to the possible existence of long economic cycles (fluctuations of economic activity with a periodicity of 50–60 years) can be found in the work of Jevons (1884). His hypothesis which postulated the existence of long economic cycles was based on the dynamics of prices for some industrial and agricultural goods.

The development of economic statistics in the beginning of our century, which was marked by the apparition of the long-term series of such major economic indicators as prices, interest rates, foreign-trade volume, output of certain industrial and agricultural products, etc., provided some empirical basis for progress in the field of long-cycles analysis.

A further step was made in the 1920s and 1930s, with the introduction of statistical indices for prices and industrial production, and national income and output data, covering several prior decades.

The works of the late 1950s and the beginning of the 1960s were also stimulated by progress in the statistical field. The contributions of Imbert (1959); Baehrel (1961) and other experts in economic history who essayed to apply the long-cycle hypothesis to pre-industrial times were made possible because of the construction of agricultural price and production series dating back as early as the middle of the thirteenth century.

Finally, looking at the more recent periods of the 1970s and 1980s, we can notice that the statistical basis of the theory was provided by the further development of national income and product statistics, long-term series of industrial production indices, as well as a number of new indicators, which became available at that time (dynamic series of innovations, rate of profit, etc.). Another feature of the modern state-of-the-art in the field of long-cycle analysis is the reference to non-economic data, reflecting, for example, war severity (measured by life losses), strike activity, poll results and other social-political indicators, including those obtained by the use of content analysis.

Thus, on the one hand, the accumulation of empirical data has always served as an important source of inspiration for the theoretical development of the long-cycle concept. On the other, it is the absence of adequate statistical data that remains crucial for the verification of the theoretical models.

Another non-negligible factor is the quality of the available long-term series. The construction of such series still remains a challenging task, and because of that the reliability of the obtained results is often questionable. Unfortunately, the methods of constructing the long-term series, which are sometimes cited by the proponents of long cycles to support their arguments, perhaps will not stand even a mild criterion of reliability.

Thus one of the major problems in long-cycle analysis seems to be the problem of overinterpretation, in other words, the adequacy of the empirical base, its theoretical validity and quality.

## 2   THE THEORETICAL MODELS

The modest scope of the present paper does not allow us to present a comprehensive overview of the vast number of the existing long-cycle models. Let us simply mention that the range of factors included by different authors in their theoretical models to explain the mechanism of the long cycle is broad enough to include technological and technical innovations, demographies, geographical discoveries, migration, peculiarities of agricultural production, structural changes in the economy, investment processes, monetary sector and price formation, influence of socio-political factors, and many others.

In this paper we are going to outline only the main lines of the modern analysis of long cycles.

### 2.1   The Innovation Process

The irregular character of the innovation process was pointed out in the 1920s by Kondratiev (Kondratiev and Oparin, 1928). In the same decade an interesting statistical analysis of invention and innovation cycles was provided by another Russian economist Rainoff (1929) although unfortunately this work is almost unknown to modern researchers. In the 1930s the innovation issue was developed by Schumpeter (1939), who connected innovation cycles with changes in entrepreneurial activity. During the 1970s and 1980s important results in the field of research on technical innovations were obtained by Mensch (1975); Kleinknecht (1981a, 1981b, 1987); Freeman, Clark and Soete (1982); Haustein and Neuwirth (1982), and others.

Trying to develop a *closed* theoretical model of the innovational long cycles, these authors met some substantial problems. For example, in Mensch's schemes it appeared to be necessary to suppose periodical exogenous growth of demand for innovations, but that opens the possibility for mass dissemination of basic technologies.

The attempts to close an innovational model of long cycles largely resemble a macroeconomic version of the standard schema of the product life-cycle (in this particular case the life-cycle of the set of products produced with the help of basic innovations). It is significant that a number of authors (for example, Marchetti, 1980; Nakicenovic, 1987) directly link long-term fluctuations of economic activity with the product life-cycles of different industries.

Beyond the frame of the theoretical model in this case remains the question: what determines the duration of the period of saturation of the market with goods and services, and why in the different countries and under different economic conditions must this period eternally be equal to approximately fifty years?[1] Within this theoretical model the interrelations of economic forces giving life to the long cycles – movements of prices and price expectations, interest rate, profit, personal incomes, etc. – is developed to the least extent. A more detailed critique of the innovational concept of long cycles can be found, for example, in Rosenberg and Frischtak (1984).

## 2.2  Investment Mechanism

The founders of the theory of long cycles frequently connected long-term cyclical upswing with the mass renewal of plant and equipment. The material basis of the long cycles, as was supposed by Kondratiev by analogy with the 'usual' business cycle, can be the turnover (circulation) of those elements of fixed capital, which are characterised by the most prolonged duration of their functioning (Kondratiev and Oparin, 1928, pp. 60–1). During recent years this idea got further development in several works, among them in some Marxist interpretations of long cycles (see, for example, Menshikov and Klimenko, 1985).

The formal description of such a type of relationship can be found in the works of Forrester and the group of researchers from the Massachusetts Institute of Technology (Forrester, 1981; Forrester *et al.*, 1985; Sterman, 1987, and others). These works seems to satisfy the demand for a closed analytical model of long cycles. Modern methods of simulation analysis allow these researchers to demonstrate very clearly the consequences of several seemingly simple assumptions.

At the same time such an approach inevitably comes across several insufficiencies inherent in simulation models in general. Unfortunately the hypothesis of coexistence of several assumptions used in this model cannot be verified. That is why in such schemes of long cycles one model cannot be said to be more (or less) realistic than an alternative one.

The key role in the basic Forrester's acceleration-type model is performed by the intricate system of lags, linking production of investment goods with the demand for those goods. That is why it is especially interesting to analyse the consequences connected with possible changes of these lags. In this light it is difficult to limit ourselves to such statements as:

None of these factors that give rise to the long wave depends significantly on faster communications or details of technological change. The policies and industrial structure that generate the long-wave capital-construction cycle have changed very little since 1800 (Forrester, 1981, p. 327).

It seems worth adding that in spite of extensive research practically no authors have succeeded, as far as we know, in demonstrating 50-year fluctuations in productive investments (at least as clearly as in the case of 'usual' business cycles). This may be partially explained again by the absence of satisfactory statistical data.

## 2.3 Fluctuations of the Demand for Raw Materials and Agricultural Products

Yet Van Gelderen (1913, p. 450) noted that the long-term expansion of industrial production displays the lagging of production of raw materials and reveals a tendency for the rise of prices for those goods. The same idea was developed by Kondratiev (1928). Detailed analysis of this thesis has been provided by W. Rostow (Rostow, 1975, 1978; Rostow and Kennedy, 1979).

According to Rostow, the fast growth of prices for organic and mineral raw materials changes terms of trade of different sectors of the economy and of different countries. Consequent general decline of economic activity is accompanied by the reduction of demand for primary materials, while somewhat rigid, inflexible production of these goods continues to grow for some time. An oversupply of raw and intermediate products proves to be more or less prolonged. So the terms of trade of those sectors (and countries) have to change in the opposite direction. Structural shifts in this phase of the long cycle are accompanied by the appearance of the new leading sectors in national economies (countries in the world economy). Intensive growth of the new industries stimulates the new rise in the demand for agricultural products and mineral raw materials, and so on.

The long-term fluctuations of prices has attracted attention of many researchers for a long time. In Rostow's book *The World Economy* (1978) one can find a large empirical material which, according to author's logic, ought to prove the main idea: fluctuations of prices for primary materials are accompanied by the periods of accelerated and decelerated growth of the world economy, and by periodic changes of the leading sectors of the economy.

The approach developed by Rostow seems to be rather interesting; we should like to refer, for example, to the study of long cycles in the frame of the world economy as a whole, and to the long-term changes in the relations between primary and secondary sectors of the economy. Rostow's study attracts attention to some substantial aspects of the problem which are given relatively less attention in other theories of long cycles.

But even the statistical data included in Rostow's book show that the form of the long-term price fluctuations in the eighteenth and nineteenth centuries differs greatly from that in the twentieth century. More realistic is the reference to the movement of relative prices and, more specifically, Rostow's assumption of the existence of more or less regular fluctuations of the terms of trade of the industries producing and consuming primary materials.

The largest disparities between Rostow's schemes and real facts seem to appear in our century, especially after the Second World War. It may be sufficient to note a kind of paradox which was discussed in many surveys on long cycles: according to Rostow's criteria the 1950s and 1960s belong to the downswing phase, and the 1970s to the upswing phase of the long cycle.

In this theoretical model the question of the causes and factors determining the approximately 50-year duration of the fluctuations again remains unanswered. Is it certain that the transition to the resources-saving type of economic growth and improvement of the situation in the primary materials markets always needs at least two or three decades? It might be useful to refer to the experience of the past few years: the downswing phase of the fluctuations in the prices for agricultural and mineral materials has been renewed after a much shorter time span.

## 2.4   The Role of Demographic Factors

Recently several authors have asserted that an active role in the long-cycle mechanism can be played by demographic factors (see, for example, Tylecote, 1987; Waterman, 1987). More than two centuries ago Adam Smith wrote that intensive growth of incomes contributes to the lowering of mortality and to the increase of the birth-rate. Under current socio-economic conditions in the industrially developed countries fluctuations of income perhaps do not exert a strong influence on the changes in mortality but still, seemingly, provide some influence on changes in the birth-rate. At the same time, as is shown by Tylecote (1987), synchronous swinging influence on the movement of the saving ratio can be provided by the processes of ageing of the population, migration, etc.

This approach correctly points out a non-neutral character of the demographic changes in the process of economic growth. Under some circumstances such changes can probably enforce or dampen the long-term fluctuations of economic activity. But in these schemes the long-term fluctuations of incomes have an exogenous character; that is why this theoretical model also appears not to be closed.

Up to now there have been practically no serious empirical studies of the long-term demographic fluctuations; among the few exceptions we can mention the provocative work of Keyfitz (1972).

### 2.5 The Role of Socio-political Factors

As a representative example of this group of theoretical models we can use the works of Mandel (1975, 1980). In these works long-term fluctuations are connected with the movement of profit rate. Nevertheless from the very beginning Mandel excludes the very movement of the profit rate from his empirical analysis, reducing the problem to the statement that the dynamics of production can be used as an indicator of rising (or falling) rate of profit. It is evident that such an approach implies serious difficulties for the empirical verification of the initial hypothesis.

The decline of the profit rate during the downswing phase of the long-wave Mandel explains by the growth of the capital/labour ratio, which in turn is connected with mass renewal of plant equipment (under conditions of an aggravating economic situation?).

As a matter of fact, cyclical movement seems to be disrupted: according to Mandel, endogenous *economic* processes capable of pulling the economy out of the downswing phase cannot exist. Mandel (1980, p. 21) believes that the inner logic of the laws of the capitalist development can explain only the transition from expansion to stagnation, but cannot explain the transition from stagnation to expansion. So he appeals to the influence of non-economic forces: wars, counterrevolutions, class struggle, etc.

This causes a lot of questions which unfortunately are not answered by Mandel. For example, why must there regularly occur – approximately once in a half-century – such very specific socio-political events as 'counterrevolution' or other events, prescribed for that time by this schema? Besides that the indetermination of the theoretical model seems to make impossible the empirical verification of the key assumptions of this model.

Goldstein (1988) in his fundamental work made an interesting attempt not only to integrate different models of long economic cycles, but also to establish the interrelations between long-term fluctuations of economic activity and wars. In contrast to the works of Mandel, Goldstein tries to combine theoretical models with empirical analysis.

Nevertheless the empirical part of this work and theoretical schemes seemingly need further explanations. The author himself points out, for example, that the Second World War does not fit well with his analytical assumptions and appears to be an exception. In principle, the direct binding of the war conflicts – especially world wars of the modern time – to the acceleration of prolonged economic growth seems to be rather an oversimplification.

It is possible to include in this group of theoretical models the works of Namenwirth (1973), and Weber (1981), describing the role of changes in the social consciousness; we can refer also to the works of the researchers from the Fernand Braudel Center (New York University at Binghamton) – see, for example, Silver (1989) – assuming a cause-and-effect connection between social and class conflicts and long cycles, as well as some other studies.

\*    \*    \*

As can be seen even from the brief enumeration of the main theoretical schemes, they cannot be treated as quite incompatible. Each of the groups of models, seemingly, reflects some aspects, sometimes substantial, of the long-term economic growth and development. That is why the idea of integration of different schemes into the united theoretical model of long cycle seems so attractive.[2] But the integrative approach encounters several problems, because the theoretical models mentioned above differ not only in their object, but also in their methodology of analysis. Following the logic of each scheme and dating of long cycles proposed by different authors, we would rather come to the suggestion of the simultaneous existence of several *different* long cycles, which reveal themselves in different sectors of the economy and social life (in many cases such fluctuations, seemingly, cannot be treated even as synchronous) than to the conclusion that these models simply describe different elements (sides) of the same unique long cycle.

## 3 EMPIRICAL VERIFICATION AND METHODS OF ESTIMATION

The empirical analysis of long cycles inevitably comes across several complicated problems. Many of these problems, as far as we know, were raised and considered for the first time in the discussion of Kondratiev's report, made in Moscow in February 1926 at the Economic Institute (see Kondratiev and Oparin, 1928).

Since cyclical fluctuations were from the very beginning treated as the deviations from a trend, the central place in the discussion belonged to the problem of the economic nature of the assumed trend. What are the criteria which could provide the best methods for its estimation? The definition of the trend played a crucial role in Kondratiev's empirical analysis; his wording was clear-cut:

> In principle the theoretical curve can reflect real general tendencies of the evolutionary development of the economy. But we cannot say that the theoretical curves that we have derived exactly reflect them. Up to now we have no method of determination; we cannot determine how precisely the theoretical curve reflects real economic tendencies of the economic evolution. We can only say how well the derived theoretical curve reflects the characteristic features of the empirical series which are given to us (Kondratiev and Oparin, 1928, p. 13).

This question seems to be one of the principal problems of empirical studies, and we are afraid that progress in the analysis of this problem during the past sixty years has not been very impressive. Up to now the theory of long cycles is to the minimal extent integrated with the theory of economic dynamics, and the selection of the 'best' trend curve in long-cycle studies is still based primarily on the criterion of best fit.

Kondratiev's co-author Oparin also mentioned several practical problems of the statistical estimation of trend. The general form of the trend crucially depends on specific features of the investigated time span: does it include one or several complete cycles, or are there non-complete cycles 'at the tails' of our curve (see Kondratiev and Oparin, 1928, pp. 87–90)? So we have to conclude: before the start of empirical analysis a researcher has not only to be persuaded of the existence of long cycles but to have (*a priori*?) information on the more or less exact dating of these cycles.

In addition the choice of the trend curve cannot be treated as quite neutral for the procedure of separation of regular fluctuations. Oparin showed that a transition from one form of the trend to another can create 'artificial' cycles or dampen (even eliminate) 'real' cycles (ibid, pp. 226–7). Up to now – to the extent to which specification of one or another form of the trend curve is based only on the criterion of fit – technical considerations can determine the treatment of the substantive issues,[3] including among others the problem of the existence of long cycles.

But even if we take for granted the interpretation of long cycles simply as deviations from the long-term equilibrium growth path there remains the question of how to take into account the influence of specific historical events on the process of economic growth. The period under investigation is mostly too long to be described by a single trend curve; that is why researchers often have to subdivide – proceeding from some additional assumptions – the investigated time span into several subperiods and to estimate the trend curve for each subperiod. It is clear that this approach introduces additional influences into the procedure for the identification of long cycles.

But even when the transition from real statistical data to stationary series has been left behind, there still remain a lot of problems. And again the main difficulties seem to be not of a purely technical character, but rather connected with an insufficient accuracy of assumed definitions.

In real life it is surely impossible to find two absolutely identical cycles even of the highest frequency, and our conclusions on the existence of cyclicity usually refer to more or less regular reiteration of some general tendencies. It is clear that the comparison of long periods of time always has to reveal more than the usual specific differences between these periods. So the criteria used here must be flexible enough and at the same time must be especially clear-cut to allow us to draw conclusions on the existence of regular fluctuations.

A standard method which is used for the identification of such fluctuations – spectral analysis – in such a situation can prove to be 'too strict' (inflexible). Besides that, the reliability of the spectral analysis of long economic cycles is usually limited by the inadequate number of observations. That is why the negative results obtained in the search for long cycles in the movement of real variables – industrial production, GDP and GNP at constant prices, etc. – by spectral methods (see, for example, Van Ewijk, 1982) can hardly be treated as sufficient arguments against the existence of long cycles.

One of the most interesting results obtained in these studies is a low coherence of the long-term fluctuations of prices and real variables (in the business cycles of five to ten years duration the coherence between these variables was pretty high – with the exception of recent stagflation). But even here some reservations about the methods of estimation seem to be quite appropriate.

Enumerating the methods of identifying the long-term fluctuations in non-stationary series, we have to mention the use of linear frequency filters. This method was used in the long-cycle analysis of David and Solar (1977), which considered the rates of growth in the cost of living and real wages in the USA for 1774–1974. During recent years, the linear filter technique (based on the method developed by Stier, 1980) has been used for long-cycle analysis in the works of Metz (1987 and other) and Gerster (1988).

The use of linear filters allows researchers to 'soften' demands for the stationarity of the series and for a large number of observations. Besides, the use of the filters allows one to link both 'filtered' components (with the determined frequency) and the deviations from the 'filtered' curve, to the real time-scale.

Nevertheless the results obtained by the linear-filter method do not seem very hopeful. In most cases researchers did not succeed in revealing substantial fluctuations with a periodicity close to fifty to sixty years. Some series demonstrate, rather, fluctuations with a period of no more than twenty-five to thirty-five years, which is closer to the Kuznets cycles. But David and Solar (1977) obtained more promising results: in the case of a one-sided high-frequency filter (which means the elimination of fluctuations with a period less than twenty-four years) they revealed more prolonged fluctuations in the deviations from the 'filtered' curve. This result is consistent with the theoretical approach asserting that we must not split trend and long cycles as the latter include changes of the trends (Kuczynski, 1989).

The development of the theory of business cycles stimulated many students to use this experience in studies of long cycles. One of the most important works in this field was prepared by Burns and Mitchell (1946). In the following years substantial (in our opinion) results were obtained by Van der Zwan (1980) and some other scholars.

In these studies, however, the long cycles to a large extent lack their own features, becoming a secondary characteristic of the usual business cycles; they are supposed only to shift the growth path and/or modify short-term cyclical upswings and downswings of business activity. But authors using these truncated versions of models of the long cycle, as far as we know, did not succeed in obtaining reliable proofs of the existence of such long cycles (see, for example, the general conclusions of Burns and Mitchell, 1946, p. 465; Van der Zwan, 1980, p. 198). A little more hope for the discovery of derived long cycles comes from the estimates made by Van Duijn (1980, 1983), Delbeke (1982), and other authors who try to form aggregate long cycles by combining five or six adjacent business cycles (this tradition can be traced back to the works of De Wolff, 1924; and Schumpeter, 1939). But even in these cases the results seem to be not very promising (see Van Duijn, 1980, p. 231; Delbeke, 1982, p. 21).

Under this approach the definition of long cycles is significantly modified in comparison with, for example, the work of Van Ewijk (1982). The point is that Burns and Mitchell (1946) and Van der Zwan (1980) used predetermined (*a priori*) datings of long cycles. And the negative results obtained in these works could simply imply the necessity of using another benchmark for long cycles. The approach used by Van Duijn and his followers practically excludes any base for dating long cycles beyond the given framework of the reference business cycles. Differences between business cycles are used to identify the particular phases of aggregate long cycles ('cycles of cycles'). Such an approach to the study of long cycles, treating these fluctuations as cycles of a higher order can be fruitful, but it does not correspond very well with the majority of the theoretical models described above.

Another truncated version of the long-cycles model has been used by Kuczynski (1980); Bieshaar and Kleinknecht (1984); Kleinknecht (1987); Solomou (1986, 1987), and some other researchers. Here the concept of long cycle is simply reduced to the assumption of the regular alternation of periods of relatively more and less high rates of economic growth.

In the book by Kleinknecht (1987) quite a large number of statistical series are tested according to such criteria. The results are rather ambiguous. In some cases they are negative: thus, the movement of world industrial production only during 1893–1939 was consistent with the hypothesis of the regular change of periods of high and low growth rates; no signs of distinct long waves (of the proposed type) were found in the British economy, nor in the movement of American GNP and German NNP during the nineteenth century. At the same time in the movement of Italian GDP one and a half long cycles were found, in the Swedish GDP two cycles, and in Belgian industrial production 2.5 cycles.

Detailed estimates made by Kleinknecht give evidence that many variables were strongly influenced by the acceleration of economic growth at the turn of the century (1893–1913), on the one hand, and by the Second World War and the Great Depression – which seriously diminished the average rate of growth in 1914–39 – on the other hand. For the period prior to the 1890s the results, as Bieshaar and Kleinknecht (1984, p. 293) show, remain undetermined.

Observing the methodology of such an approach, we have to point out that the results of these estimates can be influenced, strictly speaking, not only by the fifty year long cycles (treated as fluctuations in the rates of growth), but also by cycles of a lesser duration – first, by the Kuznets cycles. In all these estimates the choice of upswing and downswing periods was again predetermined by out-of-model considerations.

The search for criteria to be used for the identification of long cycles shows an obvious tendency towards more and more permissibility. The truncated versions of long-cycle concepts use the difference between rates of growth in adjacent business cycles (Van Duijn, 1983) or the sign of the difference between rates of growth in adjacent phases of the long cycle (Bieshaar and Kleinknecht, 1984) as test criteria. But interpretation of the long-term downswing phase as an economic situation with a somewhat lower rate of growth can hardly be treated as a proper recession which looks so gloomy in the majority of theoretical models of long cycles.

## 4 DEFINITIONS AND DATING OF LONG CYCLES

It is a bit amusing to note that until now two primary problems of the study of long cycles remains unsolved: their definition and their dating.

To begin with, there exist terminological problems which, however, also reflect conceptual indeterminateness of the object under investigation. The phenomenon is named by different authors as: 'long cycles'; 'long waves'; 'Kondratiev cycles'; 'Kondratiev waves'; 'Schumpeter's long cycles'; 'long swings'; 'trend periods'; 'big (large) cycles of conjuncture'; 'cyclical rhythms'; 'long-term fluctuations'; 'low-frequency fluctuations', and so on. There are also more specific

names, originated from the analysis of specific statistical data; definitions of some of them, such as 'waves of innovations', seem to be
especially vague.

The definition of the very phenomenon – long economic cycles –
can include, as has been shown above, the alternation of periods of
high and low rates of economic growth (economic activity, etc.) or
long-term upswings and downswings of the economy (prices, etc.).

The permissible periodicity of long economic fluctuations is usually
defined as forty to sixty years. But in the case of fluctuations with the
period, for example, of thirty to thirty-five years, some researchers
(Solomou, Metz) treat them as Kuznets cycles, and others (e.g.
Imbert) as Kondratiev cycles.

Some authors (Imbert and others) consider that long cycles appeared as early as the middle of the thirteenth century. Other
students (including Kondratiev) suppose that such fluctuations can be
traced back only to the end of the eighteenth century. A third group
(Kleinknecht and others) believes that long cycles exist only in
developed market economies. Several economists (of whom Van
Duijn is one) believe that there were two different types of long
waves ('price' and 'real'), which intersected only in the last quarter of
the nineteenth and the beginning of the twentieth century. There is
also the point of view that long cycles must be treated as a purely
historical phenomenon which does not exist at the present time.

What is the sphere of the manifestation of long cycles? Are they
only a price phenomenon, or can they be traced in the movement of
real variables? Or, as some researchers treat them, are long cycles
the global characteristic of the development of the socio-economic
system as a whole?

Again, there is no uniform treatment of the level of the phenomenon – whether long cycles appear only on the national level, or
develop within an international, world-scale framework.

Thus one of the main problems for the future development of the
concept of long cycles is a more accurate and clear-cut definition of
the object.

A controversial situation still remains in the identification and
timing of long cycles. Different dating schemes exist which apparently are not strictly comparable. Several main types of dating
schemes used in the economic literature are presented in Figure 11.1.

Scheme 1a ('rise-fall') in Figure 11.1 is usually used in the studies
dealing with more or less stationary variables (prices, interest rates,
etc.). A variant of this approach is represented by scheme 1b; here

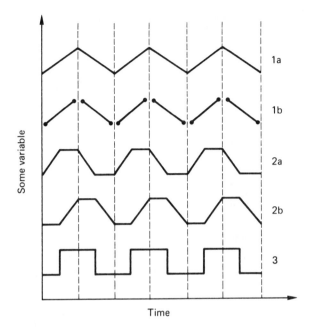

*Figure 11.1*   Schemes of the long cycles

the turning-points of long cycles are defined not by particular years, but by time intervals (such a scheme was used by Kondratiev). The timing of long cycles based on these schemes is given in Tables 11.1 and 11.2.

The more refined dating of long cycles (first proposed by Schumpeter) includes not just two, but four or five different phases. The timing of different phases is either linked to the dating of business cycles (see Section 3 above), or is defined according to the general economic situation. Such ambiguity leads to significant differences in dating under this approach. Tracing the links between this scheme and the previous one, we might also mention that some authors treat the upper turning-phase as part of the upswing (scheme 2a in Figure 11.1), others as part of the downswing (scheme 2b). The timing of long cycles based on this approach is given in Tables 11.3 and 11.4.

The third basic scheme of dating (which again is a dichotomous one) is used mostly in the recent works starting with Mandel (1975). Here high and low *levels* of some variables (particularly rates of economic growth) are used for the discrimination of different phases

*Table 11.1* Two-phase scheme of dating of long cycles, pre-industrial period (based on price dynamics)

| Turning-points | Wagemann (1931) | Imbert (1959) | Baehrel (1961) | Mauro (1964) | Braudel (1972) | Ebeling, Irsigler (1976) | Frank (1978) | Irsigler and Metz (1984) |
|---|---|---|---|---|---|---|---|---|
| Lower | – | 1286/93 | – | – | – | – | – | – |
| Upper | – | 1313/22 | – | – | – | – | – | – |
| Lower | – | 1335/44 | – | – | – | – | – | – |
| Upper | –. | 1360/70 | – | – | – | – | – | 1360 |
| Lower | –' | 1380/90 | – | – | – | – | – | 1394 |
| Upper | – | 1391/09 | – | – | – | – | – | |
| Lower | – | 1410/20 | – | – | – | – | – | |
| Upper | – | 1435/40 | – | – | – | – | – | 1435 |
| Lower | – | 1457/64 | – | – | 1460 | – | – | 1450/65 |
| Upper | – | 1480/83 | – | – | 1483 | – | – | 1487/94 |
| Lower | – | 1507/10 | 1507 | – | 1509 | 1510 | – | 1505/18 |
| Upper | – | 1530 | 1536 | – | 1529 | | – | 1523/34 |
| Lower | – | 1540 | | – | 1539 | | – | 1534/44 |
| Upper | – | 1556/58 | | – | 1559 | | – | 1544/69 |
| Lower | – | 1569/74 | 1564/73 | – | 1575 | | – | 1569/86 |
| Upper | – | 1585/95 | 1594 | 1590 | 1595 | 1586 | – | 1586/91 |
| Lower | – | 1613/20 | 1625 | 1620 | 1621 | 1620 | – | 1608/13 |
| Upper | – | 1636/54 | 1655 | 1640 | 1650 | 1642 | – | 1635/55 |
| Lower | 1690 | 1684/90 | 1689 | 1690 | – | 1668 | 1689 | 1676/80 |
| Upper | 1720 | 1709/15 | 1725 | 1720 | – | 1698 | 1720 | 1702/15 |
| Lower | 1730 | 1733/43 | 1754 | 1730 | – | 1736 | 1747 | 1721/25 |
| Upper | 1763 | 1769/72 | 1785 | 1775 | – | 1770 | 1762 | 1762/72 |
| Lower | 1790 | 1787/92 | – | 1792 | – | 1785 | 1790 | 1774/84 |

*Notes:* 1. Double dating is based on different price series (in the table we give intervals in which peaks and troughs of different series appear)
2. Our summary of datings for this period is largely based on works of Goldstein (1988) and Zschoke (1985).

*Table 11.2* Two-phase scheme of dating of long cycles, industrial period (based on price dynamics)

| Turning-points | Kondratiev (1925) | Burns and Mitchell (1946) | Rostow (1978) | Goldstein (1988) |
|---|---|---|---|---|
| Lower | 1787/93 | 1789/93 | 1790 | 1790 |
| Upper | 1810/17 | 1808/20 | 1815 | 1814 |
| Lower | 1844/51 | 1843/51 | 1848 | 1848 |
| Upper | 1870/75 | 1864/73 | 1873 | 1872 |
| Lower | 1890/96 | 1895/96 | 1896 | 1893 |
| Upper | 1914/20 | 1920/26 | 1920 | 1917 |
| Lower | – | 1932/35 | 1935 | 1940 |
| Upper | – | – | 1951 | |
| Lower | – | – | 1972 | |
| Upper | – | – | 1978(?) | 1980 |

*Table 11.3*  Four-phase scheme of dating of long cycles (based on business cycles dating and general conjuncture)

| | Schumpeter (1939) Kuznets (1940) | Van Duijn (1983) | Cleary and Hobbs (1983) | Van Roon (1986) |
|---|---|---|---|---|
| Prosperity | 1787–1800 | 1782–1802 (war 1802–15) | | |
| Recession | 1802–13 | 1815–25 | 1815–25 | – |
| Depression | 1814–27 | 1825–36 | 1825–40 | – |
| Recovery | 1828–44 | 1836–45 | 1840–50 | – |
| Prosperity | 1845–57 | 1845–66 | 1850–65 | |
| Recession | 1858–69 | 1866–73 | 1865–75 | 1869–79 |
| Depression | 1870–85 | 1873–83 | 1875–95 | 1879–93 |
| Recovery | 1866–97 | 1883–92 | 1895–1900 | 1893–1903 |
| Prosperity | 1898–1911 | 1892–1913 (war 1913–20) | 1900–20 | 1903–11 |
| Recession | 1912–25 | 1920–29 | 1920–25 | 1911–21 |
| Depression | 1926–39 | 1929–37 | 1925–30 | 1921–36 |
| Recovery | 1940–. . . | 1937–48 | 1930–60 | 1936–49 |
| Prosperity | – | 1948–66 | 1960–80 | 1949–63 |
| Recession | – | 1966–73 | – | 1963–73 |
| Depression | – | 1973–. . . | – | 1973–. . . |
| Recovery | – | – | – | – |

*Notes*: 1. Names of phases differ among different authors.
2. Kuznets and Van Duijn start long cycle with prosperity phase, while Cleary and Hobbs, and Van Roon start them with recession phase.

of long cycles (scheme 3 in Figure 11.1). Such a dating of long cycles is represented in Table 11.5.

Beside the differences among particular dating schemes, there are disagreements in dating within each scheme (see Tables 11.1–11.5). The discrepancies can sometimes reach several decades (especially in the twentieth century!).

The dating of long cycles depends, first of all, on the kind of empirical data used. As a matter of fact the majority of students of

*Table 11.4*  Five-phase scheme of dating of long cycles (based on dating of business cycles)

| | Van Duijn (1983) | Poletayev and Savelyeva (1988) | |
|---|---|---|---|
| | | Depression | 1772–83 |
| Prosperity 1 | 1782–92 | Recovery | 1783–93 |
| Prosperity 2 | 1792–1802 | Upswing | 1794–1803 |
| | (war 1802–15) | Prosperity | 1803–12 |
| Recession | 1815–25 | Instability | 1812–25 |
| Depression | 1825–36 | Depression | 1825–37 |
| Recovery | 1836–45 | Recovery | 1837–48 |
| Prosperity 1 | 1845–57 | Upswing | 1848–57 |
| Prosperity 2 | 1857–66 | Prosperity | 1857–66 |
| Recession | 1866–73 | Instability | 1866–73 |
| Depression | 1873–83 | Depression | 1873–86 |
| Recovery | 1883–92 | Recovery | 1886–92 |
| Prosperity 1 | 1892–1903 | Upswing | 1892–1903 |
| Prosperity 2 | 1903–13 | Prosperity | 1903–12 |
| | (war 1913–20) | | |
| Recession | 1920–29 | Instability | 1912–29 |
| Depression | 1929–37 | Depression | 1929–38 |
| Recovery | 1937–48 | Recovery | 1938–49 |
| Prosperity 1 | 1948–57 | Upswing | 1949–58 |
| Prosperity 2 | 1957–66 | Prosperity | 1958–67 |
| Recession | 1966–73 | Instability | 1967–74 |
| Depression | 1973–. . . | Depression | 1974–82 |
| Recovery | – | Recovery | 1982–. . . |
| | | Upswing | – |
| | | Prosperity | – |
| | | Instability | – |

*Note*: Van Duijn does not include the wars of 1802–15 and 1913–20 in regular phases of long cycles.

*Table 11.5*  Two-phase scheme of dating of long cycles (based on rates of economic growth)

|  | Mandel (1975, 1980) | Amin (1975) | Kuzcynski (1980) | Van Duijn (1983) | Kleinknecht (1987) |
|---|---|---|---|---|---|
| High rates | 1847–73 | 1850–70 | 1850–66 | 1845–72/73 | 1847–73 |
| Low rates | 1873–93 | 1870–90 | 1866–96 | 1872/73–90/95 | 1873–93 |
| High rates | 1893–1913 | 1890–1914 | 1896–1913 | 1890/95–1913 1920–29 | 1893–1913 |
| Low rates | 1913–39 (1913–48) | 1914–48 | 1913–51 | 1929–48 | 1913–39 |
| High rates | 1939–67/68 (1948–67/68) | 1948–67 | 1951–69 | 1948–73 | 1939–74 |
| Low rates | 1967/68–. . . | 1967–. . . | 1969–. . . | 1973–. . . | 1974–. . . |

long cycles are still dealing with what may be called 'specific long cycles'. Here we again come to the necessity of enlarging and better systematising the empirical base of the research. That can be useful not only for dating, but also for revealing causal relationships among different variables. A good example here is the work on the construction of the data bank of reference business cycles, which exerted a noticeable influence not only on empirical, but also on theoretical studies of the business cycle.

**Notes**

* The authors want to thank Professor Joshua S. Goldstein for his valuable remarks on this paper.
1. Mensch in his work especially notes that his 'metamorphosis model' can describe non-regular fluctuations.
2. It is not out of place to mention here that even in the works of the founders of the theory of long cycles – Van Gelderen, Kondratiev, and others – we can find the implicit idea of the simultaneous functioning of different mechanisms of long cycles.
3. An interesting analysis of the problem of trend specification in long-cycle studies can be found in Reijnders (1988).

298 *Political Economy of Long Waves*

**References**

Amin, S. (1975) 'Toward a Structural Crisis of World Capitalism', *Socialist Revolution*, vol. 5, pp. 9–44.

Baehrel, R. (1961) *Une croissance: La Basse-Provence rurale (fin du XVIe siècle – 1789)* (Paris: SEVPEN).

Barr, K. (1979) 'Long Waves: A Selective Annotated Bibliography', *Review*, vol. II, no 4, pp. 675–718.

Bieshaar, H. and Kleinknecht, A. (1984) 'Kondratieff Long Waves in Aggregate Output? An Econometric Test', *Konjunkturpolitik*, vol. XXX, no 5, pp. 279–303.

Braudel, F. (1972) 'History and the Social Sciences', in P. Burke (ed.) *Economy and Society in Early Modern Europe: Essays from Annales* (New York: Harper & Row).

Burns, A. F. and Mitchell, W. C. (1946) *Measuring Business Cycles* (New York: National Bureau of Economic Research).

Cleary, M. N. and Hobbs, G. D. (1983) 'The Fifty-Year Cycle: A Look at the Empirical Evidence', in C. Freeman (ed.) *Long Waves in the World Economy* (London: Butterworth).

David, P. A. and Solar, P. (1977) 'A Bicentenary Contribution to the History of the Cost of Living in America', *Research in Economic History*, vol. II, pp. 1–80.

Delbeke, J. (1981) 'Recent Long-Waves Theories: A Critical Survey', *Futures*, vol. XIII, no 4, pp. 246–57.

Delbeke, J. (1982) 'Long Waves and Leading Sectors in the Belgian Industrialization Process: 1831–1913', in *Proceedings of the Eighth International Economic History Congress* (Budapest: B3:17).

De Wolff, S. (1924) 'Prosperitats – und Depressionperioden', in O. Jenssen (ed.) *Der Lebendige Marxismus* (Jena: Thuringer Verlagsanstalt).

Ebeling, D. and Irsigler, F. (1976) *Getreideumsatz, Getreide- und Brotpreise in Koln, 1368–1797* (Cologne: Bohlau-Verlag).

Forrester, J. (1981) 'Innovation and Economic Change', *Futures*, vol. XIII, no 4, pp. 313–21.

Forrester, J. *et al.* (1985) 'An Integrated Approach to the Economic Long Wave', in G. Blanchi, G. Bruckman, and T. Vasko (eds) *Long Waves, Depression and Innovation: Implications for National and Regional Economic Policy* (Laxenburg, Austria: IIASA).

Frank, A. G. (1978) *World Accumulation, 1492–1789* (New York: Monthly Review Press).

Freeman, C., Clark, J. and Soete, L. (1982) *Unemployment and Technical Innovation* (London: Frances Pinter).

Gerster, H. J. (1988) *Lange Wellen wirtschaftlicher Entwicklung* (Lang, etc.).

Goldstein, J. S. (1988) *Long Cycles: Prosperity and War in the Modern Age* (New Haven, Connecticut: Yale University Press).

Haustein, H.-D. and Neuwirth, E. (1982) 'Long Waves in World Industrial Production, Energy Consumption, Innovations, Inventions, and Patents and Their Identification by Spectral Analysis', *Technological Forecasting and Social Change*, vol. 22, pp. 53–89.

Imbert, G. (1959) *Des mouvements de longue durée Kondratieff* (Aix-en-Provence: La pensée universitaire).

Irsigler, F. and Metz, R. (1984) 'The Statistical Evidence of "Long Waves" in Pre-Industrial and Industrial Times', *Social Science Information*, vol. XXIII, no 2, pp. 381–410.

Jevons, W. S. (1884) *Investigation in Currency and Finance* (London: Macmillan).

Keyfitz, N. (1972) 'Population Waves', in T. N. E. Greville (ed.) *Population Dynamics* (New York: Academic Press).

Kleinknecht, A. (1981a) 'Innovation, Accumulation and Crises: Waves in Economic Development?', *Review*, vol. IV, no 4, pp. 683–711.

Kleinknecht, A. (1981b) 'Observations on the Schumpeterian Swarming of Innovation', *Futures*, vol. XIII, no 4, pp. 293–307.

Kleinknecht, A. (1987) *Innovation Patterns in Crisis and Prosperity: Schumpeter's Long Cycle Reconsidered* (London: Macmillan).

Kondratiev, N. D. (1925) 'Big Cycles of Conjuncture'; in Russian: Кондратьев. Н.Д. (1925) 'Большие циклы конъюнктуры'. Вопросы конъюнктуры, vol. I, pp. 28–79. (English translation with minor differences: Kondratieff, N. D. (1979) 'Long Waves in Economic Life', *Review*, vol. II, no 4, pp. 519–62).

Kondratiev, N. D. (1928) 'Dynamics of Prices for Industrial and Agricultural Goods'; in Russian: Кондратьев. Н.Д. (1928) 'Динамика цен промышленных и сельскохозяйственных товаров. (К вопросу о теории относительной динамики и конъюнктуры)'. Вопросы конъюнктуры, vol. IV, pp. 1–85.

Kondratiev, N. D. and Oparin, D. I. (1928) *Big Cycles of Conjuncture: Reports and Their Discussion at the Economic Institute*; in Russian: Кондратьев, Н. Д, Опарин, Д.И.(1928) Большие циклы конъюнктуры: Доклады и их обсуждение в Институте экономики (Москва: Красная пресня). (Part of this book was published in English: Kondratiev, N. D. (1984) *The Long Wave Cycle*, New York: Richardson & Snyder).

Kuczynzki, Th. (1980) 'Have there been Differences between Growth Rates in Different Periods of the Development of the Capitalist World Economy Since 1850?', in J. M. Clubb and E. K. Scheuch (eds) *Historical Social Research*, vol. 6 (Stuttgart: Klett-Cotta).

Kuczynski, Th. (1989) 'Great Depressions as Transitional Phases within the Capitalist Mode of Production – the Interaction of Socio-economic and Techno-economic Factors', paper presented at the international conference '*The Long Waves of the Economic Conjuncture – The Present State of the International Debate*' in Brussels, Belgium.

Kuznets, S. S. (1940) 'Schumpeter's Business Cycles', *American Economic Review*, vol. XXX, no 2, pp. 257–71.

Mandel, E. (1975) *Late Capitalism* (London: New Left Books).

Mandel, E. (1980) *Long Waves of Capitalist Development: The Marxist Interpretation* (Cambridge: Cambridge University Press).

Marchetti, C. (1980) 'Society as a Learning System: Discovery, Invention, and Innovation Cycles Revisited', *Technological Forecasting and Social Change*, vol. XVIII, no 2, pp. 267–82.

Mauro, F. (1964) *L'Expansion européen: Aspects économiques* (Paris:

Presses Universitaires de France).

Mensch, G. O. (1975) *Das Technologische Patt: Innovationen uberwingen die Depression* (Frankfurt: Umschau) (English translation: Mensch, G. O. (1979) *Stalemate in Technology: Innovations Overcome the Depression* (Cambridge, Massachusetts: Ballinger).

Menshikov, S. and Klimenko, L. (1985) 'On Long Waves in the Economy', in G. Blanchi, G. Bruckman, and T. Vasko (eds) *Long Waves, Depression and Innovation: Implications for National and Regional Economic Policy* (Laxenburg, Austria: IIASA).

Metz, R. (1987) 'Kondratieff and the Theory of Linear Filters', in T. Vasko (ed.) *The Long-Wave Debate* (Berlin: Springer Verlag).

Nakicenovic, N. (1987) 'Technological Substitution and Long Waves in the USA', in T. Vasko (ed.) *The Long-Wave Debate* (Berlin: Springer Verlag).

Namenwirth, J. Z. (1973) 'Wheels of Time and the Interdependence of Value Change in America', *Journal of Interdisciplinary History*, vol. III, no 4, pp. 649–83.

Poletayev, A. V. and Savelyeva, I. M. (1988) 'Long Waves in the Development of Capitalism'; in Russian: Полетаев, А., Савельева, И. (1988) 'Длинные волны в развитии капитализма', Мировая экономика и международные отношения, vol. 5, pp. 71–86.

Rainoff, T. Y. (1929) 'Wave-like Fluctuations of Creative Productivity in the Development of West-European Physics in the 18th and 19th Centuries', *ISIS*, vol. XII(1), no 37, pp. 287–319.

Reijnders, J. (1988) *The Enigma of Long Waves* (Utrecht: Drukkerij Elinkwijk BV).

Rosenberg, N. and Frischtak, C. R. (1984) 'Technological Innovation and Long Waves', *Cambridge Journal of Economics*, vol. VIII, pp. 7–24.

Rostow, W. W. (1975) 'Kondratieff, Schumpeter, and Kuznets: Trend Periods Revisited', *Journal of Economic History*, vol. XXXV, no 4, pp. 719–53.

Rostow, W. W. (1978) *The World Economy: History and Prospect* (London: Macmillan).

Rostow, W. W. and Kennedy, M. (1979) 'A Simple Model of the Kondratieff Cycle', *Research in Economic History*, vol. IV, pp. 1–36.

Schumpeter, J. A. (1939) *Business Cycles: A Theoretical, Historical and Statistical Analysis of the Capitalist Process* (New York: McGraw-Hill).

Silver, B. J. (1989) 'Class Struggle and the Kondratieff', paper presented at the international conference '*The Long Waves of the Economic Conjuncture – The Present State of the International Debate*' in Brussels, Belgium.

Solomou, S. (1986) 'Kondratieff Long Waves in Aggregate Output? A Comment', *Konjunkturpolitik*, vol. XXXII, no 3, pp. 179–84.

Solomou, S. (1987) *Phases of Economic Growth, 1850–1973: Kondratieff Waves and Kuznets Swings* (Cambridge: Cambridge University Press).

Sterman, J. D. (1987) 'The Economic Long Wave: Theory and Evidence', in T. Vasko (ed.) *The Long-Wave Debate* (Berlin: Springer Verlag).

Stier, W. (1980) *Verfahren zur Analyse saisonaler Schwankungen in okonometrischen Zeitreihen* (Berlin: Springer Verlag).

Tylecote, A. (1987) 'Generational Factors in an Evolutionary Theory of the Long Wave', paper presented at the international conference '*Life Cycles and Long Cycles*' in Montpellier, France.

Van der Zwan, A. (1980) 'On the Assessment of the Kondratieff Cycle and Related Issues', in S. K. Kuipers and G. J. Lanjouw (eds) *Prospects of Economic Growth* (Amsterdam: North-Holland).

Van Duijn, J. J. (1980) 'Comment on Van der Zvan Paper', in S. K. Kuipers and G. J. Lanjouw (eds) *Prospects of Economic Growth* (Amsterdam: North-Holland).

Van Duijn, J. J. (1983) *The Long Wave in Economic Life* (Boston: Allen & Unwin) (1st edn, 1979).

Van Ewijk, C. (1982) 'A Spectral Analysis of the Kondratieff Cycle', *Kyklos*, vol. XXXV, no 3, pp. 468–99.

Van Gelderen, J. (alias J. Fedder) (1913) 'Springvloed: Beschouwingen over industriele ontwikkeling en prijsbeweging', *De Nieuwe Tijd*, vol. XVIII, pp. 253ff, 369ff, and 445ff.

Van Roon, G. (1986) 'Cycles, Turning Phases and Societal Structures: Historical Perspective and Current Problems', in C. Freeman (ed.) *Design, Innovation and Long Cycles in Economic Development* (New York: St Martin's Press).

Wagemann, E. (1931) *Struktur und Rhythmus der Weltwirtschaft: Grundlagen einer weltwirtschaftlichen Konjunkturlehre* (Berlin: Reimar Hobburg).

Waterman, A. M. S. (1987) 'On the Malthusian Theory of Long Swings', *Canadian Journal of Economics*, vol. XX, no 2, pp. 257–70.

Weber, R.Ph. (1981) 'Society and Economy in the Western World System', *Social Forces*, vol. LIX, no 4, pp. 1130–48.

Weinstock, U. (1964) *Das Problem der Kondratieff–Zyklen* (Berlin: Duncker & Humblot).

Zschocke, A. (1985) 'Kondratieff Cycles in the Pre-industrial Period: A Bibliography', *Newsletter on Long Waves* (FBC, Binghamton) no 2, pp. 14–24.

# Comment

## Richard M. Goodwin
UNIVERSITÀ DEGLI STUDI DI SIENA, ITALY

This excellent survey points out a number of important difficulties in long wave analysis.

Mandel's problem of the lower turning-point relates to a central issue in most economic cycle theories. When the economy is depressed, there is little incentive for the investment needed to initiate an upswing. In my view the solution to this is offered by Schumpeter's notion of innovations. Precisely when profits are low and capacity is in excess, there is strong reason to look for new methods or products.

The fact of serious irregularity or aperiodicity constitutes a major analytic problem unless one adopts the hypothesis of chaos, where it is no problem. Beyond this there are other advantages: thus one can avoid the danger of spurious results from fitting any particular trend. With a chaotic attractor one can generate a unitary explanation of irregular, alternating growth, where there is no need to fit a 'best' trend. Likewise the question of disputed dating of long waves is largely avoided in the sense that there is no exact periodicity, leaving ample room for different interpretations.

The authors take a poor view of innovations as an explanation of long waves. With this view I disagree: after all, growth is mainly from technology and that is innovation. The dominant innovations, like steam and steel, all took the long gestation periods required by the half-century-cycle theory.

# 12 A War-Economy Theory of the Long Wave

Joshua S. Goldstein

SCHOOL OF INTERNATIONAL RELATIONS
UNIVERSITY OF SOUTHERN CALIFORNIA

## INTRODUCTION

Long waves of roughly fifty years in economic and social life have intrigued many scholars because they offer an alternative perspective from which to view history and the present situation – an alternative to either static or linear projections of the future. Past empirical studies of long waves have agreed on the dating of long waves historically but not on the scope of those waves in terms of variables encompassed, relevant time-periods, or causal mechanisms (see review in Goldstein, 1988: ch. 3). I have sought to advance the empirical evidence relevant to long waves by sorting and testing conflicting hypotheses in the long-wave debate against about fifty historical time-series (Goldstein, 1988). Based on the most salient lagged correlations among variables found in my empirical analysis, I adduced a set of causal dynamics among variables that could account for the sequence of phenomena making up the long wave – as best that sequence could be inferred from spotty empirical data. The adduced theory is a tentative one, with many remaining loose ends and anomalies. But it is better-grounded empirically than past long-wave theories.

My theory of long waves centres on the relationship between war and economic growth in the world system. Periods of severe war follow phases of robust economic growth and lead to phases of stagnant growth. The empirical evidence that war plays a central role in long waves is quite strong. Long waves in prices can be explained largely by the inflationary effects of recurrent wars. Economic innovations, capital investment, and real wages also play reinforcing roles in generating long waves, in my view – and all are also affected by

303

major wars. The theory thus builds on, rather than contradicts, other long-wave theories stressing innovation, over-investment, and class struggle.

In this paper, I investigate the adduced causal dynamics among war and economic variables directly, setting aside the idea of long waves (as the expression of those underlying dynamics in the historical behaviour of the system). That is, I begin from the micro level of shorter-term relations among the variables in a system, rather than the macro level of how that system behaves over the long term. First I will summarise these causal dynamics, posited in my long wave theory. Then I will present evidence from a new analysis of several of the longest and highest-quality historical time-series in the period 1750–1935, using VAR modelling.

Finally, I will discuss the question of whether the underlying causal dynamics continue to operate in the present-day world system, despite the unusual nature of the most recent long wave. In terms of a four-phase dating scheme of long waves, I argue that the 1940–68 'expansion' phase was distorted by the extension of the core of the world system to America, which poured huge new economic resources into the European war system at the time of the Second World War. Despite this disruption, there is some evidence that long-wave dynamics continue in the present.


# 1 GOLDSTEIN'S LONG-WAVE THEORY

My theory posits causal dynamics among war, production, prices, real wages, technical innovation, and capital investment. These variables are all conceived at a global level of analysis – i.e. in the core of the world system, roughly equivalent to the 'Great Power system' in politics or the 'leading industrial countries' in economics.

## 1.1 War and Prices

Long waves in prices, more than in any other economic or political phenomenon, have attracted attention to the phenomenon of long cycles. Price waves are clearly visible in many untransformed historical price-series (including that of Kondratieff in the 1920s), whereas long waves in production, innovation, and other aspects of economic or social life have been sharply debated and require more controversial methodologies. As for the price waves, some critics of long waves argue that the price peaks about every fifty years are merely the by-product of severe wars, and hence are not 'endogenous' economic cycles.

The bulk of evidence supports the idea that wars cause the long waves in prices. Figure 12.1 is a graph of Levy's (1985) data on Great Power war fatalities, which I transformed into a 500-year time-series. The long-wave dating for prices – my 'base dating scheme' – is a composite of the dates given by Braudel (1972), Frank (1978), Kondratieff (1935), and Mandel (1980), with a minor modification (Goldstein, 1988). The price peaks in this scheme are shown at the top of Figure 12.1 as vertical arrows. On the graph of Great Power war battle fatalities, I have marked the recurrent, particularly severe and prolonged wars as 'war peaks' (WP). The dates and peak wars are listed in Table 12.1. Clearly each spurt of inflation ending a long-wave price upswing corresponds with a high severity of war in the Great Power system. The only exception is the Second World War which I will discuss later.

Wallerstein's three periods of 'world war' are shown at the bottom of Figure 12.1: the Thirty Years' War, Napoleonic Wars, and the First and Second World Wars. I call these 'hegemonic wars' because they are struggles for the dominant position in the world system. Out of each war has emerged a new hegemon – the leading country on the winning side that survives with its economy intact and reorganises the world system around itself, while its adversaries and allies are drained by war. The three hegemons were the Netherlands, Britain, and the USA.

It is tempting to assign the struggle for hegemony – including the great hegemonic wars ('world wars', 'global wars', 'systemic wars', etc.) – a place in the long wave. Several past schemes have tied *pairs* of long waves to hundred-year cycles of war. However, in my view the relationship is more irregular. There is no fixed number of long waves that makes up a cycle of hegemony. Rather, there is a longer-term cycle, the rise and fall of hegemony, which does not appear strongly linked to long waves in a causal sense. The two cycles, of course, overlap in that hegemonic wars are also war peaks in the long wave (again, except the Second World War). But other long-wave war peaks occur at times of intermediate hegemony, adjusting but not rewriting the political arrangements in the world system.

What accounts for the regularity of war recurrence? I find explanations based on endogenous 'war cycle' mechanisms, such as the 'social memory of war' or the 'alternation of generations', incom-

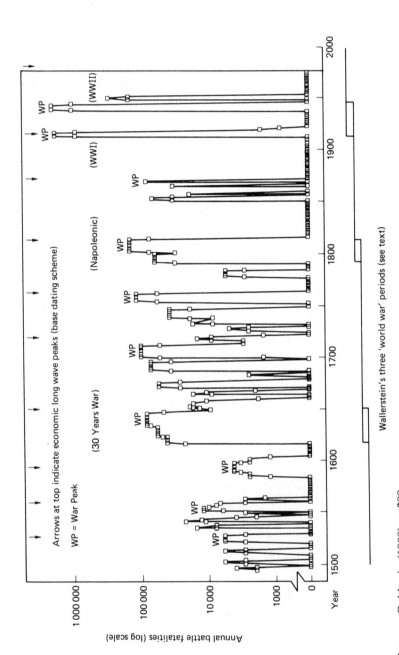

*Source:* Goldstein (1988) p. 290

*Figure 12.1* Great Power war severity, 1495–1975

*Table 12.1* Dating of long war cycles, 1495–1975

| Cycle | Starting date of war cycle | Peak war years | Length (years) | Ending date of corresponding long wave phase period |
|-------|------|------|------|------|
| 1 | (1495) | 1521–1529 | (35) | 1528 |
| 2 | 1530 | 1552–1556 | 28 | 1558 |
| 3 | 1558 | 1593–1604 | 47 | 1594 |
| 4 | 1605 | 1635–1648 | 44 | 1649 |
| 5 | 1649 | 1701–1713 | 65 | 1719 |
| 6 | 1714 | 1755–1763 | 50 | 1761 |
| 7 | 1764 | 1803–1815 | 52 | 1813 |
| 8 | 1816 | 1870–1871 | 56 | 1871 |
| 9 | 1872 | 1914–1918 | 47 | 1917 |
| 10 | 1919 | 1939–1945? | (27) | (1968/80?) |

| Cycle | Peak wars | Annual fatality rate at peak (thousands) |
|-------|------|------|
| 1 | First and Second Wars of Charles V (Ottoman War v. Hapsburgs)[a] | 13 |
| 2 | Fifth War of Charles V (Ottoman War v. Hapsburgs)[a] | 22 |
| 3 | War of the Armada (Austro-Turkish War)[a] | 11 |
| 4 | Thirty Years' War: Swedish/French Phase | 88 |
| 5 | War of the Spanish Succession | 107 |
| 6 | Seven Years' War | 124 |
| 7 | Napoleonic Wars | 156 |
| 8 | Franco–Prussian War | 90 |
| 9 | First World War | 1934 |
| 10 | Second World War | 2158 |

[a] Dating of war peaks in cycles 1–3 based primarily on intra-European wars rather than those against Turkey. Wars against Turkey are included in the statistics, however, and are shown above in parentheses.
*Source*: Goldstein (1988) p. 241.

plete. These contributing factors notwithstanding, I have proposed that the war cycle cannot be explained independently of economics. While prices merely respond to war, trends in economic production both affect and respond to the severity of Great Power wars. Prosperity gives the Great Powers the wherewithal to fight bigger wars.

Big wars, however, drain the world economy, which must be slowly rebuilt over decades. Periodic big wars also serve as regulating 'shocks' to cycles of capital investment and technical innovation, and they drive down real wages.

## 1.2   War and Production

The growth of world production appears to vary in a manner consistent with this war-growth theory of the long wave, although the changes in growth rates are generally not dramatic. Upswings of faster and more robust growth in production *precede* upswings in war and prices, which in turn precede production downswings marked by slower and less stable growth. The production waves appear to lead war/price waves by about a quarter of a cycle (ten to fifteen years) on average. These production waves are less sharply defined than the price waves, resembling 'swells' rather than the more extreme peaks and troughs in prices. Wojtyla (1988) illustrates one possible dating scheme (see Table 12.2) which leads my price dating by ten to fifteen years on average, and which seems to show alternating phases of economic growth in leading industrial countries (based on Maddison's data).

Production upswings, then, provide the economic surplus in the world system to fill the 'war chests' of the Great Powers. Severe wars drain those war chests and end the robust growth of the world economy (through the obvious disruption and destruction wrought by war, which is not fully compensated by the full mobilisation of economic resources for the fight). Toward the end of the war upswing, as production has already begun stagnating, sharp world-wide inflation often results from the severity of war (which increases demand and reduces supply); this phase of 'stagflation' has historical precedents before the 1970s (around 1920, 1872, 1815). Finally, as wars give way to peace (often in a flurry of bankruptcies), the world economy recovers and eventually a new period of robust economic growth gets under way.

The central dynamic of the long wave, then, is the long-term 'lagged negative feedback loop' of world economic growth and Great Power wars. I posit that this central dynamic is reinforced by three other such feedback loops involving variables that affect production and are affected by war – real wages, innovation, and capital investment.

*Table 12.2*   Growth rates by production phase periods

| Kondratieff phase* | Average growth rate for contending Great Powers | Germany | France | UK | |
|---|---|---|---|---|---|
| Downswing 1790–1830 | 1.5% | 1.3% | 0.8% | 2.4%+ | |
| Upswing 1830–1860 | 2.0 | 1.9 | 1.8 | 2.2+ | |
| Downswing 1860–1890 | 1.8 | 2.3+ | 1.1 | 2.0 | |
| Upswing 1890–1910 | 2.1 | 3.1+ | 1.5 | 1.6 | |
| | | | | | *USA* |
| Downswing 1910–1950 | 1.7 | 1.5 | 1.2 | 1.4 | 2.8+ |
| | | *Western Europe* | | | *USSR* |
| Upswing 1950–1970 | 4.6 | 5.0 | | 3.5 | 5.2+ |
| Downswing 1970–Date | 2.3 | 2.4 | | 2.5+ | 2.0 |

* This dating for production phases leads price phases by 10 to 15 years.
+ Leader

*Source*:  Based on data in Angus Maddison *Phases of Capitalist Development* (Oxford University Press, 1982); Angus Maddison 'A Comparison of Levels of GDP Per Capita in Developed and Developing Countries, 1700–1980: *Journal of Economic History*, vol. XLIII, no 1, March 1983.

*Source*:  Wojtyla (1988:5)

## 1.3   War, Production, Prices and Real Wages

Although my empirical analysis for real wages extends only to two British series, it shows evidence of an inverse correlation of real wages with the price phases of the long wave. When prices rise, real wages fall. This timing makes particular sense in relation to the timing of Great Power wars – during the biggest wars, with high taxation and inflation, real wages fall way behind prices; during peacetime, economic resources are channelled back to the civilian economy and workers end up better off in real terms. In short, workers suffer in wartime.

The long waves in real wages should, in principle, bear some

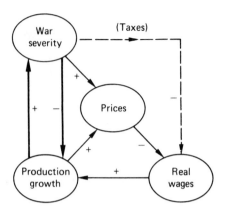

*Source*: Goldstein (1988) p. 260.

*Figure 12.2*   Adduced causality, production/war/prices/wages

relation to long waves of 'class struggle' described by some researchers (e.g. Mandel, 1980). However, I have not been able to identify that relationship to date.

Figure 12.2 maps out the adduced causal dynamics at the core of the long wave. Most important is the cycle in which production growth stimulates war severity, but war severity dampens production growth in the world system. War severity also affects prices (positively) and real wages (negatively, both directly and by way of prices). Real wages appear, from the lagged timing, to have a positive effect on production – a plausible connection since better-paid workers would be more productive. Finally, I adduce a direct, positive effect of production on prices (as well as the indirect effect through war). This connection rests on the idea that as a production upswing proceeds, demand increases while supply at some point begins to experience limits.

**1.4   Innovation and Capital Investment**

Two other economic phenomena come into play in this account of long-wave dynamics. First, an innovation cycle reinforces the long wave in that a higher rate of innovation stimulates (with some lag) stronger economic growth, but strong economic growth in turn dampens the innovation rate. This is the majority view among long-wave scholars (e.g. Mensch, C. Freeman, Van Duijn) focusing on

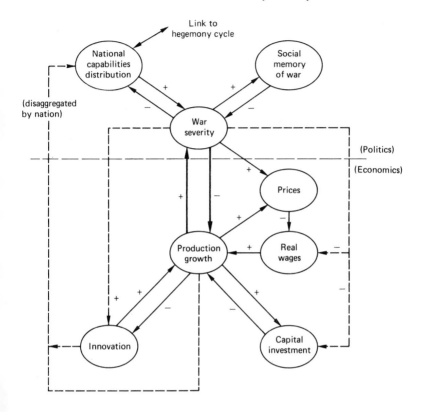

*Source*: Goldstein (1988) p. 275

*Figure 12.3*   Theoretical model of long-wave dynamics

innovation. My empirical evidence on the timing of innovations, although sketchy, is consistent with this interpretation. The timing suggests that innovations are highest in the rebuilding phase after post-war stagnation. I tried to test whether inventions lead innovations, as some researchers believe; but the data on patents gave anomalous results (British long waves of invention being half a cycle out of phase with American ones).

Second, a capital-investment cycle also reinforces the long wave. Production upswings lead to upswings of capital investment, ultimately leading to overinvestment and retrenchment, dampening production growth. The Massachusetts Institute of Technology (MIT) group suggests that this cycle of over- and under-investment (their 'self-ordering of capital') may extend the wavelength of the long wave (Sterman, 1983).

Figure 12.3 illustrates my causal model of long waves with the inclusion of innovation and capital investment. Also shown in the figure are two possible influences on war that may also help regulate the timing of the long wave. The first, social memory of war, has been mentioned above. The second is the possible effect of 'national capabilities distribution' (in the Great Power system) in perpetuating the war-cycle component of the long wave. Immediately after a severe war, the capabilities of winners usually far overshadow those of losers. Under these conditions a severe war is unlikely (Organski's power transition theory); rather, war is likely to occur after the low-capability countries have recovered and embarked on long-term growth that brings their capabilities within striking distance of adversaries. Thus war severity disequalises national capabilities distribution, which in turn dampens war severity (which allows capabilities to equalise, thus increasing war severity). National capabilities are affected by relative national rates of innovation and production growth, in addition to the effects of war. The national capabilities distribution also connects with the hegemony cycle, but (as mentioned above) I consider this only a weak causal connection. The most important point of Figure 12.3 is that an adequate model of the long wave must bridge economics and politics.

## 2    A NEW STATISTICAL ANALYSIS

In order to explore further the causal connections among the key variables of the long wave, I have conducted a new analysis using VAR modelling. The VAR model is essentially a multivariate, multi-equation reduced-form statistical model in which each variable is regressed on its own past behaviour and the past behaviour of every other variable in the system. This method was developed by economist Christopher Sims (1980), and its applications to political science are discussed by Freeman, Lin, and Williams (forthcoming).

The data I used in this exploratory exercise consisted of several of the best time-series (highest quality and longest duration) from my earlier analysis (described and listed in Goldstein, 1988, Appendices A, B). For each of six variables of interest, I chose one time-series. In one case (world industrial production) I spliced together two series

(1740–1850 and 1850–1975) by multiplying the second series by the ratio of the two in 1850. The six series were:

| War | Logged war severity (from Levy) | 1495–1975 |
| Production | World industrial production (spliced) | 1740–1975 |
| Prices | British wholesale price index | 1750–1975 |
| Innovation | Haustein's list of innovations | 1764–1975 |
| Real wages | S. English real wage index | 1736–1954 |
| Investment | US private building volume | 1830–1957 |

The use of US private building volume as a measure of world investment was particularly questionable, and the time-frame covered by that series is considerably less than the other series. Therefore, I dropped capital investment from this analysis, pending better data. This left five variables, spanning the years 1764–1954.

In specifying the time-frame and number of included lags in the model, I used a Bayesian approach of imposing prior theoretical expectations. One must decide how many lags of the independent variables should be included on the right-hand side of each equation. There are statistical tests to induce this from the data, but since my theory calls for up to 10–15 lags I began by simply using 15 lags. That is, the lagged effects of one variable's past behaviour in influencing another variable's current behaviour may extend up to fifteen years (just over one quarter of a cycle). My theory has no lagged effects longer than this.

Since in my theory, the Second World War is considered unusual and because the war years have many extremes in the time series that would have a heavy influence on the statistical results, I decided not to include the years after 1935 in the analysis. The years 1936–54 would add few degrees of freedom and might well introduce an instability that would mask earlier patterns. The Second World War in any case cannot be fully included with 15 lags in the model and data up through only 1954. This left a time-frame for the five-variable VAR model of 1764–1935. While VAR analysis allows the testing of time-stability within the time-frame covered (to see whether the coefficients change significantly at a certain candidate break-point), preliminary tests merely show that the great wars (Napoleonic, and the First and Second World Wars) are unstable relative to the peaceful years. Of course I could not use only peaceful times in this analysis, so I relied on my prior analysis which suggested omitting the Second World War but assuming that the prior 150 years could be modelled as one system (even though the sudden changes in the system induced by war and peace do no make for 'stability' in the coefficients). Allowing for the fifteen years of lags in variables, the actual analysis at this point covered the period 1779–1935, or 157 years.

The VAR model is estimated for all five equations using ordinary least squares (OLS) (which works when the same lagged variables make up the right-hand side of each equation). For each variable taken as the dependent variable (one equation), the significance of each other variable (as an independent variable) is assessed in the form of an F-fest for the joint significance of the coefficients on all fifteen lagged terms on that variable. These F-tests, then, are statistically significant if the behaviour of a given variable over the past fifteen years is correlated with the present behaviour of another variable (taking into account the independent effects of the second variable's own past behaviour and that of all other variables in the model).

The statistically significant correlations in the five-variable VAR model are diagrammed in Figure 12.4. Each causal arrow points from an independent variable (past fifteen years) toward the dependent variable (present) it affects. The significance level of the F-statistic is indicated by the width of the arrow. Each of the five variables was also significantly affected by its *own* recent past behaviour (autoregressive), and this is not shown on the figure.

These causal arrows are supplemented by a simulation of the VAR model to identify the *kind* of response which one variable has to another. In this simulation, a hypothetical positive shock is induced in one variable at a time, and its subsequent effect on all the variables is traced in the moving average responses of those variables when the estimated model is simulated. The shock is ahistorical, but based in magnitude on the standard deviation of the residuals from historical data. The simulation requires an 'ordering' of variables specifying how the shock will propagate through the system; to check for robustness I used one ordering based on 'forward timing' along the long wave, and a second reversed ordering (the effects of shocks were robust against both orderings). Based on the response to the hypothetical shock, I have put a plus or minus sign (or in some cases a notation) by each causal arrow in Figure 12.4 (below I will show graphs of the moving average responses to the shocks).

Turning now to the actual relationships found significant in Figure

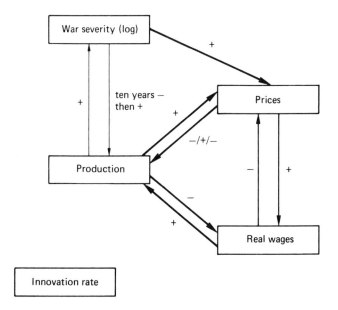

*Note*: Arrows indicate direction of causality (forward through time) suggested by lagged correlations. Statistical significance shown by size of arrow is given by the F-test on the joint (1–15) lagged coefficients for each variable in each equation.

Statistical significance:

⟶ Less than 0.01
⟶ Less than 0.05
⟶ Less than 0.10

Notations by arrows indicate direction of (moving average) response in the second variable, to a hypothetical shock in the first variable, in a VAR simulation. (+ indicates response in kind; – indicates opposite response).

*Figure 12.4* Significant lagged correlations (over 1–15 lags taken jointly) in VAR model of five long-wave variables, 1779–1935.

12.4, there was good support for the relationships postulated in my theory (Figure 12.2 above):

1. The two-way relationship of war and production was significant – although the direction of response of war to production was

unclear and the postulated negative response of production to war lasted only about ten years.

2. The one-way causation from war to prices was highly significant and positive as postulated in the theory.
3. The positive effects of production on prices, and of real wages on production, were significant in the VAR model, although there were also significant reverse linkages not postulated in the theory.
4. Prices did exert a significant influence on real wages, but a positive one; this is because the negative effect of prices on real wages is instantaneous, while the effect seen here, over 1–15 years, is the partial return of real wages toward where they were before the price shock (instantaneously) changed them.

In the model wages also had a significant reverse effect on prices. Surprisingly, no significant relationships involving innovation were found in the model (perhaps just because of data quality).

Since innovation did not appear significant in the five-variable model, I dropped it from the analysis and created a four-variable VAR model. This allowed the time-frame to be extended to 1750–1935, which after allowing for 15 lags left an analysis of 1765–1935, or 171 years. In this four-variable model, with a slightly longer time-frame, the degrees of freedom are increased.

Using this four-variable model, I then checked whether the 15 lags could be shaved down somewhat to increase degrees of freedom. Using Sims's modified likelihood test to check whether additional lags significantly change the estimated model, I tested 10, 12, and 15 lags, staying within the general confines of my theory (roughly a quarter of a cycle maximum for lagged effects). 12 lags turned out to be significantly different (at .01) from 10 lags, but 15 was not significantly different from 12. Thus I reduced the specification of 15 lagged terms to 12 for each independent variable.

The results of this four-variable analysis are shown in Figure 12.5 (the graphs of moving average response curves are included on Figure 12.6):

1. Both the positive link from production to war and the negative link from war to production are still significant.
2. The positive effect of recent war on present prices is still extremely significant.
3. Unlike the five-variable model, here war exerts a significant, negative effect on real wages, as in the theory.

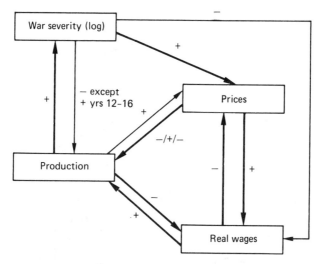

*Note*: Arrows indicate direction of causality (forward through time) suggested by lagged correlations. Statistical significance shown by size of arrow is given by the F-test on the joint (1–12) lagged coefficients for each variable in each equation.

Statistical significance:

⟶ Less than 0.01
⟶ Less than 0.05
⟶ Less than 0.10

Notations by arrows indicate direction of (moving average) response in the second variable, to a hypothetical shock in the first variable, in a VAR simulation. (+ indicates response in kind; – indicates opposite response).

*Figure 12.5*  Significant lagged correlations (over 1–12 lags taken jointly) in VAR model of four long-wave variables, 1762–1935.

4. The two-way interaction of production with prices and production with real wages resembles the five-variable model (the effects of production on prices, and wages on production, are still positive as theorised.
5. The price-wage interaction is also similar to the five-variable model.

As a further test, I ran a VAR model identical to the four-variable model just discussed except that only 5 annual lags, rather than 12,

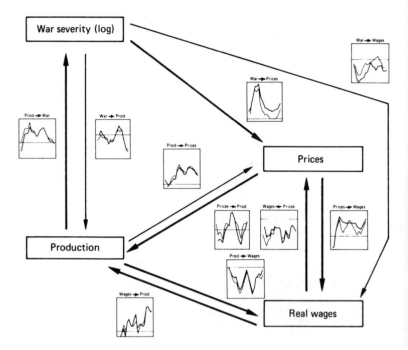

*Note*:  Arrows indicate direction of causality (forward through time) sug-
        gested by lagged correlations. Statistical significance shown by size of
        arrow is given by the F-test on the joint (1–12) lagged coefficients for
        each variable in each equation.

                          Statistical significance:

                          ──────▶  Less than 0.01
                          ──────▶  Less than 0.05
                          ──────▶  Less than 0.10

        Graphs by each arrow indicates moving average response in the
        second variable, to an orthogonalised shock in the first variable, in a
        VAR simulation. Solid lines represent main ordering of variables;
        dashed lines represent reverse ordering.

*Figure 12.6*  Significant lagged correlations (over 1–12 lags taken jointly)
              in VAR model of four long-wave variables, 1762–1935, with
              MAR responses

are included for each variable. Although this model is presumably mis-specified, it opens, in a sense, a window on shorter-term causal connections while becoming blind to longer-term effects beyond five years.

According to my theory, the lagged correlations between war and production, postulated as operating over a ten-to-fifteen year period, should disappear in the 5-lag model. This is exactly the case in the results of the 5-lag VAR analysis, shown in Figure 12.7. The production-war connection is no longer significant, and war becomes the only 'exogenous' variable in the system if we consider just the short-term interactions (one-to-five years). Only in considering longer-term effects (one to twelve years, Figure 12.5 & 12.6) do we see that war is endogenous, responding to changes in production. All this fits my long-wave theory well, and calls in question models of the economic long wave which leave out war.

Finally, the contemporaneous correlations of residuals in the VAR model reflect very short-term causal effects on a time-frame of less than one year (thus appearing contemporaneous in annual data). The correlations are:

| | |
|---|---|
| Prices – real wages | −0.32 |
| War – prices | +0.12 |
| War – real wages | −0.10 |
| War – production | −0.23 |
| Prices – production | +0.24 |
| Production – real wages | 0.00 |

Here the statistics say nothing about the directions of causality which I will instead draw from those adduced in my theory. The price–wage correlation confirms that the *immediate* effect (not the delayed effects after one-to-fifteen years) of prices on wages is negative, as one would expect. The residual correlations also suggest same-year effects of war on prices (positive), on production (negative), and on real wages (negative). There is also a same-year positive correlation of production and prices, the causal direction of which is unclear.

These new analyses were undertaken for exploratory purposes. I consider the results a success in largely supporting my long-wave theory. The causal diagrams that emerge from a VAR analysis of selected time-series contain almost all the relationships postulated in my long-wave theory. The main exceptions were the failure to establish any relationships using Haustein's list of innovations, and

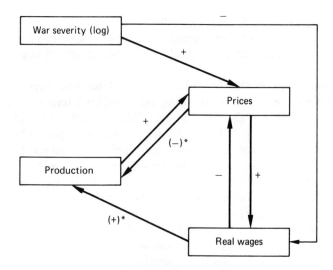

* In reverse ordering simulation, response is − then +.

*Note*: Arrows indicate direction of causality (forward through time) suggested by lagged correlations. Statistical significance shown by size of
arrow is given by the F-test on the joint (1–5) lagged coefficients for
each variable in each equation.

Statistical significance:

⟶ Less than 0.01
⟶ Less than 0.05
⟶ Less than 0.10

Notations by arrows indicate direction of (moving average) response
in the second variable, to a hypothetical shock in the first variable, in a
VAR simulation. (+ indicates response in kind; − indicates opposite
response).

*Figure 12.7*  Significant lagged correlations (over 1–5 lags taken jointly) in
VAR model of four long-wave variables, 1755–1935.

the unexpected reverse feedbacks among production, prices, and wages.

The elements of the theory concerning war are supported, overall,
by the VAR analysis. War is affected by, and in turn affects, production. War exerts a one-way influence on prices (positive), and on
real wages (negative). In the short time-frame, war seems to be exogenous, driving prices and real wages; but in fact war is endogenous and
responds to production on a time frame of up to twelve years.

## 3   A FOUR-PHASE DATING SCHEME

Given the important time-lags among variables in this theory, we must abandon the simple two-phase dating scheme for long waves. Figure 12.8 illustrates the timing sequence of the variables in my long-wave theory. There is not simply an '*A*' phase and a '*B*' phase, but a series of lagged phases.

Concentrating on the crucial production and war variables, which lag each other by about a quarter of a cycle, we can define a four-phase scheme of the long wave:

1. *Expansion* – production, investment, war severity, and prices all rise; innovation is stagnant; real wages flatten out.
2. *Stagflation* – war severity is high, prices rise rapidly, and production and investment stagnate (stagflation); innovation is low; real wages fall.
3. *Stagnation* – production growth is low and uneven; investment is low; war severity declines; inflation is low (or prices even decline); innovations begin rising; real wages recover.
4. *Rebirth* – production growth picks up again, investment follows; prices are low, war severity is low; innovation is high; real wages are high.

The traditional conception of long waves in terms of synchrony of prices and production gives rise to an *A*-phase, *B*-phase rendition of all-round economic expansion or stagnation. These phases do occur – they are phases 1 and 3 above – but account for only half of the story. The other half is in certain ways even more interesting. The war phase and the rebirth phase seem to represent extremes of the undesirable and desirable points in the long wave.

This four-phase timing may be tentatively matched with historical dates. The beginning dates of 'expansion' and 'stagnation' would come from the price troughs and peaks listed in my base dating scheme (Goldstein, 1988) – except that I would change 1917 to 1920, which seems a better date for the *price* peak. The following dating is put forward as a starting-point, and may need adjustment:

| Expansion | 1790–1803? | 1848–60? | 1893–1910 | 1940–68 |
| War | 1803?–14 | 1860?–72 | 1910–20 | 1968–80 |
| Stagnation | 1814–30 | 1872–(?) | 1920–33 | 1980–95? |
| Rebirth | 1830–48 | (?)–1893 | 1933–40 | ?1995–2010? |

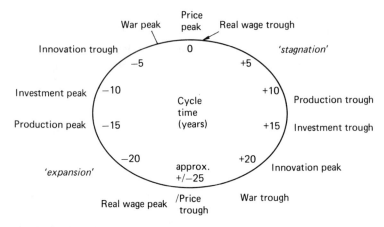

*Source*: Goldstein (1988) p. 259.

*Figure 12.8*   Sequence and timing of idealised long wave


In this scheme, as I have mentioned, the Second World War does not fit into the normal long-wave timing. It comes at the beginning, rather than the end, of an expansion phase, and hence follows too closely on the First World War. Or, put more accurately, it is too big a war for coming so soon after the First World War. How was the world system able to afford such a big war at this point in time? And how, following that monstrously large war, could the world system resume robust growth to finish out the expansion phase, rather than skipping to stagnation? The answer has to be a great and relatively sudden influx of economic surplus, of the 'nerves of war', into the Great Power system. This is what happened as the core of the world system expanded to incorporate the USA (and to a lesser extent Russia and Japan) in the early twentieth century. The USA paid for much of the Second World War and for most of the post-war economic aid which put Europe and Japan back on track to sustained growth.

Given the disruption to the long wave around the Second World War, it is not clear that the world has returned to 'normal' dynamics since then. Perhaps the events of the twentieth century have broken the long-wave dynamic once and for all. If so, any insights into the present or projections into the future would be of little use. Nonetheless, there are ways in which the long-wave dynamic seems to continue – the Vietnam War (on top of the Cold War) in the late

1960s, the 'stagflation' on schedule in the 1970s, the end of robust world economic growth in the 1970s and 1980s, and the downturn of inflation in at least some key economies in the 1980s.

If this timing sequence is correct, we are now in the 'stagnation' phase of stagnant production, low inflation, and reductions in Great Power war (or in the cold war, which has been the economic equivalent of a low-intensity, drawn-out Great Power war). The historical analogies to our present phase are in 1920–33, or perhaps more appropriately (as I argue in Goldstein, 1988) in the 1870s and 1880s.

In such a sequence, the Reagan military build-up of the 1980s is counter-cyclical. That build-up could not last and, after less than a decade, came to a halt under a cloud of national debt. The Reagan policy of priming economic growth by cutting taxes and increasing military spending led to massive deficits in part because the underlying production-downswing phase could not respond strongly enough to such stimulation. On the other hand, the policy did not trigger high inflation because the underlying price-downswing phase (notable in decreasing oil prices in the late 1980s) kept inflation under control and production creeping forward despite the drain of increased military spending.

The US military build-up of the 1980s appears as a delayed 'last gasp' of the war-stagflation phase. It has, at best, applied counter-cyclical pressure to smooth out the transition to out-and-out stagnation. At worst, it has delayed true stagnation by a few years but increased its potential severity. The policy has also thwarted the real wage increases that should be the due of workers in this phase, as the economy readjusts away from war.

The debt for those years must still be paid off or written off, and this may hold back the coming of 'rebirth' and perhaps bring financial instability, even crashes. But the long-term picture, which even the US frenzy of spending did not change, is that the world economy and the world military system are moving toward a truly 'peacetime' economy for the first time since before the Second World War. That is, the world may finally demobilise from the last great war in a way that was done quickly after most wars in centuries past. The 'permanent' war economy may be long-lived but not immortal after all. Thus, the peaceful character of these years offers one consolation for continuing stagnation and possible financial collapses in the early 1990s. By 1989 these trends have clearly emerged, and it is 'no accident' (as the Soviets like to say) that the trends have moved furthest and fastest in that greatest of military economies, the Soviet Union.

A second consolation in this late stagnation period is the high rate of innovation as new sectors are arising to carry the next wave of prosperity. The most interesting of these innovations may be occurring in the biotechnology, electronics, telecommunications, and space industries (the latter and much of the rest depending on the ability of political leaders to resist militarising space).

If this difficult transition through 'stagnation' can be navigated successfully, we may look forward to the 'best of times' in the rebirth phase around the turn of the century. This all-important time of peace *and* prosperity for the great powers may offer the best hope for restructuring the war system in fundamental ways. Those years may offer a 'window of opportunity', toward which we should now be aiming, to get off the merry-go-round of Great Power war once and for all.

### Note

* Acknowledgements: For their comments on and criticisms of an earlier draft of this paper, I thank John Freeman, David Gordon, Giovanni Arrighi, Richard Goodwin, Dina Zinnes, Paul Pudiate, Andra Rose, André Gunder Frank, Alfred Kleinknecht, Thomas Kuczynski, Beverly Silver, Andrey Poletayev, Stanislav Menshikov, Ernest Mandel, and Immanuel Wallerstein. A previous version of this paper was presented at the 'Long Wave Debate' conference, Vrije Universiteit Brussels, 12–14 January 1989.

### References

Braudel, Fernand (1972) *The Mediterranean and the Mediterranean World in the Age of Philip II* (London: Collins).
Frank, André Gunder (1978) *World Accumulation, 1492–1789* (New York: Monthly Review Press).
Freeman, Christopher, Clark, John and Soete, Luc (1982) *Unemployment and Technical Innovation* (London: Frances Pinter).
Freeman, John R., Lin, Tse-min and Williams, John (forthcoming) 'Vector Autoregression and the Study of Politics', *American Journal of Political Science*.
Goldstein, Joshua S. (1988) *Long Cycles: Prosperity and War in the Modern Age*. (New Haven: Yale University Press).

Haustein, Heinz-Dieter and Neuwirth, Erich (1982) 'Long Waves in World Industrial Production, Energy Consumption, Innovations, Inventions, and Patents and Their Identification by Spectral Analysis', *Technological Forecasting and Social Change*, no 22, pp. 53–89.

Kondratieff, Nikolai D. (1935) 'The Long Waves in Economic Life', *Review of Economic Statistics*, vol. 17 no 6 (November) pp. 105–15.

Levy, Jack S. (1983) *War in the Modern Great Power System, 1495–1975* (Lexington, Kentucky: University Press of Kentucky).

Mandel, Ernest (1980) *Long Waves of Capitalist Development* (Cambridge: Cambridge University Press).

Mensch, Gerhard (1979) *Stalemate in Technology: Innovations Overcome the Depression* (Cambridge, Massachusetts: Ballinger).

Sims, Christopher (1980) 'Macroeconomics and Reality', *Econometrica*, vol. 48, no 1, pp. 1–48.

Sterman, John D. (1983) 'A Simple Model of the Economic Long Wave', MIT System Dynamics Group, working paper D–3410, March.

Van Duijn, J. J. (1983) *The Long Wave in Economic Life* (Boston: Allen & Unwin). (From the Dutch version of 1979.)

Wojtyla, Henry L. (1988) 'Going for Growth and Global Diversification: An Investment Strategy for the Post-Reagan Era', Investment Strategy Special Report (New York: Rosenkrantz, Lyon, and Ross) 17 August 1988.

# Comment

Richard M. Goodwin
UNIVERSITÀ DEGLI STUDI DI SIENA, ITALY

This paper convinced me of an intimate connection between long waves and wars. The two are quite distinct phenomena, with each being much affected by the other. A buoyant economy makes wars more possible; also some parts of the economy benefit from wars while others are damaged. Nonetheless it seems to me dubious to try to 'explain' the long wave by wars. This only shifts the responsibility for the half-century periodicity from economics to military behaviour, which surely offers a much weaker plausibility of explanation. Marx would say that shifts in economic power challenge existing political hegemony and hence can lead to war.

# Comment

Carsten Heyn- Johnsen
UNIVERSITY OF AALBORG, DENMARK

Goldstein's encompassing theory of the long wave comes very close to being a genuine theory of history – or at least to providing a major part of such a theory.

One could doubt the chances of accomplishing the same theory as in our days and in our science. We have the big books and holy books with an elaborated 'theory' of the history of man and the world, but they are all considered as, at most, pre-scientific.

Professors Entov and Poletayev have pointed to a number of difficulties confronting us when we try to substantiate the ideas of a long wave. I believe these problems grow the more centuries we want to cover with our models. How are we to interpret and eventually compare incompatible datas?

Goldstein proposes to establish a causal link between the dynamics of production and the social phenomenon of war. An increase in production is the necessary condition for starting a war, and major wars condition the further development of production, major wars being the benchmarks in time.

It is seen from Goldstein's presentation that the production–war nexus breaks down in the period after the last experienced major war, the Second World War. So we hope we can ignore that nexus as a part of a general theory of history.

But perhaps the reciprocal nexus war–growth of production is still worth considering?

If we restrict ourselves to that part of the history which could have both long waves and a rising trend in production that is, the epoch from Adam Smith via Marx to Joseph Schumpeter – industrial capitalism – there is a very nice book by Ferenc Janossy which seems to tell a plausible story; in German translation 'Das Ende der Wirtschaftswunder', 1966, Frankfurt.

Janossy's basic hypothesis is that 'all high growth rates in production and/or productivity occur in periods of reconstruction after social catastrophes.' A 2 per cent annual growth in productivity is seen as the maximal sustainable rate in the long run. In an analogy with the mechanical watch the growth rate is the result of the force of a spring and regulation by an escapement. The spring is innate to man, it is of a socio-anthropological origin *à la* Adam Smith. The historical–institutional conditions of capitalism as described by Marx and Schumpeter allow the inherent disposition in man to unfold.

The escapement is made up of a fundamental condition for the existence of societies. A long-run rise in productivity of 2 per cent per annum is a doubling in thirty-five years. This doubling is the combined result of qualitative and mere quantitative changes in labour-force qualifications. To have a society means to have a dialogue between its members, and in Janossy's view a dialogue between generations of twenty-five to thirty-five years will not be possible if we assume more than doubling in productivity. So the trend in productivity growth would be around 2 per cent. Society cannot sustain a higher growth rate, if mothers should be able to talk with their offspring and teachers able to teach.

The straightforward observation which on this background leads to higher growth rates in reconstruction periods is that the labour force will not unlearn or dequalify during the catastrophe, it is just the man-made capital that could be destroyed.

As the potential job structure follows the 2 per cent trend, the adequate equipment will be produced, if necessary, at a higher speed to cope with the inherited qualification structure. Rates of 5–10 per cent are possible in these periods of reconstruction, but they have to come down when the actual path hits the trend. The trend on its side will be stable as long as the 'spring' and 'escapement' are stable.

With this general model and some empirical estimates, Janossy made a forecast of 'Das Ende des Wirschaftswunder' for the BRD in the mid-1960s. The forecast came true. The theory is plausible and supports the war-production nexus in Goldstein's theory of the long wave. But it is of course not a long wave in itself.

# Part VII

# The Time-Series of Economic and Political Fluctuations: A Theoretical Analysis and an Empirical Exploration

# 13 Permanent and Transitory Components in Macroeconomics

Marco Lippi    and    Lucrezia Reichlin*

UNIVERSITÀ DI
MODENA

OFCE, PARIS

## INTRODUCTION

The Keynesian approach to macroeconomics, which prevailed until the end of the 1960s, distinguished quite neatly between those forces that drive the economic system along its long-run path and forces causing fluctuations around that path. Macroeconomists were mainly concerned with these latter, and since excessive fluctuations were considered as undesirable, or even politically and socially dangerous, the most important aim was to provide suitable techniques to reduce their amplitude.

Representations and estimates of the trend were obtained using relatively simple tools, mainly by fitting elementary functions of time. Thus, while population growth, accumulation of capital, technical progress, were summarised in functions like:

$$T_t = a + bt,$$

(after log transformation), business cycles were thought of as a stationary variable superimposed on $T_t$.

The strong criticism of the Keynesian approach which developed at the beginning of the 1970s, and which originated the 'new classical macroeconomics', was directed at the way fluctuations were explained, without calling into discussion the issue of the shape of the trend. Papers as influential as Lucas (1973) or Sargent (1978) started their econometric analysis after having detrended the data using traditional techniques; deterministic detrending was also used in VAR analysis.[1] Thus, while explanations of fluctuations diverged, no novelty was introduced in the treatment of the trend.

A major break in this respect occurred at the beginning of the 1980s. Starting from an important paper by Nelson and Plosser (1982), an impressive number of works came out, in which a closer link was established between macroeconomic theory and statistical time-series analysis, while, at the same time, some new economic problems on the interpretation of non-stationary data were posed.

First of all, the traditional detrending procedure was questioned. It turned out that if the hypothesis of a stochastic trend was tested against the usual deterministic trend, the former was almost never rejected by macroeconomic data. But as soon as both the permanent and the transitory components were modelled as stochastic variables whose changes occurred with the same frequency, two questions could be posed that did not make sense in the traditional framework:

(i) what is the relationship between permanent and transitory changes?
(ii) what is the relative importance of permanent and transitory changes in explaining the variation of the output?

In particular, Nelson and Plosser claimed that a substantial portion of the growth rate of the US output was accounted for by the permanent component. They also suggested, as an economic consequence of this finding, that 'real factors' should be considered as the main causes of both economic growth and fluctuations, in contrast to explanations of the cycle based on monetary or demand theories.

In the literature following Nelson and Plosser the question was reformulated focusing on a single quantity, the so-called 'size of the unit root', which may be defined as the long-run effect of a unit shock to GNP. Accordingly, the debate centred on whether the size of the unit root was smaller or greater than one, where in the second case the real business-cycle viewpoint seemed to be corroborated, while monetary or Keynesian theories seemed to be consistent with the first.

In this paper we will review the debate and make two points. First, the relative importance of trend and cycle in the GNP can be assessed on the sole basis of the size of the unit root only if it is assumed – as almost all the literature we shall review has done – that the trend is a pure random walk. In Section 7 we shall see that this assumption is based upon the usual picture of the productive system as a single representative firm. We shall argue that if such a construction is abandoned and the real processes by which technical innovations are diffused amongst firms are taken into consideration, then the random walk representation of the trend cannot be maintained; rather, a specification for the permanent component must be sought in a more general class of processes. The latter may provide economically sensible decompositions into trend and cycle, where the trend variance is small relative to the cycle variance, while the 'size of the unit root' may be greater than one. Second, the debate has been carried out on the hypothesis that economic time-series belong to the class of difference stationary processes. However, macroeconomic theory suggests several interesting examples of processes not belonging to this class. When these are considered, the issue of the multiplicity of decompositions between trends and cycles becomes even more apparent.

We will only deal with univariate models, but our arguments extend easily to multivariate analysis. The paper does not contain new estimation results; we shall limit ourselves to a discussion of the models employed up to now, and to an outline of directions for future research. Finally, as a by-product, we shall show that temporal aggregation may cause dramatic changes in the size of the unit root; this, we shall argue, contributes to considerably reducing the importance of such a measure of the permanent component in a macro-economic series.

## 1   THE GENERAL FRAMEWORK

A brief general premise is necessary. Almost all the trend-cycle decompositions we shall refer to belong to the so called Slutsky–Frisch approach to the business cycle. This is based upon two fundamental elements: serially uncorrelated random shocks (white noise), and propagation mechanisms. More precisely, the time variables considered are thought of as realizations of stationary stochastic processes that admit the following representation:

$$y_t = b + a(L)\,\varepsilon_t \qquad\qquad (1)$$

(the Wold representation) where:

(i) $\varepsilon_t$ is a white noise;
(ii) $a(L)$ is analytic in an open set containing the unit circle;
(iii) $a(L)$ has no roots of modulus smaller than one;
(iv) $a(0) = 1$.

It must also be recalled that the class of stationary processes actually considered in macroeconomics is limited to ARMA processes (autoregressive, moving average), i.e. those processes that admit a representation like the following:

$$y_t = k + \frac{M(L)}{N(L)}\,\varepsilon_t$$

where $N(L)$ and $M(L)$ are finite polynomials. Conditions (ii) and (iii) above become, respectively: $N(L)$ has no root of modulus smaller or equal to one; $M(L)$ has no root of modulus smaller than one; it is also assumed that $N(0) = M(0) = 1$, which implies (iv) above.

Accordingly to the Slutsky–Frisch approach, most of the decompositions into trend and cycle have taken the following shape (the works on segmented trends we shall consider below constitute an exception):

$$y_t = T_t + c_t \tag{2}$$

where $c_t$ is a stationary ARMA, while $T_t$ is non-stationary but $(1 - L)T_t$ is stationary and admits an ARMA representation:

$$(1 - L)T_t = b + \frac{m(L)}{n(L)}\,v_t \tag{3}$$

where $m(L)$ and $n(L)$ fulfil the assumptions above and, in addition, $m(1) \neq 0$; this last restriction will be justified below. Last, even though only implicitly, it is generally assumed that $(1 - L)T_t$ and $(1 - L)c_t$ are co-stationary. If the variance of $v_t$ is zero then $T_t$ is deterministic.

## 2   THE BEGINNING OF THE DEBATE

To fix our ideas let us now identify $y_t$ with the logarithm of real aggregate output. This variable is clearly non-stationary. The problem consists in how to model such non-stationarity. The rival models, in their simplest shapes, are:

$$T_t = a + bt \tag{4}$$

$$T_t = b + T_{t-1} + v_t \qquad (5)$$

where $b$ is assumed non-zero in (4), while $v_t$ is assumed to be a non-zero white noise in (5).

Processes (4) and (5) are both particular cases of (3). However, there is a crucial difference between (4) and (5): if (4) is assumed to be the trend, the output will follow a stationary oscillation around a straight line, whereas if the trend has shape (5) such a line does not exist. This may be seen by rewriting (5) as:

$$T_t = T_0 + bt + v_t + v_{t-1} + \ldots + v_1$$

It is clear that the distance of $T_t$ from any straight line has no finite variance.

More generally, if we start with decomposition (2)–(3), then:

(A) If $v_t = 0$ the trend has shape (4) discussed just above and traditional detrending, i.e. regression on $t$ and a constant, is recommended (notice that $b \neq 0$, otherwise $y_t$ would be stationary); if the operator $(1 - L)$ were applied to $y_t$ the variable obtained, $b + (1 - L)c_t$, would possess a unit root in its moving average representation (the latter would be non-invertible) and this, in turn, would have undesirable consequences on the estimation of the ARMA coefficients of $(1 - L)y_t$. In this case $y_t$ is called 'trend stationary', TS from now on.

(B) If $v_t \neq 0$ application of the operator $(1 - L)$ to $y_t$ produces the variable $b + (m(L)/n(L))v_t + (1 - L)c_t$. The consequences of traditional detrending will be discussed below. Co-stationarity of $(1 - L)T_t$ and $(1 - L)c_t$, together with the assumption that $m(1) \neq 0$, imply that $(1 - L)y_t$ has an ARMA representation:

$$(1 - L)y_t = k + \frac{M(L)}{N(L)} \varepsilon_t \qquad (6)$$

in which $M(1) \neq 0$. In fact, the co-stationarity assumption permits consideration of the spectra of $(1 - L)T_t$ and of $(1 - L)c_t$ and of their cross-spectrum. As $c_t$ is stationary, both the spectrum of $(1 - L)c_t$ and the cross spectrum vanish at the zero frequency. Therefore, at the zero frequency, the spectrum of $(1 - L)y_t$ equals the spectrum of $(1 - L)T_t$. As $m(1) \neq 0$ the latter does not vanish at the zero frequency, so that $M(1)$ cannot vanish. Processes for which $v_t \neq 0$, $m(1) \neq 0$, are called 'difference stationary', DS from now on.

In summary:

**Assume that $y_t$ is non-stationary while $(1 - L)y_t$ is a stationary ARMA with representation (6): (i) $y_t$ admits representation (2)–(3) with $v_t \neq 0$ if and only if $M(1) \neq 0$; (ii) $y_t$ admits representation (2)–(3) with $v_t = 0$ if and only if $M(1) = 0$ (in this case $b \neq 0$).**

To complete the proof of (i) we just observe that if $(1 - L)y_t$ admits a representation (6) in which $M(1) \neq 0$, then, trivially, we may put $T_t = y_t$, $c_t = 0$. As regards (ii), notice that integration of a stationary process with a unit in its moving average polynomial results in a stationary process.

Lastly, we recall that DS processes are often said to posses an autoregressive unit root. The reason is clear from (6); multiplying by $N(L)$ and putting $\bar{N}(L) = (1 - L)N(L)$, we obtain:

$$\bar{N}(L)y_t = \bar{k} + M(L)\varepsilon_t$$

This is an autoregressive-moving average representation of $y_t$, in which the autoregressive polynomial possesses a unit root that cannot be cancelled because $M(1) \neq 0$.

Let us now come to the beginning of the debate. Assume that the trend is as in (5) and, for simplicity, that $c_t = 0$, so that $y_t = T_t$. If a researcher is convinced that the model for the trend is (4), then, first he will detrend the data by a regression on $t$ and a constant term. Second, he will erroneously interpret the residual series as a realisation of a stationary process. Consequently, a spurious transitory component will result. The idea that detrending based on a misspecified trend shape could be responsible for exaggeration of the importance of the cycle in macroeconomic time series was central in the papers by Nelson and Plosser (1982) and Beveridge and Nelson (1981), which gave rise to the debate.

Also crucial was the possibility of testing for unit roots, that had been developed in the late 1970s by Dickey and Fuller (1979, 1981). This means the possibility of testing the hypothesis that $y_t$ is DS against the hypothesis that $y_t$ is TS.

The Dickey–Fuller test was extensively applied in the papers just quoted to the most important US macroeconomic series. Almost invariably, model (5) was not rejected. Moreover, this was the main statement in Nelson and Plosser's paper – once (5) was assumed, the fraction of the variation of the GNP explained by the cycle component turned out to be small, if not negligible, as compared with the fraction explained by the permanent component. This point must be developed in some detail.

## 3  NELSON AND PLOSSER'S PROPOSITION

Thus, Nelson and Plosser's first result was that the real GNP does not admit a traditional decomposition with a trend as in (4). Therefore the correct transformation in order to achieve stationarity consisted in taking differences, i.e. considering the series $y_t - y_{t-1}$, instead of the residuals from a linear trend. Following Box–Jenkins methodology Nelson and Plosser analysed the autocorrelation function of $y_t - y_{t-1}$ and found out that the first order autocorrelation was significantly positive, whereas autocorrelations corresponding to longer lags were not significantly different from zero. They concluded that a model like:

$$(1 - L)y_t = k + (1 + \tau L)\varepsilon_t \tag{7}$$

was appropriate. When estimating, obviously they found a positive $\tau$.

The subsequent step was to put the question as to which decomposition into trend and cycle was consistent with model (7). More precisely, they started with a decomposition like (2)–(3), which we rewrite using their notation:

$$c_t = \psi(L)u_t \tag{8}$$

$$(1 - L)T_t = b + \theta(L)v_t \tag{9}$$

where $\psi(L)$ and $\theta(L)$ are rational functions of $L$ fulfilling all the conditions necessary for the stationarity of $c_t$ and $(1 - L)T_t$. Furthermore, they assumed that $(v, u_t)$ is a white-noise vector, i.e. that $u_t$ and $v_t$ are white-noise scalars and that $\operatorname{cov}(u_{t-k}, v_t) = 0$ for any $k \neq 0$; however, they allowed a non-zero $\operatorname{cov}(u_t, v_t)$. This is a rather severe restriction on the dynamic interrelationship between trend and cycle, but we do not want to discuss this point here.

By combining (7) with (2), (8), (9) the resulting decomposition (omitting the constant term) is:

$$(1 + \tau L)\varepsilon_t = \theta(L)v_t + (1 - L)\psi(L)u_t \tag{10}$$

Analysing (10) Nelson and Plosser reached the following conclusions:

(a) $\theta(L)$ must be a polynomial of order one, while $\psi(L) = 1$.
(b) (Nelson and Plosser's proposition) A decomposition like (10) in which the variance of the trend (differenced)$^2$ is very small as compared with the variance of the cycle (differenced) is not possible.[3] This applies, in particular, to decompositions in which trend and cycle are orthogonal at all leads and lags.

In Section 4 we shall give a simple explanation of these results, as well as some critical remarks. Let us now develop some consequences of them. First, to appreciate fully the importance of proposition (b), it must be pointed out that, after all, a stochastic trend, instead of a deterministic one could have been harmlessly incorporated into the traditional dichotomic point of view if the trend had been very small in variance relative to the cycle (both differenced), i.e. if it had been very smooth relative to the cycle. In other words, a trend like (9) – instead of a deterministic function of time – considered by itself, is neutral as regards its economic implications. But Nelson and Plosser went much further with statement (b). Not only did they claim that the trend was stochastic, but their analysis of equation (10) appeared to provide strong suport for real business-cycle theories, in which productivity shocks causing permanent changes in output were at the same time the main source of fluctuations, leaving little room for additional *independent* causes, were they monetary shocks, demand shocks or any other causes of fluctuation (we shall return to this point in Sections 5 and 7).

This idea of a single cause generating both trend and fluctuations is quite evidently expressed in the trend-cycle decomposition that was proposed in the nearly contemporaneous paper by Beveridge and Nelson (1981). Such a decomposition may be easily derived from rather elementary considerations. Assume that $y_t$ is DS and that

$$(1 - L)y_t = a(L)\ \varepsilon_t$$

is the Wold representation of $(1 - L)y_t$. As $y_t$ is DS, $a(1) \neq 0$. Now observe that:

$$a(L) = a(1) + (1 - L)b(L)$$

where $b(L)$ is uniquely determined as the expansion of $[a(L) - a(1)]/(1 - L)$. The decomposition proposed by Beveridge and Nelson was:

$$(1 - L)y_t = a(1)\,\varepsilon_t + (1 - L)b(L)\varepsilon_t$$

where the trend is the random walk $T_t = T_{t-1} + a(1)\varepsilon_t$. This decomposition has the remarkable property that the white noises driving the trend and the cycle components are perfectly correlated.[4]

Beveridge and Nelson (1981) showed that $a(1)\varepsilon_t$ may be interpreted as the long-run effect of $\varepsilon_t$ on $y_t$ (see pp. 154–8). More precisely, if we consider $E_t(y_{t+k})$, i.e. the prediction of $y_{t+k}$ based on the history of the process up to $y_t$, then $E_t(y_{t+k}) - E_{t-1}(y_{t+k})$ tends to $a(1)\varepsilon_t$ as $k$ tends to infinity. Therefore $a(1) > 1$ implies a long-run magnification of the shocks affecting $y_t$.

Before continuing let us recall that if $y_t$ is DS and $(1 - L)y_t = a(L)\varepsilon_t$ is the Wold representation of $(1 - L)y_t$, the quantity $a(1)$ is usually referred to as the 'size of the unit root' of $y_t$.[5]

## 4 AN ELEMENTARY SPECTRAL EXPLANATION OF THE PROBLEM

Let us now return to Nelson and Plosser's statements. As regards (a), they limit themselves to observing that: 'The presence of first-order autocorrelation only in $(1 - L)y_t$ implies (*barring fortuitous cancellations*) that $\theta(L)$ is first order and $\psi(L)$ is zero order' (p. 155, emphasis added).

This argument does not appear to be convincing. If we start, for instance, assuming that $\theta(L)$ and $\psi(L)$ are polynomials of order two, then in order to obtain an MA(1) in (10), their coefficients must fulfil a restriction (the fortuitous cancellation). However, notice that this restriction will be trivially satisfied when $\theta(L)$ and $\psi(L)$ are, respectively, an MA(1) and an MA(0). Thus, if a more general dynamic shape is assumed for $\theta(L)$ and $\psi(L)$ – but this is implicit in the 'fortuitous cancellation' argument – the cancellations needed to obtain statement (a) are no more fortuitous than those necessary to make $\theta(L)$ an MA(1) and $\psi(L)$ an MA(0).[6]

Let us now consider statement (b). We shall give a simple and heuristically useful explanation of it, based on the simplifying

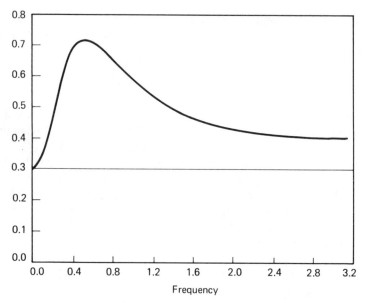

*Figure 13.1*   Spectral density of $v_t + (1 - L)\psi(L)u_t$

assumption that trend and cycle are orthogonal at all leads and lags, which implies that the covariance $\text{cov}(u_t, v_t)$ vanishes. To begin with let us take the simplest example of stochastic trend, i.e. assume that $\theta(L) = 1$, so that the trend is the pure random walk $T_t = T_{t-1} + v_t$, and the decomposition is:

$$(1 - L)y_t = v_t + (1 - L)\psi(L)u_t \tag{11}$$

Moreover, assume that $v_t$ and $u_t$ are white noises orthogonal at all leads and lags. The spectral density of $(1 - L)y_t$ will look like Figure 13.1, where the rectangle at the bottom represents the spectal density of $v_t$, while the spectral density of the cycle is on top of the rectangle. Now, the spectral density of the process estimated by Nelson and Plosser, i.e. (7) with a positive $\tau$, is given in Figure 13.2 by the curve AB. It is clear that a decomposition like (11) is imposs-ible for (7).

Nelson and Plosser, as we have seen, allowed for slightly more general decompositions like:

$$(1 - L)y_t = (1 + \tau L)\varepsilon_t = (1 + \mu L)v_t + (1 - L)u_t$$

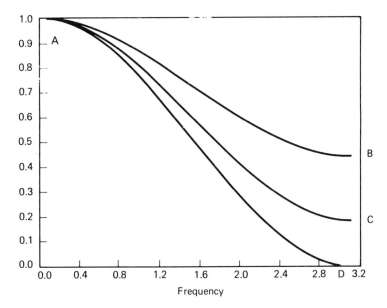

*Figure 13.2* Spectral density of $(1 + \tau L)\varepsilon_t$, $\tau > 0$, various $\tau$

It is easily seen that $\mu$ must be positive (otherwise the first autocorrelation of $(1 - L)y_t$ would be negative) and bigger than $\tau$ (otherwise the negative first-order autocorrelation due to $(1 - L)u_t$ would not be compensated). The spectral density of the permanent component will therefore be represented by curves like AC, while the spectral density of the cycle will be given by the difference. The variance of the trend is (up to a factor) the area under AC, while the residual area under AB is the variance of the cycle. The picture very clearly shows Nelson and Plosser's results in the case of orthogonal components. In fact, the maximum for the cycle variance is obtained when $\mu = 1$ (line AD for the trend).

Some simple calculations lead to Nelson and Plosser's conclusion when $u_t$ and $v_t$ are not orthogonal (even though $(u_t\ v_t)'$ remains a white noise). We will not report them here. Rather, an important feature of Figure 13.2 must be pointed out. All lines representing possible permanent components intersect the vertical axis exactly where the spectral density of the process itself does. This is a general fact. Consider the decomposition:

$$(1 - L)y_t = (1 - L)T_t + (1 - L)c_t$$

and assume that: $(A)c_t$ is stationary; $(B)T_t$ is non-stationary while $(1 - L)T_t$ is stationary; $(C)$ $(1 - L)c_t$ and $(1 - L)T_t$ are co-stationary and possess a joint ARMA representation. Thus we have:

$$\begin{pmatrix} (1 - L) \ T_t \\ (1 - L) \ c_t \end{pmatrix} = \begin{pmatrix} A(L) & B(L) \\ C(L) & D(L) \end{pmatrix} \begin{pmatrix} \mu_t \\ v_t \end{pmatrix}$$

where $A(L)$, $B(L)$, $C(L)$, $D(L)$ are rational functions of $L$, while $(\mu_t \ v_t)'$ is a vector white noise. Now regress $\mu_t$ on $v_t$:

$$\mu_t = kv_t + \omega_t$$

with $\text{cov}(\omega_t, v_t) = 0$. Consequently:

$$(1 - L)c_t = C(L)\mu_t + D(L)v_t = (kC(L) + D(L))v_t + C(L)\omega_t$$

Now, the spectral density of $(1 - L)c_t$ vanishes at the zero frequency, because $c_t$ is already stationary. Therefore, as $\omega_t$ and $v_t$ are orthogonal, both $C(1)$ and $D(1)$ must vanish. If $g(\lambda)$ is the spectral density of $(1 - L)y_t$:

$$g(\lambda) = |kA(z) + B(z) + kC(z) + D(z)|^2\sigma_v^2 + |A(z) + C(z)|^2\sigma_\omega^2$$

where $z = e^{-i\lambda}$. At $\lambda = 0$ we have:

$$g(0) = |kA(1) + B(1)|^2\sigma_v^2 + |A(1)|^2\sigma_\omega^2$$

which is the spectral density of $(1 - L)T_t$ at $\lambda = 0$. Summing up:

**Under assumptions (A), (B), (C) above, the spectral density of $(1 - L)y_t$ and the spectral density of $(1 - L)T_t$ concide at $\lambda = 0$.**

Thus in any decomposition into trend and cycle the trend spectral density must intersect the vertical axis exactly where the spectral density of the series itself does.

Now, it is important to point out that the height of the spectral density of $(1 - L)y_t$ at $\lambda = 0$ does not in general, contain, sufficient information in order to provide an assessment regarding the ratio between the variance of the trend and the variance of the cycle. In Nelson and Plosser's case a statement about such a ratio can be inferred from the spectral density of $(1 - L)y_t$ at $\lambda = 0$, but only because of: (i) the particular dynamic shape of $(1 - L)y_t$, and (ii) the particular shape assumed both by the trend and the cycle (Nelson and Plosser's statement (a)). As we shall see in the next Sections, if the first or the second, or both, of these assumptions are relaxed (for the first see Section 5, for the second Section 7) statement (b) no longer appears to be a necessary implication of the data.

But let us now briefly outline the most important objections that have been raised against Nelson and Plosser's findings. A first line of research (Harvey, 1985; Watson, 1986; Clark, 1987; Cochrane, 1988) starting with the acceptance of a DS model, has developed the idea that fitting an ARMA model does not in general ensure a good fit of the spectral density at a particular frequency, the zero frequency in our case. Different models and direct estimation of the spectral density at $\lambda = 0$ have been proposed, all leading to the conclusion that the importance of the trend component had been overestimated by Nelson and Plosser.

A second line of research (see Perron, 1987; Rappoport and Reichlin, 1987; Hamilton, 1989) calls into question the dichotomy between linear deterministic and stochastic DS trends. In particular, the first two papers mentioned, consider as a possible representation of the trend a function $a + bt$, where now $a$ and $b$ are allowed to change. These changes correspond to fairly infrequent 'epochal' shifts of regime. Once a segmented trend is identified and estimated, the residual is a stationary variable, with possible variations in parameters across different regimes.

## 5 HOW BIG IS THE RANDOM WALK IN THE GNP?

In the work we are going to review in the present Section: (i) the stochastic trend, as opposed to deterministic functions of time, is taken for granted; (ii) the dynamic shape of the stochastic trend is confined to the pure random walk, i.e. $T_t = T_{t-1} + v_t$, or to its second order version.[7] This second feature of the models proposed is a drastic simplification with respect to Nelson and Plosser's work. As we have seen, Nelson and Plosser had allowed the trend to assume any dynamic shape whatever. The reduction to an MA(1) (not a pure random walk anyway) had been obtained on the basis of the estimated shape of $(1 - L)y_t$ and the 'cancellation' argument we have discussed above. This aspect of Nelson and Plosser's paper appears to be forgotten in the subsequent debate. In Section 7 we shall try to give a motivation for this. Here we shall show how such a simplification caused a shift from the question 'how big is the ratio between the variances of the trend and the cycle' to the question 'how big is the size of the unit root'.

## 5.1

Nelson and Plosser had based their conclusions on the correlogram of $(1 - L)y_t$: only the first autocorrelation was significantly different from zero. Harvey (1985) observed that the Box–Jenkins identification procedure, which in this case recommended discarding all autocorrelations beyond the first, may imply a severe bias as regards the long-run features of the series.

This point requires further analysis. Start again with the Wold representation:

$$(1 - L)y_t = a(L)\varepsilon_t$$

We have seen, using elementary considerations on the spectral density shape, that in Nelson and Plosser's model $a(1) > 1$, i.e. $\tau > 0$, implies that it is impossible to decompose $y_t$ into a pure random walk and a cycle, where the two components are orthogonal at all leads and lags. This result holds in general:

**If $a(1) > 1$, then, irrespective of the shape of $a(L)$, a decomposition into a pure random walk and a stationary cycle, where these processes are orthogonal at all leads and lags, is not possible.**

To prove this, let us express $a(1)$ in terms of the spectral density at $\lambda = 0$. The spectral density of $(1 - L)y_t$ is:

$$g(\lambda) = |a(z)|^2\sigma_\varepsilon^2$$

(remember $z = \exp(-i\lambda)$). Thus:

$$a(1) = \sqrt{\frac{g(0)}{\sigma_\varepsilon^2}} \tag{12}$$

Notice that estimating the spectral density at $\lambda = 0$ and $\sigma_\varepsilon^2$ leads to an estimation of $a(1)$ (this is the basis of Cochrane's paper which we shall refer to below).

Let us now consider the ratio under the square root. The denominator may be obtained from the spectral density $g(\lambda)$ by the Kolmogorov formula (see, e.g., Hannan, 1970, p. 137):

$$\sigma_\varepsilon^2 = \exp\left\{ \frac{1}{2\pi} \int_{-\pi}^{\pi} \log\left[g(\lambda)\right] d\lambda \right\}$$

If an orthogonal decomposition into a random walk and a cycle were possible (i.e. trend and cycle are orthogonal at all leads and lags) we would have $g(\lambda) > g(0)$ almost everywhere in $[-\pi, \pi]$, so that:

$$\sigma_\varepsilon^2 > \exp\left\{ \frac{1}{2\pi} \int_{-\pi}^{\pi} \log\left[g(0)\right] d\lambda \right\} = g(0)$$

Thus we have proved that if such a decomposition exists then $a(1) < 1$, which is an equivalent way of stating our proposition.[8]

We may conclude that if we restrict ourselves to the question as to whether or not a decomposition into a random walk and a cycle is possible, the two processes being orthogonal at all leads and lags, then we may put the problem in the form: 'how big is the random walk?', or, more precisely, 'is $a(1)$ bigger or smaller than one?'.

Notice however, that while $a(1) > 1$ decisively rejects the decomposition, $a(1) < 1$ is not sufficient for its existence. Consider, for instance, a process whose spectral density is as in Figure 13.3: the decomposition is impossible, although $a(1)$ is smaller than one. This may be seen by a simple visual inspection of the log of the spectral density graph (Figure 13.4), from which it immediately turns out that the arithmetic mean of $\log[g(\lambda)]$ is greater than $\log[g(0)]$. But this is tantamount to saying that the geometric mean of $g(\lambda)$ – i.e. $\sigma_\varepsilon^2$, by Kolmogorov formula – is smaller than $g(0)$.

Now we may return to the debate and to Harvey's argument, which we restate using Cochrane's (1988) paper. Consider again equation (12). Then observe that:

$$g(0) = \sigma^2 + 2 \sum_{k=1}^{\infty} \sigma(k)$$

where $\sigma^2$ is the variance of $(1 - L)y_t$ and the $\sigma(k)$ are the autocovariances. Now, Box–Jenkins modelling, although based on the estimated $\sigma(k)$s, simply does not aim at an accurate estimation of the

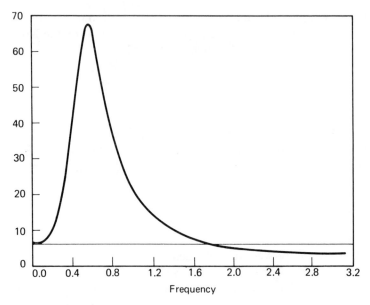

*Figure 13.3*    Random walk plus orthogonal cycle not possible, but $a(1) < 1$

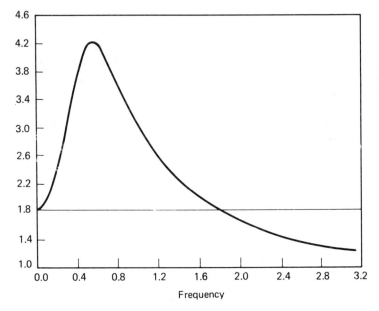

*Figure 13.4*    Log of the spectral density in Figure 13.3

above sum. More precisely, once a particular restriction on the ARMA shape is chosen – on the basis of the estimated σ(k)s – maximum likelihood estimation may well sacrifice accuracy for certain frequency bounds.[9] Cochrane proposed direct estimation of the spectral density at λ = 0. When applied to the yearly figures of US GNP that Nelson and Plosser had analysed, Cochrane's estimation led to an $a(1)$ smaller than one. On the other hand, using the same method, but on quarterly data, Campbell and Mankiw again obtained an $a(1)$ greater than one (we shall return to this issue below, when discussing the effect of time aggregation on $a(1)$).

Harvey had proposed the estimation of unobserved component models where the trend has the form:

$$T_t = T_{t-1} + d_{t-1} + w_t$$
$$d_t = d_{t-1} + q_t \qquad (13)$$

i.e. a random walk whose drift is itself a random walk,[10] while the cycle is an ARMA(2,1). Watson (1986) and Clark (1987) also estimated unobserved component models. In particular, Watson used a random walk trend ($d_t$ constant): thus, as the cycle and the trend were assumed to be orthogonal at all leads and lags – this feature being common to all the unobserved component models we are mentioning – a spectral density as in Figure 13.1 was obtained and, of course, $a(1) < 1$. Notice, however, that such a result is imposed *a priori* in this case. Objections to the unobserved component models were raised by Nelson (1987), who argued that unobserved component models tend systematically to overestimate the importance of the cyclical component (Nelson made an attempt to extend the argument raised against the use of deterministic trends).

A clear graphic presentation of the discussion is contained in Figure 13.5, which we report from Watson (1986). The spectral density corresponding to an ARIMA model (the monotonic decreasing curve) and to an unobserved component model (both estimated by Watson using the same data) are plotted together. They perform almost equally well as regards the likelihood, but $a(1) > 1$ in the first, whereas $a(1) < 1$ in the second, due to the sharply different behaviours near the zero frequency. Watson concludes that 'data are not very informative about the long-run characteristics of the process' (Watson, 1986, p. 73).

In Section 7 we shall propose a more general trend component

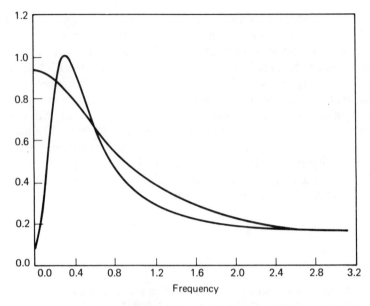

*Figure 13.5*   Spectral densities corresponding to two different methods of estimation applied to the same data set

based on economic considerations. In particular, we shall argue that a smoother process, as compared with the pure random walk, is highly plausible. This will lead to the idea of a decomposition whose shape has been stylised in Figure 13.6, in which the lower line represents the spectral density of the trend. As an easily understandable consequence, the magnitude $a(1)$ will become less and less interesting.[11]

### 5.2

A considerable reduction of the importance of $a(1)$ results also from the consideration of temporal aggregation. In fact, temporal aggregation may cause a sizeable cut down of $a(1)$ if $a(1) > 1$ and a magnification if $a(1) < 1$. Thus temporal aggregation contributes to making the issue more confused.

To understand the above statement consider first the case:

$$(1 - L)y_t = \frac{1}{1 - 0.9L} \varepsilon_t$$

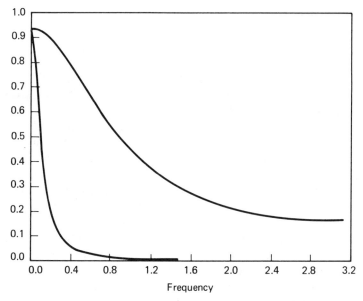

*Figure 13.6* More general trend-cycle decompositions

Here $a(1) = 1/(1 - 0.9) = 10$. Now, suppose the process $y_t$ is monthly and we aggregate over 12 months. The aggregate process will follow an ARMA model whose autocorrelation will decay at a considerably lower rate than 0.9. Thus a lower $a(1)$ may intuitively be expected. Precisely, this will be 2.04.[12]

On the other hand, if we start with the process $T_t + u_t$, where $T_t = T_{t-1} + v_t$, $u_t$ and $v_t$ being white noises orthogonal at all leads and lags, and $\sigma_u^2 = 5\sigma_v^2$, we have $a(1) = 0.36$, while after aggregation over 12 months $a(1) = 1.18$.[13]

Lastly, the first example, in which temporal aggregation leads to a reduction of $a(1)$, and an example we shall show in Section 7, in which temporal aggregation reduces $a(1)$ from above 1 to below 1, may perhaps help in explaining the contrast we mentioned above between the results obtained by Campbell and Mankiw (quarterly data) on the one hand, and Cochrane (yearly data) on the other.

## 6   IS THERE A UNIT ROOT?

As we have already observed, most of the models studied in the discussion raised by Nelson and Plosser belong to the DS class. This was due to the results obtained when testing DS against TS specifications and therefore, we shall argue, also to the limits imposed on the alternative to the DS hypothesis.

First, it should be noted that there is no economic motivation for restricting the choice of trend models to these two particular cases. On the contrary, both economic history and macroeconomic theory suggest that trends may take alternative shapes. For example, it is often suggested that the average rate of economic growth is subject to unfrequent changes as a result of shifts in policy regimes or major technological discoveries; this view would correspond to processes which are neither DS nor TS. It then becomes natural to ask whether the general finding on the presence of a unit root is due to the narrowness of the alternative hypotheses being tested.

Rappoport and Reichlin (1987, 1989) have stressed that the two alternative models of the trend being tested, the linear trend and the random walk, correspond to two extreme views on the frequency of changes of the rate of economic growth between which there lies an entire range of intermediate cases. In order to obtain a more general dynamic shape they modelled the trend as follows:

$$T_\tau = a_t + b_t t \tag{14}$$

with the condition $a_{t-1} + b_{t-1} (t - 1) = a_t + b_t(t - 1)$, which implies $a_t - a_{t-1} = (t - 1)(b_{t-1} - b_t)$ (so that the changes of $a_t$ are entirely determined by the changes of $b_t$) and

$$T_t - T_{t-1} = b_t \tag{15}$$

Equation (15) includes the TS model as the special case when $b_t$ is a degenerate random variable. At the other extreme, if $b_t$ is normally distributed with constant mean and finite variance, then with probability one the trend growth rate changes each period, and the process is DS. Between these two extremes there are processes whose slope, $b_t$, is not constant, but changes less frequently than the data are sampled ('segmented trends'). The authors have shown that if the true process is subject to $k$ deterministic changes in slope and we consider an alternative with $k - 1$ changes, these tests will favour the DS model against the misspecified alternative.

More generally, Reichlin (1989a) has shown that the bias is not just due to this simple characterisation of the alternative hypothesis, but it is present for any continuous function that is arbitrarily close to the true function. The proposition shown is the following. Assume that the alternative hypotheses are:

1. a continuous function $g(t)$ arbitrarily close to the true function $f(t)$;
2. a random walk.

Then, if enough observations can be made, $g(t)$ will be rejected in favour of a random walk.

The presence of a bias of standard Dickey–Fuller tests when the true process is a segmented trend with one break has also been shown in Monte Carlo experiments by Perron (1987) and Hendry and Neale (1989). Both authors show that when the true process corresponds to this case the power of the test decreases. Simulations by Reichlin (1989b) indicate that the power of unit root tests decreases with the number of segments of the true process.

These results are supported by empirical applications. Both Rappoport and Reichlin (1989a) and Perron (1987) have considered processes with deterministic regime changes and tested against the DS hypothesis. Christiano (1989) and Reichlin (1989b) have used bootstrapping techniques for testing for structural breaks in US GNP. With the exception of Christiano, all authors conclude that, when tested against the hypothesis of a TS model with one structural break, the unit-root hypothesis cannot be accepted for most series examined.

Recently, processes with stochastic regime shifts have been considered by Hamilton (1989) who has suggested that these are a better characterisation of macroeconomic data than linear DS models.

The literature considering alternative models for the trend is still limited to a restricted class of processes. Moreover, the question that has been crucial within the DS literature – i.e. the relative variance of trend and cycle – has not an obvious equivalent in the framework of generalised deterministic or stochastic trends. However, as we shall try to argue in the next section, the discussion should concentrate on the economic meaning of trend-cycle decompositions, and discard conventional measures.

## 7   HETEROGENEITY OF PRODUCERS AND MORE GENERAL TREND PROCESSES

The problem of discriminating between different representations of the trend component leads us beyond the simple issue of statistical testing, and raises general questions on the economic meaning to be attributed to the permanent component and its variations.

On this ground, although both generalised deterministic functions of time and pure random walks reproduce relevant aspects of economic reality, neither of them are fully satisfactory. We have mentioned that examples such as segmented trend processes allow the consideration of sizeable changes which arrive with a lower frequency than that of the observations, such as, for instance, technological revolutions. However, if we concentrate our attention on technical progress as a major source of permanent change, it is plausible first, that, within each regime productivity changes follow a unit-root process rather than a deterministic function of time, but second, that, productivity changes are not adequately represented by a pure random walk.

In the present section we will motivate the latter assertion and therefore, from now on, we will abstract from the problem of possible changes in regime and concentrate on the dynamics within each segment.

### 7.1

As we have seen, Nelson and Plosser observed a significant autocorrelation only at lag one. Thus they concluded that the process was MA(1), that the trend could only take the shape MA(1), and that the variance of the trend was a substantial part of the variance of $(1 - L)y_t$. Other authors objected that the Box–Jenkins identification rule led to overestimating the importance of the trend component in the GNP. Yet in all such work the trend component took the particular shape of a random walk (or of a process like (13)).[14]

To explain why the pure random walk $T_t = b + T_{t-1} + v_t$ has been almost unanimously considered as a good representation of the permanent component two convergent reasons must be mentioned. The first may be traced to the statistical concern with parsimonious parameterisation and identification. The second reason regards both the economic meaning which has been attributed to $T_t$, and the assumption of the representative agent, which are standard in recent macroeconomics.

At the risk of oversimplification let us summarise this issue as follows. Technology is given by a standard Cobb–Douglas production function. Such a function contains a stochastic multiplicative coefficient, whose meaning is that of total factor productivity. Now – this is the crucial point – that coefficient is also interpreted as 'the stock of neutral technological progress at time *t*'. Moreover, it is assumed that 'knowledge arrives in random amounts'.[15] The consequence is that the stock of neutral technical progress follows a random walk and that *therefore* total factor productivity follows a random walk. Finally, total factor productivity is implicitly identified with the main source of permanent variation in the GNP, so that the permanent component of the latter is modelled as a random walk.

As regards this line of reasoning, first notice that knowledge is assumed to arrive with the same frequency as the observations. Moreover, it is important to point out that in order to get the equation 'accumulated knowledge=actual level of productivity' we must *rule out* two very important features of observed technical progress:

(a) once a new method of production has been introduced at the firm level, productivity increases usually follow learning processes;
(b) since the final result of such processes is not known in advance, and since firms are heterogeneous, arrivals of new knowledge are not absorbed by all firms at the same time; on the contrary, diffusion of new methods of production is a complex, and definitely non-instantaneous process.

The assumption of the representative agent – or of many identical agents – which is usual in macroeconomic modelling, explains why the second source of non-coincidence has been ruled out both by real business-cycle theory and by alternative interpretations. It must be pointed out that the first source of non-coincidence has also been neglected.

Now, if we do not accept the common assumption of a representative producer and, on the contrary, we base our reasoning on relevant heterogeneity among producers, then the representation of productivity growth will also change. Technical innovations will no longer be absorbed simultaneously by all firms. Rather, they will give rise to processes that may be given a shape like the following:

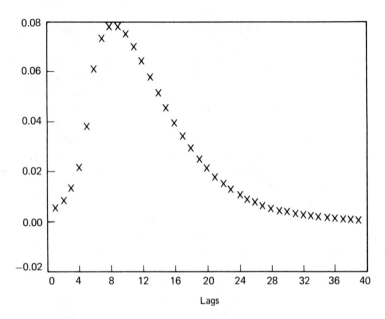

*Figure 13.7*   The coefficients $d_i$

$$T_t = b + T_{t-1} + d(L)w_t \qquad (16)$$

where $w_t$ is white noise. The pattern of the coefficients $d_i$ has been stylised in Figure 13.7, while in Figure 13.8 the corresponding cumulated sum exhibits the well known *S*-shape. Here $\bar{w}_t = w_t + b/d(1)$ is the rate of change of the productivity at the firm level due to the introduction of a new method of production. The coefficient $d_i$ is the fraction of the industry that introduces the new method with lag $i$ with respect to its first introduction. Therefore $\Sigma d_i = 1$.[16]

Some comments upon (16) are necessary:

(A) As stated above, we are reasoning within one regime; therefore productivity changes $\bar{w}_t$ must be interpreted as normal improvements within a given technological 'epoch'. A unit-root process, instead of a linear trend, is a consequence of the obvious assumption that such permanent changes are of variable size.

(B) If we continue to make reference to aggregate output, then a high frequency for the occurrences of $\bar{w}_t$ is plausible: some new method is being continuously introduced somewhere within the

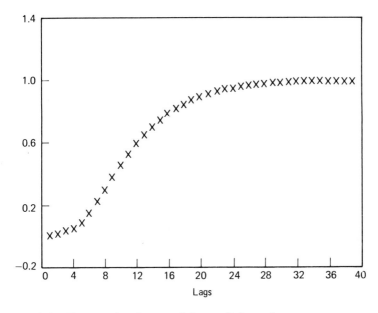

*Figure 13.8* The cumulated sums of the coefficients $d_i$

economy; incidentally, this provides a reason for the use of a monthly frequency in the exercise that follows and for the insistence on the effects of temporal aggregation on $a(1)$. Naturally, serious problems of aggregation over different industries arise. In fact, the functions $d(L)$ will generally differ across industries. This problem will not be taken into consideration here.[17]

A vision of economic growth that insists on firms' heterogeneity can certainly be based on empirical grounds. Within the history of economic analysis the key reference is Schumpeter and his view of the creative role of entrepreneurs. Recent works by Nelson and Winter (1982), Silverberg *et al.* (1988) and Arthur (1989) amongst others, put across models of diffusion of technological progress which are based on the assumption of heterogeneity across adopters of alternative technologies and where the technological path of the firm and of the industry is determined by the interaction between the firm itself and the environment. Naturally, all these models describe diffusion processes instead of an instantaneous increase in productivity.

The questions raised by this literature go far beyond the scope of the present paper. Here we limit ourselves to mentioning the above works, and to pointing out that they provide a strong economic basis for going beyond the dichotomy between deterministic trends and pure random walks, and introducing processes like (16) as stylised representations of the way new technical knowledge causes productivity increases.

**7.2**

Diffusion processes may quite naturally produce spectral densities that are highly concentrated around $\lambda = 0$. By way of example, we shall take into consideration the following family of processes. Let $m$ and $q$ be positive integers and $k_1, k_2, \ldots k_{m+1}$ be positive real numbers. Now consider all the processes $d(L)w_t$, where:

$$d(L) = d_0 + d_1 L + d_2 L^2 + \cdots + d_m L^m + \frac{d_{m+1} L^{m+1}}{(1 - \alpha L)^q}$$

with $1 > \alpha > 0$, while:

$$d_1 = k_1 d_0, \, d_2 = k_2 d_0, \, \ldots \, d_{m+1} = k_{m+1} d_0$$

As we keep fixed $m$, $q$ and the coefficients $k_i$, the members of the family vary with the parameters $d_0$, $\alpha$ and $\sigma_w^2$. Adding the condition:

$$\sum d_i = d_0 \left[ (1 + k_1 + \cdots + k_m) + \frac{k_{m+1}}{(1 - \alpha)^h} \right] = 1 \qquad (17)$$

$d_0$ is seen to be a function of $\alpha$: it never vanishes as $0 \leqslant \alpha < 1$, it is always smaller than one and tends to zero as $\alpha$ approaches 1. Thus the family is in fact two-dimensional, and is conveniently parameterised by $\alpha$ and $\sigma_w^2$.

In the Mathematical Appendix we prove that, given one such family, and given a positive real $A$, there is a member of the family whose variance is smaller than any preassigned positive real and whose spectral density equals $A$ at $\lambda = 0$.

The functions $d(L)$ just described are constituted by a finite stretch of arbitrary coefficients followed by an exponential tail. They are quite flexible to describe diffusion processes. For instance, the pattern in Figures 13.7 and 13.8 has been obtained from:

$$d(L) = d_0 \left( 1 + 1.5L + 2.5L^2 + 4L^3 + \frac{6L^4}{(1 - \alpha L)^2} \right) \qquad (18)$$

with $\alpha = 0.8$. Now the meaning of Figure 13.6 can be fully understood. Assume that $(1 - L)y_t$ is ARMA and that $g(\lambda)$ is its spectral density. There are infinitely many ways in which $g(\lambda)$ can be decomposed into a permanent and a transitory component, these being orthogonal at all leads and lags, while the variance of the permanent component can be as small as we want.[18] Lastly, it must be pointed out that both pure random walks and deterministic linear trends are limits of processes like (16). Thus the sharp dichotomy between stochastic and deterministic trends fades away. Moreover, as $d(L)$ may approximate $(1 - L)^{-1}$, by adding a white noise to (16), processes like (13) may also be viewed as limits of diffusion processes.

### 7.3

Diffusion processes can be finitely parameterised or approximated by ARMA processes. Provided the identification conditions are met, they might be used to specify the trend component in unobserved component models. We have not carried out such an attempt formally. Rather, we present a simple exercise whose aim is to illustrate the ideas developed so far.

The permanent component was modelled as:

$$(1 - L)T_t = \theta(L)\mu_t, \quad \theta(L) = \frac{1}{(1 - \alpha L)^2}$$

which produces the pattern of Figure 13.9 for the coefficients $d_i$. For the cycle, which is assumed to be orthogonal to the trend at all leads and lags, we adopted the usual shape:

$$(1 - \psi_1 L - \psi_2 L^2)c_t = u_t$$

so that:

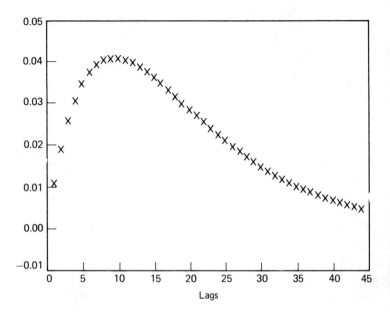

*Figure 13.9*   The coefficients of $(1 - \alpha L)^{-2}$

$$(1 - L)y_t = \theta(L)v_t + \frac{1}{\psi(L)} u_t \qquad (19)$$

$u_t$ and $v_t$ being orthogonal at all leads and lags. We took the following autocorrelation structure as a benchmark:

1   0.34   0.04   −0.18   −0.23   −0.19   0.01

which is the correlogram estimated by Nelson and Plosser for real US GNP, yearly figures, over the sample 1909–70. Interpreting the coefficients of our model as corresponding to a monthly process, the following autocorrelations for the resulting annual process were calculated[19]

1   0.45   −0.09   −0.23   −0.20   −0.13   −0.07

using the following values for the parameters:

$\alpha = 0.95$

$\sigma_v^2 = 1.0$

$$\psi_1 = -1.8989$$

$$\psi_2 = 0.9025$$

$$\sigma_u^2 = 12.5 \times 10^3$$

The ratio between cycle and trend variances is 32.9 for the monthly process, 19.5 for the yearly process. The size of the unit root, i.e. $a(1)$, is 3.5 for the monthly process, 1.8 for the quarterly process, only 0.71 for the yearly process (this is the result to which we were referring at the end of Section 5).

Some comments are necessary. First, the memory of $\theta(L)$ is very high. This explains why $\sigma_u^2/\sigma_v^2$ must be so large in order to get 32.9 as the cycle-variance ratio. Second, note that time-aggregation considerably lowers such ratio (from 32.9 to 19.5).

Let us now come to the reduction in $a(1)$. In Figure 13.10, after normalisation, monthly and annual spectral densities are plotted together (the smoother corresponding to the annual process of course), while the corresponding logs are plotted in Figure 13.11.[20] The reason for $a(1) < 1$ for the annual process and $a(1) > 1$ for the monthly process is easily seen (in Section 6 we observed that the sign of $a(1) - 1$ depends on the mean of the log of the spectrum).

Notice finally that as the spectra cross the horizontal line through $g(0)$, a decomposition into a pure random walk and a cycle must be excluded.

There is no point in discussing the 'goodness of fit'; this was only an exercise with very simple processes,[21] the parameters corresponding to few adjustments after an initial guess, not an estimation. Moreover, the assumption of independence between trend and cycle should be released in an economically sensible model. Nonetheless, comparing Figure 13.10 with the spectra of Figure 13.5, it is apparent how our model could compete with the others. Its spectral density has a shape very similar to that of Watson's (1986) model, but it is not constrained, as Watson's is, by the impossibility of crossing the horizontal line through $g(0)$.

## CONCLUDING REMARKS

We have seen that in the last decade an attempt has been made to unify the explanation of the permanent change of aggregate output and of the fluctuations around the permanent component. This

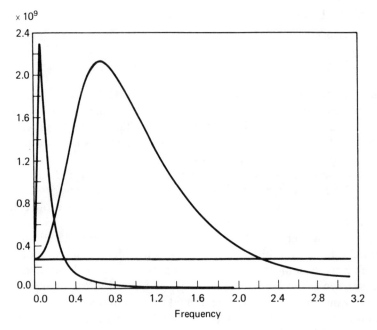

*Figure 13.10*   The effect of time aggregation on the spectral density
of (19)

theoretical development has been paralleled by empirical work trying
to show that macroeconomic data were consistent with the real
business-cycle theory.

Several strong objections have been raised against these findings.
Within the DS framework, recent work on the 'size of the unit root' –
which has become the central issue in this area – has shown that the
first results were not robust when Box–Jenkins identification and
estimation were substituted by unobserved component modelling or
direct estimation of the spectral density around the zero frequency.
Thus, depending on the approach, both values higher than one and
values much smaller than one were obtained.

On the other hand, we have seen that concentration of the debate
on the size of the unit root is due to the general acceptance of a pure
random walk as the permanent component model, and this, in turn,
has its economic motivation in the view – widespread in macroeconomics – that the productive system is fairly well-represented by a
representative firm, which instantaneously absorbs new technological

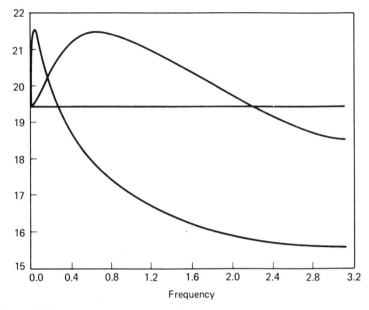

*Figure 13.11* Logs of the spectral densities in Figure 13.10

knowledge. We have suggested that if heterogeneity of agents as regards the time necessary to introduce new productive methods is considered, then the permanent component model must be sought within a more general class as compared with random walks. Consequently, the size of the unit root is no longer a decisive quantity: in fact, a big size of the unit root is consistent with a very low variance of the trend relative to the series itself, i.e. with the existence of substantial independent causes of variation of the output.

The size of the unit-root issue appears even less crucial when more general models than DS or TS are considered, as occurs in the literature on generalised deterministic or stochastic trends. This literature, though embryonic, provides a framework in which the impact of technical progress on macroeconomic series could be treated satisfactorily. In fact, not only, as we have argued, do diffusion processes represent more sensible models of technical change as compared with pure random walks, but also the idea of a stationary arrival of technological knowledge should be put into discussion along the lines suggested in the works on generalised trends.

**Appendix**

**1.** Let

$$x_t = (1 - L) y_t = \frac{M(L)}{N(L)} \varepsilon_t$$

be stationary. Aggregation over 12 months implies taking first the series:

$$w_t = (1 - L^{12}) (1 + L + L^2 + \ldots + L^{11}) y_t$$

$$= (1 + L + L^2 + \ldots + L^{11})^2 x_t$$

and then selecting, say, $t = k \times 12$, for $k$ integer. The spectral density of $w_t$ is:

$$g_w(\lambda) = |1 + z + z^2 + \ldots + z^{11}|^4 \; \frac{|M(z)|^2}{|N(z)|^2} \; \sigma_\varepsilon^2$$

The $k$th autocovariance of the time aggregated series is the $(12 \times k)$th autocovariance of $w_t$, and may be calculated as:

$$C_k = \frac{1}{2\pi} \int_{-\pi}^{\pi} g_w (\lambda) \cos (12k\lambda) d\lambda)$$

If the decay of the covariances $C_k$ is fast, then a small number of such covariances will be sufficient to obtain a fairly accurate approximation of the spectral density of the aggregate process. Once such spectral density has been obtained, Kolmogorov formula may be applied to obtain $a(1)$ both for the original and the time-aggregated process. Obviously no further problem arises if the series is given as the sum of a trend and a cycle or if aggregation is over 3 months.

All numerical results reported in the paper were obtained using GAUSS System Version 2.0.

**2.** Suppose that the following decomposition into orthogonal components holds:

$$(1 - L)y_t = a(L)\varepsilon_t = \theta(L)v_t + (1 - L)\psi(L)u_t$$

We have:

$$\sigma_\varepsilon^2 = \exp \left( \frac{1}{2\pi} \int_{-\pi}^{\pi} \log \left[ |\theta (z)|^2 \sigma_v^2 + |(1 - z)\psi(z)|^2 \sigma_u^2 \right] d\lambda \right)$$

$$= \exp \left( \frac{1}{2\pi} \int_{-\pi}^{\pi} \log \left[ |\theta (z)|^2 \sigma_v^2 \left( 1 + \frac{|(1 - z)\psi(z)|^2 \sigma_u^2}{|\theta(z)|^2 \sigma_v^2} \right) \right] d\lambda \right)$$

$$= \sigma_v^2 \exp\left(\frac{1}{2\pi} \int_{-\pi}^{\pi} \log\left[1 + \frac{|(1-z)\psi(z)|^2 \sigma_\mu^2}{|\theta(z)|^2 \sigma_v^2}\right] d\lambda\right)$$

$$= \sigma_v^2 H$$

where $H \geqslant 1$. Since $g(0) = a(1)^2 \sigma_\varepsilon^2 = \theta(1)^2 \sigma_v^2$, we have:

$$a(1) = \frac{\theta(1)}{\sqrt{H}} \tag{20}$$

This formula says that, if trend and cycle are orthogonal (at all leads and lags), the measure of the long-run effect of $\varepsilon_t$ is obtained by reducing the corresponding measure for the trend component, i.e. $\theta(1)$, by the factor $1/\sqrt{H}$, which is smaller than or equal to one; the bigger the cycle component with respect to the trend, the smaller $1/\sqrt{H}$. Notice that $H = 1$ if and only if there is no cycle component ($\sigma_u^2 = 0$) (in particular, (20) says that if the trend is a pure random walk, i.e. $\theta(1) = \theta(L) = 1$, then $a(1)$ is always smaller than one, unless the cycle vanishes).

**3.** Let $A$ be a given positive real. If the spectral density of the process $d(L)w_t$ must equate $A$ at $\lambda = 0$ we must have:

$$A = \left((d_0 + d_1 + d_2 + \ldots + d_m) + \frac{d_{m+1}}{(1-\alpha)^q}\right)^2 \sigma_w^2$$

$$= \left((1 + k_1 + k_2 + \ldots + k_m + \frac{d_{m+1}}{(1-\alpha)^q}\right)^2 d_0^2 \sigma_w^2 \tag{21}$$

It will be shown below that, indicating with $B$ the variance of $d(L)w_t$:

$$B \leqslant \left(1 + k_1^2 + k_2^2 + \ldots + k_m^2 + \frac{k_{m+1}^2}{(1-\alpha^2)(1-\alpha)^{2q-1}}\right) d_0^2 \sigma_w^2 \tag{22}$$

Elimininating $d_0 \sigma_w^2$ we obtain:

$$B \leqslant \frac{(1-\alpha)^2 [(1 + k_1^2 + k_2^2 + \ldots + k_m^2)(1-\alpha^2)(1-\alpha)^{2q-1} + k_{m+1}^2]}{(1-\alpha^2)[(1 + k_1 + k_2 + \ldots + k_m)(1-\alpha)^q + k_{m+1}]^2}$$

As $k_{m+1} \neq 0$, and as $(1-\alpha)^2/(1-\alpha^2) = (1-\alpha)/(1+\alpha)$, it is possible to find $\tilde{\alpha}$, $1 > \tilde{\alpha} > 0$, such that $B$ is smaller than any preassigned positive real number. Once $\tilde{\alpha}$ is determined, $d_0$ is also determined by (17), while $\sigma_w^2$ is determined by (21).

Lastly, as regards (22), consider the variance of $(1 - \alpha L)^{-q} w_t$. This is equal to $(2\pi)^{-1} \sigma_w^2 R$, where:

$$R = \int_{-\pi}^{\pi} \frac{1}{|1 - \alpha e^{-i\lambda}|^{2q}} \, d\lambda$$

We have:

$$R = \int_{-\pi}^{\pi} \frac{1}{|1 - \alpha e^{-i\lambda}|^{1}} \quad \frac{1}{|1 - \alpha e^{-i\lambda}|^{2}} \, d\lambda$$

$$\leq \frac{1}{(1 - \alpha)^{2q-1}} \int_{-\pi}^{\pi} \frac{1}{|1 - \alpha e^{-i\lambda}|^{2}} \, d\lambda$$

where the disequality has been obtained by substituting the maximum over $[-\pi, \pi]$ to the second factor in the first integral. But the remaining integral has the familiar value $(2\pi)(1 - \alpha^2)^{-1}$.

## Notes

\* We would like to thank F. Canova, L. Christiano, M. Forni, C. Giannini, L. Gutierrez, A. Kirman, A. Maravall, B. Salanié and M. Woodford for helpful comments.
1. See, in particular, Sims (1980).
2. The first difference of $T_t$ has finite variance, while $T_t$ has infinite variance.
3. As Nelson and Plosser (1982) put it: 'the variation in actual output changes is dominated by the secular component . . . rather than the cyclical component . . .' (p. 155).
4. In the particular case of (7) we have: $(1 - L)y_t = (1 + \gamma)\varepsilon_t - (1 - L)\gamma\varepsilon_t$. Notice that the variance of the trend is $(1 + \gamma)^2\sigma_\varepsilon^2$, while the variance of the series is $(1 + \gamma^2)\sigma_\varepsilon^2$. Thus, since $\gamma > 0$, we get that the trend is noisier than the series itself, which is paradoxical from the traditional viewpoint.
5. Remember that $a(1)$ does not vanish. More precisely, $a(1)$ must be positive. This is easily seen in the ARMA case, i.e. where $a(L) = M(L)/N(L)$. Both numerator and denominator must factor into monomials like $(1 - \alpha L)$. If $\alpha$ is real, then, since $|\alpha| < 1$, we have $1 - \alpha > 0$. If $\alpha$ is non-real, then also $(1 - \bar{\alpha}L)$ belongs to the factorisation. But $(1 - \alpha)(1 - \bar{\alpha}) = |1 - \alpha|^2 > 0$.
6. This argument is developed in more detail in Forni (1989).
7. An exception will be mentioned in Section 7. It must be pointed out that we are not taking into account the works on fractional differencing as an alternative to the current views on the non-stationary component in the GNP; see, on this point, Diebold and Nerlove (1988).
8. For a more general version of the proposition just proved see Appendix, 2.
9. See Cochrane (1988) and Sims (1972).
10. Harvey's preferred model was different, but this is inessential for the present purposes.

11. We would like to thank F. Canova who drew our attention to a paper by D. Quah (1988), in which a very similar point is independently made and developed.
12. See the Appendix.
13. This result may be easily checked directly by elementary methods. Aggregation of $T_t$ leads to an ARIMA (0, 1, 1) whose variance (after differencing) is 1156 times the variance of $v_t$, while aggregation of $c_t$ (i.e. $u_t$ in this case) leads to a white noise whose variance is only 12 times the variance of $u_t$. This example could be used against Nelson and Plosser's conclusion, but only to a limited extent. In fact, with models like the one just above the $a(1)$ of the yearly process can never go beyond 1.26, and this figure is obtained when $u_t = 0$.
14. As a remarkable exception we shall mention a hint to a more general trend shape contained in Campbell and Mankiw (1987). Their estimated $a(1)$ was well higher than 1. Nonetheless, in the concluding remarks they observed that if the permanent component had the shape: $(1 - \alpha L)^{-1} v_t$, then a high fraction of the variance of $(1 - L)y_t$ could be due to the cycle component. We shall see below that such possibility can be given an interesting economic meaning.
15. We are quoting from Long and Plosser (1983) p. 61, which has been, together with Kydland and Prescott (1982), a most influential paper in this area. Kydland and Prescott modelled the permanent component by $(1 - \varrho L)$, with $\varrho$ slightly smaller than one, but this was due to their employment of an existence theorem requiring stationarity (see p. 1352, footnote 10). For a very clear presentation of the way technical progress gets incorporated into the production function see also King, Plosser, Stock, Watson (1987).
16. It should be noted that even simple consideration of different vintages of existing capital stock would lead to ruling out a pure random walk as a representation of productivity growth.
17. For the consequences of aggregation on macrodynamics see Granger (1980), Lippi (1988). See also Chapter 2 (Granger) and Chapter 3 (Lippi and Forni) in Barker and Pesaran (forthcoming).
18. For instance, if $h(\lambda)$ is any rational spectral density with $h(0) = g(0)$, $h(\lambda) \leq g(\lambda)$, then $(1 - L)y_t$ can be thought of as the sum of two orthogonal (at all leads and lags) components whose spectral densities are, respectively, $h(\lambda)$ and $g(\lambda) - h(\lambda)$.
19. The resulting annual process here means: (1) aggregation over 12 months; (2) discarding all terms of the series but, say, those corresponding to $t=0, 12, 24, \ldots$ On this point see Appendix, 1.
20. Both spectra have been divided by their value at $\lambda = 0$. Although these joint plots are suggestive (in particular Figure 13.11), it must be pointed out that they correspond to different units of time.
21. In particular, the cycle, with $c_t$ depending only on its lagged values one and two months before, seems too naive.

## References

Arthur, W. B. (1989) 'Competing Technologies, Increasing Returns, and Lock-In by Historical Events', *Economic Journal*, no 99, 116–31.

Barker, T. S. and Pesaran, M. H. (eds) (forthcoming) *Disaggregation in Economic Modelling* (London: Routledge & Kegan Paul).

Beveridge, S. and Nelson, C. R. (1981) 'A New Approach to the Decomposition of Economic Time Series into Permanent and Transient Components with Particular Attention to Measurement of the Business Cycle', *Journal of Monetary Economics*, no 7, pp. 151–74.

Campbell, J. Y. and Mankiw, N. G. (1987) 'Are Output Fluctuations Transitory?', *Quarterly Journal of Economics*, no 102, pp. 857–80.

Christiano, L. J. (1988) 'Searching for a Break in GNP', Working Paper no 2695, National Bureau of Economic Research.

Clark, P. K. (1987) 'The Cyclical Component of the US Economic Activity', *Quarterly Journal of Economics*, no 102, pp. 798–814.

Cochrane, J. H. (1988) 'How Big is the Random Walk in GNP?', *Journal of Political Economy*, no 96, pp. 893–920.

Dickey, D. A. and Fuller, W. A. (1979) 'Distribution of the Estimators for Autoregressive Time Series with a Unit Root', *Journal of the American Statistical Association*, no 74, pp. 427–31.

Dickey, D. A. and Fuller, W. A. (1981) 'Likelihood Ratio Tests for Autoregressive Time Series with a Unit Root', *Econometrica*, no 49, pp. 1057–72.

Diebold, F. X. and Nerlove, M. (1988) 'Unit Roots in Economic Time Series: a Selective Survey', Finance and Economics Discussion Series, (Washington, DC: Federal Reserve Board).

Forni, M. (1989) 'Trend, Cycles and "Fortuitous Cancellations": a Note on Paper by Nelson and Plosser', Dipartimento di Economia Politica, Modena.

Granger, C. W. J. (1980) 'Long-Memory Relationships and the Aggregation of Dynamic Models', *Journal of Econometrics*, no 14, pp. 227–38.

Hamilton, J. D. (1989) 'A New Approach to the Economic Analysis of Non-Stationary Time Series and the Business Cycle', *Econometrica*, no 2, pp. 357–84.

Hannan, E. J. (1970) *Multiple Time Series* (Chichester and New York: Wiley).

Harvey, A. C. (1985) 'Trends and Cycles in Macroeconomic Time Series', *Journal of Business and Economic Statistics*, no 3, pp. 216–27.

Hendry, D. F. and Neale, A. J. (1989) 'The Impact of Structural Breaks on Unit-root Tests', manuscript, Nuffield College, Oxford.

King, R. G., Stock, J. H., Plosser, C. I. and Watson, M. (1987) 'Stochastic Trends and Economic Fluctuations', Working Paper no 2229, National Bureau of Economic Research, April.

Kydland, F. E. and Prescott, E. C. (1982) 'Time to Build and Aggregate Fluctuations', *Econometrica*, no 50, pp. 1345–70.

Lippi, M. (1988) 'On The Dynamic Shape of Aggregated Error Correction Models', *Journal of Economic Dynamics and Control*, no 12, pp. 561–85.

Long, J. B. Jr, and Plosser, C. I. (1983) 'Real Business Cycles', *Journal of Political Economy*, no 91, pp. 39–69.

Lucas, R. E. Jr (1973) 'Some International Evidence on Output–Inflation Trade-offs', *American Economic Review*, vol. 68, no 3, pp. 326–34.

Nelson, C. R. (1987) 'Spurious Trend and Cycle in the State Space Decomposition of a Time Series with a Unit Root', NBER Technical Working Paper # 63.

Nelson, C. R. and Plosser, C. I. (1982) 'Trends and Random Walks in Macroeconomic Time Series: Some Evidence and Implications', *Journal of Monetary Economics*, 10, 139–62.

Nelson, R. and Winter, S. (1982) *An Evolutionary Theory of Economic Change* (Harvard, Massachusetts: The Belknap Press of Harvard University Press).

Perron, P. (1987) 'The Great Crash, the Oil Price Shock and the Unit Root Hypothesis', mimeo, Université de Montreal.

Quah, D. (1988) 'The Relative Importance of Permanent and Transitory Components: Identification and Some Theoretical Bounds', mimeo, Department of Economics, Massachusetts Institute of Technology.

Rappoport, P. and Reichlin, L. (1987) 'Segmented Trends and Nonstationary Time Series', Working Paper no 87/319, European University Institute.

Rappoport, P. and Reichlin, L. (1989) 'Segmented Trends and Nonstationary Time Series', *Economic Journal*, no 395, pp. 168–77.

Reichlin, L. (1989a) 'Structural Change and Unit Root Econometrics', *Economic Letters* (forthcoming).

Reichlin, L. (1989b) 'Does GNP Have Breaks? Some Simulation Results', mimeo, OFCE, Paris.

Sargent, T. J. (1978) 'Rational Expectations, Econometric Exogeneity and Consumption', *Journal of Political Economy*, no 86, pp. 673–700.

Silverberg, G., Dosi, G. and Orsenigo, L. (1988) 'Innovation, Diversity and Diffusion: A Self-Organisation Model', *Economic Journal*, no 98, pp. 1032–54.

Sims, C. A. (1972) 'The Role of Approximate Prior Restrictions in Distributed Lag Estimation', *Journal of the American Statistical Association*, no 67, pp. 169–75.

Sims, C. A. (1980) 'Macroeconomics and Reality', *Econometrica*, no 48, pp. 1–48.

Watson, M. W. (1986) 'Univariate Detrending Methods with Stochastic Trends', *Journal of Monetary Economics*, no 18, pp. 49–75.

# 14 Politics Matter After All: Testing Alesina's Theory of RE Partisan Cycles on Data for Seventeen Countries

Martin Paldam*
AARHUS UNIVERSITY, DENMARK

## 1 INTRODUCTION

This paper is an attempt to address the following two large questions:

(a) Do left and right governments follow different policies, i.e. *does politics matter?*
(b) Will different policies lead to systematically different outcomes, i.e. *do policies matter?*

The two questions are analysed empirically on a large cross-country data base using a theoretical framework known as the *Alesina rational expectations* (RE) version of the *partisan cycle theory*. The data base covers thirty-eight annual observations for four main series for seventeen OECD countries as explained in Section 3 which also discusses the test procedure.

The theoretical framework belongs to the family of *political business cycles* as are briefly surveyed in Table 14.1. We want to analyse (a) and (b). We therefore use the theory of partisan cycles (introduced by Hibbs, 1977) that takes off from the idea that governments have *different ideologies*, and that cycles are generated because *governments change*. The link between the different policies, as generated by the different ideologies, and the different outcomes depends crucially on the expectations regime assumed. In the original Hibbs-version of the theory there are no expectations. The result is

*Table 14.1*   A taxonomy of political business cycles[a]

| Type – Duration – Name | Election cycles[b] 1 EP | | Partisan cycles[c] 2 EPs | |
|---|---|---|---|---|
| | NM-cycle | Actual | Hibbs | Alesina[d] |
| Reference | Nordhaus (1975) MacRae (1977) | Paldam (1979 and 1981a) | his 1977 and five later versions | his 1987 and five later versions |
| Main mechanism | Gs manipulate economies to win elections[e] | Election campaigns force parties to promise + promises implemented by Gs | Gs change between parties + Gs implement different targets | Election outcome surprise + Gs have different targets + wage contracts |
| Expectations | Voters myopic AE, price–wage-setters AE, Gs perfect foresight | ? | No expectations or (in other versions) AE | RE, but asymmetric reaction speed of Gs and other agents |
| Form of cycles | First contraction so expansion before election | Expansion in second year | Trends during EP in key variables | Post-election blips lasting 1–2 years |
| G profit | Vote profit | Vote profit? | Ideological profit | Ideological profit |
| Politics matters | No | No | Yes | Yes |
| Policies matter | Yes | Yes | Yes | Just enough |
| Empirical existence | No | Yes, weak | Yes, weak except USA[f] | Yes, stronger[g] |
| Main problem | Agents have different expectations | Lack of theory | Lack of expectations | Other observations, see below |

*Notes*: EP is election period, G government, AE adaptive expectations, and RE rational expectations.

[a] The early history of the theories, covering the pioneers Kalecki (1943) and Åkerman (1946), is discussed in Paldam (1981a).

[b] Two different attempts to include RE in the NM-cycle are Minford and Peel (1982) and Cukierman and Meltzer (1986).

[c] Partisan cycles demand that parties have different ideologies lead-

ing to different policies. The reasons why ideologies are different will not be discussed.

[d] Alesina's model is virtually the same as Hibbs's, but with RE. The cycle may appear with 1 EP, see text.

[e] The model assumes a VP-function, i.e. that economic conditions determine the election result. The VP-literature is covered in Paldam (1981b) and Lafay, Lewis-Beck and Norpoth (1990).

[f] Tests for the USA (and UK) are found in the articles by Hibbs (already mentioned) and for many countries in Paldam (1991a).

[g] Tests are found below, in Alesina (1989) and Alesina and Roubini (1991) and, for the USA, in other of the papers by Alesina and various co-authors. Note that both Hibbs and Alesina find their cycle to be strong for the USA – I only find the Hibbs cycle in the US data.

that the key economic variables come to contain ideologically determined trends.

As the reader may have guessed the least favourable regime for obtaining cycles is a RE-regime. However, elections always have an element of surprise. If we further assume that some agents are contractually prevented from adjusting immediately to the new information, while others, such as the new government, can act immediately, we do get a minimal partisan cycle even when all agents have RE. However, all we are likely to observe are short-run 'blips' in the politically important variables just after the election, as will be further discussed in Section 2. The post-election blips might last one or two years; but then all variables follow their 'natural' path.

This was first discovered by Alesina (1987) and he has later developed his model in a series of papers that provides a whole set of model variants taking various institutions and economic theories into account. In Section 2 we attempt to strip his model down to the absolute minimum in order to find what has to be true if the basic idea is correct. Section 3 then presents the data and the non-parametric test used. Section 4 displays the pattern of the data over the average right and left government so that the reader can see if there is something like the predicted pattern in the 'raw' data. Section 5 contains the test results and finally Section 6 compares the results with the findings in Alesina (1989), Alesina and Roubini (1991) and in Paldam (1991a) analysing whether the same data contain the Hibbs no-expectations partisan cycle.

## The Purpose of Our Study and Some Additional Points

The main purpose of this study is to examine how significant the Alesina partisan cycle is in a large data set. Our data set covers all governments in the seventeen main developed countries between 1948 and 1985. It proved easy to classify all governments as left ($-1$), right ($+1$) and left/right coalition ($0$). With these data we then study the trends and post-election blips in the following economic series: unemployment $u_{i,t}$, real growth $y_{i,t}$, inflation (consumer price rises) $p_{i,t}$, and public consumption growth $c_{i,t}$. In each case $i$ is a country index and $t$ is time.

One major problem might be the *international elements* in the series. As a certain fraction of each series is internationally generated and not due to domestic policies one wonders what that means to the possibility of observing such cycles? To control for this factor we have, corresponding to each series $x_{i,t}$, calculated a series, $x_{i,t}^a$, for the trade weighted 'abroad', seen from the point of view of the relevant country $i$. We have then calculated $x_{i,t}^d = x_{i,t} - x_{i,t}^a$, as the domestic component of $x$. This procedure is further defined in Section 3.1. All trend-tests are made on both:

[s1]   the *raw series*: $u_{i,t}$, $p_{i,t}$, $c_{i,t}$ and $y_{i,t}$ and on

[s2]   the *domestic components* of these series: $u_{i,t}^d$, $p_{i,t}^d$, $c_{i,t}^d$ and $y_{i,t}^d$.

A second major problem might be that governments are different in seemingly relevant ways – apart from being left and right. Many governments are re-elected and so weak that it is dubious if they have any possibility of following a consistent policy at all. Therefore, we make all tests for three types of governments – as will be further discussed in Section 2.6.

[g1]   *All* left and all right governments – including minority governments and re-elected ones.

[g2]   *Stable* left and right governments – including re-elected governments.

[g3]   *First* left and right governments after a change – including minority governments.

## 2 PARTISAN CYCLES – THE HIBBS AND THE ALESINA THEORIES

As already outlined, the theory of partisan cycles requires that the following four conditions are fulfilled:

(C1)   *Governments change* between parties having different orientation.

(C2)   Each government pursues an *ideologically determined policy*.

(C3)   An *expectations* condition which allows policies to influence economic outcomes in a systematic way. This condition appears in different versions – (C3.H) and (C3.A) – in the Hibbs and the Alesina theories.

(C3$\frac{1}{2}$)   There is a minimum of a Phillips curve.

The first three conditions will be discussed in subsections 2.1, 2.2 and 2.3. Then we put together the two versions of the theory in 2.4 and 2.5. The discussion will concentrate on two variables: unemployment $u$ and inflation $p$ and we take a government period to be years. Later we also include public consumption $c$ and real growth $y$, and we look at the government periods actually occurring. Bold type is used to indicate the path of the variables over the government period; $\mathbf{u} = [u_1, u_2, u_3, u_4]$ and $\mathbf{p} = [p_1, p_2, p_3, p_4]$. These three conditions are all necessary and together they are (with some minor assumptions to be mentioned) sufficient for producing partisan cycles. It is easy to check (C1) independently; but (C2) and (C3) are both quite controversial, and a lot of evidence exists *pro et contra*, allowing different people to hold different, but well-substantiated, opinions. We shall therefore concentrate on these conditions below.

The fourth condition (C4) is that both versions of the theory need a minimum of a Phillips-curve: if a left government reduces unemployment $u \downarrow$, by increasing public spending $c \uparrow$, then we should get increasing inflation $p \uparrow$. Conversely, if a right government reduces inflation $p \downarrow$ and public spending $c \downarrow$, then unemployment should rise $u \uparrow$. Note that all we need is that this mini-Phillips-curve holds within one government period. Nothing is assumed as to the dynamics of the Phillips-curve outside one election period.

## 2.1   (C1) The Government Change Condition

We know from many studies that the average government loses votes. In Paldam (1986) the loss from ruling is analysed for our cross-country sample. It appears that the average government loses 1.6 per cent of the vote, the loss has a s.d. of 4.5 per cent. The distribution of the losses from ruling is remarkably stable over time and across countries. It does not appear to depend upon the voting system, the party system, on the size of the vote for the government at the last election etc.[1] It is not really clear why there is a loss like this,[2] but several hypotheses exist.

One theory which explains the cost of ruling, in a highly relevant way, is the theory of the 'kick-the-rascals-out' asymmetry in the voter reactions, first found by Mueller (1970); see also Bloom and Price (1975). Voters punish governments for the 'bad' outcomes they produce more than they reward them for the 'good' outcomes produced. Mueller also coined the colourful name for the effect: the *kick-the-rascals-out* asymmetry. Hence, let us imagine two outcomes produced by two governments termed the left and the right: $[u^l, p^l]$ and $[u^h, p^h]$. The left outcome pushes down unemployment, so that $u^l$ gets a downward trend, but in the process an upward trend occurs in $p^l$, the rate of inflation. For the right government, the important goal is to reduce inflation, so $p^h$ gets a downward trend, and consequently $u^h$ gets an upward trend. The kick-the-rascals-out asymmetry says that the right government is punished for the high unemployment it produces more than it is rewarded for the low inflation produced, while the left government is punished for the inflation it generates more than it is rewarded for the low unemployment it obtains. Hence, it is clear that there will be fairly regular changes between left- and right-wing governments, if the kick-the-rascals-out asymmetry is true. However, this is a rather dubious theory empirically.[3] We do not, fortunately, need the kick-the-rascals-out asymmetry in order to get partisan cycles. All we need is the simple, extremely well-established fact, that governments lose votes by ruling. It is easy to check the data and see that power does change between parties in most of the seventeen countries.

It should be noted that the Alesina version of theory is less dependent upon actual changes taking place than upon the *surprise element* in the election outcome (as will be discussed later). However, it is unlikely that the agents will continue being surprised of the election result if the government is always re-elected.

*Table 14.2*  Expected trends in the variables according the ideology

| Series: | | Left government | Right government |
|---|---|---|---|
| $u$, | unemployment | downwards | upwards |
| $p$, | inflation | upwards | downwards |
| $c$, | growth in real public consumption | upwards | downwards |
| $y$, | real growth rate | ?? | ?? |

## 2.2  (C2) The Ideologically Determined Policy Condition – From Ideology to Policy

The ideological dimension in politics we shall apply in the present study is the *left/right-dimension*. It will be assumed that this is, by far, the most important ideological dimension in politics. For three of the variables – u, p and c – it is clear what the dimension predicts. This is indicated in Table 14.2. However, it is less clear what a left/right dimension lets us believe about real growth, y. Maybe, the left ideology will automatically rise y as u goes down as per Okun's law; but on the other hand it is right to be pro-business, and hence to promote growth in the private sector.

A lot of research, (see, for example, Castles, 1981) shows that the averages of the key economic variables $A(\mathbf{u})$ and $A(\mathbf{p})$ are not significantly different under governments of different orientation. The result is a standard one both in time-series and in cross-section covering local governments. It is known as the *politics-doesn't-matter result*. Some people dislike this result, and it surely flies in the face of a lot of casual observation. Politicians from different parties certainly claim that they pursue rather different policies. Party programmes are different, the discussions on party conferences are different, etc. However, two arguments have been presented to explain the politics-doesn't-matter-result:

1. The *median-voter theorem* says that when the two parties (blocks) fight for the majority they end up fighting the same 'middle' voter. Consequently, both parties come to follow the same policies, the policies most appealing to the median voter. A lot can be said both for and against this explanation; but it is worth pointing out that the politics-doesn't-matter-result is the main empirical evidence for the median voter theorem, so there is some circularity in the proofs.

2. The *RE-theory*, in its extreme version, argues that even when
   policies may be different this is unlikely to make outcomes different when everybody recognises that governments keep changing.
   That brings us to the third condition:

### ?.3   (C3) The Expectations/Actions Conditions – from Policy to Jutcome

A key result in the RE-literature is the policy inefficiency result (see,
for example, Begg, 1982).[4] It is an extreme result, appearing if:

  (i) all reactions in the economy are symmetrical;
 (ii) expectations are rational, in the sense that the agents consider
      the costs of improving their expectations to be very small rela-
      tive to the gains they may win from the improvement.
(iii) From (i) and (ii) it follows that all information that exists in the
      market is quickly disseminated to everybody.

The gist of the argument is that under RE all agents in the
economy take every predictable future policy-change into consideration in their actions, and the effect of any systematic policy therefore
shows up as a discrete jump in the relevant endogenous variables at
the time the information that such a policy will be pursued becomes
available and is believed. Election results are never fully predictable,
so at election day new information becomes available. However, to
the extent that the cycles are fully predictable they are already taken
into consideration in advance.[5]

So under RE we should therefore expect jumps in the relevant
variables at election day; as the series adjust to the levels that are
'natural' under the said regime. On the other hand, the voters cannot
fail to know that the government elected will rule for only a limited
period. Hence, the jump at election day may be only a short time-blip
in the series before it returns to its long-run 'natural level'. The sizes
and directions of the *post-election blips* are what Alesina (and Sachs)
have tried to model.[6] The more perfect and symmetrical the economy
is, the smaller the blip. However, there is one reason to expect the
blip to be significant: it is the fact that except at certain points in time
many agents are constrained by contracts or adjustment costs to act.
The key example of a constrained group of agents is the group of
unions/workers who have wage contracts covering, in the typical
case, a two-year period. Most other adjustment constraints have a

shorter period; but it appears reasonable to look for blips lasting one to, at most, two years. It is also justified empirically below.

### 2.4 Assembling the Hibbs Theory

In the start of the section we listed three conditions (C1), (C2) and (C3) for getting a partisan cycle. The Hibbs theory uses a strict version of (C3):

(C3.H) *An anti-RE condition*: policies influence economic outcomes systematically throughout the full government period.

It is worth pointing out that there have gradually emerged large amounts of sample evidence about the way people actually form expectations (see, for example, Jonung and Laidler, 1988, for a brief introduction to the particularly large Swedish evidence). The sample evidence is differently interpreted, but it would be hard, indeed, to claim that the evidence is strongly in support of the RE-theory. The patterns observed show an amazing variation between the expectations of different people, adding up to something that on average looks a lot like fairly myopic, adaptive expectations. Hence it is not difficult to argue that people form expectations in the way that is far from the one predicted by RE-theory,[7] that people have different and often incomplete information, learn slowly etc.

The shape of the cycles depends upon the details of the models used. Hibbs's first version of his model has no expectations, but he argued that there may be some lags in the reactions to give the pattern shown on Figure 14.1. Above we have tried to set out the theory with as little modelling as possible, in order to pinpoint the key assumptions. However, in the main version of the theory the cycles look like a sinus-curve extending over two election periods, and with the elections taking place near the maximum and the minimum. It takes some time for a new government to start influencing events, then the target-variable adjusts to its desired new level. In other versions there is a quick immediate jump and then a slow further adjustment, etc. In all cases, however, there are the trends set out in Table 14.2. Tests for the basic type of Hibbs's partisan cycle are developed and applied in Paldam (1991a).

*The Hibbs non-expectations cycle — ideological trends*

(a) **The path of unemployment u**

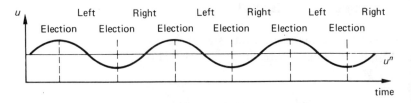

(b) **The path of inflation p**

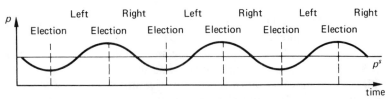

*Note:* Cycles last two governments of different orientation, the agents in the economy are steered by the government.

*The Alesina RE cycle — post election blips*

(c) **The path of unemployment u**

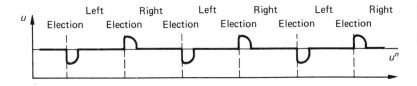

(d) **the path of inflation p**

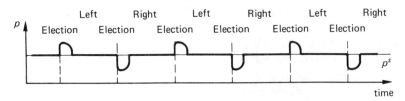

*Note:* The agents have RE, but agents have asymmetrical adjustment lags due for contracts adjustment costs, etc., $u^n$ in the natural rate of unemployment giving a constant inflation $p^s$.

*Figure 14.1*   Illustrating the two theories of partisan cycles

## 2.5   Assembling the Alesina Theory

The Alesina version of the theory uses conditions (C.1) and (C.2), but now (C.3) becomes:

(C.3A) All agents have RE, but they are not all able to adjust immediately to major pieces of new information, such as an election result.

The result, as already explained, are post-election blips lasting one to, at most, two years. The government elected immediately starts to pursue its ideologically determined policy, and as the agents manage to take the policy into consideration, the effects of the policy disappear. The size of the blips depends on three factors:

(i) the size of the surprise – i.e. if the election outcome has been predicted with a great probability then all agents have already had time to adjust; but if the surprise has been great then the blip will be great, too;

(ii) the institutional system of contracts, etc.;

(iii) the difference between the ideologies of the parties.

We have no systematic data on the three factors (i), (ii) and (iii) and we are therefore unable to make estimates involving the size of the jumps, so we have constructed a non-parametric blip-test. It is presented in Section 3.3, while the test results are presented in Section 5. The direction of the blips is clear to predict in the Alesina theory. The variables jump in the direction desired by the government. This gives the picture depicted on Figures 14.1c and 14.1d. When the two types of the partisan cycle are compared something interesting emerges:

The *trends in the variables become the reverse* in the two versions of the cycle. Consider for example, the path of unemployment under a left government: if the partisan cycle is of the Hibbs type, unemployment is adjusted from the former high level to the new low level, so the trend is negative. If the partisan cycle is of the Alesina type unemployment jumps down immediately and then rises to the natural level as the agents manage to adjust. Hence, the trend is positive.

## 2.6    The Three Types of Governments – Definitions and Relevance

As already mentioned, we have classified all governments in left (−1), mixed coalitions (0) and right (+1). Using this classification we distinguish between three types of left and right governments:

[*g*1]  *All* left and all right governments – including minority governments and re-elected ones.

[*g*2]  *Stable* left and right governments – including re-elected governments. Two criteria have to be fulfilled for a government to be stable: (i) It should have a majority – i.e. the parties in the government should have a majority in the main chamber (in the US, both chambers) of the parliament. (ii) It should rule for a normal election period, i.e. the full statutory period minus half a year.

[*g*3]  *First* left and right governments after a change – including minority governments. A change is defined as either of the two possibilities: (i) from left (−1) or a mixed coalition (0) to right (+1), or (ii) from right (+1) or a mixed coalition (0) to left (−1).

When going through the two theories it appears that the most relevant type of government is [*g*3] the first government. However, it is not clear whether the other two types are irrelevant. In the Hibbs theory a re-elected government may very well adjust its goals. By getting a larger support it may implement a more ideological policy, etc. In the Alesina theory the size of the surprise is crucial, and it may very well be that a re-election comes as a big surprise and then we get a blip to the same side as the last blip. If a government keeps getting re-elected the surprise must decrease; but strictly speaking one may get a one-period or a two-period cycle in the RE-case. Hence, it is interesting to run the tests for all three types of governments.

## 3    THE DATA AND THE TWO BLIP TESTS: $\zeta_1$ AND $\zeta_2$

The data covers all government periods, as defined in sub-section 3.2 from 1948 to 1985, for the following seventeen OECD-countries: (1) Australia; (2) Austria; (3) Belgium; (4) Canada; (5) Denmark; (6) Finland; (7) France; (8) Germany; (9) Holland (the Netherlands); (10) Ireland; (11) Italy; (12) Japan; (13) New Zealnd; (14) Norway;

(15) Sweden; (16) UK, and (17) the USA. In the following the index $i = 1, \ldots, 17$ refers to the countries.

## 3.1 The Four Economic Series: The 'Raw' Series and the 'Domestic' Component

$p$   inflation rate, i.e. the percentage rise in the consumer price index (CPI) of the country. It is calculated as the implicit deflator for private consumption as found in the OECD tables of National Accounts.

$p^d = p - p^a$, domestic component of price rises. Here $p^a$ is the trade-weighted price rises abroad.[8]

$u$   unemployment rate, in percentage of labour force as per the OECD Labour Force Statistics.

$u^d = u - u^a$, domestic component of unemployment. Here $u^a$ is the trade-weighted unemployment abroad.

$c$   the percentage rise in general government consumption, from the OECD tables of National Accounts.

$c^d = c - c^a$, domestic component of rises in public consumption. Here $c^a$ is the trade-weighted rises in public consumption abroad.

$y$   the real growth rate, i.e. the percentage rise of the gross domestic product in base/factor prices, from the OECD tables of National Accounts.

$y^d = y - y^a$, domestic component of real growth. Here $y^a$ is the trade-weighted real growth rate abroad.

The idea behind the domestic versions of the series is that all economic time-series contain international elements (see Paldam, 1983). To see how a government influences the economy one therefore has to adjust the series to 'take out' the international element and consider the domestic component only. The way we have obtained the domestic component is somewhat crude; but nevertheless it should give an approximation to the desired series.

## 3.2 The Political Data: Governments, Periods, Left/Right and Majority Measures

For each election period we include the last *government* $G_{i,j}$ before the election, except in (a few) cases of short-run governments of civil servants appointed with the sole purpose of providing 'neutral' rule while an election takes place.

For each government we define the *government period* $T_{i,j}$, by using the 'division point' of 1 July: if the government is appointed before 1 July of a certain year this is the first government year, if the appointment is later the following year is the first government year. The same principle is used to define the last government year. In Australia and New Zealand where the statistics are compiled using a different year the division-point is adjusted accordingly. Hence, for each government $G_{i,j}$ we obtain a government period $T_{i,j}$ of 1, 2, 3, 4 or (in a few cases) 5 years. To speak of a trend we need a $T_{i,j}$ lasting at least 2 years, so the governments with a period of less than 2 years are excluded.[9]

For each of the included governments – of which there are $n_i$ in country $i$ – we have collected the following data:

$T_{i,j}$  government period, constructed as explained.

$L_{i,j}$  $= -1$, 0 or $+1$. The left/righ variable defined relative to the political spectrum of the country. It is $-1$ when the government is left, 0 if it is a left/right coalition, and $+1$ if it is right. The variable is further discussed in Høst and Paldam (1990).

$M_{i,j}$  $= 1$ or 0. Indicates if the government has a majority or not. In all countries (except the USA) the government can be formed only if there will be no majority against it in the parliament. However, this does not necessarily mean that a government has an actual majority on which it can rely. $M_{i,j} = 1$ if the party/ parties in the government form a majority in the (main chamber of the) parliament.[10]

### 3.3  The Blip Scores $\zeta_1$ and $\zeta_2$ for one Government

Consider the four observations $x = [x_1, x_2, x_3, x_4]$, of the series $x$ for one particular government period $T$. We now want to analyse if there is an upward post-election blip in $x$ during $T$. To examine this possibility we need to consider $x_0$ and $x_{-1}$ and the corresponding $x^d$-observations. We say that there is an upward one-period blip if:

$$x_1 > (x_0 + x_{-1})/2, \quad \text{and similar for } x^d \tag{1}$$

there is an upward two-period blip if:

$$x_1 > (x_0 + x_{-1})/2 \text{ and } x_2 > (x_0 + x_{-1})/2, \tag{2}$$

and similarly for $x^d$

In the first case we look at one 'pair' ($\Gamma = 1$) and obtain $D = +1$ or $-1$ if (1) holds or fail, or zero if there is a tie, and we can now calculate $\zeta_1 = D/\Gamma$. In the same way we make two comparisons ($\Gamma = 2$) in (2) and get $D = +2, +1, 0, -1$ or $-2$, as the score. We can now calculate $\zeta_2 = D/\Gamma$.

Note that by using the domestic components, the $x^d$-series, we come to delete all international movements in the series, and hence to consider the 'abroad'-series as the reference series. By taking the average of the two pre-election observations we should have as good an estimate of the natural level as we can get, according to the theory.

Obviously, by considering one government there is a 50 per cent probability to get a $\zeta_1 = +1$ for (1) completely by chance. In the same way there is a 25 per cent probability to get $\zeta_2 = +1$ for (2) by chance. The possibilities for getting significant results therefore rest entirely upon combining results for many governments.

### 3.4  Combining Results from Many Governments

If we can take each blip test to be independent of the other blip tests they can be combined simply by adding the nominators and the denominators: The combined $\zeta_1$ for all left governments is simply $\zeta_1 = \Sigma D/\Sigma\Gamma$, where the sum covers all left governments. Similarly the combined $\zeta_2$ for all right governments is simply $\zeta_2 = \Sigma D/\Sigma\Gamma$, where the sum covers all right governments, etc. Under the independence assumption the outcome follows the binomial distribution and we can test if there is a significant number of blips to a given side simply by comparing with the cumulated tail of the binomial distribution $B(n, 0.5)$, where $n = \Sigma\Gamma$ and the 0.5 indicates that there is the same probability for getting either result. In fact, $\Sigma D$ is not the number of results to the expected side; but the *difference* between the number to the expected side and the number to the other side. We therefore have to make a small transformation of the standard table. The resulting significance points are given in Table 14.3.

The independence assumption in the relevant form is as follows for the $\zeta_1$-test: Given that there is a blip, as measured by formula (1), in one particular left (right) government, does this influence the probability that a similar blip is observed in any other left (right) government? In most cases the governments included in a combined test are so distant in space and time that independence can safely be assumed: the existence of a blip in the $x$-series in Norway in 1973, does

*Table 14.3*   Percentage points for $\zeta_1$ and $\zeta_2$ under the independence assumption

| | Significance level | | | | | Significance level | | | |
|---|---|---|---|---|---|---|---|---|---|
| $\Gamma$ | 5 | 2.5 | 1 | 0.5 | $\Gamma$ | 5 | 2.5 | 1 | 0.5 |
| 5 | 1.00 | – | – | – | 40 | 0.30 | 0.35 | 0.40 | 0.45 |
| 10 | 0.80 | 0.80 | 1.00 | 1.00 | 50 | 0.28 | 0.32 | 0.36 | 0.40 |
| 15 | 0.60 | 0.60 | 0.73 | 0.73 | 60 | 0.23 | 0.30 | 0.33 | 0.37 |
| 20 | 0.50 | 0.50 | 0.60 | 0.70 | 80 | 0.20 | 0.25 | 0.28 | 0.30 |
| 25 | 0.44 | 0.44 | 0.52 | 0.60 | 100 | 0.18 | 0.22 | 0.26 | 0.28 |
| 30 | 0.33 | 0.40 | 0.47 | 0.53 | 140 | 0.16 | 0.19 | 0.21 | 0.23 |
| 35 | 0.31 | 0.37 | 0.43 | 0.49 | 200 | 0.13 | 0.15 | 0.17 | 0.19 |

*Note*:   The table is for one-sided tests. It is symmetrical and one reaches the corresponding two-sided tests by taking the 2.5 per cent column for the 5 per cent test, etc. The table is constructed from the standard binominal test-table as explained in text.

not seem to depend upon whether or not we find a blip in the same series in 1957 in Italy – that is, *except* if the theory tested is right, and the two years are each the first year of a government. Consequently, there are, at most, a couple of cases in each combined test, where there is the possibility of a dependence. Obviously, the problem is a small one.

The independence assumption is more critical for the $\zeta_2$-test, for here we make comparisons for two consecutive years for the same country as per formula (2). So here the reader should take the test-results to be more debatable.

## 4   THE AVERAGE PATHS OF THE FOUR VARIABLES DURING FIRST LEFT AND RIGHT GOVERNMENTS

The purpose of this section is to take a look at the path of the four series over the period of the average left and right government. The look is provided in the 16 curves drawn on the eight sub-figures of Figure 14.2. Our theories predict, and the tests presented below show, that both types of partisan cycles are strongest in the first governments, so we only show the results for these governments, but the corresponding figures for all governments are found in Paldam (1991a).

The statutory period for a government is between three and five years in the seventeen countries. In most countries it is possible to call an early election, and it frequently happens. Therefore, only very few government periods extend to five years, so this possibility is disregarded in the calculations behind Figure 14.2. However, there are enough data to draw the four-year periods (sub-figures A to D) separately from the three-year periods (sub-figures a to d). In both cases we have added two years to both sides of the government period for comparison:

The reader should note that the figures are all cross-country averages covering the cases found, irrespective of the years and countries. All that matters is that it is a first left government lasting four years, a first right government lasting four years, etc. Hence, the reader should disregard the levels of the curves on all the graphs. However, it is interesting and relevant to look at *the development in each curve over time*.

## 4.1 Discussing Figure 14.2

The paths depicted on Figure 14.2 present a fairly unclear picture in the sense that one can see different cycles in the different series and for the government periods of different length. Consider first unemployment in the two cases: here a clear Hibbs-cycle appears in the paths of the right governments, but it is difficult to see a pattern looking like the ones predicted by any of the two types of partisan cycles in the paths of unemployment under the left governments. For the inflation rates the paths under the four-year governments look like an Alesina cycle but the paths under the three-year governments look like a Hibbs cycle, therefore it is hard to draw any conclusion.

For the real growth rate the picture is fairly weak; but there is a tendency for the trend to be upward under the right governments and downward under the left governments. Also there might be an Alesina cycle in the left four-year governments, but the data are rather thin here. Of more interest is the path of public consumption. Here there seems to be no clear case either; but for the three-year governments there appear to be something almost like a reverse partisan cycle. Furthermore, the picture for the four year-governments look very different from the picture under the three-year governments.

All in all it is therefore difficult to reach firm conclusions from Figure 14.2. We have also made similar drawings for the domestic

386 *Time-Series of Economic and Political Fluctuations*

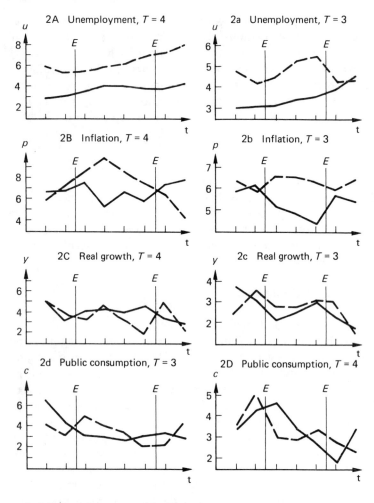

Paths under left ●– –● and right ─── governments.
The *E*s are the elections before and after *T*

*Note:* Sub-figures with capitals *A* to *D* cover averages over the 4 first left and the 15 right governments ruling 4 years, i.e. where *T* = 4. The corresponding figures with small letters *a* to *d* cover the 9 first left and the 9 first right governments where *T* = 3.

*Figure 14.2*   The paths of the four variables over first left and first right governments

components of the series; but the pictures found are no clearer. The next section tests for Alesina RE partisan cycles, while the same data are analysed for Hibbs partisan cycles in Paldam (1991a). It is perhaps not surprising – considering Figure 14.2 – that we do find a significant number of both cycles in the data.

## 5   THE RESULTS: TESTS FOR THE ALESINA PARTISAN CYCLE

Tables 14.4 to 14.6 contain our tests of the Alesina RE-cyle. In each of the tables there are three sets of three columns. The three sets of columns are for our *three types of governments*: [g1] *all* governments, [g2] *stable* governments and [g3] *first* governments.

As the surprise element is crucial to the theory we have included Japan even when all Japanese governments in the period included are right,[11] so that we have no first government. In all the other sixteen countries we have at least two of the three possible types of governments: $(-1)$ left governments, $(0)$ left-right coalition governments and $(+1)$ right governments. In Belgium, Finland, France, Italy and the Netherlands we have only the possibilities $(0)$ and $(+1)$.

For the one-year blip we get one observation, $\Gamma(\zeta_1) = 1$, per government, so for [g1] all left governments there are on average only 3 per country, as $\Sigma\Gamma(\zeta_1, \text{left}) = 51$, while there are 5.5 right, as $\Sigma\Gamma(\zeta_1, \text{right}) = 93$, and 1.5 mixed coalitions. When we consider [g3] first left governments we have only $\Sigma\Gamma(\zeta_1, \text{left}) = 21$, and first right only $\Sigma\Gamma(\zeta_1, \text{right}) = 34$ cases. If all governments lasted at least two years $\Sigma\Gamma(\zeta_2)$ – testing for two-year blips – would have been exactly twice the corresponding $\Sigma\Gamma(\zeta_1)$. However, some governments last less than two years so, in principle we only have:

$$\Sigma\Gamma(\zeta_1, i) \leq \Sigma\Gamma(\zeta_2, i) \leq 2\Sigma\Gamma(\zeta_1, i) \tag{3}$$

where $i$ = left, right, and one government type [g1], [g2] or [g3] is considered.

The three sets of columns are each divided in three columns. {C1}, {C2} and {C3}:

{C1} $\Gamma$ gives the number of governments in comparisons made.
      Since Tables 14.4 and 14.5 only give the results for the one-year

*Table 14.4*   Tests for one-year Alesina RE-cycles in unemployment

| | All governments | | | Stable governments | | | First governments | | |
|---|---|---|---|---|---|---|---|---|---|
| | $\Gamma$ | $\zeta_1(u)$ | $\zeta_1(u^d)$ | $\Gamma$ | $\zeta_1(u)$ | $\zeta_1(u^d)$ | $\Gamma$ | $\zeta_1(u)$ | $\zeta_1(u^d)$ |
| *Left government/expected sign for $\zeta_1$ is negative* | | | | | | | | | |
| 1. Australia | 3 | 0.33 | 1.00 | 3 | 0.33 | 1.00 | 2 | 0.00 | 1.00 |
| 2. Austria | 4 | 0.00 | −0.50 | 3 | 0.33 | −0.33 | 1 | −1.00 | −1.00 |
| 3. Belgium | − | | | − | | | − | | |
| 4. Canada | 7 | −0.14 | −0.43 | 5 | 0.20 | −0.20 | 2 | −1.00 | −1.00 |
| 5. Denmark | 8 | −0.25 | −0.50 | 2 | 0.00 | 0.00 | 4 | −0.50 | −0.50 |
| 6. Finland | − | | | − | | | − | | |
| 7. France | − | | | − | | | − | | |
| 8. Germany | 3 | −0.33 | −0.33 | 3 | −0.33 | −0.33 | 1 | −1.00 | −1.00 |
| 9. Holland | − | | | − | | | − | | |
| 10. Ireland | 3 | −0.33 | −0.33 | 2 | −1.00 | 0.00 | 3 | −0.33 | 0.33 |
| 11. Italy | − | | | − | | | − | | |
| 12. Japan | − | | | − | | | − | | |
| 13. New Zealand | 2 | 0.00 | −1.00 | 2 | 0.00 | −1.00 | 2 | 0.00 | −1.00 |
| 14. Norway | 5 | 0.20 | −0.60 | 2 | 0.00 | −1.00 | 1 | −1.00 | −1.00 |
| 15. Sweden | 9 | −0.33 | 0.11 | 2 | 0.00 | 1.00 | 1 | 1.00 | −1.00 |
| 16. UK | 4 | −0.50 | −1.00 | 3 | −0.33 | −1.00 | 2 | −1.00 | −1.00 |
| 17. USA | 3 | −0.33 | −0.33 | 2 | 0.00 | 0.00 | 2 | 0.00 | 0.00 |
| $\Sigma$ | 51 | −0.18 | −0.29* | 29 | −0.03 | −0.17 | 21 | −0.43 | −0.43(*) |
| *Right governments/expected sign for $\zeta_1$ positive* | | | | | | | | | |
| 1. Australia | 11 | 0.09 | −0.09 | 11 | 0.09 | −0.09 | 1 | 1.00 | 1.00 |
| 2. Austria | 1 | −1.00 | −1.00 | 1 | −1.00 | −1.00 | 1 | −1.00 | −1.00 |
| 3. Belgium | 6 | 0.67 | 0.00 | 5 | 0.60 | 0.20 | 4 | 1.00 | 0.00 |
| 4. Canada | 4 | 0.00 | 0.00 | 1 | 1.00 | 1.00 | 2 | 0.00 | 0.00 |
| 5. Denmark | 5 | 0.60 | 0.20 | 1 | 1.00 | 1.00 | 4 | 1.00 | 0.50 |
| 6. Finland | 2 | 0.00 | 1.00 | 1 | −1.00 | 1.00 | 1 | 1.00 | 1.00 |
| 7. France | 7 | 0.71 | 0.14 | 3 | 0.33 | 0.33 | 1 | 1.00 | 1.00 |
| 8. Germany | 5 | −0.20 | 0.20 | 5 | −0.20 | 0.20 | 1 | 1.00 | 1.00 |
| 9. Holland | 4 | 0.00 | 0.50 | 4 | 0.00 | 0.50 | 3 | −0.33 | 0.33 |
| 10. Ireland | 7 | −0.14 | −0.14 | 4 | 0.00 | 0.00 | 4 | 0.50 | 0.00 |
| 11. Italy | 4 | 1.00 | 1.00 | 1 | 1.00 | 1.00 | 1 | 1.00 | 1.00 |
| 12. Japan | 12 | −0.17 | −0.17 | 11 | −0.09 | −0.09 | no changes | | |
| 13. New Zealand | 9 | −0.33 | −0.33 | 9 | −0.33 | −0.33 | 2 | 0.00 | −1.00 |
| 14. Norway | 3 | 0.33 | −0.33 | 2 | 0.00 | −1.00 | 2 | 0.00 | −1.00 |
| 15. Sweden | 2 | 0.00 | 0.00 | 0 | 0.00 | 0.00 | 1 | 1.00 | 1.00 |
| 16. UK | 6 | 0.00 | −0.33 | 6 | 0.00 | −0.33 | 3 | 0.33 | −1.00 |
| 17. USA | 5 | −0.20 | −0.60 | 2 | 0.00 | −1.00 | 3 | −0.33 | −0.33 |
| $\Sigma$ | 93 | 0.10 | −0.03 | 67 | 0.01 | −0.04 | 34 | 0.41 | 0.00* |

*Table 14.5* Tests for one-year Alesina RE-cycles in price rises

| | All governments $\Gamma$ $\zeta_1(p)$ $\zeta_1(p^d)$ | | | Stable governments $\Gamma$ $\zeta_1(p)$ $\zeta_1(p^d)$ | | | First governments $\Gamma$ $\zeta_1(p)$ $\zeta_1(p^d)$ | | |
|---|---|---|---|---|---|---|---|---|---|
| *Left government/expected sign for $\zeta_1$ is positive* | | | | | | | | | |
| 1. Australia | 3 | 0.33 | 0.33 | 3 | 0.33 | 0.33 | 2 | 0.00 | 1.00 |
| 2. Austria | 4 | 0.00 | −0.50 | 3 | −0.33 | −0.33 | 1 | 1.00 | −1.00 |
| 3. Belgium | − | | | − | | | − | | |
| 4. Canada | 7 | 1.00 | 0.43 | 5 | 1.00 | 0.20 | 2 | 1.00 | 0.00 |
| 5. Denmark | 8 | 0.25 | 0.00 | 2 | 0.00 | −1.00 | 4 | 0.00 | 0.00 |
| 6. Finland | − | | | − | | | − | | |
| 7. France | − | | | − | | | − | | |
| 8. Germany | 3 | 0.33 | 0.33 | 3 | 0.33 | 0.33 | 1 | 1.00 | 1.00 |
| 9. Holland | − | | | − | | | − | | |
| 10. Ireland | 3 | 0.33 | 0.33 | 2 | 0.00 | 0.00 | 3 | 0.33 | 0.33 |
| 11. Italy | − | | | − | | | − | | |
| 12. Japan | − | | | − | | | − | | |
| 13. New Zealand | 2 | 1.00 | 0.00 | 2 | 1.00 | 0.00 | 2 | 1.00 | 0.00 |
| 14. Norway | 5 | −0.20 | 0.60 | 2 | −1.00 | 1.00 | 1 | 1.00 | −1.00 |
| 15. Sweden | 9 | −0.11 | −0.33 | 2 | −1.00 | −1.00 | 1 | −1.00 | 1.00 |
| 16. UK | 4 | 0.50 | 0.50 | 3 | 0.33 | 0.33 | 2 | 1.00 | 1.00 |
| 17. USA | 3 | −0.33 | −0.33 | 2 | −1.00 | 0.00 | 2 | −1.00 | 0.00 |
| Σ | 51 | 0.25 | 0.10(*) | 29 | 0.10 | 0.03 | 21 | 0.33 | 0.24 |
| *Right governments/expected sign for $\zeta_1$ negative* | | | | | | | | | |
| 1. Australia | 11 | 0.27 | 0.27 | 11 | 0.27 | 0.27 | 1 | −1.00 | −1.00 |
| 2. Austria | 1 | −1.00 | −1.00 | 1 | −1.00 | −1.00 | 1 | −1.00 | −1.00 |
| 3. Belgium | 6 | 0.00 | −0.33 | 5 | −0.20 | −0.60 | 4 | 0.00 | 0.00 |
| 4. Canada | 4 | 1.00 | 0.50 | 1 | 1.00 | 1.00 | 2 | 1.00 | 0.00 |
| 5. Denmark | 5 | 0.20 | 0.20 | 1 | 1.00 | 1.00 | 4 | 0.50 | 0.00 |
| 6. Finland | 2 | −1.00 | −1.00 | 1 | −1.00 | −1.00 | 1 | −1.00 | −1.00 |
| 7. France | 7 | 0.43 | 0.43 | 3 | 0.33 | 0.33 | 1 | −1.00 | −1.00 |
| 8. Germany | 5 | −0.60 | 0.20 | 5 | −0.60 | 0.20 | 1 | −1.00 | 1.00 |
| 9. Holland | 4 | −0.50 | −0.50 | 4 | −0.50 | −0.50 | 3 | −1.00 | −1.00 |
| 10. Ireland | 7 | 0.14 | 0.14 | 4 | 0.00 | 0.00 | 4 | 0.00 | 0.00 |
| 11. Italy | 4 | −0.50 | 0.50 | 1 | −1.00 | −1.00 | 1 | 1.00 | 1.00 |
| 12. Japan | 12 | −0.33 | −0.17 | 11 | −0.45 | −0.27 | no changes | | |
| 13. New Zealand | 9 | 0.33 | 0.11 | 9 | 0.33 | 0.11 | 2 | 1.00 | 0.00 |
| 14. Norway | 3 | −0.33 | −0.33 | 2 | −1.00 | 0.00 | 2 | −1.00 | 0.00 |
| 15. Sweden | 2 | 0.00 | −1.00 | 0 | 0.00 | 0.00 | 1 | −1.00 | −1.00 |
| 16. UK | 6 | 0.00 | 0.00 | 6 | 0.00 | 0.00 | 3 | 0.33 | 0.33 |
| 17. USA | 5 | 0.20 | 0.20 | 2 | 1.00 | 0.00 | 3 | −0.33 | 0.33 |
| Σ | 93 | 0.01 | 0.03 | 67 | −0.07 | −0.04 | 34 | −0.12 | −0.12 |

*Table 14.6* Comparing the results for the sum-line

| $x = u, p,$ $y, c$ | All governments $\Gamma$ | $\zeta_i(x)$ | $\zeta_i(x^d)$ | Stable governments $\Gamma$ | $\zeta_i(x)$ | $\zeta_i(x^d)$ | First governments $\Gamma$ | $\zeta_i(x)$ | $\zeta_i(x^d)$ |
|---|---|---|---|---|---|---|---|---|---|
| *Left governments* | | | | | | | | | |
| Unemployment $u$ – expected sign negative | | | | | | | | | |
| $\Sigma\zeta_1$ | 51 | –0.18 | –0.29* | 29 | –0.03 | –0.17 | 21 | –0.43 | –0.43(*) |
| $\Sigma\zeta_2$ | 94 | –0.09 | –0.15(*) | 56 | 0.04 | –0.04 | 36 | –0.28 | –0.33* |
| Price rises $p$ – expected sign negative | | | | | | | | | |
| $\Sigma\zeta_1$ | 51 | 0.25 | 0.10(*) | 29 | 0.10 | 0.03 | 21 | 0.33 | 0.24 |
| $\Sigma\zeta_2$ | 94 | 0.21 | 0.04* | 56 | 0.04 | 0.00 | 36 | 0.28 | 0.06(*) |
| Real growth rate $y$ – expected sign unclear | | | | | | | | | |
| $\Sigma\zeta_1$ | 51 | 0.06 | 0.25(*) | 29 | 0.10 | 0.17 | 21 | –0.14 | –0.05 |
| $\Sigma\zeta_2$ | 94 | 0.02 | 0.28* | 56 | 0.11 | 0.21(*) | 36 | 0.17 | 0.33(*) |
| Growth in public consumption $c$ – expected sign positive | | | | | | | | | |
| $\Sigma\zeta_1$ | 51 | –0.06 | –0.02 | 29 | 0.03 | 0.24 | 21 | –0.33 | –0.14 |
| $\Sigma\zeta_2$ | 94 | 0.06 | 0.06 | 56 | 0.07 | 0.21 | 36 | –0.06 | 0.17 |
| *Right governments* | | | | | | | | | |
| Unemployment $u$ – expected sign positive | | | | | | | | | |
| $\Sigma\zeta_1$ | 93 | 0.10 | –0.03 | 67 | 0.01 | –0.04 | 34 | 0.41 | 0.00* |
| $\Sigma\zeta_2$ | 162 | 0.26 | 0.06(*) | 122 | 0.20 | 0.07 | 56 | 0.54 | 0.14* |
| Price rises $p$ – expected sign negative | | | | | | | | | |
| $\Sigma\zeta_1$ | 93 | 0.01 | 0.03 | 67 | –0.07 | –0.04 | 34 | –0.12 | –0.12 |
| $\Sigma\zeta_2$ | 162 | 0.00 | 0.09 | 122 | 0.02 | 0.07 | 56 | –0.14 | –0.04 |
| Real growth rate $y$ – expected sign unclear | | | | | | | | | |
| $\Sigma\zeta_1$ | 93 | –0.05 | –0.16 | 67 | –0.04 | –0.22(*) | 34 | –0.06 | –0.24 |
| $\Sigma\zeta_2$ | 162 | –0.09 | –0.20* | 122 | –0.03 | –0.21* | 56 | –0.18 | –0.21 |
| Growth in public consumption $c$ – expected sign negative | | | | | | | | | |
| $\Sigma\zeta_1$ | 93 | 0.05 | –0.05 | 67 | 0.10 | 0.01 | 34 | –0.12 | –0.29(*) |
| $\Sigma\zeta_2$ | 162 | –0.02 | –0.01 | 122 | 0.05 | 0.02 | 56 | –0.07 | –0.25(*) |

*Note*: $\zeta_1$ tests for one-year blips and $\zeta_2$ tests for two-year blips.

blip test $\zeta_1$ this corresponds to the number of governments, i.e. in Australia there are three left governments of which all had a majority, but only two first left governments, it means that one was re-elected.

{C2} $\zeta_1(x)$ gives the results for the raw series.

{C3} $\zeta_1(x^d)$ gives the results for the corresponding domestic component.

The following signs are used to indicate significance of the two tests for $\zeta(x)$ and $\zeta(u^d)$:

* If at least one of the tests is significant, with expected sign, at the 5 per cent level.
(*) If at least one of the tests is significant, with expected sign, at the 10 per cent level.
! If at least one of the tests is significant, but with wrong sign, at the 5 per cent level.
(!) If at least one of the tests is significant, but with wrong sign, at the 10 per cent level.

Table 14.6 gives only the $\Sigma$-lines, but here we include the results for all four series and for both the one- and two-year blips $\zeta_1$ and $\zeta_2$.

## 5.1 Discussing the Test Results

Tables 14.8 and 14.9 give the results for the one-year blips, using $\zeta_1$, in the unemployment rate and the inflation rate, while Table 14.10 gives the results for the $\Sigma$-line for both tests $\zeta_1$ and $\zeta_2$ for all four series. Several points are interesting to note:

(A1) None of the results for the individual countries gives significant results, but there are so few that it is almost impossible to get significance. However, for the $u$- and the $p$-series the $\Sigma$-lines are significantly different (at a high level) between left and right governments in the direction expected.
(A2) In most cases the test results are stronger for the raw series than for the domestic components, as in the Hibbs-cycle tests. We shall discuss this point in the conclusion below.
(A3) Comparing the three types, $[g1]$, $[g2]$ and $[g3]$, the results are always strongest for the first governments $[g3]$ – the ones that Alesina terms 'regime shifts'.[12]
(A4) The results for the one-year and the two-years blips are almost equally good; but to the extent that there is a systematic difference, it is to the advantage of the one-year-blip.
(A5) The USA constitutes an exception. There are no signs of the Alesina cycle in the USA. But the USA is the country where the Hibbs-cycle performs the best, so it is no wonder that the USA is the country analysed by Hibbs in his original paper presenting the partisan cycle.

Altogether, this would seem to indicate that the Alesina-type partisan cycle is a fairly strong phenomenon. However, there are several awkward pieces of evidence that are clearly a part of the empirical picture of post-election blips; but which nevertheless seem to belong to a different story. We shall briefly mention two such awkward pieces of evidence.

### 5.2    The Labour Market Climate and Political Changes

The first one is that in a significant number of cases, left political victories have been followed by a wave of strikes.[13] The evidence is presented in Paldam and Pedersen (1982 and 1984). The most dramatic cases have occurred when the change to the left was deemed to be particularly large. The two most famous cases (where the level of strikes rose more than 20 times) – France in 1936 and Chile in 1970 – are outside our data. We can probably say that these cases constitute genuine regime shifts; but significant coefficients occur in half the countries covered.

A key reason why post-election blips occur in the Alesina theory is that wages cannot adjust before a wage-contract expires. However, strikes lead to wage-drift, so what we see is clearly a grassroot attempt to adjust wages to the new possibilities. This gives a post-election inflation blip; but through a mechanism that is very different from the one modelled by Alesina. In fact, it is the contract-constrained labour market that reacts to the government change and not the government.

### 5.3    Some Concrete Stories

The second one follows when we look at cases. Two of the most prominent cases of a post-election left-wing blip occurred in France in 1981/82 and Sweden in 1982/83: In France the blip took place during the first years of the left government, starting in mid-1981 after the two victories of Francois Mitterand – at the presidential and the parliamentary elections – after many years of non-socialist rule. In Sweden the blip occurred during the first two years of the Social Democratic government of Oluf Palme returning to power after six years of right governments (a shocking event in Sweden, interrupting forty years of Social Democratic rule). When one read up the relevant issues of the Economist and the OECD Economic Surveys the two stories look very similar (and, furthermore, they look like many similar stories).

The stories run like this:

1. The left has been in opposition for a long time, but now they have a *Big Plan* for a new policy. The plan calls for an expansion which will increase employment substantially. The plan furthermore contains some trick which is supposed to make the expansion unproblematic, i.e. it prevents inflation and a balance-of-payments deterioration.
2. The left then wins the election and starts to implement the Big Plan.
3. The expansion actually occurs; unemployment goes down, but the trick does not work: the rate of inflation goes up and the balance-of-payments deteriorates.
4. After a year or two the plan is abandoned, and the bad old 'conservative' policy is reintroduced.

One may argue that this is in accordance with the theory; but the story does not reflect rational expectations on the part of all agents. In fact, the majority of the voters (or at least a crucial number of swing-voters) turns out to have irrational expectations. Whether the leaders of the left believe in the 'Big Plan' is hard to know; but the whole point surely is that a crucial number of agents have expectations that are wrong in a systematic way.

### 5.4 Conclusion as Regards the Alesina Partisan Cycle

We conclude that there is an 'animal' in the data looking a lot like the Alesina RE partisan cycle. It is not confined to a few countries; but it is, as yet, a fairly debatable creature, which should be further investigated.

## 6 CONCLUSIONS

The results are easy to sum up: *some key variables, notably unemployment and inflation, contain a significant number of cases of post-election blips, where the direction depends upon the orientation of the government*, as predicted by Alesina's theory of RE-partisan cycles (where RE stands for rational expectations). The blips are probably closer to one year than two years long. The findings are well in accordance with the literature (see Alesina, 1989; and Alesina and Roubini, 1991) except for the USA as will be discussed in a moment, but our results cover a larger data set and the analysis uses a different statistical technique.

It is hard to say if one should have expected to find a relatively strong or weak partisan cycle in the USA. On the one hand is the impression that the difference between left and right is relatively small in the USA, so we expect to find stronger cycles elsewhere. On the other hand the US economy is relatively closed, and therefore the US series are likely to contain relatively exogenous international elements, so domestic cycles should stand out more clearly. However, our attempt to purge the series of the international elements did make the results marginally weaker in the average country.

In Paldam (1991a) the same data are analysed for Hibbs NE Partisan Cycles (where NE stands for no expectation). They should, as explained in Sections 1 and 2 above, appear as ideologically generated trends in the series. Since trends give more structure to test we get much more degrees of freedom in the tests; but we nevertheless find that the NE-version of the partisan cycle is weaker, but still significant, in the data than the RE-version. The RE-cycle is, in fact, a more commonly found phenomena than Hibbs's original NE-cycle. As for the RE-cycle it also decreased the significance of the NE-cycles when the series were purged for the international elements.

It is worth mentioning that earlier work (Paldam, 1979 and 1981a) using data for 1948 to 1975 only, testing for one-period election cycles, did find that many economic variables have a weak, but significant, cyclicality over the average election period; but, as mentioned in Section 1, this cycle did not look as it should according to the theory.

The Alesina RE-version of the partisan cycle looks remarkably different from Hibbs's NE-version of the theory,[14] as shown in Figure 14.1. It is clear from the detailed results that most often we get either the one or the other in the results or a particular government. In most countries we find specimens of both types of cycles. However, the US data appear to contain only the Hibbs-type NE-cycle. This is contrary to the findings of Alesina himself (see his 1987 and all later papers mentioned). Perhaps the explanation is that Alesina gets the best results for the growth rate of real GDP – our $y$ variable – and that he takes account of the mid-term elections. We find that the results for $y$ are relatively weak, and the mid-term election only appears in our analysis as a factor that may change the stability of the US government (i.e. it only enters in the definition of $g2$). In any case it should be noted that the results for the USA *are an outlier*, as is often the case in comparative economic studies.

This leaves us in a situation that is not altogether pleasant. On the one hand, we have found significant partisan cycles. On the other hand, we have found that both types of partisan cycles are significant. The only real difference between the two versions of the partisan cycle is the way that expectations are formed. It would have been an important result if we had found such clear difference between the number of cases where the two types of cycles appear that we could have drawn strong conclusions as to how expectations are formed. Our results do give an edge to rational expectations; but it is far from being a clear victory.

Let us finally return to the two questions posed in the first lines of the paper: does politics matter? and do policies matter? We can now answer both questions in the affirmative: *yes, politics matters*, and *yes, policies matter*; but we have to add to both answers: *but not very much*.

**Notes**

* Flemming Nielsen has provided research assistance. The paper is one of a sequence of two, where the other Paldam (1991) tests for Hibbs's non-expectations theory of partisan cycles using the same data. The two papers are written with about 30 per cent overlapping so as to be independently readable. The text has benefited from discussions with Jan Rose Sørensen, Jan Trosborg (who has recalculated my analysis, using a more normal regression technique – almost as Alesina and Roubini, 1991) and, in particular, Doug Hibbs. I am grateful also for help from Viggo Høst, and comments from Alberto Alesina, Michael Beenstock, Sven Berg, Daniel Heymann and Ben-Zion Zilberfarb.
1. However, the loss has a larger s.d. in presidential systems (i.e in the USA) than in parliamentary systems.
2. If, for a moment, we look upon the average loss in a RE-perspective it appears logical that the average government rules exactly as the rational voter must have expected. Hence, it is illogical that it should lose 1.6 per cent of the vote.
3. The kick-the-rascals-out asymmetry has not fared well in subsequent research. It has actually (almost) disappeared in the subsequent large literature on the VP-function. It is interesting to note, however, that the VP-function in the particularly flexible form modelled by Hibbs produces

a result as requested by the kick-the-rascals-out asymmetry.

4. Depending upon the pay-off from having one's expectations improved one gets a whole spectrum of RE-models: the adaptive pattern of expectation formation is the extreme case where the pay-off from improved expectations is small relative to the cost. We follow the tradition of concentrating on the reverse extreme, where the costs of improving one's expectations are small relative to the pay-off. We shall reserve the name RE for that case.

5. It is perhaps a problem to know just how large movements in the policy variables the agents may absorb – it is easy to imagine changes known, for example, two years in advance, that are so big that it is impossible for most agents to make the full adjustment at the day the policy change is announced. But it is obvious that such small cycles as the ones we are discussing must be absorbable.

6. A literature analysing this idea is already quickly emerging (though most is available only as working papers as this is being written), see, for example, the references in Sørensen (1988).

7. Another formulation would be to claim that most people can gain very little from having improved expectations, and that it is time-consuming to improve one's expectations, so that it is entirely rational to have myopic, adaptive expectations on the mass level. And as we know that politicians, trade union leaders, etc., have to sell their policies to their clients at the mass level, then surely the mass level must influence policy-making at the top level too.

8. The trade weights are constructed with five years apart, using a matrix giving the sum of all imports and exports from and to each of the seventeen countries to and from each of the others. By setting the rest of the world to zero, and normalising each row in the matrix to sum to 1, we have the weights used. The years in between are reached by linear interpolation. The construction of the series is further discussed in Paldam (1990).

9. This means that we exclude a few governments which break down, presumably because they fail to agree upon a policy.

10. In the USA a majority demands a majority in both houses in our definition.

11. The first and only socialist government in Japan (from 1949 to 1952) is at the start of the period, a period where Japan was also ruled by the US military government of Douglas MacArthur.

12. The author does not like the term 'regime shift', as it is used in different ways by different authors. However, it has a special meaning in the RE-literature. And to use the term for government shifts between parties having different ideologies makes more sense than most other uses.

13. The strikes appear as an increase in $s_n$, the sheer number of conflicts, measuring labour unrest at the grassroot level.

14. In the newest development Hibbs (1991) presents a model that has RE formed by a learning process; thereby the Hibbs model converges towards the Alesina formulation.

# References

Åkerman, J. (1946), *Ekonomiskt skeende och politiska forändringan* (Lund.) (also *Kyklos*, vol. 1, 1947).

Alesina, A. (1987) 'Macroeconomic Policy in a Two-Party System as a Repeated Game', *Quarterly Journal of Economics* vol. 102: 651–677.

Alesina, A. (1988) 'Macroeconomics and Politics', *NBER Macroeconomic Annual 1988* (Cambridge, Massachusetts: MIT Press).

Alesina, A. (1989) 'Politics and Business Cycles in Industrial Democracies', *Economic Policy*, no 8.

Alesina, A. and Sachs, J. (1988) 'Political Parties and the Business Cycle in the United States, 1948–1984', *Journal of Money, Credit and Banking*, vol. 20, pp. 63–82.

Alesina, A. and Rosenthal, H. (1988) 'Partisan Cycles in Congressional Elections and the Macroeconomy' (forthcoming) in the *American Political Science Review*, June 1989, pp. 63–82.

Alesina, A. and Roubini, N. (1991) *Political Cycles*, Conference Paper, NBER.

Begg, D. K. H. (1982) *The Rational Expectations Revolution in Macroeconomics. Theories & Evidence* (Oxford: Phillip Allen).

Bloom, H. S. and Price, H. D. (1975) 'The Effects of Aggregate Economic Variables on Congressional Elections' (an article in the discussion on Kramer, 1971) *American Political Science Review*, vol. 69, pp. 1232–69.

Castles, F. C. (1981) 'How does Politics Matter?: Structure or Agency in the Determination of Public Policy Outcomes', *European Journal of Political Research*, vol. 9, pp. 119–32.

Cukierman, A. and Meltzer, A. H. (1986) 'A Positive Theory of Discretionary Policy: The Cost of a Democratic Government and the Benefits of a Constitution', *Economic Inquiry*, vol. 24, pp. 367–88.

Hibbs, D. A., Jr (1977) 'Political Parties and Macroeconomic Policy', *American Political Science Review*, vol. 71, no 4, pp. 1467–87 (reprinted in Hibbs, 1987a).

Hibbs, D. A., Jr (1986) 'Political Parties and Macroeconomic Policies and Outcomes in the United States', *American Economic Review*, papers and proceedings, vol. 76, 66–70.

Hibbs, D. A., Jr (1987a) *The Political Economy of Industrial Democracies* (Cambridge, Massachusetts: Harvard University Press).

Hibbs, D. A., Jr (1987b) *American Political Economy: Macroeconomics and Electoral Policy in the United States* (Cambridge, Massachusetts: Harvard University Press).

Hibbs, D. A., Jr (1991) *The Partisan Model of Macroeconomic Cycles: More Theory and Evidence for the United States*, Conference Paper, FIEF, Stockholm.

Høst, V. and Paldam, M. (1990) 'An International Element in the Vote? A Comparative Study of seventeen OECD countries 1946–85, forthcoming in *European Journal of Political Research*, vol. 18, no 1 or 2.

Jonung, L. and Laidler, D. (1988) 'Are Perceptions of Inflation Rational? Some Evidence from Sweden', *American Economic Review*, vol. 71, pp. 1080–87.

Kalecki, M. (1943) 'Political Aspects of Full Employment', reprinted in *Selected Essays: On the Dynamics of the Capitalist Economy* (Cambridge: Cambridge University Press 1971).

Kramer, G. H. (1971) 'Short-Term Fluctuations in US Voter Behavior, 1896–1964', *American Political Science Review*, vol. 65, pp. 131–43.

Lafay, J. D., Lewis-Beck, M. and Norpoth, H. (eds) (1991) *Economics and Elections in United States and Western Europe* (Michigan: Michigan University Press).

MacRae, D. C. (1977) 'A Political Model of the Business Cycle', *Journal of Political Economy*, vol. 85, pp. 239–63.

Minford, P. and Peel, D. (1981) 'The Political Theory of the Business Cycle', *European Economic Review*, vol. 17, pp. 253–70.

Mueller, J. E. (1970) 'Presidential Popularity from Truman to Johnson', *American Political Science Review*, vol. 64, pp. 18–34.

Nordhaus, W. D. (1975) 'The Political Business Cycle', *Review of Economic Studies*, vol. 42, pp. 169–90.

Paldam, M. (1979) 'Is there an Election Cycle? A Comparative Study of National Accounts', *Scandinavian Journal of Economics*, vol. 81, pp. 323–42.

Paldam, M. (1981a) 'An Essay on the Rationality of Economic Policy: The Test-Case of the Electional Cycle', *Public Choice*, vol. 37, pp. 287–305.

Paldam, M. (1981b) 'A Preliminary Survey of the Theories and Findings on Vote and Popularity Functions', *European Journal of Political Research*, vol. 9, pp. 181–99.

Paldam, M. (1983) 'The International Element in Economic Fluctuations of 20 OECD-Countries 1948–75', *Regional Science and Urban Economics*, vol. 13, pp. 429–54.

Paldam, M. (1986) 'The Distribution of Election Results and the Two Explanations of the Cost of Ruling', *European Journal of Political Economy*, vol. 2, no 1, pp. 5–24.

Paldam, M. (1990) 'Wage Rises and the Balance of Payments: A Study of the Reaction Lags', Working Paper, Institute of Economics, Aarhus University, Denmark.

Paldam, M. (1991a) 'Politics Matters After All (2). Testing Hibbs' Theory of Partisan Cycles on Data for 17 Countries', in A. L. Hillman (ed.) *Markets and Politicians* (Boston: Kluwer).

Paldam, M. (1991b) 'How Robust is the Vote Function? A Comparative Study of 197 Elections in the OECD Area 1948–85', in Lafay, Lewis-Beck and Norpoth (1991).

Paldam, M. and Pedersen, P. J. (1982) 'The Macroeconomic Strike Model: A Study of Seventeen Countries, 1948–1975', *Industrial and Labor Relations Review*, vol. 35, no 4, pp. 504–21.

Paldam, M. and Pedersen, P. J. (1984) 'The Large Pattern of Industrial Conflict – A Comparative Study of 18 Countries, 1919–79', *International Journal of Social Economics*, vol. 11, no. 5, pp. 3–26.

Sørensen, J. R. (1988) 'The Political Business Cycle in a Rational Expectations Model with two Political Parties', paper for the European Public Choice Meeting 1989.

# Comment

Carsten Heyn-Johnsen
UNIVERSITY OF AALBORG, DENMARK

## ECONOMIC FLUCTUATIONS AND POLITICS – WHAT CONNECTIONS?

Time-series of economic data show fluctuations. At least since the Book – the old part of it – was thought out, people expect and even observe some regularity in these fluctuations. That fat and lean years follow one another is a part of our conception of life, whether we are ubiquitarians or not.

In economics we have tried to rationalise and model these fluctuations as cycles for at least 150 years. The endeavour has been either:

(i) to show how exogenous shocks trigger off cycles. It is the impulse-propagation picture, where the impulse is exogenous and the propagation is determined by the economic system, i.e. endogenous; or to

(ii) have the economic system producing the fluctuations by itself as one of the characters of the said system.

If we include the historical and societal fact of government in our analysis, be it as an exogenous impulse-producing agent or as a part of the economic system, the question could be framed, 'does the institution of government influence the economic time-series, and if so, how?'

For a start, one would – without the aid of too much sophistication – assume that a potent government, i.e. a government with a workable parliamentary majority, will pursue its goals in diverse political areas. Many of these endeavours could have identifiable economic and even macroeconomic ramifications.

In our context the question is, will the actual policy of governments change the course of the economy over time as compared with the figment of a course, that would install itself in the absence of any government at all or a government that, in some relevant sense, was

399

neutral *vis-à-vis* what we conventionally understand by the economic sphere.

To be more specific – in the real world – will the inevitable state or governmental interference in the economic sphere even change the counterfactual course in a way that manifests itself as cycles?

To answer this question we have first to conceptualise and quantify the imagined dynamic course of the economy. In short, we have to establish a 'reference path'. To separate analytically what empirically occurs as an assumed combined result, is a task for speculative, pure theory.

The next step would be to expose the actual governmental actions. Our assumption would imply that they express the goals of the government either as means or ends in themselves. *If* these actions move the economy on a path that differs from the reference path, they could generate cycles, provided that the actual path is not sustainable for political or pure economic reasons. In the more encompassing political business-cycle theories of the Marx–Kaleckian variety, where distribution is the focal point, the distinction between political and economic reasons is of course meaningless.

By contrast, in the dominating business-cycle theories the economic reasons for the unsustainability of the Political path are stressed. The empirical hidden course – the reference path – is set to play a dominating role as a causal force in the economy, which will sooner or later redress every deviation from the reference path. This is expressed in various ways in Paldam's short survey of these theories. Here some remnants of the Phillips curve will do the job, or rational expectation equilibrium may be brought in. It can be conditioned by some degree of myopia, to overcome the otherwise consequential inefficiency of any policy, eventually with the agent's faculty of learning from experience kept intact, to prevent a deviation to last too long. Rates of change in different quantities are coined natural or long run values, etc.

This all points to the obvious, *chosen* theoretical necessity of an economic force to generate the cycle, once politics has caused a deviation from the reference path. But it seems that the political business-cycle theories apply economic theory in a rather casual way. And in the paper at issue, not much is done to purge the different-named versions from inconsistencies in the encircling of a reference path. Predictably this causes some trouble in interpretation of the alleged findings.

Paldam's paper sets out to test the plausibility of the so-called partisan cycles, (re)introduced in the discussion by Hibbs and Alesina, on data covering seventeen OECD-countries for the period 1948–85 – a rather comprehensive range.

What is tested is whether *changes* in the political orientation of government generate cycles. Governments are classified as right or left following their presumed scales of preferences, with the components: rate of unemployment, inflation, growth in real income and public consumption. The distinction right and left is taken as ideological in a quite pedestrian way.

To be right-wing means, for example, that to minimise the rate of inflation is a more important goal than to increase employment and vice versa for the left-wing. So if, as is assumed in this case, there is a real, active, trade-off between unemployment and inflation, a shift from right to left in government will reduce unemployment and enhance inflation, and vice versa. Both these opposite outcomes must be unsustainable, if we have the expected cyclical results.

## The Hibbs Version

In Paldam's presentation the Hibbs version of the partisan cycle has this unsustainability as a political phenomenon. The assumed inflation–unemployment trade-off calls forth a change in policy through elections. The stylised sequences are: right-wing policy → rising unemployment, election → left-wing policy → rising inflation, election → right-wing policy → rising unemployment, etc. The cycle in the two time-series is extended over two election periods.

The shift in government is endogenised by an assumed assymetric behaviour of the electorate. There has to be a change in government in the right-left dimension, as it is defined, to call forth the cycles. 'However, this is a rather dubious theory empirically'. But even then, the indisputable fact that governments do change, will ensure that the cycle establishes itself sooner or later. According to Paldam's own findings, there is even a stable relation, 'the losing votes by ruling' with an average loss of 1.6 per cent of the voters per election.

For some of the politically more stable countries – for example, Scandinavia – this leads to a partisan cycle with a duration of dozens of years. For these cases the force of the imagined reference path seems to have lost its power altogether, at least in an empirical sense. To anyone who is not a scholar in this special area it seems that this elaborate version of the partisan cycle, as it is thought out and inadequately supported by immediate empirical knowledge, can only be upheld as a case of *sapiente sat*.

We find that for a scholar it is somewhat disturbing too, this is reckoned by Paldam in his explicit reintroduction of the causal power of the reference path. There will be cycles looking like the Hibbs-cycle independent of changes in government, provided that we endogenise the policy along the lines proposed by Paldam: 'policies of repeated governments will change, perhaps in a systematic way as to converge to the long-run paths of the variables'.

So Paldam is inclined to contemplate a change in policy without a change in government; at least it is worth while to test for this possibility.

From here it is only a minor jump to the Alesina version of the partisan cycle – a shift in the time-series without a shift in policy.

**The Alesina Version**

Choosing the assumption of rational expectations – an assumption that by empirical luck in theoretical ill-luck has shown its vast area of non-applicability (Jonung and Laidler (1988) – to give theoretical leeway for partisan cycles necessitates the assumption of some temporary constraints on the behaviour of the public. Paldam mentions contracts as a possible real constraint.

In this construction, a change in government in the right–left direction will have an instantaneous effect on our data. There will be a jump to a new level. Necessity will force the data back to the assumed equilibrium trend at a speed determined by the nature of the constraints. The resulting empirical path is the Alesina blip. It will materialise irrespective of the actual policy or change in policy. Any deviation from the assumed equilibrium will be redressed, as the actions of the public neutralise the policy.

**The Paldam Test Results**

By organising the data for a Kendall test, eight time-series for each of the seventeen countries plus the recorded periods of right or left governments, Paldam tests for the Hibbs and Alesina type of coincidence in the time-series. The conclusion is that the Hibbs version is not too convincing for countries other than the USA. This conclusion is expressed rather cryptically 'But the USA is the country where the

Hibbs cycle performs best. So it is no wonder that the USA is the country analysed by Hibbs' (ibid. p. 391).

How does Paldam want us to interprete this? No wonder that Hibbs was misled by using the US-data-induction for an erroneous generalisation; no wonder that the US-data are used to substantiate a speculative preconception. Be this as it may, the Alesina version of the partisan cycle is a more important phenomenon than the Hibbs version.

Accepting the results of the statistical tests we see a degree of concatenation in time between changes in government and the trend in the selected time-series. The results depend on the assumption that the data sets for different periods of government are *independent*. And, as far as the paper takes us, on a not-too-clear treatment of the fact that there can be ties in the data. This is the impression to which one is led reading the passage where Paldam mentions that there is an equal probability of 50 per cent for a rise or fall in the value of consecutive observations. This excludes the possibilities of ties. If these ties were included in the test, what *a priori* probability should the, now three, possible outcomes be assigned?

What the assumption of independence and this exclusion imply for the asserted significance of the coincidence of governments and trends, let alone any causality therein, is not quite clear in Paldam's paper. Probably it is not out of the question that a sensitivity test, on these two caveats, could disturb the part of Paldam's conclusion already mentioned.

One might add that, although the test chosen by Paldam reveals that if the trends in the data are significant and compatible with the assumed or expected directions, the amplitude of the deviations of the cycles or blips disappear in the preparation of the raw data for this test. It is quite possible to have significant trends and at the same time to have insignificant amplitudes: that is, to have variations between consecutive observations that lie within an expected area of measurement errors. With data for seventeen countries for the named period, this possibility seems highly probable. The paper does not allow an evaluation of this.

Leaving this aside, there are some more fundamental points to be made on the concluded significance of the Alesina blips.

**What 'Animal' are we Looking For?**

In the data Paldam sees 'an animal looking a lot like the Alesina RE partisan cycle' (ibid, p. 393). This is acknowledged as somewhat paradoxical. As we know from the study by Jonung and Laidler (1988) the public cannot be assumed to be informed at a level which makes it sensible to rely on a behaviour in accordance with the hypothesis of rational expectations. But if there are Alesina blips, they can only be brought about, be rationalised by alluding to a rational-expectation equilibrium exercising its normative power on the public's behaviour. If the 'animal' is there – that is, if the results of the test can be upheld, it looks very much like a case of measuring and testing without a consistent theory. For instance, do we get any hints on where we should look for it in the taxomony of species? Therefore, the conclusion '*Politics matters*', to assert even a causality, seems – at least to a non-scholar in this particular field – premature.

This brings us to the last point: '*yes, policies matter*' (Paldam, p. 395) It is a rather strange procedure to have not much more than the presupposition that 'politics matters' and then, as the next step, to transform this into a fact from which the much stronger statement, 'policies matter' follows. This latter is undoubtedly meant to be a statement expressing a causality from deliberately executed policies to changes in economic trends.

Even if one is catholic to an extreme in the matter of research methods in the social sciences, it seems devastatingly platonic-Friedmanian (Chicago-Milton) to picture deliberately executed policies, called ideology, by the assumed effects of these policies only. To conclude that policies matter, without recording these policies by their deliberately executed elements rather than their assumed effects, seems somewhat inconclusive. And Paldam gives us only the data on public consumption as a direct clue to the policies actually carried through.

It would undoubtedly enhance the possibility of reaching intelligible conclusions on the posed question: 'do policies matter?', if these policies were directly incorporated in the testing procedure. Albeit the data-collection would inevitably be rather hard work the reward would be some conclusive elements contributing to the general endeavour to grasp the phenomenon of empirical shifts in trends in economic time-series.

## Note

* In his presentation at the conference Professor Paldam included results of the test of the Hibbs cycles as well. I have taken the liberty of including my comments on these since the contrast seems interesting.

## Reference

Jonung, L. and Laidler, D. (1988) 'Are Perceptions oʟ Inflation Rational? Some Evidence from Sweden', *American Economic Review*, vol. 71, pp. 1080–87.

# Part VIII

# Panel Discussion and Closing Speech

# 15  Panel Discussion

# A Will the Business Cycle Ever Be Obsolete in Industrial Societies? I

Michael Bordo

UNIVERSITY OF SOUTH CAROLINA, USA

Varied answers to this question can be derived from the papers at this conference. On one hand the answer depends on how one defines cycles. If one views cycles as some regular phenomenon demarcated by time duration as people used to do – that is, set up a chronology beginning at the long end of the spectrum with Kondratieff or long-wave cycles of fifty years or more and then Kuznets cycles (of twenty years), Juglar cycles (of nine years), Kitchin cycles (of three to four years), inventory cycles (eighteen months) etc., the answer might be yes. However, as exhibited in the discussion on long waves or the recent literature critically evaluating NBER reference-cycle chronologies, there is considerable doubt that such phenomena exist. If one views cycles as economic fluctuations – irregular disturbances – then it seems likely we will always have them as long as we live in a stochastic world with changing tastes, technologies, national disasters, wars, imperfect government policies, etc.

Closely related to this are the methods used to identify and measure fluctuations – to distinguish between trends and cycles. In this respect I found the paper by Lippi and Reichlin to be the most useful at the conference. It summarises the recent literature in the neoclassical real business-cycle tradition using time-series analysis. Although the evidence suggests that real GNP can be characterised by a difference stationary process, the importance of permanent changes in it in the total variation of real GNP is questionable.

An answer to the question posed by this panel also depends on the theoretical approaches taken to explain cyclical phenomena (economic fluctuations). What are the key causes of such fluctuations and how are they propagated? The conference's answers to these questions are varied. If you believe in Keynesian fixed-price models, then any nominal or real shocks will lead to changes in output. The addition of dynamic elements gives a cycle. This also holds if one follows new Keynesian lines with small frictions or new classical lines with asymmetric information – both assuming rational expectations. Real business-cycle models with continuous market-clearing and productivity shocks also give fluctuations.

Perhaps a more important issue than which is the best story is whether the underlying model is one where the economy if left alone returns to stability in a reasonable length of time (after being shocked), or whether prolonged instability and some outside (government) intervention is required.

Several useful papers at this conference combined theory with evidence. Thus the two historical papers by Capie and Eichengreen provided evidence respectively on whether monetary forces and the exchange-rate regime are important determinants of the cycle, while Paldam and Hibbs provided empirical insights into the existence and nature of political business cycles. However a question not answered by either was whether cycles were caused or exacerbated by political factors.

A key theme which dominated the conference and which is perhaps basic to an answer to the question posed is methodological – how do you model the cycle? Some argued for a general dynamic non-linear systems approach stressing the theory of chaos.

A final theme is the endogenous/exogenous nature of fluctuations. One view is that shocks are external to basic microeconomic organisms, another view suggested by John McCall's thought-provoking lecture is that there are fluctuations in human organisms at the neurological level which lie at the basis of preferences. Such fluctuations may be at the root of instability in economic activity.

# B Will the Business Cycle Ever Be Obsolete in Industrial Societies? II

Bjorn Thalberg
UNIVERSITY OF LUND, SWEDEN

In attempting to answer the question, I would wish to resume a connection with certain sessions of this conference. As my point of departure, I take the introductory survey by Professor Velupillai (Chapter 1). Velupillai mentioned, as the first mathematical model of the cycle, Frisch's model (in the *Festschrift* to Cassel, 1933); stressing *inter alia*, the dichotomy between impulse and propagation mechanism, which Frisch elaborated, but which goes back at least to the famous rocking-horse analogy of Wicksell (1918). The Frisch class of model is interpreted in terms of linear models with exogenous shocks (even though Frisch himself did not advocate linearity, and operated in fact with a kind of ceiling on upward expansion). As a second type of basic mathematical model of the cycle, Velupillai noted the non-linear model of Goodwin which appeared in 1951 – the year before the IEA Conference on 'The Business Cycle in the Post-war World' in Oxford in 1952.

At the Oxford conference, it may be noted, the participants could claim that for the time being the business cycle was in fact obsolete since the long post-war boom could be expected to last for a few more years. This prediction followed convincingly from the simple non-linear model of Goodwin. Production of capital goods, even running at capacity, still needed quite some time to eliminate the enormous gap between desired and existing level of capital stock which had developed during the 1940s as a result of extraordinary wear and tear, lack of replacement investments, a wave of technical inventions, as well as an extraordinary population growth and a strong demand for public investments. However, even though cyclical fluctuations were not an actual problem of the day, the participants of the Oxford conference considered it a basic problem of industrial economies which would sooner or later reappear.

411

The suggested simple explanation of the very long post-war boom illustrates the explanatory power of Goodwin's basic model. The Frisch model also accounts in a simple and elementary way for some fundamental features of the cycle phenomenon. In this model, the propagation mechanism, which represents structural properties of the economy, converts shocks into cyclical fluctuations around a possible steady-state path, i.e. cyclical fluctuations which, because of the more or less independent erratic shocks, are so irregular and unpredictable that it may be almost futile to make a forecast of the phase of the cycle for more than say three quarters ahead (a confidence interval for longer periods may include the whole amplitude). The Frisch model thus explained an old experience, mentioned by the way by Muth in his seminal article on rational expectations, that economists as a rule are not capable of making a profit from commodity speculation, selling information, etc. (a fact which, in contrast, Muth took as evidence that people have rational expectations).

The very structure of the Frisch model, i.e. that the cycle is explained, in Frisch's own words, by a 'synthesis between the stochastical point of view and the point of view of rigidly determined dynamical laws', may give us an idea why cyclical fluctuations will always be present in industrial economies. Most probably, what we describe as erratic shocks which cause variables to differ from their steady-state levels will also be a realistic phenomenon in the future. Shocks of different kinds and strength, we may safely continue to assume, are all the time impinging on our model of the economy. If this model, i.e. the propagation mechanism, generates damped time-paths, the shocks keep cyclical fluctuations alive. If, in contrast, intrinsic forces of the propagation mechanism tend to produce un-damped solutions, non-linearities in the form of more or less rigid 'ceilings' and 'floors', are necessary part of a realistic model. In this case, cyclical fluctuations can be explained even in the absence of erratic shocks.

Moreover, as discussed in the session on political business-cycle theories, cyclical fluctuations may also come about as a result of systematic changes in economic policy variables. This theory rests on such very plausible assumptions as that politicians like to be re-elected, and that low unemployment and rapid growth appeal to voters, particularly on the voting day. This certainly is, and will continue to be, an independent source of cycles, even though the politicians are generally not able to control the economy as closely as they hope.

Thus, looking at the simple ideas behind the basic theories of the cycle, one obviously gets the feeling that the answer to the above question must be in the positive. However, since the cyclical fluctuations are highly irregular and unpredictable, people may occasionally find other names for the cycle phenomenon as well as other methods to analyse it, but basically the phenomenon remains the same.

**References**

Cassel G. (1933) Economic Essays in *Honour of Gustav Cassell* (London: George Allen & Unwin).
Wicksell K. (1918) Review of K. Perander: 'Goda och Dåliga Tider', *Ekonomisk Tidskrift*, vol. 19, pp. 66–75.

# C  Some Basic Aphorisms around Business Cycles

## Helge Brink
UNIVERSITY OF AALBORG, DENMARK

'Presumably not' seems to be a fairly safe and robust answer to the question if business cycles will ever be obsolete in industrial societies. But one will probably also be in a low-risk position even if the answer is sharpened to 'most certainly not'. And economists may draw consolation from this answer, since it might appear frustrating if business cycles vanished before we understood their full nature.

There is little doubt, however, that the character of the business cycle will change, especially if 'advanced societies' is substituted for 'industrial societies'. For instance, if one considers a robot economy it is doubtful whether there is any meaning to the word 'unemployment'. Nevertheless, there may still be some kind of business cycles in a post-industrial, diversified, specialised and market-organised society. In any case the story told in Charles Kindleberger's lecture will apply for quite a while, so we may safely go home from this conference and declare that . . . 'there will be business cycles for our time'.

A few years ago the main themes of a conference like this would most probably have centred on dichotomies such as real–monetary, equilibrium–disequilibrium, market-clearing – non-market-clearing; and the various consequences for economic policy would have been traced out. It was a surprising fact of this conference that such topics were relegated from centre stage, deposed by a renewing discussion about how to analyse business cycles. The talks given by Kumaraswamy Velupillai, Ralph Abraham and Richard Goodwin were leading in this respect, and each of them highly illuminating and inspiring. Even so there may be reasons to be cautious – a caution which is most certainly shared by some of the aforementioned.

Let me illustrate the competition between two important partitions by Figure 15.1 diagram which, with apology to Axel Leijonhufvud, I shall call the *Danish flag*. The columns refer to the familiar distinction between theories with market-clearing prices and those without.

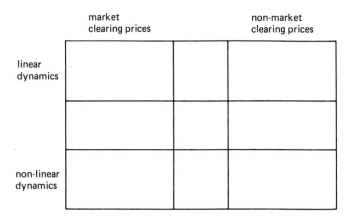

*Figure 15.1*   The Danish flag

The rows delineate the important difference between two methods of analysing the business cycle: linear dynamic models with stochastic shocks, and non-linear dynamic models, recently being analysed by the new mathematical tools for handling chaotic motions. These tools have highlighted important and complicated aspects of some – not necessarily complicated – non-linear dynamical systems, such as their ability to mimic stochastic motion and their critical dependence on (small) variations in initial conditions and parameter values. No wonder, then, that economists, like professionals in other sciences, have passionately welcomed this promising procedure. In the upper right corner of the flag we would find Keynesian versions of the business cycle such as most multiplier–accelerator models. However, forty years ago Goodwin had already moved to the lower right square and stayed there, convinced but rather lonely until the new wave of non-linear dynamical analysis. The upper left square would be occupied by new classical models of the business cycle, and they too may be dragged down by the irresistible gravity of the new body of mathematical thought. No doubt one could also find intermediate cases belonging to the cross of the flag, but to make the point the two-by-two cases will suffice.

While the horizontal barrier now seems highly permeable the vertical is still impenetrable. It is perhaps the most important barrier between different 'schools' of economic thought, and it is testimony to the underdeveloped state of economic theory that it has been with us almost as long as economics itself. It has a profound influence on

*Table 15.1*

| Causes | Sciences |
| --- | --- |
| Nature | physics, geography meteorology, ecology |
| Human nature | biology, psychology biopsychology, ethics |
| Human institutions | sociology, political science, economics |

the way we think about economic institutions and the way economic policy is being recommended and conducted. For example, are business cycles, though not obsolete, perhaps unimportant or even desirable as the most efficient response to exogenous disturbances? Surely, the answer is 'yes' from a market-clearing point of view and 'no' from the opposite view. In the latter case we have involuntary unemployment with serious economic and social consequences for the victims, and it makes good sense to ask whether one could get rid of the business cycle itself or at least mitigate its results.

It is in this state of affairs that it may be sidetracking to embrace the new tools with entirely unreserved enthusiasm. They seem much like an inexhaustible resource that may turn into a totem to which economic thinking and models must submit, at the promise of maximising the number of published articles, subject only to very loose constraints of relevance. This is not in any way to deny the vital importance of the new possibilities in dynamical analysis; it will surely become a vehicle for gaining insight into very complicated structures and for helping intuition in forming new ideas and methods. But it would be a pity if this prospect should hide the need for more basic work in economic theory.

Economics is a rather complacent science. This is so although, looking at the 'most basic' causes of business cycles it seems obvious that other sciences ought to be central to economic thinking. A list of the deeper sources of business cycles and the adjacent sciences or disciplines may look something like Table 15.1. Other branches of knowledge could have been listed, but those mentioned do have a relevance to the following.

If one includes, 'possible technologies' under the heading '*nature*' it becomes a very comprehensive concept. Until very recently it may have been fairly safe to regard 'nature' as given, and exploitable without limits. It has, however, become increasingly clear that nature has become endogenous to mankind's economic activities influencing the entire biosphere. We do not know, as yet, if a major disaster is approaching, but no one can any longer deny that it is a serious and perhaps likely possibility. Nevertheless, it is not reflected in economic thinking, either in pure growth models or in combined growth-cycles models. How should these models be changed or modified to take into account the erosion of their own foundation? Of course, I do not know the answer, but I know that the question has been swept under the carpet.

*Human nature* has long been taken to be thoroughly understood by economists. By contrast psychologists and philosophers are still struggling to grasp it. Unfortunately, the answers from our neighbouring sciences do not correspond too well with the single-minded concept of rational maximising individuals. It is true that some economists, notably Herbert Simon, have tried to follow new routes, and John McCall's work suggests other interesting research strategies; but otherwise economics is glued to the axiom of rational maximising behaviour.

The importance of this complaint can only be judged in the context of a microfoundation for macrodynamics. This discussion cannot be pursued here, but as an example new classical business-cycle theory is explicitly built on the individual rational maximiser. Indeed, it is a *sine qua non* for that theory, and the results are bound to reflect it. So also in macroeconomics, it is important that one's view of human nature reflects something also to be found in reality. That this is the case in economics is open to serious doubt.

*Human nature*, of course, is not sufficient in itself to create business cycles. Crusoe did not inflict cycles on himself. Neither did they appear after the arrival of Friday, since Defoe could not possibly imagine any rival practice to Crusoe's benevolent autocracy. There was no choice of institutions, as with ants and bees where business cycles, to the best of my knowledge, are also not found.

Human institutions are likely to be chosen for reasons other than economic efficiency. Even so they *may* give rise to efficiency, just as they *may* cause inefficiency as well as economic cycles. In the latter cases the question of economic policy arises, whether it is seen as a medium for improving economic performance, or as an institution which is the cause rather than the cure of inefficiency and cycles. These bifurcated views on economic policy are but a repercussion of the dichotomy of market-clearing versus non-market-clearing prices. As discussed above this separation was not a central theme of the conference, and consequently economic policy was reduced to a dinner-topic.

So the absence of policy discussions is hardly evidence of a sudden mass-psychosis resulting in collective conversion to 'policy ineffectiveness propositions'. However, it may be true that there was a certain relief, that we did not have to go 'through it all' again with the only prospect of increasing animosity more than scientific knowledge. If this interpretation is right, is it not a silent cry for more work on the foundations of our science, and its relation to other sciences?

As already stated economics is a rather complacent science. This, however, has to be qualified. The self-righteousness is shown only to the closest kin, the social sciences and humanities. Contrary to this the more distant physics is worshipped, and mathematics is exploited, sometimes thoughtlessly so. This qualification brings our two themes together. Economics, and consequently business-cycle theory, is in danger of over-exploiting one resource, not always usable, while at the same time underutilising another, possibly promising or even necessary.

# D Contribution to the Round Table

Marco Lippi
UNIVERSITÀ DEGLI STUDI DI MODENA

At the cost of over-simplification I begin by recalling that research on business cycle in the past two decades has concentrated upon two distinct approaches: the first – and more followed – is based on linear stochastic equations, while the second is underpinned by the analysis of deterministic non-linear equations. The issue, independently of whether the first or the second approach is taken up, consists in the attempt to reproduce the main features of aggregate macroeconomic data: within the linear-stochastic approach exogenous random shocks reproduce that irregularity in cycle period and amplitude which is typical of the macroeconomic time-series pattern; within the domain of non-linear models it has been shown that very complex dynamical patterns may be produced by means of quite simple equations.

In this short talk I shall first of all underline a weakness which, in my opinion, affects most of the recent literature, independently of whether it belongs to the first or to the second approach: namely, systematic neglect of the heterogeneity of economic agents, and consequent resort, more or less implicitly, to the representative agent; second, I shall suggest that the explicit introduction of hetero-geneity into the picture, instead of being only an analytic complica-tion, may represent a source of very interesting interpretations of macroeconomic data.

## 1 THE NEW MACROECONOMICS

Let us consider first the so-called 'new macroeconomics'. As is well-known new macroeconomics came over the stage with a sharp criticism toward Keynesian ad-hoceries, putting over as a scientific standard for macroeconomic models that:

1. economic agents optimise intertemporal objective functions;

2. agents are able optimally to exploit all the information to which they have access; this idea led to rational expectations;
3. prices and quantities are instantaneously set according to the Arrow–Debreu general equilibrium system.

Rational expectations had first been employed to explain the failure of macroeconomic models: in fact, under rational expectations the parameters of the processes generating the right-hand variables enter the behavioural equations (Lucas's critique). It might be argued – and it might have been argued when rational expectations were introduced – that such phenomena affect the relationships between aggregate macroeconomic data for reasons that go far beyond the rational expectations example. Indeed, the possibility that the parameters of an estimated macroequation were 'corrupted' by the covariances of the independent variables was well known since Theil's book on aggregation,[1] and has often been raised in various forms as an important issue: temporal aggregation, systematic sampling, unobserved components, aggregation over agents in a dynamic framework, all produce undesirable effects on all exogeneity relationships,[2] independently of any assumption on expectations formation. When considered as just one of the sources of such complication Lucas's critique could have been easily added to the list of reasons leading to strongly recommend sobriety in interpreting macroeconomic data.

But this is only what might have been argued, whereas the prevailing opinion of macroeconomists took a completely different route. The problem raised by Lucas was solved – i.e. it was shown, even though under very special assumptions, that the deep parameters might be recovered. Thus, from the initial negative role rational expectations became a crucial ingredient of macroeconometric models and could be submitted to statistical tests, even though jointly with other hypotheses. This might seem a happy conclusion if we forget those very special assumptions underlying the models: on one hand quite sophisticated intertemporal models for individual agents, but, on the other hand, total homogeneity: i.e. one single producer or consumer, according to the problem dealt with. Elsewhere I have made an attempt to show that the introduction of differences among agents into the dynamic models analysed in the new macroeconomics produces aggregation problems that are very difficult, if not impossible, to overcome.[3]

Naturally, once this sort of over-simplification is adopted, the claim that the macromodel is based on the Arrow–Debreu general equilibrium theory is not a very interesting statement. In fact, interesting issues within general equilibrium theory come out only when heterogeneity of agents and goods is taken into consideration. I shall recall here the well-known consequences of capital goods heterogeneity, which was at the centre of a heated debate in the 1960s and the early 1970s; and also the difficulties for *tâtonnement* processes which arise in pure consumption Walrasian models when only slight differences across the agents are allowed.[4]

In conclusion, I shall only observe that there is little point in employing such heavy guns to deal with individual agents if the whole model breaks down as soon as different tastes, incomes, dynamic reaction across agents are seriously considered.

## 2 NON-LINEAR EQUATIONS

Let me now come to the second approach: non-linear equations. I would like to quote here a passage from Lorenz's paper, which was discussed in a previous session: 'many recent business-cycle models are formulated in discrete time because this time concept appears to be adequate when the economic decision process is reduced to a single (or representative) optimising agent in the neoclassical tradition. However, when more than a single agent is involved, a continuous-time concept is the more adequate framework for studying dynamical phenomena because (optimal or non-optimal) individual decision processes and appropriate actions overlap and do not take place in periods with identical length and starting-points'.

I think this is a very clear argument in favour of continuous-time models. However, it must be admitted that the representative agent is usual also in the non-linear, possibly non-neoclassical, approach, and that this may have very serious consequences. Let us consider the issue of whether an empirical time-series has been generated by a stochastic or a deterministic non-linear equation. The idea underlying the possibility of testing such hypotheses is the following: in spite of a random aspect, if the data are generated by a deterministic non-linear equation they will contain a structure, and the latter should be detectable. Now, let us consider highly aggregated macroeconomic time-series like, for example, GNP or the consumer price index. Even if we assume that the individual series are generated by non-linear deterministic equations, but we allow for differences between individual microparameters, the structure will in general be lost through aggregation over huge numbers of microvariables. To understand the reason for this it will be sufficient to remember that the spectral representation of a stochastic process is nothing other than the reconstruction of the process as a sum of infinite cosine waves, and the latter do possess a very simple structure. I think that the above argument can be given a more rigorous form by stating that detection of structure in highly aggregated macroeconomic data would need an enormous number of observations, far beyond the sample size that is usually available.

## 3  MODELLING THE BUSINESS CYCLE

In conclusion, I want to express some scepticism upon modelling the business cycle without explicitly modelling differences and interactions between economic agents. Moreover, even though I am aware that I am referring to embryonic works, I would like to mention here, as examples of the opposite attitude, two recent papers by Silverberg *et al.* and by Arthur.[5] Neither of these articles contains complicated intertemporal optimisation schemes; rather, they are characterised by the effort to model relationships between different agents in a non-trivial way. In both cases important features of empirical technical change are reproduced, in particular the fact that adoption of a new productive method is not instantaneous is theoretically accounted for. The paper which L. Reichlin and I presented at this Conference contains an attempt – quite naïve, I feel bound to say – to analyse the consequences of such a vision of technical change on the interpretation of macroeconomic data.

### Notes

1. H. Theil, *Linear Aggregation of Economic Relationships* (Amsterdam, 1954).
2. See C. Sims, 'Discrete Approximations to Continuous Distributed Lags in Econometrics', 1970, *Econometrica*, no 38, pp. 545–64; M. Nerlove, P. M. Grether and J. L. Carvalho. *Analysis of Economic Time-Series*, (New York: John Wiley 1979) M. Lippi, 'On the Dynamic Shape of Aggregated Error Correction Models', 1988, *Journal of Economic Dynamics and Control*, no 121 pp. 561–85.

3. See Lippi, 'On the Dynamic Shape . . .'.
4. More precisely, even when all agents have the same preferences and different but collinear endowments (i.e. agents are endowed with different quantities of the same basket of goods). On this point see the recent article by A. Kirman, 'The Intrinsic Limits of Modern Economic Theory: The Emperor Has No Clothes', *Economic Journal*, vol. 99 (Conference 1989) pp. 126–39. For a general assessment of the Walrasian system, both as regards its original formulation and its modern version, see B. Ingrao and G. Israel, *La mano invisible*, 1987, Bari (an English translation is forthcoming).
5. G. Silverberg, G. Dosi and L. Orsenigo, 'Innovation, Diversity and Diffusion', 1988, *Economic Journal*, no 98 pp. 1032–54; W. B. Arthur, 'Competing Technologies, Increasing Returns, and Lock-In by Historical Events', 1989, *Economic Journal*, no 99, pp. 116–31.

# 16 Non-Linear Dynamics and Economic Evolution

Richard M. Goodwin
UNIVERSITÀ DEGLI STUDI DI SIENA

Since I am to be dealing with an aspect of evolution, I hope I may be forgiven for approaching the topic through my own evolution. When I was young I often said 'There is no bore like an old bore – but now, for some reason or other, I rarely repeat that view (though I have just done so)! So I shall be brief.

I entered Harvard in 1930 during the onset of possibly the worst-ever cyclical decline. It was an appropriate and interesting time to begin the study of business cycles; as a lapsed Marxist, I see a clear, causal link between the Great Depression and the birth of more rigorous and somewhat more mathematical business-cycle theories. Likewise I accept that my lifelong preoccupation with those theories springs from the dramatic impact of that period on the life and dim prospect of employment of my contemporaries and myself. My own initiation into serious study of economic cycles came chiefly through a marvelous seminar conducted during the year 1936–7 by Jacob Marschak in Oxford: we concentrated on a superior survey of the subject by Jan Tinbergen in *Econometrica*. In that seminar Marschak stated the rule that no one was allowed to use a concept for which he could not produce some numbers, or else state how, in principle, they could be found. At the same time I was being personally taught by Roy Harrod, who produced a small book on the *Trade Cycle*, from which I found my analytic problem for future use. He dynamised Keynes's statical *General Theory* by adding the accelerator to the multiplier, stating that the economy once growing would accelerate and thus grow faster than the full-employment barrier and hence break down. So having acquired a method from Marschak, I acquired my problem from Harrod, who had no idea how to formulate such a problem. Nor, I may add, had I, so that in my spare time I applied myself to it for the next decade. Happily I met Phillipe Le Corbeiller who

424

worked in the same physics laboratory as I did. He had written a short note in an early issue of *Econometrica* which told economists that they needed non-linear methods to deal with cycles – a warning totally ignored by economists, including Frisch, who shuld have known better. As a result I succeeded in combining the multiplier with the accelerator in such a way as to produce a limit cycle, thus providing an explanation for the continued existence of cycles in capitalism.

All previous theories of limit cycles had two non-linearities, an upper and a lower, usually in the form of a cubic. But my Harrod problem had only one non-linearity, that is, full employment. After some time, I managed to persuade myself, and finally Le Corbeiller that whereas two non-linearities were sufficient, only one was necessary and sufficient for a limit cycle.

Already in that multiplier–accelerator model of 1948, I introduced technological progress, so that the fixed point of the cycle was moved upward in the course of time. In 1952 at a conference in Oxford of the IEA on business cycles, I tried to deal with 'the simultaneous existence and mutual conditioning of economic growth and economic cycles'. (reprinted in my *Essays in Economic Dynamics*). I used a consumption function with hysteresis which helped to produce fluctuating growth.

At the First World Congress of the Econometric Society in Rome in 1965, I presented a significant improvement on the 1952 model, by formulating a model in terms of two variables defined as ratios. In that way I could have a stationary analysis of the dynamics in which, however, the variables were independent of scale and so defined as to produce growth. The system was an economic, non-stationary variant of the Lotka–Volterra prey–predator theory. At that point I felt that I had resolved Harrod's problem. Much later, however, Dick Day convinced me that chaotic analysis is important for economics, and it is in this form that I offer the following.

It is useful to visualise this remarkable conceptual advance in the following simple way. Poincaré generalised an equilibrium point to an equilibrium motion; a chaotic attractor generalises the motion to a bounded equilibrium region towards which all motions tend, or within which all motions remain; the conception of equilibrium is more or less lost since all degrees of aperiodic, or erratic fluctuations can occur within the region. The special relevance of this to economics is that it offers not *one* but *two* types of explanation of the pervasive irregularity of economic time-series – an endogenous one in addition to the conventional exogenous shocks. It will no doubt prove to be an exceedingly difficult and subtle problem for econometricians to disentangle the two. To me as an innocent un-econometric bystander, the answer seems simple and self-evident! Consider the Great Depression of the 1930s: can anyone seriously specify the exogenous shock which set that process in motion? And again, what shock produced the unanticipated, short, sharp cycle of 1937–8, so totally different in magnitude, shape and duration from its companion cycle? These two appear to me to be typical examples of chaotic dynamics. By the 1950s, I thought I had finally arrived at my goal of understanding cycles, only to be told that they no longer existed; both Schumpeter and Hansen, with their diametrically opposed views, were largely forgotten. Now in the 1980s, we are repeating the 1952 conference on business cycles! Chaotic dynamics warns us that we predict for the next two decades at our peril. Long ago Norbert Wiener, with the simplicity available only to mathematicians, said the industrial revolution removed much physical labour and that the cybernetic revolution would remove much mental labour.

When Schumpeter said that the cycle is simply the form growth takes, he was a generation ahead of most of his contemporaries – i.e. the equilibrium theorists, the cycle analysts, the growth-men. In part to embody his 'vision', I propose to consider a simple, schematic, aggregative model – an economic variant of Rössler's version of a chaotic attractor. The conditions required are:

1. an unstable fixed point but global stability;
2. endogenously generated morphogenesis in the form of changing productive structure;
3. aperiodic fluctuations in both short and long growth waves.

There are two state variables:

$v = L/N$, the ratio of employment to a constant labour force;
$u = wL/q = wa_Lq/q$, the share of wages (including salaries) in gross product, $q$, with $w$, the real wage and $a_L$ labour/output.

Net product consists solely of wages and profits; all wages and no profits being spent on consumption.

Both variables are measured in deviations from the fixed-point equilibrium, taken, for illustration, as 90 per cent of full employment. The real wage is assumed to increase faster than productivity when $v$ is positive and slower than productivity when $v$ is negative. It is helpful to think of wages as *predator* and profits as *prey*. The central dynamic is cyclical with $\dot{v} = -du$ and $\dot{u} = +hv$, $h$ and $d$ being positive constants. To the first equation is added $+fv, f > 0$, which makes the model dynamically unstable but structurally stable, thus avoiding Kolmogorov's criticism of Volterra's structurally unstable formulation. The term $fv$ can be taken to represent the accelerator or any other destablising aspect of the economy, resulting from upward and downward motion.

To the two state variables one adds a dynamical control variable, $z$, defined by $\dot{z} = +b + gz(v - c)$, with $b, g$ and $c$ positive constants, and $z$ being negatively proportional to output and employment, $v$. The controlled system then becomes

$$\dot{v} = -du + fv - ez, e > 0$$

$$\dot{u} = +hv$$

$$\dot{z} = +b + gz(v - c)$$

This is a dynamical control in contrast to the static upper and lower boundaries found in limit cycles. If $c$ be taken to be 0.05, then when unemployment goes below 5 per cent the economy is subjected to increasing downward pressure and when unemployment rises above 5 per cent, it is subjected to increasing upward pressure. The consequence of dynamical as opposed to statical control is dramatic: a stable, bounded region is defined in which chaotic motion occurs, as is illustrated in a two-dimensional projection in Figure 16.1. It is important to note that there is only *one* non-linearity and that it is defined by full employment, thus embodying the original Harrod problem.

Structural change and growth is introduced by a fifty-year Kondratiev, logistic 'swarm' of innovative capacity, $k$. There is considerable agreement that the typical course of an innovation approximates to a logistic, with maximum investment in the middle, so that $\dot{k} = +jk(1 - sk)$, $j$ and $s$ being positive. The difficulty with using this in an aggregative model is the great diversity of innovations as to timing, amplitude and duration, with the result that any aggregative series would reveal little. At that point Keynesian effective demand is needed to provide a crucial element of self-organisation. The level and growth rate of demand play a central role in all productive decisions, especially so in new and risky projects: hence a lot of

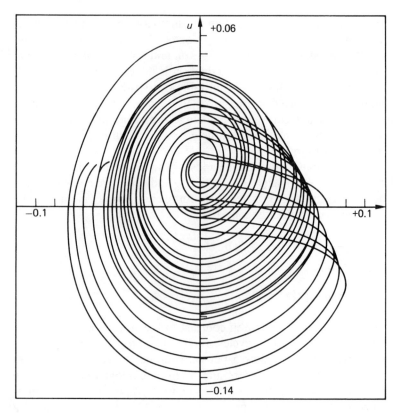

*Figure 16.1*

diverse decisions are forced to march in step. Though Schumpeter would never have admitted it, the Kahn–Keynes multiplication of expansive and contractive demand provides an essential missing link in Schumpeter's theory of the cyclical passage from one equilibrium to another.

Assuming the rate of change of productivity to be proportional to the accumulation of innovative capacity, then $m\dot{k}/k = -\dot{a}_L/a$, $m > 0$. Consequently, with a constant labour force, $\dot{v}/v = \dot{L}/L = \dot{q}/q + \dot{a}_L/a_L$, or $\dot{q}/q = \dot{v}/v - \dot{a}_L/a_L$. The complete model then becomes:

$$\dot{v} = -du + fv - ez$$
$$\dot{u} = +hv$$

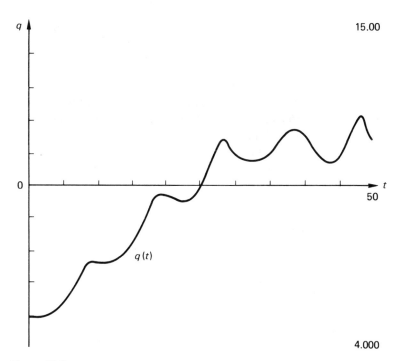

*Figure 16.2*

$$\dot{z} = + b + gz(v - c)$$
$$\dot{q}/q = (-du + fv - ez)/(v + 0.90) + mj(1 - sk)$$
$$\dot{k} = + jk(1 - sk)$$

The model is robust for economically plausible parametric changes; to illustrate, I take the following set of parameters: $d = 0.50$, $e = 0.80$, $h = 0.50$, $f = 0.15$, $b = 0.005$, $g = 85.0$, $c = 0.048$, $m = 0.16$, $j = 0.17$, $s = 0.14$. Initial conditions are 0.02, 0.03, 0, 5.0, 0.045. The resulting trajectory of output over half a century is shown in Figure 16.2. In my view it represents a fusion of some of the insights of Keynes and Schumpeter, though not in a form given by either. The end of the Kondratiev long wave, with innovatory investment approaching zero, poses the problem of how the high average level of output is maintained. Here it is solved by the upward push of earned incomes.

The Kondratiev investment is a unimodal quadratic which first eliminates and then moderates the middle-period cycles; then as it levels off, the cycle slowly re-emerges and gradually takes over as innovative investment ceases. The downside of the Kondratiev is complicated: employment/output is being cut, though at a decreasing rate; investment demand is declining, so what holds up demand and output? The equilibrium level of output has been shifted upward and does not decline to its previous level since it is dependent on the level of employment. In the middle the employment ratio is biased above its equilibrium; this raises wages, demand and output. Then as growth decelerates, the equilibrium level of employment and wages remains at 10 per cent unemployment, with its higher level of real wages and hence demand and output. Thus Schumpeter's 'vision' is confirmed, though not as he formulated it: the long wave has approximately five cycles including one large one; the real wage and output have both risen; structural change has raised both by virtue of its cyclical behaviour. What Schumpeter could not have foreseen, but no doubt would have accepted, is that each cycle is endogenously different from every other cycle, not only because of the nature of innovations. In this way history is introduced into economic analysis in an essential, even endogenous, form. By considering different values of the parameter $s$, one obtains greater or lesser growth of innovative capacity; by varying $j$ correspondingly one determines the rate of growth of productivity; by altering $m$ one makes the economic effect greater or smaller, by virtue of the capacity–output ratio. Thus one can characterise somewhat the great differences in growth rates. By altering $j$ from 0.17 to 0.22 and $s$ from 0.14 to 0.10, there results a high ('Japanese') growth and by altering $j$ to 0.15 and $s$ to 0.25 there is a low ('British') growth, as exhibited in Figure 16.3

The degree of irregularity in these examples is small, whereas the virtue of the model is that it can produce any degree of irregularity. By the modest change of initial values of $v$ and $u$ to 0 and 0.005 and $f$ to 0.18, one gets the strikingly irregular resulting time-series and phase portrait of Figure 16.4. These produce the more irregular output growths of Figure 16.5. These two examples appear to me to exhibit the generic character of the non-repeating figures one sees in economic time-series; they result, not from exogenous shocks but from the dynamic functioning of this simple model.

Such a model can be elaborated in various realistic ways but one particular change is especially important. The logistic innovative function should be bilaterally, not unilaterally coupled with output, that is, investment heavily influences demand and output, but is in its

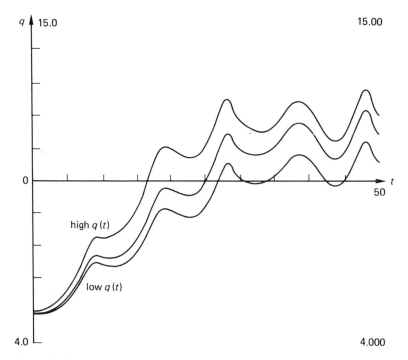

*Figure 16.3*

turn made subject to their influence. Therefore instead of assuming a constant, $j$, for new innovative capacity, one may assume a linear dependence on employment (the state of demand), thus

$$\dot{k} = (j + nv)k(1 - sk)$$

and

$$\dot{q}/q = (-du + fv - ez)/(v + 0.90) + m(j + nv)(1 - sk)$$

In this form we have a truly integrated, single theory of growth and fluctuation. The degree of irregularity can be seen in Figure 16.5 and indicated by cyclical growth rates: they were roughly, peak to peak, 26 per cent, 33 per cent, 6 per cent, 5 per cent, and trough to trough, 19 per cent, 28 per cent, 22 per cent, 23 percent, or, averaging peak and trough, 22.4 per cent, 30.7 per cent, 13.8 per cent, 14.4 per cent. The duration of each cycle, trough to trough, was roughly eight

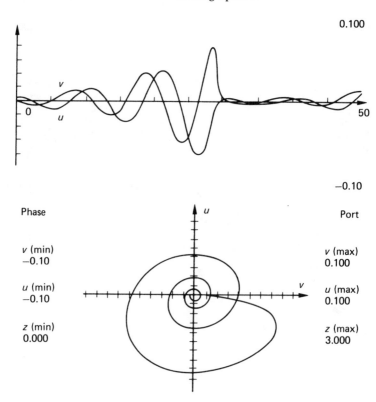

*Figure 16.4*

years, fifteen years, seven years, ten years. It will be clear that the term 'cycle' throughout this essay means only a roughly recurrent behaviour.

The foregoing model is a chaotic attractor and is obviously dynamically stable: but is it structurally stable? This is an involved question and one beyond and scope of this paper. To give a simple answer to an unsimple question, I would say it is unstable and that is why it is so interesting. The interested reader is referred to any good book on non-linear dynamics, e.g. Guckenheimer and Holmes (1983) for a more extensive treatment.

The dynamical control parameter, $z$, has been introduced simply as effective in producing versions of the irregularity characteristic of the evolution of the economy and its time-series. It can, however, be more satisfactorily considered as a concrete embodiment of the

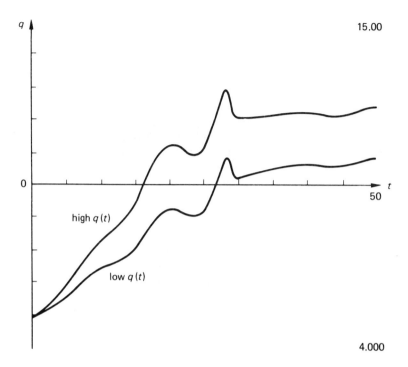

*Figure 16.5*

variable element in public net income generating expenditure. It is well-known that the normal governmental budgetary behaviour has a markedly stabilising effect on economic performance. A large part of government expenditure is substantially invariant to the short-run changes in receipts: this is in sharp contrast to the behaviour of producers and consumers. Thus public expenditure on the armed forces, administration, police, etc. is not directly related to current tax receipts, and may even vary inversely, for example, unemployment benefits and other public assistance.

Compensatory fiscal policy may appropriately be regarded as a simple type of dynamic control implemented at discrete time intervals. It aims, or should aim, at diminishing the amplitude of fluctuations in economic activity. As a result of somewhat disappointing post-war performance, there has been a decline in the expectation of major improvements from fiscal policy, and no hope of achieving a steady degree of employment. Compensatory fiscal policy has proved to be a somewhat flawed instrument, one which has not fully realised the great hopes placed on it. There are a number of evident reasons for this. First, there is the time-lag involved in collecting and processing the information necesssary to judge the state of the economy. Then there must ensue considerable time to analyse the results and to agree upon a desirable policy, a process which may involve both the executive administration and the legislature, or an effective combination of the two. Finally then, given the dynamical nature of the generation of income and output, still more time has to elapse before the full consequences of any policy are actually realised. The result is that a policy may be outdated by the time it is fully effective, so that it may happen that it is even counter-productive: such procedures are capable of making fluctuations worse instead of better. Since it is not possible simply to decide what output and employment should be and then proceed to place the economy in that position, what are required for a satisfactory, effective policy are instruments of control which are continuously variable so as to produce a gradual approach to any desired state. By contrast with static control parameters the Rössler dynamic control parameter, $z$, represents in simple form just such a procedure.

With $z$ zero, the fixed points for both $u$ and $v$ are zero. To illustrate normal government practice, let $v^* = 0.90$, so that the employment ratio, $v$, is then measured in deviations from 10 per cent unemployment, with the level of $u$ unspecified. The parameter $z$ can then be taken to represent the variations in net public deficits and surpluses: the effects on $v$ being negative, $z$ negative represents a deficit with a positive effect on employment and output, and conversely for a surplus. If the value of $c$ is 0.05, then when unemployment is less than 5 per cent public surpluses are increasing thus producing a progressive deceleration in employment and output. When unemployment is greater than 5 per cent, the government deficit is increasing thus contributing to a rising rate of employment. The real wage (or average earnings) is increasing faster than productivity whenever $v$ is positive, that is $v > v^*$, and it is increasing less rapidly than productivity when $v$ is negative.

Taking these values as representative of the effects of government budget in the absence of a compensatory policy, the behaviour of the employment ratio over a fifty-year period is shown in Figure 16.6, where the parameter values are as follows: $d = 0.50$; $f = 0.15$; $e = 0.30$; $h = 0.050$; $b = 0.01$; $g = 85.0$; $c = 0.05$, with initial conditions 0, 0.03, 0.02, 5.0 and 0.025. In this example unemploy-

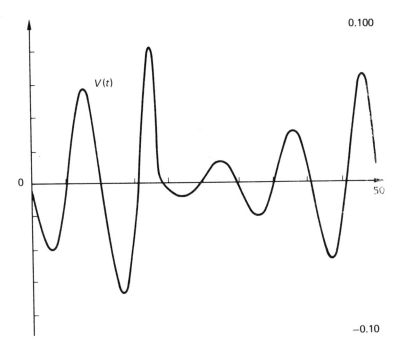

0.100

$V(t)$

0

50

−0.10

*Figure 16.6*

ment reaches a maximum of about 12 per cent and a minimum of 1 per cent over the half-century. The phase portrait is given in Figure 16.7. The degree of irregularity is considerable and enough to make prediction unreliable and policy formation very unsatisfactory. The control parameter varies continuously so that a falling $z$ means an acceleration of output and employment. On the other hand when $v > c$, $z$ is rising and decelarating $v$.

If the government policy-forming body aims to reduce the amplitude of fluctuations by instituting a compensatory policy, it should investigate the consequence of altering the government budget when $v$ is above and below smaller and smaller values of $c$. Keeping all parameters and initial values the same, for smaller and smaller values of $c$ from 0.05 to 0.01, they would find successively smaller phase portraits for $v$ and $u$, indicating smaller and smaller fluctuations to nearly constant employment and output. Very large-scale interventions are required in the early years but they rapidly diminish as the policy becomes effective. To see the dramatic results achievable by

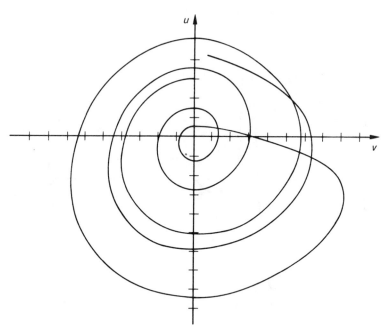

*Figure 16.7*

such continuous time compensatory fiscal policy, one can compare the system's behaviour for $c = 0.05$ with that for $c = 0.01$ (and $g = 85$ and $g = 100$). By comparing Figure 16.7 with Figure 16.8, one finds that the stable bounded region, or 'chaotic attractor', has been reduced nearly to a fixed point, which means that the waves have been substantially eliminated. The nature of the achievement of such a policy is perhaps even more clearly demonstrated in Figures 16.9 and 16.10, where the two types of behaviour for $v$ $(t)$ and $u(t)$ are plotted simultaneously. The potent interventions, not unnaturally, initially alter the course of events by adding new shorter waves but new ones of a much smaller amplitude. Then as the policy succeeds the amplitudes steadily diminish, so that after twenty-five years, they are only 10–15 per cent of their former size. The model is then extended to include a fifty-year Kondratiev in logistic form. The equally impressive effects on output are exhibited in Figure 16.11, compensated $\bar{q}(t)$ is compared with uncompensated $\bar{q}(t)$. The dynamic control initially adds some mild short waves but in such a way as to smoothe the longer-term trajectory. Then towards the end of

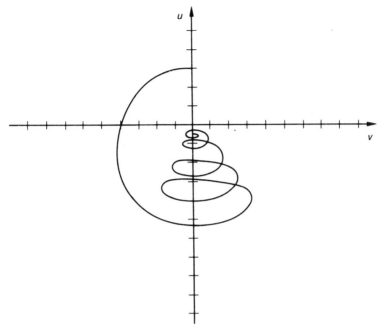

*Figure 16.8*

the long wave, the controlled behaviour becomes monotonic, approximating to the impressed logistic, whereas the uncontrolled behaviour reverts to vigorous wave motion. Thus the flexible dynamic control has its triumph towards the end by entirely erasing the three final oscillations.

That such a fiscal policy can, in principle, be astonishingly successful is thus demonstrated. And that some such result is highly desirable is also clear. However, this happy result has been achieved by stabilising unemployment at 10 per cent which is not highly desirable. The foregoing policy is one of 'derivative control' through $z$. This needs to be accompanied simultaneously by 'proportional control', that is, policies designed gradually to raise the equilibrium level, $v^*$, from 0.90 to any desired and feasible level of $v$, say 0.98. This can be done by successive increases of government or other expenditures by amounts which progressively reduce to zero the difference between actual and desired levels of unemployment (as appears to have happened as a result of the Reagan military budget). Also required is the deployment of monetary policy to avoid the inflationary result of

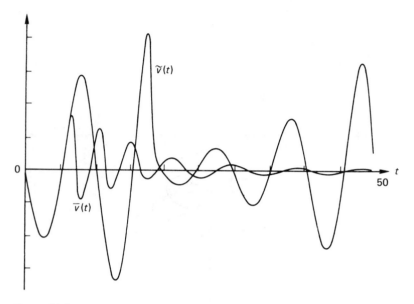

*Figure 16.9*

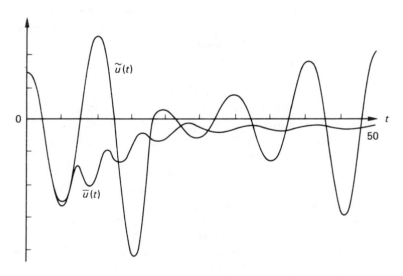

*Figure 16.10*

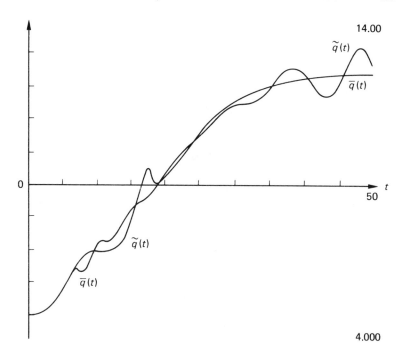

14.00

$\widetilde{q}(t)$

$\overline{q}(t)$

0

50

$t$

$\widetilde{q}(t)$

$\overline{q}(t)$

4.000

Enter value of c (0.010000)

*Figure 16.11*

the 1960s, since control of lending is so much more effective in restricting demand than in expanding it. Furthermore there must be a successful policy of forcing or persuading employers and trade unions to forego raising real wages in consequence of tightness of the labour market, in exchange for high and stable employment along with rising output.

The much more serious problems of implementing such a programme lie in the required magnitude and rapidity of the interventions. If, however, it were once agreed that such spectacular gains might accrue, then it is conceivable that the necessary, elaborate plans for increased and decreased government expenditure could be formulated and agreed in advance, so that when the need arises, they could rapidly be made operational. It has to be admitted that, on the basis of past experience, there is, politically, a very strong asymmetry between deficits and surpluses of government budgeting: for obvious reasons surpluses seem to be politically poisonous! The enormous potential advantages of some such cybernetic, adaptive policy must eventually have an impact, the difficulties notwithstanding. The example elaborated here is quite abstract, too simplified and as such impractical, but what is not impractical is the basic logic of cybernetic control for fiscal policy.

This paper, being concerned with chaotic growth through structural change, has followed Schumpeter's un-neoclassical, semi-Marxian vision of growth driven by the search for ever-renewed profit through technical change. However, he inverted Marx by maintaining a rising real wage, with profit, in the stationary state, equal to zero but kept positive by continual, cost-reducing innovations leading to cyclical growth. In spite of some theoretical difficulties, he had a quite realistic insight into the way that private capitalism works; he was no doubt helped by his disastrous experiences as Finance Minister and private banker.

If I may, in turn, invert Schumpeter – on a basis of no realism whatsoever – imagine a society based on the lust, not for wealth but for power; a society which is as efficient as managerial capitalism and as devoted to technological innovation. Being politically democratic and egalitarian, it would seek to maximise, not growth of output, but the overall well-being of its citizenry. This should be defined and measured by the free choice between work and leisure, but a free choice undistorted by the media – press, TV, radio, etc. In private capitalism these media are directed to increasing output and profit.

In such a Utopian community, there could be free individual choice between getting and spending and all the other activities, interests or pursuits of people. Such a result being difficult, there would probably have to be a democratically reached, common decision setting the number of hours of work per week or per year. In that case, the supply of labour becomes a decision variable, even for a constant population, and must be measured in man-hours not number of workers. Given such a decision, then the problem becomes one of determining output subject to a declining supply of labour, consequent on a rising productivity and a rising average earning. Since $v = a_L q / n(t)$, $\dot{v}/v = \dot{q}/q + \dot{a}_L/a_L - \dot{n}/n$. With productivity growth of $g_a = m\dot{k}/k$, and that of $n(t)$ as $g_n$, $\dot{q}/q = \dot{v}/v + g_a + g_n$. The economy, though free market, is subject to some sort of perspective control, the aim of which might be monotonic, not cyclical motion; hence with $\dot{v} = 0$. Research, being heavily subject to state subsidy and controlled with the aim of steady-state growth, would be implemented so as to give exponential rather than logistic behaviour. With a 2 per cent growth rate of productivity, there could be two extreme cases. With no change in the working week, output grows at the rate of productivity, for example, from 10 to 27.2 in fifty years with an equal growth in average earnings. This probably makes little sense for late capitalism where there is no longer any need for accumulation of capital, only substitution of newer equipment for the existing. The other extreme would be output constant with $g_n = -2$ per cent, so that in fifty years a working week of 40 hours could be reduced to 14.7 hours. To see the effects and relevance of such a choice one need only think of the consequences for the environment and natural resources. By varying the proportions of these two policies, all combinations in between these two extremes would be available.

**Reference**

Guckenheimer, J. and Holmes, P. (1983) *Nonlinear Oscillations, Dynamical Systems and Bifurcation of Vector Fields* (Berlin and New York: Springer Verlag).

# Index of Names

# Index of Subjects

accelerator models, 6, 9
*see also* multiplier/accelerator
adaptive expectations, 158, 163–7, 172, 179
addiction and dependence, 91–4
agent question, 20
agreement/conflict models, 87, 95
agricultural products, demand for, and long cycles, 283–4
arbitrage, 42, 66–7
artificial intelligence, 70, 86, 87–8
assembly methods, 96
attractors, chaotic, *see* chaos

balance of payments, 232
banks and banking, 224–5
and exchange rates, 232, 275
as lenders of last resort, 47–8, 223–4
behaviour analysis, 85–90, 94, 417
of consumers, 66, 84–5
biological neuroscience, 70, 85, 92–4, 96, 97
birth-and-death process, 70–3
brain, *see* neuroscience
Bretton Woods systems, 254

capital flows, 42, 243–7
controls on, 251–4
*see also*, money
catastrophe theory, 56–62
causal theory, 10, 18, 21
chaos theory, 29–30, 183–90, 200–3, 302, 425–41
classification of business cycle theories, 11–17, 18–19
cognitive theories, *see* neuroscience
combinatorial mathematics, 90
common knowledge and game theory, 96
communications networks, conflict resolution in, 87, 95
competitive theory of lotteries, 111
complex numbers, 77
computer neuroscience, 70, 86, 87–8
conflict
resolution of, 87, 95
*see also* war
consumers

behaviour of, 66, 84–5
tastes of, 70
continuous-time systems, 186–9
convergence theory, 95
counter-intuitive phenomena, 29
coupled oscillators, 186, 187–8
cusps and catastrophe theory, 56–62

Danish flag model, 414–15
debt, 47, 51
debt-deflation cycles, 11
delay-differential dynamics, 12
demographic factors and long cycles, 284–5
dependence and addiction, 91–4
deterministic systems, 18–19, 421
diffeomorphisms, 185
diffusion process, 77, 83
discrete-time systems, 184–5
distress, 45
distribution cycle, 11
distributional coalitions, 52
dollar area, 233
drug dependence, 92–4
dynamical systems, 12, 31–2, 56–62, 69–70
*see also* non-linear dynamics

economic policy, theory of, 21
*see also* partisan cycle
efficiency wage model, 132–3
election cycle, *see* partisan cycle
electrical network model, 67–8, 77
elementary catastrophe theory (ECT), 56–62
employment, model of, 107–8
calibration of, 114–19
critiques of, 128–34
economic environment of, 109–14
experiments with and workings of, 119–25
*see also* job search
equilibrium and business cycles
indeterminacy of, in
multiplier/accelerator model, 162–3, 176–8
locus of, 132–3
and search function, 137–49, 152–3

unit root question, 332, 350–1, 360–1
utility function, 66

VAR model, 312–20
vested interests, 52
voting, *see* partisan cycle

wages
  efficiency model of, 132–3
  and long-cycle theories, 309, 316
war-economy theory of long cycles,
  303–24, 326–8
work, *see* employment; wages